THE DOMESTICATION OF G
BIOGRAPHY AND THE ROMANTIC POET

The Domestication of Genius

Biography and the Romantic Poet

JULIAN NORTH

OXFORD
UNIVERSITY PRESS

OXFORD
UNIVERSITY PRESS

Great Clarendon Street, Oxford OX2 6DP

Oxford University Press is a department of the University of Oxford.
It furthers the University's objective of excellence in research, scholarship,
and education by publishing worldwide in

Oxford New York

Auckland Cape Town Dar es Salaam Hong Kong Karachi
Kuala Lumpur Madrid Melbourne Mexico City Nairobi
New Delhi Shanghai Taipei Toronto

With offices in

Argentina Austria Brazil Chile Czech Republic France Greece
Guatemala Hungary Italy Japan Poland Portugal Singapore
South Korea Switzerland Thailand Turkey Ukraine Vietnam

Oxford is a registered trade mark of Oxford University Press
in the UK and in certain other countries

Published in the United States
by Oxford University Press Inc., New York

© Julian North 2009

British Library Cataloguing in Publication Data
Data available

Library of Congress Cataloging in Publication Data
Library of Congress Control Number: 2009935882

Typeset by SPI Publisher Services, Pondicherry, India
Printed in Great Britain
on acid-free paper by
the MPG Books Group,
Bodmin and King's Lynn

ISBN 978–0–19–957198–7

1 3 5 7 9 10 8 6 4 2

In Memory of my Father

Acknowledgements

This book was started when I was a lecturer at De Montfort University, and completed in my current post in the School of English at Leicester University. It has been a long time in the writing and I would like to thank my colleagues at both institutions for their help and forbearance. At DMU, Judy Simons was instrumental in convincing me I should embark on the project. Kathleen Bell, Deborah Cartmell, Philip Cox, Jane Dowson, Matthew Grenby, Philip Martin, Joseph Phelan, Imelda Whelehan, and Nigel Wood gave practical, intellectual, and moral support. At Leicester University, I have been especially grateful to my Heads of School, Richard Foulkes and Martin Halliwell, for facilitating my research whenever they could. Thanks go also to Mark Rawlinson, Joanne Shattock, and Martin Stannard, for reading the completed typescript and responding enthusiastically; to Simon Morgan, for his wisdom on Victorian domesticity; to Gowan Dawson, Holly Furneaux, Elaine Treharne, and Greg Walker for friendship and sound advice; and to Alex Moseley for his computer know-how. My work on Mary Shelley as a biographer benefited from a correspondence with Nora Crook, and Chapter 5 from my contacts with other De Quincey scholars, especially Grevel Lindop, Daniel Sanjiv Roberts, and Barry Symonds. I am grateful to the Arts and Humanities Research Board for granting me a period of research leave that was vital to the completion of this project. I would also like to thank Andrew McNeillie at OUP, and my four, anonymous readers, for their encouraging and constructive comments.

I am grateful to Palgrave Macmillan, Routledge/Taylor and Francis, and Ashgate Publishing for permission to reprint material, in Chapters 3 and 5, from my essays: 'Literary Biography and the House of the Poet', in N. J. Watson (ed.), *Literary Tourism and Nineteenth-Century Culture* (London: Palgrave, 2009); 'Wooing the Reader: De Quincey, Wordsworth and Women in *Tait's Edinburgh Magazine*', in Robert Morrison and Daniel Sanjiv Roberts (eds), *Thomas De Quincey. New Theoretical and Critical Directions* (New York: Routledge, Taylor and Francis Group, 2008), 99–121; and 'Self-Possession and Gender in Romantic Literary Biography', in Arthur Bradley and Alan Rawes (eds.), *Romantic Biography* (Aldershot: Ashgate, 2003), 109–38.

For their generous permission to reproduce illustrations, I thank Peter X. Accardo, Houghton Library, Harvard University (cover image); The Special Collections of the University of Leicester (Figure 3.2); and The Keeper of Special Collections, Bodleian Library, University of Oxford (Figures 4.1, 6.1, 6.2).

I owe my greatest debts to my family. My parents, Marion and John North, were there for me throughout. My mother's interest in biography, and especially in the lives of Shelley and Byron, was my first inspiration. My father was my great example. He died shortly before the book went to press, and it is dedicated, with love, to him. My own domestic circle—William, Gabriel, and Mark—sustained me in every way during the writing of this book. To them I give my most heartfelt thanks of all.

Contents

Abbreviations

List of Illustrations

Cover image: Lithograph by J. Baillie (*c.*1840), showing Byron with his Venetian mistress, Marianna Segati. From the private collection of Peter X. Accardo. The caption is from a letter to Thomas Moore: 'Dear Tom, I really cannot go on; there are a pair of great black eyes looking over my shoulder so that I must turn and answer them instead of you'. Fiona MacCarthy writes, in *Byron: Life and Legend* (London: John Murray, 2002), 320, that 'there was an easiness, almost a domesticity' about the liaison.

Introduction

In *Records of Shelley, Byron, and the Author* (1878), Edward Trelawny recalled meeting some English travellers at his hotel in Switzerland:

I saw by their utilitarian garb, as well as by the blisters and blotches on their cheeks, lips, and noses, that they were pedestrian tourists, fresh from the snow-covered mountains, the blazing sun and frosty air having acted on their unseasoned skins as boiling water does on the lobster, by dyeing his dark coat scarlet. The man was evidently a denizen of the north, his accent harsh, skin white, of an angular and bony build, and self-confident and dogmatic in his opinions. . . . 'Waiter,' he said, 'is that our carriage? Why did you not tell us? Come, lasses, be stirring, the freshness of the day is gone. You may rejoice in not having to walk; there is a chance of saving the remnants of skin the sun has left on our chins and noses—today we shall be stewed instead of barbecued.'

On their leaving the room to get ready for their journey, my friend Roberts told me the strangers were the poet Wordsworth, his wife and sister.[1]

In the gaze of the biographer, the Romantic poet on holiday with his family is a 'pedestrian' tourist in more than one sense. Trelawny comments that he could 'see no trace, in the hard features and weather-stained brow of the outer man, of the divinity within him', but once Wordsworth's identity has been divulged, the harsh accent, dogmatic opinions, and hearty coercion of others to experience the great outdoors, produce both a shock of incongruity and of recognition. The biographer cannot see the poet's 'genius', but he mediates it to the reader nevertheless, creating a thrill of vicarious intimacy with greatness. This combination of reverence and iconoclasm, the elevated and the down-to-earth, forms a paradigm still present in biography and celebrity culture today. It finds its origins in the late eighteenth and early nineteenth centuries, when the relationship between biographer, subject, and reader shifted decisively towards its modern form. This book describes that shift as it happened within early nineteenth-century *Lives* of the poets. It looks at how literary biography constructed 'the Romantic poet' and how, in doing so, it established its own, enduring success as a popular genre.

The relationship between autobiography and Romanticism is a well-worn subject, but there has been comparatively little interest in biography at the

---

[1] Edward John Trelawny, *Records of Shelley, Byron, and the Author*, ed. David Wright (1973; 2nd edn., Harmondsworth: Penguin, 1982), 58–60.

period. The rise of the genre in the late eighteenth century is often assumed to bear a relation to the emergence of Romantic subjectivity, but critics have had doubts and difficulties in arguing for the connection. John Garraty stated baldly that 'Romanticism. . . . though it rose to prominence at a time when biography was flowering as never before . . . added little to the form'.[2] Romantic values of originality and authorial autonomy have appeared to apply to autobiography in a way that they have not to biography. As Alison Booth writes, '[c]ritics expect the iconic text, whereas biographies are transient and serial'.[3] Autobiography, the unique life story, answers this expectation. It has seemed, in the words of Laura Marcus, a 'Utopian form', a Romantic quest for the meeting of subject and object, where 'the autobiographical "I" both writes and is written'.[4] The intervention, in biography, of a third party who takes control of someone else's story, has been a vital factor in modern critical resistance to the genre.[5] It is a distrust that, as we shall see, was forcibly expressed by the Romantic poets themselves.

For a time, those who sought to define a relationship between biography and Romanticism did so by reclaiming the genre as a poetic form.[6] Annette Cafarelli mounted the first, substantial defence of early nineteenth-century biographical prose by reading it through the lens of a high Romantic poetics.[7] But, in excluding and devaluing practice that did not fit with this vision (notably the considerable legacy of Boswellism), she did not do justice to the variety of biographical writing at this time or to the complexity of its relationship with Romantic conceptions of the subject and of genius. It is striking that both Coleridge and Wordsworth believed biography to be the enemy of genius— and, in Wordsworth's case, of the poet in particular. This, on its own, suggests a powerful antagonism between biography and the Romantic poet. A desire to discover the basis of this antagonism was one of the first impetuses behind this book.

---

[2] John A. Garraty, *The Nature of Biography* (1957; 2nd edn., London: Jonathan Cape, 1958), 90.

[3] Alison Booth, *How to Make It as a Woman: Collective Biographical History from Victoria to the Present* (Chicago: University of Chicago Press, 2004), 238.

[4] Laura Marcus, *Auto/biographical Discourses: Theory, Criticism, Practice* (Manchester: Manchester University Press, 1994), 13.

[5] See Booth, *How to Make It as a Woman*, 240: 'Theoretically aware of the textual invention of the subject, the researcher nevertheless desires originating, unmediated agency, perhaps resenting having another person in the way.'

[6] e.g. Francis R. Hart, *Lockhart as Romantic Biographer* (Edinburgh: Edinburgh University Press, 1971), p. vi, characterizing Lockhart as inspired by Wordsworth and committed to 'a poetics of personality and spontaneity'.

[7] Annette Wheeler Cafarelli, *Prose in the Age of Poets: Romanticism and Biographical Narrative from Johnson to De Quincey* (Philadelphia: University of Pennsylvania Press, 1990). For Cafarelli, the representative biographies of the period were collective, anecdotal essays, by Hazlitt and De Quincey, valued by her for their affinities with Romantic poetry. She noted common ground between De Quincey's *Literary Reminiscences* and 'the intellectual and formal concerns of high Romantic poetry and criticism' and argued that the 'paramount affiliations' of these essays 'lie with the poetic tradition and the poetic use of the pastoral to allegorize nature, art, temporal change, and the passage of human life' (156).

The mythology of the poet as a solitary, autonomous, male genius has, of course, been thoroughly exposed in the last twenty years, by critics exploring the gendering of Romanticism as well as by work on authorship and the material culture of publishing at the period.[8] This book will show the extent to which the early biographies of the poets already posed this challenge to what we would now understand as 'Romantic ideology'. Biography was shaped by Romanticism, and was, I would argue, the most influential transmitter of the myth of the Romantic poet in the nineteenth century and beyond, yet *Lives* of the poets flourished in a competitive and critical relationship with their subjects. In this book I explore that relationship by looking at the first wave of *Lives* of Byron, Shelley, the Lake Poets, Felicia Hemans, and Letitia Landon, published from the 1820s to the early 1840s, by Thomas Moore, Mary Shelley, Thomas De Quincey, and others, in the context of the proliferation of biography in the print culture of the period. The 1820s and 1830s were significant decades for biography. Its profile was raised by much heralded, monumental works such as Moore's *Letters and Journals of Lord Byron* (1830), Croker's new edition of Boswell's *Life of Johnson* (1831), and Lockhart's biographies of Burns (1828) and Scott (1837–8). Biographical discourse—and literary *Lives* especially—became part of the daily fabric of reading. It appeared in a variety of formats including magazine essays and reviews, encyclopaedia articles, volumes of collective biography, individual *Lives and Letters*, and introductory material to editions of writers' works.[9] It was during these years that biography produced the 'Romantic poet' for popular consumption and that literary biography decisively asserted itself as a modern, market force. The coming together of these events was no coincidence, and it has had great significance for the course of modern biography, as it has for our understanding of the figure of the Romantic poet. The reputations of Byron, Shelley, Wordsworth, Coleridge, Hemans, Landon, and others were forged in a market competition between poetry and biography, in which biography was, in many respects, the winner. We are the inheritors of this situation, at a time when the public appetite for writers' lives matches or far outruns its eagerness to consume their works, and when *Lives* of the poets sell but the only sure way to sell poetry is to return it to biography.[10]

---

[8] See e.g. Marlon B. Ross, *The Contours of Masculine Desire: Romanticism and the Rise of Women's Poetry* (New York: Oxford University Press, 1989); Anne K. Mellor, *Romanticism and Gender* (New York: Routledge, 1993); Jack Stillinger, *Multiple Authorship and the Myth of Solitary Genius* (New York: Oxford University Press, 1991); Lee Erickson, *The Economy of Literary Form: English Literature and the Industrialization of Publishing, 1800–1850* (Baltimore: Johns Hopkins University Press, 1996); Lucy Newlyn, *Reading, Writing, and Romanticism: The Anxiety of Reception* (Oxford: Oxford University Press, 2000).

[9] Much of this material remains unexplored, although David Higgins, in *Romantic Genius and the Literary Magazine: Biography, Celebrity and Politics* (Abingdon: Routledge, 2005), has made a valuable contribution to our understanding of debates on genius in biographical prose published in the literary magazines of the 1820s and 1830s.

[10] See e.g. the huge success, relative to his other volumes, of Ted Hughes's *Birthday Letters*, an auto/biographical sequence, describing his relationship with Sylvia Plath. The *Birthday Letters* took their place in what was already arguably the most controversial debate in literary biography in the

My title, 'the domestication of genius', contains the central trope of the book and one that holds a number of meanings that will unfold in the following chapters. In my first chapter I argue that the development of biography was crucially related to the middle-class, ideological investment in domestic life, from the later eighteenth century and, decisively, in the 1830s. Linked to this, the 'domestication of genius' also refers to a widely held twentieth- and twenty-first-century view that the Victorians, in memorializing the Romantics, set out to civilize or tame them. The *Lives* of Byron, Shelley, Hemans, and Keats published in the 1820s, 1830s, and 1840s have often been belittled or dismissed as examples of a conservative, Victorian imperative to confer respectability on the Romantic subject, for the middle-class readership, by dint of censorship, editing, and invention. To put it simply, these biographers have been charged with making the Romantic poets into Victorians. Thomas Moore has been accused of enclosing Byron within the bounds of respectability, Mary Shelley and others with moulding Percy Shelley into an emasculated, unpolitical angel, Hemans's biographers as papering over the cracks in her image as a 'creature of hearth and home', Monckton Milnes and his followers with wrapping Keats 'in gentle phrases and soften[ing] the outline of his ambition'.[11] Carlyle, in 1838, was famously contemptuous of the 'mealy mouth' of contemporary biographical practice, but it was, of course, the Modernist assault on Victorian biography that reverberated in twentieth-century criticism.[12] As Richard Altick noted, biography became emblematic of aspects of Victorianism—hypocrisy and eva-siveness—that the early twentieth century sought to reject.[13] D. H. Lawrence drew the battle-lines between biography and poetry in terms of class war. Lock-hart's *Life* of Burns made him 'spit! Those damned middle-class Lockharts grew lilies of the valley up their arses, to hear them talk. . . . My word, you can't know Burns unless you can hate the Lockharts and all the estimable bourgeois and upper classes as he really did'.[14] Lytton Strachey and Virginia Woolf asserted their own newness through polemical, and enduring, caricatures of Victorian biography, as artless hagiography—'two fat volumes' of 'tedious panegyric',

20th cent. See Sarah Churchwell, 'Secrets and Lies: Plath, Privacy, Publication and Ted Hughes's *Birthday Letters*', *Contemporary Review*, 42/1 (2001), 102–48.

[11] See below, Chs. 3, 4, and 6 for discussion of these critical responses to the biographers of Byron, Shelley, and Hemans. Andrew Motion, *Keats* (London: Faber and Faber, 1997), p. xx. Hemans: 'I have been all my life a creature of hearth and home', quoted in *CM* i. 212.

[12] Thomas Carlyle, 'Sir Walter Scott', *London and Westminster Review* (1838), in *CME* iv. 29: 'How delicate, decent is English Biography, bless its mealy mouth! A Damocles' sword of *Respectability* hangs forever over the poor English Life-writer (as it does over poor English Life in general), and reduces him to the verge of paralysis.'

[13] Richard D. Altick, *Lives and Letters: A History of Literary Biography in England and America* (New York: Knopf, 1965; repr., Westport, Conn.: Greenwood Press, 1979), 289.

[14] Letter to Donald Carswell, 5 Dec. 1927, *The Letters of D. H. Lawrence*, gen. ed. James T. Boulton, 8 vols. (Cambridge: Cambridge University Press, 2002), vi. *March 1927–November 1928*, ed. James T. Boulton, Margaret H. Boulton, and Gerald M. Lacy, 231–2.

enshrining wax work effigies of goodness.[15] In the same way, more recent biographers and critics have read nineteenth-century literary *Lives* as narratives that rein in or deny the sexual and political transgressiveness of Romantic poetry, and have thereby been able, themselves, triumphantly to reassert it. Andrew Motion, promoting a new, radical Keats, will, of course, like all biographers, cast doubt on the authenticity of the previous models, but he refers particularly to the conservatism of the Victorian tradition—to Milnes, '[h]ampered by conventional morality', omitting the love affair with Fanny Brawne and 'the troublesome political dimension' of the poetry.[16] Arthur Bradley and Alan Rawes argue that Romantic biography (defined by them as the biography of Romantic subjects, from the early nineteenth century and beyond) is 'a-historical' and 'neo-conservative', engaging in a 'biological domestication' of the subject.[17]

The domestic versus the historical—it is precisely this, gendered, division that, I would argue, biography already inscribes and questions. Rachel Bowlby writes that feminists, speaking of the 'domestication' of theory, have tended to use it 'as a straightforwardly negative metaphor' implying 'simple binary oppositions and two-stage stories, whereby something initially natural, spontaneous or subversive gets pushed into a conformity or homogeneity that deprives it of whatever made it different'. Like Bowlby, I would reclaim the term as denoting far more than 'an uncomplicated and inevitable process of assimilation'.[18] In speaking of biography, I want to remain open to the value of Victorian responses to Romantic culture. I do not set out to deny the impulse of many (though not all) of these biographers to make their subjects 'respectable', but to explore its bases and its effects. The practice of writers such as Moore, Leigh Hunt, Mary Shelley, and De Quincey, but also the more ephemeral biographical literature of the period, must lead us to question the caricature of nineteenth-century biography as a simplistically repressive and politically homogeneous discourse.[19] *Lives* of the poets in the 1820s and 1830s enacted a paradoxical popularization of the conception of an

---

[15] Lytton Strachey, *Eminent Victorians. Cardinal Manning, Florence Nightingale, Dr. Arnold, General Gordon* (London: Chatto and Windus, 1918), p. viii. Virginia Woolf, 'The Art of Biography', *Collected Essays by Virginia Woolf,* 4 vols. (London: Hogarth Press, 1966–7), iv. 222. See also Woolf's essays, 'The New Biography' (1927), ibid. 229–35; and 'A Talk about Memoirs' (1920), ibid. 216–20. Her feelings about 19th-cent. biography were complex and ambivalent, not least because they involved a dialogue with her father, Leslie Stephen, editor of the *Dictionary of National Biography*. She enjoyed some Victorian literary *Lives* such as Dowden's of Shelley. See *The Essays of Virginia Woolf,* ed. Andrew McNeillie, 4 vols. (London: The Hogarth Press, 1986–94), i. 177. See Marcus, *Auto/biographical Discourses*, 90–134, for an account of 'Woolf, Strachey and the discourse of the "new biography"'; and Booth, *How to Make It as a Woman,* 225–44, for Woolf's conflicted responses to biography and their legacy for contemporary criticism.

[16] Motion, *Keats,* pp. xix–xx.

[17] Arthur Bradley and Alan Rawes (eds.), *Romantic Biography* (Aldershot: Ashgate, 2003), p. xiii. They take it as read that all biography is 'by its very nature Romantic' (p. xii).

[18] Rachel Bowlby, 'Domestication', in Diane Elam and Robyn Wiegman (eds.), *Feminism Beside Itself* (New York: Routledge, 1995), 71–91: 89.

[19] See William H. Epstein (ed.), *Contesting the Subject: Essays in the Postmodern Theory and Practice of Biography and Biographical Criticism* (West Lafayette, Ind.: Purdue University Press,

aristocracy of Romantic genius. They enshrined a version of genius as masculine, autonomous, and unreachable, but also countered it, asserting a feminine voice and the imperative of biography to mediate culture to as wide an audience as possible. Biography in practice and theory claimed that to domesticate was to democratize, to question the exclusivity of cultural production that withholds itself from general consumption, and to insist upon the connection between the public/historical and the private/domestic worlds. For many, this is the enduring pleasure of literary biography—its capacity to make this connection—to bring genius home to the reader.

By looking at *Lives* of the poets in the 1820s and 1830s we may learn much about the culture of these decades, whose reputation is rightly characterized by Richard Cronin as that of a no-man's-land between epochs, a 'lacuna' between Romanticism and Victorianism. Cronin concludes that these years were, as Virgil Nemoianu has argued, a time when '"the sheer energy of the romantic break-through is captured and tamed in a long phase of late romanticism that has a configuration of its own"'.[20] Cronin begins to look at how biography, fiction, and poetry set out to curb the perceived excesses of the Romantic poets. In *Lives* of the poets we can see this happening in particularly interesting ways, in what we might retrospectively see as a vivid clash between the 'Romantic' and the 'Victorian'. There was an acute sense in biography of the 1820s and 1830s that this was a transitional epoch in the understanding and practice of authorship. Biographers self-consciously adopted positions of lofty hindsight on these poets, looking backwards and forwards, reassessing the old, and formulating the new. One of the distinguishing generic possibilities of biography, as opposed to autobiography, is the posthumous perspective, and it was an important aspect of the competition between the biographer and the poet that this book will explore. The majority of the *Lives* I am dealing with were posthumous. As everybody knows (and the biographies are *why* they know it), Shelley, Byron, and Keats all died young. So did Felicia Hemans and Letitia Landon. The image of the poet or poetess as a doomed youth was already firmly inscribed in the poems, notably in Shelley's 'Alastor' and 'Adonais' and in such pieces as Hemans's 'The Last Song of Sappho' or Landon's 'Sappho's Song'. The early biographers of these poets capitalized on the opportunity for pathos. Their narratives were dominated by the shadow of a death foretold, by the theme of youthful promise unfulfilled but also, more tellingly, of youthful mistakes left uncorrected. Richard Monckton Milnes wrote in his *Life* of Keats,

---

1991), for one attempt to counter the reputation of biography and biographical criticism 'as conservative, if not reactionary, generic formations' (2).

[20] Richard Cronin, *Romantic Victorians: English Literature, 1824–1840* (Basingstoke: Palgrave, 2002), 2–3.

let us never forget, that wonderful as are the poems of Keats, yet, after all, they are rather the records of a poetical education than the accomplished work of the mature artist. . . . all Keats's poems are early productions, and there is nothing beyond them but the thought of what he might have become.[21]

Milnes's *Life* was published in 1848 but echoed narrative patterns already well established at least a decade earlier in the biographies of Shelley, Landon, and Hemans, amongst others, where the Romantic poet was constructed as inherently immature. This was countered by an emergent definition of Victorian authorial 'maturity': a longer life for these fated poets might have made them into grown-up authors, their works displaying an outward-looking attitude, a moral responsibility to the audience, rather than the melancholy, self-destructive, introspection that was, in some cases, their undoing. This is a familiar story of poetic maturation, of course, already present in 'Tintern Abbey', reworked obsessively by Tennyson in the 1830s and 1840s and running through early to mid-Victorian magazine reviews and criticism. One of its most famous articulations is Matthew Arnold's preface to his *Poems* of 1853. But biography enhanced and reconfigured this narrative in generically distinctive ways and was the most significant means of its dissemination, both to the popular readership and, later, within the academy. Some of the dead poets were deemed by their first biographers to have come closer than others to leaving their Romantic youth behind them. *Which* poets was, as we shall see, a matter of some significance.

Previous accounts of nineteenth-century autobiography and biography have tended to be polarized by gender. Feminist critics, from the 1980s, objected to the exclusion of female auto/biography from the canon of nineteenth-century life-writing and were instrumental in the resurrection of Victorian women's autobiography.[22] There has been less interest in women's biography, with Elizabeth Gaskell's *Life of Charlotte Brontë* (1857) the exception, although Alison Booth has produced a groundbreaking study of female collective biography.[23] Mary Jean Corbett and Linda Peterson have looked at the interactions, as well as differences, between male and female traditions of autobiography, but there has been little attempt to do the same for biography. I am indebted to this body of work on women's life-writing, and I view biography as, in many ways, a 'feminine' form, but throughout I want to stress the dialogue that existed

---

[21] Richard Monckton Milnes (ed.), *Life, Letters, and Literary Remains, of John Keats*, 2 vols. (London: Edward Moxon, 1848), ii. 52, 105.

[22] e.g. Valerie Sanders, *The Private Lives of Victorian Women: Autobiography in Nineteenth-Century England* (New York: Harvester/Wheatsheaf, 1989); Mary Jean Corbett, *Representing Femininity: Middle-Class Subjectivity in Victorian and Edwardian Women's Autobiographies* (New York: Oxford University Press, 1992); and Linda H. Peterson, *Traditions of Victorian Women's Autobiography: The Poetics and Politics of Life Writing* (Charlottesville, Va.: University Press of Virginia, 1999).

[23] Booth, *How to Make It as a Woman*. On women as the subjects of Victorian biography, see Joanne Shattock, 'The Construction of the Woman Writer', in Joanne Shattock (ed.), *Women and Literature in Britain 1800–1900* (Cambridge: Cambridge University Press, 2001), 8–34.

between male and female literary *Lives*. I give more space to male subjects than to female, because it is here that we find the bulk of biographical representation of 'the Romantic poet'. However, I have framed the chapters on Byron, Shelley, and the Lake Poets, with chapters that emphasize the importance of female *Lives* in shaping both literary biography and the poet. The very significant contribution of female biographers, including Mary Shelley, to shaping the reputations of male poets is also a thread that runs through the book. I encompass canonical male-on-male biographical writing—Boswell's Johnson, Moore's Byron, De Quincey's Coleridge and Wordsworth are all here—but in the context of a representative range of different biographical formats, many popular and ephemeral, by male and female biographers and with male and female subjects.

Chapter 1 introduces my discussion of *Lives* of the poets in the 1820s and 1830s by describing the development of biography in the late eighteenth and early nineteenth centuries in relation to domestic ideology and the literary marketplace. Chapter 2 looks at the encounter between biography and Romanticism. It focuses first on the hostile responses of Wordsworth and Coleridge to the genre, in the context of the market competition between poetry and biography, and then at contemporary celebrations of the capacity of the literary 'Life' to create an intimate relationship between reader and subject. In Chapter 3 I consider the question of how literary biography produced and was, in turn, produced by 'Byron' and Byronism. The discussion takes account of the full range of earlier nineteenth-century *Lives* of this poet—and some later—but especially of Thomas Moore's *Letters and Journals of Lord Byron*, as they constructed the relationship between genius, domestic life, and the reader. Chapter 4 extends this discussion by focusing on Mary Shelley's career as a biographer and her role in shaping the afterlives of Percy Shelley from the 1820s. It reads her fragmented attempts at a posthumous memoir (an early, unpublished sketch, followed by three influential editions of his work) in the context of the wider picture of biography at the period—looking, for instance, at the influence of William Godwin, Mary Hays, and Thomas Moore on her work. It also reads her memorialization of Shelley in relation to her major biographical publication: the essays she wrote for Dionysius Lardner's *Cabinet Cyclopaedia*. Chapter 5 explores De Quincey's gossiping and wittily critical essays on Wordsworth and Coleridge, published in *Tait's Edinburgh Magazine* in the 1830s. The focus here is on how De Quincey's biographical practice and his representation of Romantic, poetic genius were shaped by their context in a magazine aimed at a broad readership and in some respects directed at a female audience. In many ways the first posthumous *Lives* of Felicia Hemans and Letitia Landon drew together the debates set up in biographies of Byron, Shelley, and the Lake Poets, but the domestication of genius was inevitably differently inflected when the biographical subject was a female poet. The final chapter looks at issues of gender and genius in the early biographical literature on Hemans and Landon and at how these texts cast doubt on the value of masculine, Romantic genius in their attempts to articulate a new model of the poet—at once feminine, domesticated and engaged with her readers.

This book does not pretend to be an all-inclusive investigation of nineteenth-century biographies of the Romantic poets. The most significant posthumous *Lives* of Blake and Keats, for instance, fall outside the period dealt with here. Nevertheless, my introductory chapters and the individual case studies that follow aim to display, in some detail, the construction and texture of literary biography in a variety of forms and to capture what I believe to be the most representative and significant moments in the history of the genre from the 1780s to the 1840s, and in the afterlives of 'the Romantic poet'. My hope is that, in so doing, this book will go some way towards rehabilitating the image of Victorian biography, by demonstrating the capacity of this often underestimated body of literature to challenge as well as to contain.

1

Biography and Domestic Life

This chapter will look back over the shaping of biography from the later eighteenth century, in order to discover the basis of the thematic focus, in *Lives* of Byron, Shelley, the Lake Poets, Hemans, and Landon, on the clash between genius and domestic life, and of biography's ambivalent relationship with masculine, Romantic genius. Here I will be considering the practice and reception of Johnson and Boswell in relation to examples of female 'Lives', especially in the popular tradition of collective female biography. Johnson and Boswell were the presiding influences on early nineteenth-century literary biography, but not the exclusive ones and female collective biography exerted particular influences on some of the *Lives* of the poets I will be dealing with. My primary purpose in bringing canonical male biographical theory and practice together with this body of collective biography is to draw attention to the points of connection that existed between them, in order to cast fresh light on the development of biography as a genre. In brief, the following discussion proposes that a helpful way to approach biography, as it evolved in various forms from about the 1780s, is as an ideologically driven representation and publication of domestic life.

There has been some interest amongst feminist scholars in the importance of domestic life to Victorian women's autobiography. Linda Peterson, for instance, has shown how nineteenth-century female autobiographers dealt with 'the immense pressure on women to make their life writing domestic, their self-conceptions relational'.[1] There has been little recognition, however, that this was just one manifestation of a much more deeply rooted connection between the biographical and the domestic—a connection that related to the gender of the biographer and subject in much less clear-cut ways than feminist histories of women's autobiography have sometimes suggested. Here I put the case that biography, from the later eighteenth century, was shaped by its modelling and publication of the domestic subject and that, although variously inflected by differences of gender (of biographer and subject) as well as of form and

---

[1] Linda H. Peterson, *Traditions of Victorian Women's Autobiography: The Poetics and Politics of Life Writing* (Charlottesville, Va.: University Press of Virginia, 1999), 25. See also Mary Jean Corbett, *Representing Femininity: Middle-Class Subjectivity in Victorian and Edwardian Women's Autobiographies* (New York: Oxford University Press, 1992).

publishing context, this remained the matrix within which it developed.[2] The domestic sphere, as defined by biography, was not self-enclosed, but extended its influence to the public realm, most crucially in the genre's claim to find common ground between the lives of its subjects and its readers. This is visible in distinct but related ways in Johnson, Boswell, and collective female biography. The chapter is divided into two sections: the first discusses the development of biography as a product and producer of middle-class, ideological investment in domesticity and the second looks at the genre in the late eighteenth-century marketplace and at the beginnings of critical controversy over its capacity to open up private life to public view. These are the contexts within which biography's power to alarm the Romantic poets, its market success, and its self-consolidating construction of Romantic genius may best be understood.

1.1 BIOGRAPHY AND DOMESTIC IDEOLOGY: 1750–1840

Samuel Johnson, famously, in 1750 designated domestic life as the biographer's special terrain. The 'business of the biographer', as distinct from that of the 'historian', was

> often to pass slightly over those performances and incidents, which produce vulgar greatness, to lead the thoughts into domestick privacies, and display the minute details of daily life, where exterior appendages are cast aside, and men excel each other only by prudence and by virtue.[3]

For Johnson, the domestic space in biography was where the reader would genuinely come to know the great man because it signified the shared humanity of the subject and the reader.[4] The intimate view was the true one—'[t]he most authentick witnesses of any man's character are those who know him in his own family'—and the unique power of biography was to let the reader see public figures 'in their private Apartments, in their careless Hours, and observe those Actions in which they indulged their own Inclinations, without any Regard to

---

[2] Anthony John Harding, '"Domestick Privacies": Biography and the Sanctifying of Privacy, from Johnson to Martineau', *Dalhousie Review*, 85/3 (Fall 2005), 371–89, also recognizes the role of biography 'in defining and contesting the boundary between private and public' (373). I differ in emphasizing the importance of domesticity as a gendered discourse and of taking into account the contribution of 18th- and early 19th-cent. female biography in defining the domestic space.

[3] *The Rambler*, no. 60, in *The Yale Edition of the Works of Samuel Johnson*, gen. ed. J. H. Middendorf, iii–v. *The Rambler*, ed. W. J. Bate and A. B. Strauss (New Haven: Yale University Press, 1969), iii. 321. Boswell quotes this passage approvingly at the beginning of his *Life of Johnson*, see *Boswell's Life of Samuel Johnson, Together with Boswell's Journal of a Tour to the Hebrides*, ed. George Birkbeck Hill and L. F. Powell, 6 vols. (Oxford: Oxford University Press, 1934–50), i. 32.

[4] See Robert Folkenflik, *Samuel Johnson, Biographer* (Ithaca, NY: Cornell University Press, 1978), 31.

Censure or Applause'.[5] To this end, the biographer must, ideally, be the housemate of his subject, for 'nobody can write the life of a man, but those who have eat and drink and lived in social intercourse with him'.[6] Boswell's *Life of Johnson* (1791) took the reader decisively into the private apartments, by dramatizing the intimacy of biographer and subject.[7] He listed his first qualification for the task of Johnson's biographer as having had 'the honour and happiness of enjoying his friendship for upwards of twenty years' and the inauthenticity of Hawkins's biography was proved for him, first and foremost by the fact that 'they never could have lived together with companionable ease and familiarity'.[8]

Johnson's *Prefaces* (1779–81), subsequently collected as *The Lives of the English Poets* (1781–3), lacked the dramatized relationship between biographer and subject, but drew some lines of connection between their public achievement and private life that also suggested the latter as the authentic measure of the former.[9] Scenes of the poets at home implied that their works were shaped by the strengths and weaknesses of the man hidden behind closed doors—doors the biographer was empowered to open. As Kathleen Kremmerer argues, his 'Life' of Milton focused on the poet's relations with his wife and daughters, in order to attack his ideas on female education and, fundamentally, to question the poet's whole public achievement: 'By emphasizing Milton's private behavior, Johnson presents him as a hypocrite, as a man who opposed the tyranny of kings but who behaved as a tyrant in his own home'.[10] In his 'Life' of Pope, the section on Pope's character began with a description of his 'spider'-like body and with an anecdote from a female servant:

He was then so weak as to stand in perpetual need of female attendance; extremely sensible of cold, so that he wore a kind of fur doublet under a shirt of very coarse warm

---

[5] *Rambler*, no. 68 (1750), *Yale Edition*, iii. 361. Review of *Memoirs of the Conduct of the Duchess of Marlborough* in the *Gentleman's Magazine* (Mar. 1842), quoted in Samuel Johnson, *The Lives of the Most Eminent English Poets; With Critical Observations on their Works*, ed. Roger Lonsdale, 4 vols. (Oxford: Clarendon Press, 2006), i. 80.

[6] *Boswell's Life of Samuel Johnson*, ii. 166.

[7] Boswell enters his narrative roughly a sixth of the way through, racing through the first fifty-four years of Johnson's life in order to arrive at the time when they became acquainted.

[8] Ibid. i. 25, 27.

[9] There has been much debate on the degree and nature of these lines of connection. Fred Parker, 'Johnson and the "Lives of the Poets"', *Cambridge Quarterly*, 29/4 (2000), 323–37, argues that 'Johnson's format expresses the idea that the value of poetry lies in what *escapes* the biographical' (333). Others have made more convincing cases for structural and thematic connections—see e.g. James L. Battersby, 'Life, Art, and the *Lives of the Poets*', in David Wheeler (ed.), *Domestick Privacies: Samuel Johnson and the Art of Biography* (Lexington, Ky: University Press of Kentucky, 1987), 26–56; and Greg Clingham, 'Life and Literature in Johnson's *Lives of the Poets*', in Greg Clingham (ed.), *The Cambridge Companion to Samuel Johnson* (Cambridge: Cambridge University Press, 1997), 161–91.

[10] Kathleen Nulton Kremmerer, 'Domestic Relations in Samuel Johnson's *Life of Milton*', *The Age of Johnson: A Scholarly Annual*, 15 (2004), 57–8. Kremmerer shows that Johnson's sources, by contrast, focused on Milton's public achievement.

linen with fine sleeves. When he rose, he was invested in boddice [*sic*] made of stiff canvass, being scarce able to hold himself erect till they were laced, and he then put on a flannel waistcoat. One side was contracted. His legs were so slender that he enlarged their bulk with three pair of stockings, which were drawn on and off by the maid; for he was not able to dress or undress himself, and neither went to bed nor rose without help. His weakness made it very difficult for him to be clean.[11]

Here, with a fine balance of compassion and cruelty, Johnson went into the most private quarters of the poet, displaying Pope, literally and figuratively, in his undress. The passage enacted a disturbing denial of agency to the poet—the reader, voyeuristically, looks on as the maid strips him of his clothes. It ironically returned genius to the flesh in order to comment on Pope's public performance. His supportive carapace of clothes betrays the artifice of his public persona—a theme throughout the essay—here disguising a reality that is insubstantial and emasculated.

Johnson's model of biography suggests an understanding of the difference between private and public life that is founded on distinctions of social rank. His designation of the domestic as the authentic life, offers a challenge to courtly society, identified with the public sphere, and voices the interests of readers of the middling ranks. These class interests are implicated in his rejection of biography as formal panegyric and assertion of the right of the reader to intimate knowledge of the great man. He argues that an informal conversation with a servant is likely to give more insight into the great man's character than 'a formal and studied narrative, begun with his pedigree, and ended with his funeral', and even suggests that public standing is hardly necessary in order to become the subject of a biography: 'I have often thought that there has rarely passed a life of which a judicious and faithful narrative would not be useful'.[12] For Johnson, the public sphere produces an inauthentic rhetoric of deference, the private is where social hierarchies, temporarily, dissolve, uniting even the very highest with the very lowest, by virtue of their common humanity:

The prince feels the same pain when an invader seizes a province, as the farmer when a thief drives away his cow. Men thus equal in themselves will appear equal in honest and impartial biography; and those whom fortune or nature place at the greatest distance may afford instruction to each other.[13]

If biography opens a middle ground, between 'high' and 'low', a space for an imaginary social levelling, it also, in some of Johnson's practice, allows a reconfiguration of the relations between men and women.[14] The examples

---

[11] *Lives of the Most Eminent English Poets*, ed. Lonsdale, iv. 54–5.
[12] *Rambler*, no. 60 (1750), *Yale Edition*, iii. 322, 320.
[13] *Idler*, no. 84 (1759), ibid. ii. 263.
[14] Ibid. The nature of this levelling is debatable. Robert Ready, 'Flat Realities: Hazlitt on Biography', *Prose Studies*, 5/3 (Dec. 1982), 312, makes a distinction between biography as a levelling experience and a 'communal' one, where there is common ground between reader and

cited from his 'Lives' of Milton and Pope suggest Johnson associating the private sphere, specifically, with a critical, feminine perspective on masculine greatness. In both these respects his biographical theory and practice has interesting points of connection with the more widespread emergence of an ideological construction of the 'domestic' as one of the central means by which class and gender differences were being articulated in the later eighteenth century. This is a context of some significance for understanding the evolving, generic definition of biography at this time and for the *Lives* of the Romantic poets that will be the main focus of this book.

It has been argued that, throughout the eighteenth century, but especially in its later decades, middle-class identity began to be formed through the elevation of domestic, as distinct from public, life. Gary Kelly writes that the eighteenth-century

bourgeois cultural revolution used the 'domestic affections' and domesticity . . . to provide authentic social relations for the subjective self, in contrast to what were seen as the vitiated, self-interested, exploitative social relations of a courtly society . . . [15]

The domestic was also increasingly defined in relation to a gendered construction of private and public life as separate spheres, representing, respectively, feminine and masculine realms of activity and influence. There has been much distinguished scholarship mapping the emergence of this ideological understanding of the domestic. Nancy Armstrong has shown how the figure of 'domestic woman', unworldly, educated, modest by contrast to her aristocratic counterpart, was opposed to that of 'economic man' in eighteenth-century conduct literature.[16] The growth of an industrialized economy was an important factor in the articulation of these separate spheres, especially in the later eighteenth and early nineteenth centuries. As Clara Tuite writes, 'the moral ambiguities and tensions of an exploitative and profit-seeking market-place were hygienically separated from a feminized and purified realm of the home'.[17] Davidoff and Hall, in their seminal study of the subject, showed how Evangelical thinking embraced the domestic ideal as expressive of unworldliness and 'a space . . . for true family religion' and how, from the 1790s, especially in the work of Hannah More, an

subject without this interfering with recognition of the subject as the greater of the two. The distinction is hard to maintain, however, and I would argue that it is not clearly present either in Johnson's pronouncements on biography or in Hazlitt's.

[15] Gary Kelly, *Revolutionary Feminism: The Mind and Career of Mary Wollstonecraft* (Basingstoke: Macmillan; New York: St Martin's Press, 1992), 12.

[16] Nancy Armstrong, *Desire and Domestic Fiction: A Political History of the Novel* (New York: Oxford University Press, 1987). It was this literature that, Nancy Armstrong argues, 'revised the semiotic of culture at its most basic level and enabled a coherent idea of the middle class to take shape' (63).

[17] Clara Tuite, 'Domesticity', *An Oxford Companion to The Romantic Age: British Culture 1776–1832*, gen. ed. Iain McCalman (Oxford: Oxford University Press, 1999), 127.

Evangelical equation of domesticity and femininity was popularized.[18] In the Revolution controversies of the 1790s, a feminized, domestic ideal was recruited by writers from all political factions as an expression of national character.[19] Tuite argues that Burke's *Reflections on the Revolution in France* (1790) 'initiated a new language of nationalism based on domesticity', by suggesting that '"Domestic attachments" and "family affections" are the stuff that "bind" a nation'.[20] Here, and elsewhere the figure of 'domestic woman', who represented 'the values and practices of the professional middle class in particular' gradually became identified with the values of the nation as a whole.[21] This ideological construction of domestic life continued to pervade cultural production in the early 1800s, emerging decisively as a dominant cultural value from the 1830s. In this decade an explicit rhetoric of middle-class empowerment, following the Reform Bill of 1832, combined with a more secularized vision of domestic virtue and a firmer sense of the home as the woman's domain, distinct from the masculine world of work, in the writing of such 'domestic ideologues' as Sarah Stickney Ellis, Harriet Martineau, and John Loudon.[22]

    There has been considerable debate on the nature of the eighteenth- and nineteenth-century ideological construction of domesticity. Historians have drawn attention to the necessity of distinguishing between representation and social practice in speaking of middle-class domesticity at this period, and of acknowledging the slippage between the two. It has been argued that the ideal of domestic woman and of the affective family founded on companionate marriage, was not confined to the middle classes but extended to influence the social practices of the landed gentry and aristocracy, as well as the lower classes.[23] Similarly, the existence of firmly delineated 'separate spheres' of female, domestic and male, public life has been thoroughly questioned and an emphasis has been given instead to the fractured and fluid reality, in which the boundaries of private and public were permeable for both men and women.[24] The representation of domesticity, of course, was equally fractured and fluid, both in terms of class and gender. Hannah More's *Strictures on the Modern System of Female Education* (1799), which urged its female readers to

---

[18] Leonore Davidoff and Catherine Hall, *Family Fortunes: Men and Women of the English Middle Class 1780–1850* (Hutchinson Education, 1987; rev. repr., London: Routledge, 2002), 115.
    [19] Ibid. 19.
    [20] Tuite, 'Domesticity', 125.
    [21] Kelly, *Revolutionary Feminism*, 6.
    [22] Davidoff and Hall, *Family Fortunes*, 155.
    [23] See Margaret R. Hunt, *The Middling Sort: Commerce, Gender, and the Family in England, 1680–1780* (Berkeley and Los Angeles: University of California Press, 1996).
    [24] See e.g. John Tosh, *A Man's Place: Masculinity and the Middle-Class Home in Victorian England* (New Haven: Yale University Press, 1999); Kathryn Gleadle and Sarah Richardson (eds.), *Women in British Politics, 1760–1860: The Power of the Petticoat* (Basingstoke: Macmillan; New York: St Martin's Press, 2000); Eleanor Gordon and Gwyneth Nair, *Public Lives: Women, Family and Society in Victorian Britain* (New Haven: Yale University Press, 2003); Ann Stott, 'Women and Religion', in Hannah Barker and Elaine Chalus (eds.), *Women's History, Britain, 1700–1850: An Introduction* (London: Routledge, 2005), 100–23.

eschew the frivolities of fashionable life and attend to religion, education, and domestic usefulness, identified 'middle-class' women as a group in need of instruction, but was addressed, ostensibly, to the more elevated classes, who would set the best pattern both to middle and lower ranks.[25] Even by the late 1830s, Sarah Ellis felt the need to preface *The Women of England* by carefully articulating the class identity of her audience, and presented herself as the first writer on the subject of domestic femininity to address '*women*', rather than 'ladies', thereby appealing to the growing constituency of educated, but not necessarily wealthy, wives and daughters of men in trade, manufacturing industry, and the professions.[26] If the class identity of those interested in learning domestic virtue was always in the process of articulation, so was their gender. The permeability of the separate, gendered spheres of private and public life was everywhere apparent in representation, from the 1790s onwards. Cowper, one of the most important popularizers of domestic themes at this time, located the truest home of the male subject within a feminized, domestic space.[27] Conversely, in the work of Hannah More in the 1790s and Sarah Ellis in the 1830s, we find the boundaries of the domestic moving outwards, as 'woman's mission' becomes defined in terms of the extension of her moral influence, reaching beyond the home to society at large. More's conviction of the 'power' exerted by domestic woman through her moral example and especially through the education of her children, is visible in the twin epigraphs to her *Strictures on ... Female Education*.[28] The first is a quotation from Cowper, celebrating domesticity as a means to personal happiness, virtue, and reputation:

> Domestic Happiness, thou only bliss
> Of Paradise that has survived the Fall!
> Thou art not known where PLEASURE is ador'd,
> That reeling Goddess with the zoneless waist.
> Forsaking thee, what shipwreck have we made
> Of honour, dignity, and fair renown![29]

The epigraph on the facing page addresses the female reader with a more ambitious aim:

May you so raise your character that you may help to make the next age a better thing, and leave posterity in your debt, for the advantage it shall receive by your example.[30]

---

[25] Hannah More, *Strictures on the Modern System of Female Education. With a View of the Principles and Conduct Prevalent Among Women of Rank and Fortune*, 2 vols. (London: T. Cadell Jun. and W. Davies, 1799), i. 62 and see 62–6.
[26] Sarah Stickney Ellis, *The Women of England, Their Social Duties and Domestic Habits. By Mrs. Ellis* (London: Fisher, Son & Co. [1839]), 6–7.
[27] See Davidoff and Hall, *Family Fortunes*, 166.
[28] More, *Strictures*, i. 52.
[29] Ibid., p. ii.
[30] Ibid., p. iii.

Thirty years later, Ellis told 'the women of England' confidently that the 'nation's moral wealth is in your keeping'.[31] By good domestic practice they were fitted to become 'able instruments in the promotion of public and private good', at a time when capitalism threatened to eclipse moral life. The men of Britain, conquering the far corners of the earth 'have borne along with them a generosity, a disinterestedness, and a moral courage, derived in no small measure from the female influence of their native country'.[32] Her vision of women's influence, the nation's spiritual sustenance, extending in ever-widening circles to its colonies, presented a paradox of secluded, feminine domesticity that encompassed masculine, public life. The feminized, domestic space represented women's subordination, from one point of view, but was also seen as a source of female empowerment.[33] It might also be a place from which to imply a critique of the masculine, public sphere—Ellis saw domestic life as the fuel of capitalism, but also its antithesis and called for the domestic ideal to be reinvigorated by the women of England as a vanguard against a materialistic, mechanized society.[34]

There have been many explorations of the ways in which a middle-class construction of the domestic was furthered and problematized in eighteenth- and nineteenth-century fiction and conduct literature.[35] Yet there has been almost no attention to the important part played by biography in articulating the 'domestic' and still less to how the genre was shaped by domestic ideology.[36] It is no accident that biography became increasingly popular with middle-class audiences in the 1820s and 1830s when an ideological discourse of domesticity

---

[31] *The Women of England*, 18.

[32] Ibid. 38, 75–9.

[33] See ibid. 58–9 and 125, where Ellis veers between grandiose statements of women's empowerment and doubts on the merits of female intellectual ambition. She also states categorically that the sexes are not equal (302). Davidoff and Hall, *Family Fortunes*, 183, argue that '[t]he tension between subordination and influence, between moral power and political silence, was one which preoccupied all the protagonists of "woman's mission"'.

[34] See Ellis, *The Women of England*, 457, where she figures the feminine, spiritual basis of the modern material world as the vapour 'proverbial as it is for its weakness, emptiness, and nothingness in the creation', which powers a steam engine.

[35] Nancy Armstrong, in *Desire and Domestic Fiction*, uncovered the class interests implicit in the figure of 'domestic woman' and the domesticated 'sexual exchange' in 18th- and 19th-cent. conduct literature and the novel; Elizabeth Langland, in *Nobody's Angels: Middle-Class Women and Domestic Ideology in Victorian Culture* (Ithaca, NY: Cornell University Press, 1995) and 'Women's Writing and the Domestic Sphere' in Joanne Shattock (ed.), *Women and Literature in Britain, 1800–1900* (Cambridge: Cambridge University Press, 2001), 123, showed how the household represented in 19th-cent. fiction is 'a moral haven secure from economic and political storms', but also a place where women manage 'class power'; Kate Ferguson Ellis, in *The Contested Castle: Gothic Novels and the Subversion of Domestic Ideology* (Urbana and Chicago: University of Illinois Press, 1989) and Anne K. Mellor, *Romanticism and Gender* (New York: Routledge, 1993), 91, argued that Gothic fiction showed the 'dark underside of the doctrine of the separate spheres'.

[36] The exception is Harding, '"Domestick Privacies"'. See also Davidoff and Hall, *Family Fortunes*, who note in passing that '[n]umerous memoirs and biographies also immortalized the gentle influence of particular wives, mothers and daughters' and thus contributed to the formation of the domestic ideal (117).

rose to cultural prominence more generally in fiction, poetry, and conduct literature.[37] The theory and practice of Johnson and Boswell, as I have suggested, may already be related to the changing construction of domesticity. It is interesting, for example, to see how readers received their focus on domestic life as one that unsettled established boundaries of class and gender. In adopting a domestic perspective, they opened themselves to accusations of disrespect for traditional social hierarchies and, related to this, charges of effeminacy. Robert Potter in 1783, for instance, deplored Johnson's style as ungentlemanly gossip:

We are also sorry to see the masculine spirit of Dr. Johnson descending to what he perhaps in another might call 'anile garrulity.' In reading the life of any eminent person we wish to be informed of the qualities which gave him the superiority over other men: when we are poorly put off with paltry circumstances, which are common to him with common men, we receive neither instruction nor pleasure. We know that the greatest men are subject to the infirmities of human nature equally with the meanest; why then are these infirmities recorded? Can it be of any importance to us to be told how many pair of stockings the author of the *Essay on Man* wore? [38]

In 1780 Francis Blackburne, for whom Milton was an admired 'patron of public liberty', also attacked Johnson as a gossip: 'the good Doctor turns eavesdropper; and, to warn the public against the principles of the miscreant Milton, condescends to inform us of what passed in the domestic privacies of his family'.[39] Disturbed at the implications of Johnson's perspective, Blackburne went so far as to interpret this 'Life' as a feminist assault on Milton, mocking what he saw as its appeal to 'English Amazons'.[40] Boswell, too, was criticized for an interest in domestic privacies that was at once emasculating and socially subversive. Dorothea Gregory Alison wrote to Mrs Montagu on 16 March 1791, just before the *Life of Johnson* was published, deploring his 'gross gossipation' as rightly banishing him from good society.[41]

The characterization of the biographical practice of Johnson and Boswell as gossip is telling. Deborah Jones describes gossip as 'a way of talking between women in their roles as women, intimate in style, personal and domestic in topic

---

[37] See Herbert F. Tucker, 'House Arrest: The Domestication of English Poetry in the 1820s', *New Literary History*, 25/3 (Summer 1994), 521–48.

[38] James T. Boulton (ed.), *Samuel Johnson: The Critical Heritage* (London: Routledge, 1995), 297. It is significant, of course, that the stockings passage in 'Pope' relayed the revelations of a female servant, as published in the *Gentleman's Magazine* (see *Lives of the Poets*, iv. 305). See also Potter in 1789, Boulton (ed.), *Samuel Johnson*, 308, for a comparison of Johnson to Plutarch as having 'a considerable spice of the old woman'.

[39] Boulton (ed.), *Samuel Johnson*, 278, 281–2. Johnson's hostility to Milton's republicanism was repeatedly noted and often deplored as producing a distorted picture of the man and the poet.

[40] Ibid. 282.

[41] See B. R. McElderry, Jr., 'Boswell in 1790–91: Two Unpublished Comments', *Notes and Queries* (July 1962), 267–8.

and setting'.[42] The term was not so firmly gendered in the eighteenth century as now—Johnson's dictionary defines the noun as '(2) A tippling companion (3) One who runs about tattling like women at a lying-in', and the verb as (1) 'To chat; to prate; to be merry' (2) 'To be a pot companion'. However, Potter clearly sees Johnson's gossip as a descent from his usual 'masculine spirit'. It is a language that leaks domestic secrets into the public sphere and that, entertainingly, destroys public reputation. For Patricia Meyer Spacks, '[g]ossip emphasizes what people hold in common' and can therefore function as a 'resource of the subordinated', giving 'the illusion of mastery gained through taking imaginative possession of another's experience'.[43] To characterize the language of biography as gossip defines it as a feminized discourse that travels from the domestic to the public sphere and carries with it, on this journey, a disturbingly new sense of where the subject and, indeed, the biographer, stand in relation to hierarchies of class and gender. We will see later how, for all these reasons, the biographer as gossip, locating genius at the juncture of domestic and public life, became a contentious figure for the Romantic poets and their defenders.

Neither Johnson nor Boswell engaged in an overtly ideological gendering of the domestic sphere. For this we need to look at the female *Lives* being published from the later eighteenth century. The publications that might come under the heading 'female biography' between around 1780 and 1840 were diverse. Very few of them have become canonical—a notable exception being Godwin's *Memoirs* of Mary Wollstonecraft (1798).[44] Most others are still relatively unknown, although some have been resurrected latterly by historians of women's writing. They included, at one extreme, memoirs of obscure individual women, intended to illustrate an exemplary, Christian life and 'happy' death; and, at the other, scurrilous pamphlets detailing the social scheming and sexual adventures of actresses.[45] There were also literary *Lives*, as we shall see in Chapter 6, in prefaces to editions of women's poetry and in individual biographies. Perhaps the most representative—and certainly an increasingly popular form of female biography at the period—were the volumes of collected lives of 'eminent' women from ancient and modern times, eclectic mixtures of female 'worthies',

[42] Deborah Jones, 'Gossip: Notes on Women's Oral Culture', in Deborah Cameron (ed.), *The Feminist Critique of Language: A Reader* (London: Routledge, 1990), 243.

[43] Patricia Meyer Spacks, *Gossip* (1985; Chicago: University of Chicago Press, 1986), 101, 103, 22.

[44] William Godwin, *Memoirs of the Author of A Vindication of the Rights of Woman* (London: J. Johnson, 1798).

[45] Typical examples in the first category were Joseph Benson, *A Short Account of the Death of Mrs Mary Hutton, of Sunderland, who Died February 24, 1777* ([Newcastle upon Tyne?], 1777); or Thomas Dixon, *A Brief Account of the Life and Death of Barbara Walker* ([London?], 1777). By contrast see e.g. *Memoirs of Mrs. Billington, from her Birth: Containing a Variety of Matter, Ludicrous, Theatrical, Musical, and ——* (London: James Ridgway, 1792); and *The Life and Memoirs of the Late Miss Ann Catley, The Celebrated Actress: with Biographical Sketches of Sir Frances Blake Delaval, and the Hon. Isabella Pawlet, Daughter to the Earl of Thanet, by Miss Ambross* (London: J. Bird, n.d.).

predominantly royal, aristocratic, religious, and literary figures.[46] Collective
female biographies were sold on the double premiss that they offered readers
stories of extraordinary women and models of behaviour that were, whether as
positive or negative examples, of direct relevance to their own lives.[47] On the one
hand, their eclecticism strained against any reading that would contain their
subjects under the sign of 'domestic woman'. George Stewarton's entertainingly
sensational, anti-Jacobin *Female Revolutionary Plutarch* (1806), for instance,
interspersed hagiographies of female royalists with denunciations of bloodthirsty
female Revolutionaries, whose public folly was the product of their abrogation of
domestic duty.[48] It was a typical strategy. Mary Hays, coming from the opposite
end of the political spectrum, also placed figures as various as Diane de Poitiers,
Dido Queen of Carthage, the Queen of the Amazons, and Eliza Haywood side
by side in her *Female Biography* (1803).[49] Clearly, this range of biographical
representations of women, viewed as a whole, and many publications when
viewed separately, challenged a monolithic representation of femininity. The
'Advertisement' to *Eccentric Biography* (1803) made overt what was an underlying rationale of many collections:

Under the epithet *Eccentric* are properly included characters remarkable for some extraordinary deviation from the generality of the sex; and thus, the present volume contains a
variety not only calculated to entertain, but to improve, as it exhibits virtue in its greatest
purity, and vice in all its deformity: *notorious Swindlers*, being contrasted with *Ladies of
Honour*, *Women of astonishing Weakness and Credulity*, with those of *superior talents, or
learning*; others of *loose morals*, with some of *the strictest Chastity*...[50]

Yet, as even this list of eccentric subjects suggests, a bourgeois ideal of domesticated femininity was implicit in female biography, no matter how far individual
lives might deviate from it. For Hays, her Revolutionary heroine Madame
Roland's public life grew directly from her private virtues. She quoted a family
friend: '"[i]n private and domestic life she practised every virtue; her filial piety

---

[46] See Booth, *How to Make It as Woman*, 389–92, for a list of numbers of collective
women's biography published annually in Britain and America 1830–1940.
[47] See e.g. *Eccentric Biography; or the Memoirs of Remarkable Female Characters, Ancient and
Modern. Including Actresses, Adventurers, Authoresses, Fortune-Tellers, Gipsies, Dwarfs, Swindlers,
Vagrants, and Others who have Distinguished themselves by their Chastity, Dissipation, Intrepidity,
Learning, Abstinence, Credulity, &c. &c. Alphabetically Arranged. Forming a Pleasing Mirror of
Reflection to the Female Mind*, 2nd edn. (London: T. Hurst, 1803). This, the accompanying
volume to a male counterpart, included 'Lives' of Aphra Behn; Boadicea; Catherine I Empress of
Russia; Anne Catley; Cleopatra Queen of Egypt; Mrs Wollstonecraft Godwin; Mrs Angelica
Kaufman; Laetitia Pilkington; Mrs Robinson; Madam Rowland [*sic*]; and The Chevalier de
D'Eon (with an engraving of her dressed as a man).
[48] [G. L. Stewarton], *The Female Revolutionary Plutarch, containing Biographical, Historical, and
Revolutionary Sketches, Characters, and Anecdotes. By the Author of the Revolutionary Plutarch
and Memoirs of Talleyrand*, 3 vols. (London: John Murray, 1806).
[49] Mary Hays, *Female Biography; or, Memoirs of Illustrious and Celebrated Women, of all Ages and
Countries. Alphabetically Arranged*, 6 vols. (London: Richard Phillips, 1803).
[50] *Eccentric Biography*, pp. iii–iv.

was exemplary; and, united to a man twenty years older than herself, she made his constant happiness. As a mother, she was exquisitely tender. Order, economy, and foresight, presided over her domestic management."'[51] Stewarton's estimate of Madame Roland's personal and political virtues was diametrically opposed to Hays's, but he too insisted on the connection between her domestic and public life, this time as a lesson in 'how easily a domestic rebel is transformed into a political conspirator'.[52] By the time Hays was writing, there was an established tradition in collective female biography of modelling an ideal of domesticated womanhood for the emulation of female readers. The *Biographium Faemineum* (1766), an alphabetical collection of short 'Lives' of 'Illustrious Ladies', claimed to enhance the reader's own virtues through the lessons of female biography. Its title designated 'public' as well as 'private' life, the province of the female worthy, and pointed to the compatibility, in these women's lives, of 'virtue', 'piety', and 'genius'. The introduction also argued for the possibility of combining an educated, female intelligence with the roles of wife and mother.[53] Hays followed the format of the *Biographium Faemineum* but within a Revolutionary, feminist context, presenting biography as an entertaining means to women's intellectual improvement.[54] Her preface and her examples advocated an enlightened, domestic femininity—education would enhance women's experience of marriage, hence they were urged by Hays to 'substitute, as they fade, for the evanescent graces of youth, the more durable attractions of a cultivated mind'.[55] This ideal was articulated in opposition to a model of decadent (implicitly aristocratic) female vanity and neglect of mind that put them on a level with the closeted 'slaves of an Eastern haram [*sic*]'.[56] Where Johnson had argued for biographical privacies as the means by which the shared humanity of reader and subject could be communicated, Hays saw them as catering to a specifically feminine model of the reader/subject relationship. Biography, as she presented it, would be a palatable educational medium for women, who, 'unsophisticated by the pedantry of the schools, read not for dry information' but 'require pleasure to be mingled with instruction'. It would answer a specifically female need for intimate human engagement, for women's 'understandings are principally accessible through their affections'. Hence their delight in 'lively images' and 'minute delineations

---

[51] Hays, *Female Biography*, vi. 309. She is quoting the comment of M. Champagneux, a friend of Mme Roland's husband.

[52] Stewarton, *The Female Revolutionary Plutarch*, iii. 394.

[53] *Biographium Faemineum. The Female Worthies: or, Memoirs of the Most Illustrious Ladies, of all Ages and Nations, who have been Eminently distinguished for their Magnanimity, Learning, Genius, Virtue, Piety, and other Excellent Endowments, conspicuous in all the various Stations and Relations of Life, public and private*, 2 vols. (London: S. Crowder and J. Payne, J. Wilkie and W. Nicoll, J. Wren, 1766), vol i, p. x.

[54] See Hays, *Female Biography*, vol. i, 'Preface', pp. iii–viii.

[55] Ibid., p. v.

[56] Ibid., p. iv.

of character'.[57] The act of reading biography was thereby projected as an extension of the reader's already existing virtues as domestic woman, creature of the affections, interested in small-scale human interaction, to morally improving ends. The net result would be a revolution in the public standing of women, the improvement of their minds, and thus their 'advancement in the grand scale of rational and social existence'.[58]

Hays's radicalized vision was not typical of female collective biography as it developed in the first decades of the nineteenth century. More usually such publications were written in a conservative, often Evangelical context that intersected most obviously with didactic fiction and conduct literature. Mrs Pilkington's *Biography for Girls*, for instance, modelled the virtues of domestic affection, benevolence, sweetness, and charity—the chapter headings indicate the moral programme well enough: 'Louisa Harrington; or, the Victim of Pride', 'Sally Bowman; or, Filial Fondness', 'Lucy Lutridge; or, Vanity Punished'.[59] Mary Ann Kelty's *Biography for Young Ladies* (1839) exemplified the extreme of the emphasis of female biography on private virtue over public achievement, portraying its subjects as models of Christian piety, unworldliness, and the domestic affections—'virtues, which every mother would be delighted to see blossoming in her own beloved children'.[60] Nevertheless, even here there was an invitation to enter the public sphere—if only in the act of reading and possibly emulating the histories of women in public life. Thus, '[a] young lady might, from reading the life of Hannah Moore [*sic*], be desirous of imitating her ardent desire of instructing the poor; she might attend a Sunday School for that purpose, and, for trying to benefit others, God might reward her by blessing his word to her own soul'.[61]

Biography, as theorized and practised by Johnson, Boswell, and the authors of collective female biography, and as received by contemporary readers, thus made a significant contribution to the developing middle-class, ideological investment in domestic life, as a feminized but permeable space. Female collective biography certainly influenced the way that literary women were portrayed in the early nineteenth century and female poets, including Hemans and Landon, were amongst the subjects of such collections. As we shall see, Hemans, the most prominent woman poet of the late Romantic period, was memorialized in the

---

[57] Hays, *Female Biography*, vol. i, 'Preface', p. iv.
[58] Ibid.
[59] Mrs [Mary] Pilkington, *Biography for Girls; or, Moral and Instructive Examples for the Female Sex* (1st edn., London: Vernor & Hood, 1799; 3rd edn., London: Vernor and Hood, Poultrey, 1800). The companion volume, *Biography for Boys; or, Characteristic Histories, Calculated to Impress the Youthful Mind with an Admiration of Virtuous Principles and Detestation of Vicious Ones* (1st edn., London: Vernor & Hood, 1799; 3rd edn., London: J. Harris, 1808), in which boys were encouraged by the example of George Cowley to emulate his life of 'domestic tenderness', shows how at this stage the domestic virtues were, relatively uncontentiously, applied to both sexes (115).
[60] M.[ary] A.[nn] K.[elty], *Biography for Young Ladies* (London: John Kendrick, 1839), p. iv.
[61] Ibid.

1830s by biographers whose central aim was to wrestle with the relationship between her genius and her role as domestic woman. But this was not just because she was a woman poet or even because she was a prominent advocate of domesticity. The focus of biography on domestic life was by the mid-1830s well established and far from being the exclusive terrain of female *Lives*. Whilst we must take account of gender-specific factors in the construction of female genius, one of the striking features of biography in the 1820s and 1830s is the ideological congruence between *Lives* of the female and the male poets. As later chapters will show, both were seen as, in their different ways, answerable to domestic responsibility and *thereby* to public life. Biography was predicated on the interaction that More and Ellis had insisted upon between these spheres, but did not always represent the relationship between public and private realms in such a harmonious light. The posthumous reputations of Byron and Shelley, Wordsworth and Coleridge, no less than those of Hemans or Landon, were formed biographically in relation to a middle-class ideal of domesticated femininity, against which the aristocracy of masculine genius was judged—and often found wanting.

1.2 THE PUBLICATION OF 'DOMESTICK PRIVACIES'

Biography began to be defined at this period as a transgressive publication of domestic privacies. Previously critics have tended to focus on autobiography in this context. Mary Jean Corbett, for instance, has argued that autobiography 'functions generically as a mediating realm in which both the public and the private are produced for reading consumers, not as distinct realms, but as mutually constitutive' and has shown how female autobiographers had to develop strategies to circumscribe the transgression this entailed.[62] More recently James Treadwell has written that we need to understand eighteenth- and early nineteenth-century autobiography, as distinct from biography, as a newly contentious transaction, whereby private life was published without traditional justifications.[63] But such arguments characteristically sideline biography, which pre-dated autobiography, in its sophisticated and troubling capacity to create interactions between private and public life. In Treadwell's view, 'biography' at this period represented a relatively stable, culturally sanctioned genre in which the Horatian formula of pleasurable instruction operated to meliorate the potentially transgressive nature of the intrusion into private life. Autobiography was defined by its destabilization of this framework, so that even as autobiographers and reviewers tried to defend this mode, there was an uneasy awareness that

---

[62] Corbett, *Representing Femininity*, 12.
[63] James Treadwell, *Autobiographical Writing and British Literature, 1783–1834* (Oxford: Oxford University Press, 2005).

it reinflected amusement as 'prurience, voyeurism, or gossip' and privileged 'disclosure over evaluation'.[64] There are clearly interesting ways in which the biographical and the autobiographical defined themselves against one another at this period and I will return to this later. However, Treadwell's distinction between the two does not entirely hold. Biography was widely perceived at the time as the 'parent' genre of 'autobiography' and the anxieties attendant on the emergence of autobiography must be seen in the context of already existing doubts relating to biography.[65] Whilst biography was certainly the more established and respected genre, its focus on domestic life, no less than autobiography's, became the object of critical controversy, especially from the 1780s. This is an important context within which to understand the perception and practice of literary biography generally in the first decades of the nineteenth century and the *Lives* of the Romantic poets in particular.

Biography started to become differentiated, generically, from fiction and conduct literature, in the course of the later eighteenth and early nineteenth centuries by claiming a different order of historical authenticity for the lives depicted. Biographical texts began to articulate a relationship between reader and subject as an actual exchange of intimacy, a private conversation between two living subjects held within the public sphere. Greg Clingham argues that Boswell, unlike novelists of the period, 'seems to half-believe that the rhetorical, metaphorical presence of Johnson in the *Life* is in fact real and immediate, and therefore historical'.[66] Boswell advertised the 'peculiar value' of his *Life* as 'the quantity that it contains of Johnson's conversation', and his method was, famously, to recreate the authentic speaking voice of the subject through letters and dialogue.[67] The length of the *Life* was, itself, a manifestation of the living presence of Johnson, aiming to create for the reader the impression of a real-time experience of Johnson, as if they, too, were his domestic intimate:

Indeed I cannot conceive a more perfect mode of writing any man's life, than not only relating all the most important events of it in their order, but interweaving what he privately wrote, and said, and thought; by which mankind are enabled as it were to see him live, and to 'live o'er each scene' with him, as he actually advanced through the several stages of his life.[68]

---

[64] James Treadwell, *Autobiographical Writing and British Literature*, 27, 23.

[65] Treadwell, ibid. 24, claims that James Stanfield's *Essay on the Study and Composition of Biography* (Sunderland: printed by George Garbutt; London: sold by Gale, Curtis, Fenner, Cradock and Joy; Edinburgh: sold by Constable and Co., and John and James Robertson, 1813) identifies autobiography as the more problematic genre, distinct from biography, 'because its claim to provide knowledge is a seductive delusion'. In fact, Stanfield argues that both are vulnerable to authorial bias—Johnson's *Lives of the Poets* as much as Rousseau's *Confessions* (34–48).

[66] Greg Clingham, *James Boswell: The Life of Johnson* (Cambridge: Cambridge University Press, 1992), 7.

[67] *Boswell's Life of Johnson*, i. 31.

[68] Ibid. 30.

Collective histories of women also claimed a distinctive authenticity, superior to the claims of fictional discourse.[69] The excitement of affective sympathy and emulation, central to both Hays's and, later, Kelty's models of the reader/subject relationship, depended on the status of the life as historical and thus capable of producing actual, private, and public transformations in the reader's own life.

This publication of the authentic domestic life in biography became a particular problem for female subjects, as we will see in relation to Mary Shelley, Felicia Hemans, and Letitia Landon. If femininity was becoming defined by its location within the private sphere at this period, then the act of publishing a historical, as opposed to a fictionalized, female life or an abstracted code of conduct, enacted a genuine transgression. This problem was not so visible when biographical subjects were long dead, but became so in relation to women still living, or recently deceased. The best known example of this is Godwin's *Memoirs* of Mary Wollstonecraft, in which, with naïve frankness, he offered up his wife's sexual indiscretions to the public gaze and to anti-Jacobin contempt. He rapidly produced a second edition in an attempt to rescue her reputation, by further emphasizing her feminine virtues—already a prominent theme in the first edition—reinscribing her as a domestic ideal.[70] Mary Hays, who had introduced Wollstonecraft to Godwin, also stepped in with a memoir that, drawing on Godwin, tried to redeem her as a woman naturally suited to family life. Her errors and genius both stemmed from her 'extreme sensibility', a quality that also produced a 'heart . . . formed for the endearments of domestic life'.[71] Not only her happiest, but her most productive years were those spent 'in the bosom of domestic peace'.[72] In defending Wollstonecraft in this way, both Godwin and Hays attempted to reverse the act by which her private life had become sacrificed to the public sphere, but only succeeded in reproducing it for public consumption.

Whilst acknowledging the special anxieties attendant on publicity for the female subject, we should recognize that this was also true of biography with male subjects. For many readers and reviewers, Johnson's collected *Lives of the Poets* (1779–80) were celebrated as examples of pleasurable instruction, but the characterization of his biographical language—and Boswell's, after him—as gossip disrupted this comfortable vision of the function of the life story. The critical responses to Johnson's *Lives* suggest a growing sense in the 1780s of the

---

[69] Hays, admitting that she has relied on secondary sources, defends herself by writing with some contempt of the superficial novelties of fiction that she has avoided, *Female Biography*, vol. i, p. vii.

[70] See e.g. *Collected Novels and Memoirs of William Godwin*, gen. ed. Mark Philp, 8 vols. (London: Pickering and Chatto, 1992), i. 132: '[s]he was a worshipper of domestic life' (1st edn.), and 151–2 n. 128, for Godwin's explanation of Wollstonecraft's relationship with Fuseli, in the context of 'domestic charities' (2nd edn.).

[71] [Mary Hays], 'Memoirs of Mary Wollstonecraft', *The Annual Necrology for 1797–8* (London: R. Phillips, 1800), 424, 426.

[72] Ibid. 455.

disruptive potential of biography's publication of domestic life, but the moment when this really intensified was when, after Johnson's death, in 1784, he became a biographical subject himself, and the debate moved decisively towards a recognizably modern concern with issues of publicity and privacy.[73] The reception of the many *Lives* of Johnson, published between 1784 and 1791, and especially of Boswell's *Journal of a Tour to the Hebrides* (1785) and *Life of Johnson* (1791), shows the perception of biography as creating itself anew, and doing so through a new approach to private life. Mrs Montagu saw Boswell's *Tour* as a 'new invented mode of disgracing the dead & calumniating yᵉ living' and, for Hannah More, Hester Lynch Piozzi's *Anecdotes of the Late Samuel Johnson* (1786) was an example of '[t]his new-fashioned biography [which] seems to value itself upon perpetuating everything that is injurious and detracting'.[74] As James Clifford has shown, there were repeated expressions of astonishment that Johnson's biographers were apparently so intent on revealing his flaws. Thus the *New Monthly Review* commented in 1786 that

The character of Dr. Johnson has been exposed to much ridicule, by the injudicious minuteness of his biographers. They have pursued him into every retreat, and exposed him in every situation to the public eye. The veil which human weakness requires has been wantonly drawn aside, and the nakedness of their idol discovered.[75]

The dismay at the extent of the biographers' incursions into Johnson's private life—their 'injudicious minuteness' in pursuing him 'into every retreat'—was a response both to Johnson himself, as subject, and to genuine changes in biographical approach. The most famous literary figure of his times, Johnson appeared daily in the press in his lifetime, and was the subject of at least seven biographies before he died.[76] His living presence was thus brought before the public in unprecedented completeness, as his biographers competed with each other by means of claims to ever greater authenticity. Such claims, in themselves, signalled a new, and potentially worrying, sense in which the individual life could be, almost in fact, resurrected in the public domain. This was enhanced by a new prominence of domestic anecdote and a willingness to juxtapose adulation for the great man with unflattering personal details.

The *Lives* of Johnson published between 1784 and 1791 were intrinsically more careless of biographical decorum than previous biography had been and found new methods for impressing the reader with the living authenticity of the

---

[73] See James L. Clifford, 'How Much Should a Biographer Tell? Some Eighteenth-Century Views', in Philip B. Daghlian (ed.), *Essays in Eighteenth-Century Biography* (Bloomington, Ind.: Indiana University Press, 1968), 67–126 and Harding, '"Domestick Privacies"'.

[74] Quoted in Clifford, 'How Much Should a Biographer Tell?', 87, 89.

[75] Ibid. 90.

[76] See Donna Heiland, 'Remembering the Hero in Boswell's *Life of Johnson*', in Greg Clingham (ed.), *New Light on Boswell: Critical and Historical Essays on the Occasion of the Bicentenary of 'The Life of Johnson'* (Cambridge: Cambridge University Press, 1991), 194–5; and Clifford, 'How Much Should a Biographer Tell?', 84.

portrait, but it is interesting that reviewers focused their dismay on the act of publication itself as the event that, above all, generated shock. That Johnson's biographers had 'pursued him into every retreat' was, of course, only visible because they had then 'exposed him in every situation to the public eye' and responses to these biographies repeatedly referred to the act of making the private public as the crucial transgression. The *English Review* (1785) asked: 'was it meritorious, was it right or justifiable in Mr. Boswell to record and to publish his [Johnson's] prejudices, his follies and whims' and imagines how Socrates' fame might have suffered had Xenophon 'published all his infirmities to the world'.[77] In 1791 Anna Barbauld deplored the fact that Boswell had brought 'every idle word into judgment—the judgment of the public'.[78] Others took the side of the reader and welcomed the possibilities opened up by publication of the private. The *European Magazine* in 1785 argued that '[t]he observations and repartee of a Johnson, however delivered in small circles, were sure to be reported, and most probably with disadvantage and misconstruction, besides, in the sayings and opinions of such a man the public has a sort of property'.[79] Ralph Griffiths, reviewing Boswell's *Johnson* in 1792, assumed this position, demanding '[g]ive us *all*, suppress nothing'.[80]

The 1780s were a turning point in the history of biography very largely because changes in the British publishing industry were rapidly altering perceptions of what it meant to be 'published'. William St Clair places the beginnings of growth in the industry in the early 1770s and Lee Erickson argues that it took off decisively in the mid-1780s when there was an 'accelerated increase in the number of printed items coming from English publishers'—with a sudden doubling of numbers, from about 3,000 in 1780 to 6,000 in 1792.[81] With this came an expansion of the reading public that was much commented on at the time. These conditions, usually associated with the rise of the novel, were also important in driving growth in the production of biographical writing which intersected with the novel and with conduct literature in terms of its subject matter, approach, and appeal to the new readerships, including the increasingly important constituency of female readers. There was a wide variety of writing

---

[77] Quoted in Irma S. Lustig and Frederick A. Pottle (eds.), *Boswell: The Applause of the Jury 1782–1785* (London: Heinemann, 1982 edn.), 348.

[78] Clifford, 'How Much Should a Biographer Tell?', 92. See also Vicesimus Knox in 1790: 'Biography is everyday descending from its dignity. Instead of an instructive recital, it is becoming an instrument to the mere gratification of an impertinent, not to say malignant curiosity', ibid. 91.

[79] Lustig and Pottle (eds.), *Boswell*, 349.

[80] Clifford, 'How Much Should a Biographer Tell?', 93.

[81] William St Clair, *The Reading Nation in the Romantic Period* (Cambridge: Cambridge University Press, 2004), 172; Lee Erickson, *The Economy of Literary Form: English Literature and the Industrialization of Publishing, 1800–1850* (Baltimore: Johns Hopkins University Press, 1996), 7.

that we might see as coming within the broad category of the 'biographical'.[82] Brief, collective 'Lives', in themed collections, universal encyclopaedias, and magazine and periodical miscellanies, were the most prevalent forms, but there were many others, including single-subject biographies, collections of anecdotes, and literary 'Lives' prefacing collected *Works*. Literary *Lives* also seem to have become more numerous in the last decades of the century.[83] It is noticeable how many of the multi-volume collective biographies from the 1740s to the 1760s were reprinted between the 1770s and the 1790s, often in improved and enlarged editions.[84]

Brief collected 'Lives' could be perfunctory, recycling sketchy second-hand evidence and far from intrusive, whether their subjects were living or safely dead. Much biography resorted to hagiographic generalities. But other popular forms—for instance the flourishing traditions of criminal and courtesan lives— did not. The example of Johnson, both as biographer and biographical subject, alerted readers to the new directions in which biography, and literary biography especially, might turn and to the potential consequences when combined with a rapidly expanding print culture. The sheer number of biographies of Johnson appearing in a short space of time was, in itself, significant. Donna Heiland writes of a 'grimly competitive "industry"' springing up around him, posthumously. Two new biographies came out in the month of his death, three in 1785, including Boswell's *Tour to the Hebrides*. Hester Lynch Piozzi's *Anecdotes of the Late Dr. Samuel Johnson* appeared in 1786 and Sir John Hawkins's *Life* in 1787. Boswell went into print to attack both of them. He published his own *Life of Johnson* in 1791, but as Heiland points out, the quarrels of Boswell, Piozzi, and Hawkins meant that a high-profile 'battle for Samuel Johnson was well under way' by this time.[85] Boswell's *Tour* was a best-seller. Trailed extensively in the newspapers, the whole edition of 1,500 copies was sold out in the space of about two weeks and it went to a second and third edition before the end of the year. Lengthy extracts were serialized and it was reviewed more widely than any other book of 1795–6.[86] His *Life of Johnson* was, of course, even more successful. The quick succession of biographies, each spawning

---

[82] The nomenclature and understanding of genre was, of course, more fluid at the period. See e.g. James Raven, *Judging New Wealth: Popular Publishing and Responses to Commerce in England, 1750–1800* (Oxford: Clarendon Press, 1992), 45 on the lack of clear, generic distinction between history, fiction, and first-person 'memoirs'.

[83] Altick, *Lives and Letters*, 41.

[84] See e.g. *Biographia Britannica* (1747–66; 2nd edn., 1778–93); *Biographia Classica* (1740; corrected edn., 1777); Alban Butler, *Lives of the Fathers, Martyrs and other Principal Saints* (1756–9; 2nd edn., 1779–80; 3rd edn., 1798–1800); *Biographical Dictionary* (1761–2; 'greatly enlarged and improved' with the addition of 600 new lives, 1784; further edn., 1798 becoming *Chalmers's Biographical Dictionary* in 32 vols., 1812–17). All are listed in Donald A. Stauffer, *The Art of Biography in Eighteenth-Century England, Bibliographical Supplement* (Princeton: Princeton University Press, 1941).

[85] Heiland, 'Remembering the Hero', 194–5.

[86] Lustig and Pottle (eds.), *Boswell*, 345.

competitors, combined with the publicity they generated, and the numbers of readers they accrued, created a vivid demonstration of the new marketability of private life and the speed with which the act of publication might deprive an individual of control over his, or her, privacy.

After the furore that greeted the biographies of Johnson, we can see a succession of such moments, when the domestic lives of high-profile figures were exposed to public view in a sudden proliferation of print. The appearance of Godwin's *Memoirs* of Mary Wollstonecraft in 1798 was one such moment, the publication of Nelson's letters to Lady Hamilton in 1814 another.[87] The publicity surrounding Byron's separation from his wife in 1816 and again, after his death, in 1824, marked the decisive step in this perception of the biographical. These events, cumulatively, helped define the biographical act as inherently disruptive of the domestic privacy it capitalized on. The perception was growing at the beginning of the nineteenth century that no one in public life was safe from the voracious alliance of biographers, readers, and publishers, eager to market lives. Over the next thirty years, domestic lives became public property, bought, stolen (as were the Nelson/Hamilton letters), or forged (as were numerous Byron documents), published, and republished, in a relentless cycle. The desperate measures provoked by this industry from the early nineteenth century onwards are well known: the censorship and destruction of letters and journals, most famously those of Jane Austen and Byron, by family and friends, closing the boundaries of the domestic circle, obliterating private life in the name of protecting it. This was the period when the lines first began to be drawn up between the biographical subject, on the one hand, and the biographical industry, on the other. Histories of these battles have become a minor subgenre today, telling the stories, for instance, of the protracted diplomacy and warfare between biographers of Byron, Shelley, Dickens, Carlyle, and, latterly, Plath, and the representatives of their estates.[88] Lionel Trilling has called literary biography 'the paradigm of all biography' and in its inscription of an antagonism between subject and author, at least, his claim holds true.[89] Biography was nowhere more controversial at this period than in the writer's, and more particularly, the poet's life. Johnson was not entirely unconcerned at inviting his biographers into his home, but Byron's attempt to replicate his forebear's relative insouciance,

---

[87] See Joseph W. Reed, *English Biography in the Early Nineteenth Century: 1801–1838* (1965; New Haven: Yale University Press, 1966), 53–4. In 1805, the year of Nelson's death, seven biographies of him appeared and seventeen more over the next five years. The letters were stolen and sold for publication. There were rumours that Lady Hamilton herself sold them. Reed summarizes the response of the reviewers, as 'regret . . . that heroism could be destroyed by publication' (56).

[88] See e.g. Ian Hamilton, *Keepers of the Flame: Literary Estates and the Rise of Biography* (London: Pimlico/Random House, 1992); Mark Bostridge (ed.), *Lives for Sale: Biographers' Tales* (London: Continuum, 2004); Michael Millgate, *Testamentary Acts: Browning, Tennyson, James, Hardy* (Oxford: Clarendon Press, 1992).

[89] Quoted in Altick, *Lives and Letters*, p. ix.

forty years on, was a more anxious performance, revealing the pressures produced by changing conceptions of authorship in the contemporary literary marketplace. The next chapter introduces this theme by exploring the uneasy conjunction of biography and Romantic genius. It begins by reading the responses of Coleridge and Wordsworth to the genre, as defining moments in the formation of 'the Romantic Poet'.

2
Biography and the Romantic Poet

Biography represented a unique challenge to the Romantic poets. In the domesticating discourse of biography, the transcendent subject became embodied, the self-sufficient subject socialized, the masculine subject feminized. The Johnsonian model of biography and its democratizing implications became newly contentious when it met the aristocracy (literal and figurative) of Romantic genius. In biography a man and, more especially, an author might, himself, become 'published' for the consumption of the reader in a sense that he could not within poetic, fictional, or critical discourse, except in so far as it was biographical. Literary biography asserted and disrupted the autonomy of the subject in the same move: its focus on the private man underwrote and perpetuated the Romantic identification of the author with his work, but, in the very act of writing the author's life for him, the biographer usurped his self-possession. Biography claimed ownership of the subject in a peculiarly literal way. In literary biography, the domestic space opened up to threaten the autonomy of the author and the writer's life became contested property.

2.1 CONTESTED PROPERTY: COLERIDGE, WORDSWORTH, AND THE RESISTANCE TO BIOGRAPHY, 1810–1816

Mary Jean Corbett writes that the 'primary fiction about nineteenth-century authorship . . . was (and is) that the man of genius is wholly his own product'.[1] There have been a number of accounts of the ways in which male Romantic poets constructed a myth of their authorial autonomy as a defensive reaction to changes in the social and economic position of the writer. Building on the work of Marlon Ross, Mark Rose, and Lee Erickson, Lucy Newlyn has argued, persuasively, that the expansion of publishing and, with it, developments such as the professionalization of authorship, the anonymity of the marketplace, the growth of criticism as a profession, and, above all, the rise of the reader and the threat of a democratization of literary culture, produced an 'anxiety of reception' amongst Romantic writers

---

[1] Mary Jean Corbett, *Representing Femininity: Middle-Class Subjectivity in Victorian and Edwardian Women's Autobiographies* (New York: Oxford University Press, 1992), 18.

and particularly poets.[2] It was within this context that an embattled conception of the poet's ownership of himself and his work evolved. The market for poetry was comparatively healthy in the first two decades of the century, but, even during these years, publication for commercial gain was a struggle for all but a handful of exceptionally successful poets. A few—notably Scott, Byron, and Thomas Moore—were doing spectacularly well, but most, like Coleridge and Wordsworth, were struggling to make headway. It was a minority of living poets who made any money from their work in the years between the 1780s and 1830s.[3] All writers, however successful, were conscious of the increasing power of publishers and readers in the changing literary marketplace, but for poets struggling to find a readership, the inequality of the relationship was underscored.[4] Coleridge's 'revulsion at the threat which reading posed for writing' and his horror at the 'appetite for publicity' amongst readers and writers was shared by Wordsworth and other writers aware that they were dependent on a marketplace from which they felt alienated.[5] It produced, Newlyn argues, '[t]he defensive nature of Romanticism's sacralization of the author—and, more particularly, the poet'.[6] Wordsworth's agitations for the extension of copyright show that he equated 'poetic identity with private property', but, by the same token, that he acknowledged a situation in which ownership of both was contested.[7] A poet's works and thus his self were endangered by the claims of his public.

Market competition between genres was a significant factor in provoking such fears amongst the male poets of the period. The success of women's poetry and of the novel, have been seen as contributing to a perception of the feminization of the literary marketplace that threatened to undermine the status of the male poet on a number of fronts. Literary historians have also stressed the importance of a more general market competition between poetry and prose in challenging the cultural authority of poets.[8] The focus here has tended to be on fiction and criticism, but I would argue that biographical prose played a central, if little recognized, part in stimulating the anxieties of Romantic poets and in producing their defensive constructions of the author. Like women's poetry and the novel, biography was perceived by Coleridge and Wordsworth, amongst others, as a

---

[2] Lucy Newlyn, *Reading, Writing, and Romanticism: The Anxiety of Reception* (Oxford: Oxford University Press, 2000).

[3] See William St Clair, *The Reading Nation in the Romantic Period* (Cambridge: Cambridge University Press, 2004), 165, 172.

[4] See ibid. 160–7.

[5] Newlyn, *Reading, Writing, and Romanticism*, 55–6.

[6] Ibid. 14.

[7] Ibid. 98. Corbett, *Representing Femininity*, 56, extending this fear to Romantic writers more generally, argues that 'it is alienation from his own labor, his own text, that these authors fear'.

[8] See e.g. Marlon B. Ross, *The Contours of Masculine Desire: Romanticism and the Rise of Women's Poetry* (New York: Oxford University Press, 1989); Lee Erickson, *The Economy of Literary Form: English Literature and the Industrialization of Publishing, 1800–1850* (Baltimore: Johns Hopkins University Press, 1996); and Newlyn, *Reading, Writing, and Romanticism*.

commercial competitor, a popular, feminized prose form, appealing to the market in a way that their own work did not. To this extent it posed a similar threat to these other genres, but the generic associations that biography had, by this time, accrued, ensured that it offered its own, particular, challenges.

It is no coincidence that some of the major expressions of Romantic anxiety of authorship are in essays that take biography as their central theme. In 'A Prefatory Observation on Modern Biography', a brief essay, introducing his 'Life' of Admiral Sir Alexander Ball, serialized in *The Friend* in 1810, Coleridge found a powerful focus for his discontents with the contemporary reading public.[9] Biography, for Coleridge, was centrally about the public/private axis. The starting point of his essay was a passage from Bacon, seemingly advocating the inclusion of both 'public and private' actions in the history of a great man.[10] Coleridge argues that this is a misreading, perpetrated by a public who are characteristically uncritical, 'inattentive', and in need of the superior exegetical wisdom of the 'Author'. It is not Bacon's responsibility that the passage has been misinterpreted, nor even, perhaps, that of the biographers who have taken his words as a pretext for their 'huge volumes of biographical minutiae, which render the real character almost invisible, like clouds of dust on a Portrait'. It is the appetite of readers, Coleridge argues, that has led to this focus on private life, satisfying their 'senses' and their 'curiosity' and obscuring the biographer's proper object, which is to instruct his audience, by revealing the ways in which his subject was greater than them.[11] This telling reversal of Johnson's democratized vision of biography, shows Coleridge's unease with a form that threatens to relinquish control to the reader.[12]

As Coleridge worries away at anecdotal biography, his metaphors reveal a series of interlocking anxieties:

To scribble Trifles even on the perishable glass of an Inn window, is the mark of an Idler; but to engrave them on the Marble Monument, sacred to the memory of the departed Great, is something worse than Idleness.[13]

---

[9] Samuel Taylor Coleridge, 'A Prefatory Observation on Modern Biography' [Prefacing his 'Sketches and Fragments of the Life and Character of The Late Admiral Sir Alexander Ball'], *The Friend*, 21 (Thursday, 25 January 1810).

[10] *The Friend*, ed. Barbara E. Rooke, 2 vols. [no. 4 in *The Collected Works of Samuel Taylor Coleridge*, Bollingen Series LXXV, gen. ed. Kathleen Coburn] (London and Princeton: Routledge and Kegan Paul and Princeton University Press, 1969), ii. 285.

[11] Ibid.

[12] See, by contrast, Johnson's relaxed attitude to authorship and ownership: 'For the general good of the world ... whatever valuable work has once been created by an authour, and issued out by him, should be understood as no longer in his power, but as belonging to the publick', *Boswell's Life of Samuel Johnson, Together with Boswell's Journal of a Tour to the Hebrides*, ed. George Birkbeck Hill and L. F. Powell, 6 vols. (Oxford: Oxford University Press, 1934–50), ii. 259.

[13] *The Friend*, ed. Rooke, ii. 286.

The popular biographer, as scribbler of trifles, has lowered himself to become one with his readership. Graffiti is a careless, public writing, a democratic language that may reveal intimate secrets or make subversive political statements—an apparently ephemeral defacement that has a habit of staying around. Anecdotal biography, by surviving into posterity, might permanently deface the monumental *Life* and the posthumous reputation of the great man at its centre. This vision is picked up in the more familiar figure of the biographer as gossip. '[G]arulous Biography' is equivalent to 'gossiping', a spoken discourse which has all the properties of graffiti.[14] For Coleridge, both suggest the qualities he fears in contemporary print culture: a debased literary currency, spreading uncontrollably, eroding the division between public and private life. But the equation of biography with gossip, of course, adds the suggestion of anecdotal biography as a feminized, domestic discourse, extending dangerously into the public sphere. Coleridge's essay compounds this fear by imagining biographical gossip working in a reverse trajectory too. Having exposed private life to public view, biography then insinuates gossip back into the home:

> For a crime it is . . . thus to introduce the spirit of vulgar scandal, and personal inquietude into the Closet and the Library, environing with evil passions the very Sanctuaries, to which we should flee for refuge from them! . . . And both the Authors and Admirers of such Publications, in what respect are they less Truants and Deserters from their own Hearts . . . than the most garrulous female Chronicler, of the goings-on of yesterday in the Families of her Neighbours and Towns-folk?[15]

The passage describes a far-reaching breach of privacy. The gentleman at home reads biographies that violate the privacy of others and is, in the process, himself violated. His personal, domestic space should signify his autonomy—his ownership of self—but here he cowers, like Austen's Mr Bennet, in his library, besieged by a democratized and feminized print culture. Biography's feminine leakage of domestic secrets is no trivial crime for Coleridge. The essay becomes progressively alarmist—the demand for biography is a 'mania', and a 'disease', and there is a hint too, in the vision of closet and library environed with 'evil passions', of the nationalistic rhetoric and iconography of the 1790s—the home as homeland—and of popular biography, its readers and authors, as fifth-columnist traitors.[16]

In a passage that suggests continuities between early nineteenth- and early twenty-first-century perceptions of a growing celebrity culture, Coleridge designates his times as 'the age of personality' and deplores the fact that the public and the private have collapsed into one another—for the class of '*public* Characters',

---

[14] *The Friend*, ed. Rooke, ii. 286.
[15] Ibid. 286–7.
[16] Ibid. 286. The hint was picked up and elaborated more explicitly by Wordsworth in 1816—see below.

deemed fair game for biographers, 'has encreased so rapidly . . . that it becomes difficult to discover what Characters are to be considered as private'.[17] It is significant that Coleridge should place biography as central to his culture's appetite for subjective life. He was not alone in this opinion, which was echoed by Hazlitt, for instance, a decade later—and it suggests that the persistent focus of Romantic studies on the autobiographical, at the expense of the biographical, needs readjusting.[18] Coleridge's 'age of personality' is not an age of introspection. He explicitly describes the modern disease as that of 'busying ourselves with the names of *others*' [my italics].[19] The 'autobiographical' was beginning to be perceived as a distinct mode of writing at this period, but always as a branch of biography, so that it was, typically, within discussions of biography that the province of the autobiographical began to be defined.[20] A recognition of the extent of Romantic interest in the broader category of the biographical is especially relevant when approaching Wordsworth, the poet most closely associated, still, with autobiography. Only one of his essays—his *Letter to a Friend of Robert Burns* (1816)—is commonly mentioned in the context of biography, but his interest in the subject extends into other areas of his work too. Before turning to the *Letter*, his most open discussion of these issues, I want to suggest that, although they are not usually read in this way, his 'Essays Upon Epitaphs' were also an important meditation on biography and the poet.[21]

The three 'Essays Upon Epitaphs' were written between about December 1809 and late February 1810, when the first of them was published, in *The Friend*, with an introductory paragraph, possibly by Coleridge.[22] This was just over a month after Coleridge's 'Prefatory Observation on Modern Biography'

---

[17] Ibid.

[18] See e.g. William Hazlitt, 'Spence's Anecdotes of Pope', *Edinburgh Review* (May 1820), in *The Complete Works of William Hazlitt*, ed. P. P. Howe, 21 vols. (London: Dent, 1930–4), xvi. 152–81.

[19] *The Friend*, ed. Rooke, ii. 286.

[20] See e.g. Wordsworth's *A Letter to a Friend of Robert Burns: Occasioned by an Intended Republication of the Account of the Life of Burns, by Dr. Currie* (London: Longman, Hurst, Rees, Orme and Brown, 1816), discussed below. See also James Field Stanfield, *An Essay on the Study and Composition of Biography* (Sunderland: printed by George Garbutt; London: sold by Gale, Curtis, Fenner, Cradock and Joy; Edinburgh: sold by Constable and Co., and John and James Robertson, 1813), see e.g. 30 ff.

[21] The essays have, of course, been read in the context of autobiography—see e.g. Paul De Man, 'Autobiography as De-Facement', in *The Rhetoric of Romanticism* (1979; New York: Columbia University Press, 1984), 67–81. Annette Wheeler Cafarelli, *Prose in the Age of Poets: Romanticism and Biographical Narrative from Johnson to De Quincey* (Philadelphia: University of Pennsylvania Press, 1990), 185 alludes to Wordsworth's analogies between epitaph and biography in the 'Essays', in the context of De Quincey's debts to the biographical sketches in *The Excursion*.

[22] The first 'Essay Upon Epitaphs' was published in *The Friend* (22 Feb.) and reprinted as a footnote to *The Excursion*, v. 978 (1814). The second and third essays were also held in readiness for Coleridge's journal, but it ceased publication before they could appear. Coleridge then wanted them to appear in the supplemental numbers of *The Friend* (1812), but they remained unpublished until 1876 when they were printed in *The Prose Works of William Wordsworth*, ed. Alexander B. Grossart, 3 vols. (London: Edward Moxon, 1876), ii. 41–75. For further details of the inception of the essays, see *PWW* ii. 45–7 and *The Friend*, ed. Rooke, ii. 336 n.

and the language and argument of both suggest that the pieces were in dialogue with each other.[23] Coleridge, as we have seen, figures the dignified *Life* as a 'Marble Monument'; Wordsworth cites a definition of epitaph as 'epitomized biography' and refers to Chiabrera, whose epitaphs he translates at the opening of the first essay, as a 'funereal Biographer'.[24] Like Coleridge, Wordsworth focused a personal anxiety of reception on the question of biographical record—how an individual life should be memorialized and thus preserved, within the public sphere, but also how, in entering that sphere, it might be threatened with extinction. His personal desire to live in the minds of his readers, and his fear that he will not, are a tangible presence in the essays. Epitaphs have arisen, he argues, from a deep-rooted need in man 'to live in the remembrance of his fellows', stemming from an intimation 'that some part of our nature is imperishable'.[25] Epitaph, a biographical record framed in Christian terms, sanctifies the yearning of the writer for immortality.

Wordsworth's ideal epitaph, like Coleridge's conception of dignified biography, is a panegyric, but the good epitaph, as an affirmation of man's immortality, must, for Wordsworth, be written and received in a spirit, not merely of reverence, but of love. His favoured epitaphs are of ordinary people, written by family or friends and engraved on stones in secluded churchyards. These memorials are, technically, available to all, but in practice, seen by few. Those who do read them are already bound to the deceased by kinship or friendship or, if strangers like himself, by sympathy. This is a consoling vision of a coterie readership and of biography as a private, affective exchange in the face of the reality of a marketplace where *Lives*—and reputations—were increasingly being produced and consumed by strangers, in a spirit far from sympathetic. Contrary to Coleridge, who despairs at the critical obtuseness of the masses and wants biography to highlight the ways in which great men rise above their readers, Wordsworth insists that 'an epitaph is not a proud writing shut up for the studious: it is exposed to all . . . concerning all, and for all'.[26] It is 'grounded upon the universal intellectual property of man;—sensations which all men have felt and feel in some degree daily and hourly'.[27] This appears to be a democratic riposte to Coleridge's hierarchical vision of the author/subject/reader relationship, but Wordsworth is closer to Coleridge than he might appear. The reader in

---

[23] The 'Essays Upon Epitaphs' stemmed in part from discussions with Coleridge in 1799 and from Coleridge's notes on 'Tombs by the Roadside & Tombs in Church yards', see *PWW* ii. 45. The 'Essays' were also a response to Johnson's essay on the Epitaphs of Pope, appended to his essay on 'Pope' in the *Lives of the Poets*.
[24] *PWW* ii. 89. The first definition is from John Weever, *Ancient Funerall Monuments within the United Monarchie of Great Britaine, Ireland, and the Islands adiacent . . . Whereunto is prefixed a Discourse of Funerall Monuments* (1631).
[25] *PWW* ii. 50.
[26] Ibid. 59.
[27] Ibid. 78.

the graveyard is a sentimentalized vision of what Wordsworth calls 'the People', as opposed to the 'Public'.[28] Wordsworth's fantasy of biography as a universal language of love, rising above the marketplace to affirm the transcendence of the biographical subject, is also, clearly, defensive. It is an expression of his awareness of the perishability of the individual life, and especially the writer's life, once published, since, as he writes in *The Prelude*, textual 'shrines' are 'frail'.[29] In the 'Essays Upon Epitaphs' idealized, epitaphic biography is always threatened by a counter-vision of the destructive reality of modern biography.

The third 'Essay Upon Epitaphs' discusses the importance of sincerity in the language of epitaph and contemplates the damage done by insincere epitaph. Wordsworth finds numerous examples of these in the second-rate imitators of Dryden and Pope, many of them anthologized in Vicesimus Knox's compilation, *Elegant Extracts*. Such epitaphs suggest 'our Countrymen, through successive generations, had lost the sense of solemnity and pensiveness (not to speak of deeper emotions) and resorted to the Tombs of their Forefathers and Contemporaries only to be tickled and surprised'.[30] To make a joke of out of the life of another man is the ultimate desecration, replacing continuity of human sympathy with ephemeral pleasure. It is an example of Wordsworth's association of such corrupted feeling with popular print culture. *Elegant Extracts*, as he points out, 'is circulated every where and in fact constitutes at this day the poetical library of our Schools'.[31] This produces an insidious threat to readers and to the subjects of the epitaphs, for

Language, if it do not uphold, and feed, and leave in quiet, like the power of gravitation or the air we breathe, is a counter-spirit, unremittingly and noiselessly at work to derange, to subvert, to lay waste, to vitiate, and to dissolve.[32]

This well-known passage has not usually been read in the context of Wordsworth's opinions on biography, but it shows interesting affinities with Coleridge's reference to anecdotal biographers as 'wretched misusers of language' and his analogies between anecdotal biography, graffiti, and gossip.[33] For both it is the mass dissemination of biographical record, with its unique power to preserve

---

[28] For this distinction, see 'Essay, Supplementary to the Preface' (1815), *PWW* iii. 84. By the 'Public' he appears to mean the literary world. The 'People' are a less tangible, projected ideal of the readership, representing nationhood, essential humanity, a divinely justified 'Vox Populi'.

[29] *The Prelude* (1805), v. 44–8: 'Oh, why hath not the mind | Some element to stamp her image on | In nature, somewhat nearer to her own? | Why, gifted with such powers to send abroad | Her spirit, must it lodge in shrines so frail?'. The 'shrines' are a figure for man's works, including 'The consecrated works of bard and sage' (l. 41), but also for the mortal body. The lines preface the passages describing a dream in which an Arab with two 'books' representing Geometry and Poetry, flees from destruction.

[30] *PWW* ii. 84.

[31] Ibid. 84.

[32] Ibid. 85.

[33] *The Friend*, ed. Rooke, ii. 286.

or destroy a life, that raises the spectre of language as an annihilating 'counter-spirit'.

Wordsworth also shares Coleridge's distaste for Boswellian detail of character analysis. He persistently contrasts the true spirit of epitaph with the urge to analyse character. He remembers his sensations contemplating the idealized inscriptions in a country graveyard, when he wondered, smilingly, ' "Where are all the *bad* People buried?" '[34] But he makes a show of having suppressed his reverie on the buried complexities of human nature, arguing that harmonious banalities hold a greater truth than searching character analysis, without generosity of spirit, ever could. They are 'a far more faithful representation of homely life . . . than any report which might be made by a rigorous observer', deficient in sympathy.[35] Wordsworth doubts if minute character analysis of those we love is ever 'a common or natural employment' and least of all in the moment of bereavement—'the writer of an epitaph is not an anatomist, who dissects the internal frame of the mind'.[36] The strength of feeling suggested by the dissection metaphor is typical of the 'Essays' when Wordsworth contemplates the particularized biographical record. It is a resistance to the way that biography embodies in order to socialize the subject: to compose a probing epitaph is to treat the mind as if it were merely flesh, to lay it open on the operating table. Details of individual character demystify the life, destroy it as an integrated, imperishable whole.

In 'Essays Upon Epitaphs' this perception is visible in the desire to expel all signs of character analysis from epitaph, to the extent that, finally, epitaph itself is all but erased. At one point Wordsworth submerges troubling details of individual character beneath an unruffled sea.[37] At another he brings down a sublimating mist. In epitaph:

The character of a deceased friend or beloved kinsman is not seen, no—nor ought to be seen, otherwise than as a tree through a tender haze or a luminous mist, that spiritualises and beautifies it; that takes away, indeed, but only to the end that the parts which are not abstracted may appear more dignified and lovely; may impress and affect the more.[38]

This kind of abstraction, says Wordsworth, is only reflective of one's emotions on learning of the death of any man, even an enemy, when '[e]nmity melts away; and, as it disappears, unsightliness, disproportion, and deformity, vanish'.[39] It is a vision of transcendence—of the flesh and of the marketplace—escape from the destructive insincerities that circulate in anthologies such as *Elegant Extracts*. But the tropes of effacement, suggestive of the inevitable erosions even of gravestone inscriptions, have unsettling reverberances, in an argument which invests so

---

[34] *PWW* ii. 63. The quotation comes from Charles Lamb, *Rosamund Gray* (1798).
[35] *PWW* ii. 64.
[36] Ibid. 56–7.
[37] See ibid. 63–4.
[38] Ibid. 58.
[39] Ibid.

much in the idea of permanence. If all detail of the individual is obscured, what exactly will be left to the memory? What is the power of epitaph to preserve after all? Wordsworth's consideration of various examples of epitaph, good and bad, shows persistent dissatisfaction with the form. Few specimens are without fault of some kind—few are quite sincere, quite spare enough. At the end of the third essay his culminating example of epitaph appears on a memorial stone, almost hidden from view. The terse inscription and the brief life are nearer to a denial than to a record of memory:

In an obscure corner of a Country Church-yard I once espied, half-overgrown with Hemlock and Nettles, a very small Stone laid upon the ground, bearing nothing more than the name of the Deceased with the date of birth and death, importing that it was an Infant which had been born one day and died the following. I know not how far the Reader may be in sympathy with me, but more awful thoughts of rights conferred, of hopes awakened, of remembrances stealing away or vanishing were imparted to my mind by that Inscription there before my eyes than by any other that has ever been my lot to meet with upon a Tomb-stone.[40]

What remains of this child's life, pared away almost to silence, is Wordsworth's own, moving epitaph. His words compensate for the lack of biographical record but also celebrate its absence. The less that is publicly known of a life, the more opening there is for private meditation.

The difficulties of self-substantiation in Romantic autobiography have been the subject of much critical investigation, but more recognition needs to be given to the fact that biography formed one of those difficulties and, in doing so, produced an articulation of the autobiographical. The meditations on biographical record in 'Essays Upon Epitaphs' lead Wordsworth, defensively, to connect a writer's immortality with the ability to author himself. He not only recommends that the writer's best epitaph is his own work, but quotes Milton's sonnet 'On Shakespear' which denies the need for memorial monuments created by other men (although, of course, creating one itself) and asserts the ability of the poet to construct his own best memorial: 'Thou in our wonder and astonishment | Hast built thyself a livelong monument'.[41] Six years later, Wordsworth addressed the subject of biography directly in *A Letter to a Friend of Robert Burns* (1816) and here his resistance to the genre produced a more developed definition of what it was to be an autobiographical poet.

In the *Letter* Wordsworth deplored the way in which Burns's reputation had been damaged by revelations of his private life, including his drunkenness, in James Currie's 'Life' of the poet and its reviews.[42] Even more obviously than in

---

[40] Ibid. 93.

[41] Ibid. 62.

[42] James Currie's 'Life' of Burns in his edn. of Burns's *Works*, 4 vols. (Liverpool and Edinburgh: J. McCreery and W. Creech, 1800), i. 33–336. For full details of the circumstances of composition of the *Letter*, see *PWW* iii. 111–13.

Coleridge's essay, this concern was driven by Wordsworth's own anxiety of reception. His subject was, after all, what biography has done, and might do, to the reputation of a poet. He had openly identified himself with Burns in 'Resolution and Independence', as the self-created genius—'By our own spirits are we deified' (l. 47)—who was the victim of poverty.[43] His interest in extending the posthumous copyright of authors, for the sake of their dependants, seems to have been initiated by the poor sale of *Poems in Two Volumes*, in which 'Resolution and Independence' was first published, and became connected in his mind with the plight of Burns's wife and children.[44] Currie's 'Life', which prefaced his edition of the collected *Works* of Burns, focused Wordsworth's concern at the vulnerability of the poet in the modern marketplace and the powers of the popular, biographical edition to determine the life and afterlife of a poet. In 'Essay, Supplementary to the Preface' (1815), Wordsworth's major discussion of the conflict between genius and popular acclaim, he had attacked the most famous of all biographical editions—that prefaced by Johnson's *Lives of the Poets*—as an example of the incompatibility of popularity and poetic greatness. The collection created a poetic canon that bore no resemblance to the one he would have chosen. It included no mention of Chaucer, Spenser, Shakespeare—'to our astonishment the *first* name we find is that of Cowley!'[45] It was a canon driven by questionable popular taste and market forces:

The booksellers took upon themselves to make the collection; they referred probably to the most popular miscellanies, and, unquestionably, to their books of accounts; and decided upon the claim of authors to be admitted into a body of the most eminent, from the familiarity of their names with the readers of that day, and by the profits, which, from the sale of his works, each had brought and was bringing to the Trade.[46]

Currie's biographical edition raised similar fears of the sacrifice of genius to a debased consumer culture.

In his *Letter* Wordsworth represented Currie as a good man in himself, but a poor judge of the readership for whom he wrote. He had revealed Burns's weaknesses to 'multitudes' who were ill-equipped to understand them.[47] His 'Life' was symptomatic of contemporary biography's exploitation of the childish appetites of the new readerships for the domestic life of genius:

---

[43] He drew on Currie's biography for this poem, especially on the portrayal of Burns as a poet whose tragedy was the want of regular employment and financial independence. See Julian North, 'Leeches and Opium: De Quincey replies to "Resolution and Independence" in *Confessions of an English Opium-Eater*', *Modern Language Review*, 89/3 (July 1994), 576–7.

[44] See Erickson, *The Economy of Literary Form*, 61–2. See also e.g. letter to J. Forbes Mitchell, 21 Apr. 1819, in *The Letters of William and Dorothy Wordsworth*, ed. Ernest de Selincourt (2nd rev. edn.), iii. *The Middle Years*, pt. 2. *1812–1820*, rev. Mary Moorman and Alan G. Hill (Oxford: Clarendon Press, 1970), 533–6.

[45] *PWW* iii. 79.

[46] Ibid. 79.

[47] Ibid. 119. See also 120 on the incapacity of 'the mass of mankind' to interpret Burns's letters.

The life of Johnson by Boswell had broken through many pre-existing delicacies, and afforded the British public an opportunity of acquiring experience, which before it had happily wanted[48]

The echoes of Coleridge's 'Prefatory Observation' are clear, but intensified by Wordsworth's embattled sense of the poet's struggle to assert his life as his own property in the face of biography's appropriative power. In words that recall the 'Essays Upon Epitaphs', Wordsworth presented biographers as the usurpers of the right of any subject to speak for himself:

Silence is a privilege of the grave, a right of the departed: let him, therefore, who infringes that right, by speaking publicly of, for, or against, those who cannot speak for themselves, take heed that he opens not his mouth without a sufficient sanction.[49]

But Wordsworth's concern is, more specifically, with the way that *literary* biography speaks for its subjects. He argues that biographies of authors, and particularly poets, are to be discouraged on the grounds that 'if their works be good, they contain within themselves all that is necessary to their being comprehended and relished'.[50] We have heard this argument before in the 'Essays Upon Epitaphs', but in the *Letter* Wordsworth finds some poets more vulnerable to biographical investigation than others. Homer, Virgil, or Shakespeare are relatively impervious, but poets such as Burns are not, since

Neither the subjects of his poems, nor his manner of handling them, allow us long to forget their author. On the basis of his human character he has reared a poetic one, which with more or less distinctness presents itself to view in almost every part of his earlier, and, in my estimation, his most valuable verses. This poetic fabric, dug out of the quarry of genuine humanity, is airy and spiritual:—and though the materials, in some parts, are coarse, and the disposition is often fantastic and irregular, yet the whole is agreeable and strikingly attractive. Plague, then, upon your remorseless hunters after matter of fact (who, after all, rank among the blindest of human beings) when they would convince you that the foundations of this admirable edifice are hollow; and that its frame is unsound![51]

In this passage Wordsworth's resistance to biography produces a definition of what we might recognize as the autobiographical poet. His metaphor is architectural. The poet is a fanciful, do-it-yourself builder, erecting a transcendent structure on foundations that are not just earthly and human but are himself. He is, in fact, his own property. The biographer and the reader of biography are outsiders who want to tear the edifice down—surveyors who would reduce the poet's creation to something merely material and ephemeral. The figure is continued in a passage which has clear parallels with Coleridge's vision of biography as invasion in 'A Prefatory Observation'. Wordsworth deplores the

---

[48] Ibid. 120.   [49] Ibid. 121.
[50] Ibid. 122.   [51] Ibid. 123.

coarse intrusions into the recesses, the gross breaches upon the sanctities, of domestic life, to which we have lately been more and more accustomed.[52]

The poet's self as property becomes a domestic interior assailed by biographers and the reading public. The invasion metaphor is amplified here. Wordsworth speaks of the guarded domestic space as a sign of English liberty. He worries that the popularity of this new biography may indicate a 'state of public feeling' in which 'lovers of licence rather than of liberty' have prevailed over those who evince 'one of the noblest characteristics of Englishmen, that jealousy of familiar approach, which, while it contributes to the maintenance of private dignity, is one of the most efficacious guardians of rational public freedom'.[53] The *Letter* finishes with an extended attack on Francis Jeffrey for his condemnation of Burns, and soars into a comparison of the critic to Napoleon and Robspierre, 'these redoubtable enemies of mankind'.[54] The domestic space by now represents the ability of poet, man, and country to govern themselves, and the misguided biography of Dr Currie, in undermining all three, has become nothing less than the instrument of imperial conquest and despotic power.

As was immediately apparent to contemporaries, the essay's strength of feeling derived from Wordsworth's personal grievance against Jeffrey for his damaging reviews of *Poems in Two Volumes, The Excursion*, and *The White Doe of Rylestone.*[55] It is significant that Jeffrey criticized Wordsworth's poetry on the grounds of the poet's inattention to the needs of the reader.[56] In the *Letter*, Wordsworth responded by taking the position of the embattled author, fending off a public whose demand for biography, rather than poetry, represented a significant threat to his creative autonomy. It was, therefore, quite specifically against biography as a popular form that Wordsworth attempted to define Burns's, and thereby his own, voice as an autobiographical poet. His effort throughout the *Letter* was to return ownership of self to the poet. He allows Burns to speak for himself, by quoting from his autobiographical poetry, rather than from the biographical accounts of his life. He quotes from 'A Bard's Epitaph', which he interprets as Burns's own memorial and which he praises accordingly as 'a sincere and solemn avowal—a public declaration *from his own will*—a confession at once devout, poetical, and human' (Wordsworth's emphasis).[57] The word 'own', in fact, resonates throughout the *Letter* which is, as a whole, an anxiously reiterative claim to self-possession. For Wordsworth, autobiography is paradoxically the truer reflection of a life for the very reason that it

---

[52] *PWW* iii. 122.
[53] Ibid.
[54] Ibid. 128.
[55] See ibid. 58–60 and 112–13.
[56] See e.g. [Francis Jeffrey], Review of *The Excursion, Edinburgh Review*, 24 (Nov. 1814), 1–30. Jeffrey, by contrast to Wordsworth, became a notable defender of the value of literary biography.
[57] *PWW* iii. 126.

softens the unkind mirror image cast by contemporary biography. As in 'Essays Upon Epitaphs', he urges a model of biography, produced and received in a spirit of love. The ideal candidate to write the life of the poet is a 'bosom friend of the author. . . . Such a one, himself a pure spirit, having accompanied, as it were, upon wings, the pilgrim along the sorrowful road, which he trod on foot', or a family member—Wordsworth nominates Burns's brother Gilbert.[58] The ideal readers of biography are, likewise, 'the considerate few' who are bonded in sympathy with the poet and his works.[59] This reconstitutes the domestic space invaded by popular biography as one controlled by the poet. The biographer and the readership have moved so far within the poet's private circle that they have become almost indistinguishable from him. Indeed, it is hard to escape the impression that, for Wordsworth, the ideal biographer of a poet is the poet himself.

The dismay of Wordsworth and subsequent writers at the power of biography to invade and appropriate their lives, was in part a perception that the poet might not be able to reject biography, that his career might become dependent on it. Even Wordsworth entertained the possibility of a biography of himself whilst still alive, allowing Barron Field to submit a manuscript for comment—and then rejection.[60] The more writers became reliant on the publicizing offices of the biographer in the course of the century, the more they became wary of them. Not only the objections voiced by Coleridge and Wordsworth, but the terms in which those objections were made, were echoed by writers long afterwards. Elizabeth Barrett Browning, protesting against herself and Robert becoming the subjects of memoirs, used the same language of contested property: 'because our books belong to the public . . . do our persons? do our lives? I have a right to my life, I think, till I am dead'.[61] In Robert Browning's 'House' (1876) he figured the autobiographical poem as the poet's home, opened up to inquisitive tourists, and his resistance to biographical readings as a defence of his private, domestic space:

> No, thanking the public, I must decline.
> A peep through my window, if folk prefer;
> But, please you, no foot over threshold of mine![62]

---

[58] Ibid. 120. He suggests that the reprint of Currie's 'Life' be placed as an appendix, 'subsidiary' to the poetry, rather than a preface, and replaced by a sympathetic memoir by his brother.

[59] Ibid. 119.

[60] Wordsworth had Field to stay at his home, Rydal Mount, but this did not prevent him writing on 16 Jan. 1840 to bar publication, adding: 'One last word in matter of authorship; it is far better not to admit people so much behind the scenes, as it has been lately fashionable to do.' See Geoffrey Little (ed.), *Barron Field's Memoirs of Wordsworth* (Australian Academy of the Humanities, Monograph 3) (Sydney: Sydney University Press, 1975), 17. See below, Ch. 5 for Wordsworth's furious response to De Quincey's biographical essays on him.

[61] Letter to Mary Howitt (1856), quoted in Corbett, *Representing Femininity*, 57.

[62] The poem was written as a reply to Dante Gabriel Rossetti's self-revealing sonnet sequence, 'The House of Life', as it appeared in his *Poems* (1870).

As we shall see, the conception of biography as an invasion and appropriation of private space materialized in literary *Lives*, in the motif of the biographer's visit to the poet's home.

Wordsworth's *Letter*, published just before the scandal of Byron's separation from his wife and the 'Poems on His Own Domestic Circumstances' (1816), attracted more publicity than it might otherwise have done and produced interesting responses, some of which are discussed below. But, important as they were, the perceptions of Coleridge and Wordsworth were only part of a larger, cultural shift towards a relationship of competitive dependency between writers and their biographers. The next section looks at the state of biography in the literary marketplace in the 1820s and 1830s and at the extent to which the fears of Coleridge and Wordsworth were realized in the competition between biography and poetry that began to emerge at this period.

2.2 POETRY AND BIOGRAPHY IN THE MARKETPLACE, 1820–1840

The market for volumes of new poetry declined sharply from the mid-1820s and by 1830 almost no publishers were taking it on.[63] By 1837, William St Clair writes:

> The only new books written in verse which the main London publishers would consider were those financed by authors 'on commission'. . . . Murray, whose fortune had been built on publishing Scott and Byron, declined even to read offered manuscripts, and Longman, who had published Bloomfield, Campbell, James Montgomery, Moore, Southey, and Wordsworth, withdrew from literary publishing.[64]

Between 1830 and 1858, Edward Moxon stood virtually alone as a publisher of original poetry.[65] As has been widely recognized, the major reason for this decline was the competition provided by the expanding periodical press. In the post-war years and especially during the 1820s, periodicals became the most profitable form of publishing.[66] Between 1815 and 1832 over twenty new journals came into production—the quarterly and monthly literary reviews, followed in the 1830s by cheap weekly magazines.[67] The popular literary annuals, with their mixture of verse, essays, and short stories, became the most lucrative way of publishing poetry after the mid-1820s, with the *Keepsake* of 1829 including contributions from Coleridge, Wordsworth, Southey, Scott, and

---

[63] See Erickson, *The Economy of Literary Form*, 26, 28–9, 38.
[64] St Clair, *The Reading Nation*, 413.
[65] Erickson, *The Economy of Literary Form*, 38.
[66] Ibid. 7.
[67] Ibid. 28, 80. The quarterlies were in decline after 1831, see ibid., 90.

(posthumously) P. B. Shelley.[68] Through the periodical press, prose forms, notably essays and reviews, short stories, and in the 1830s serialized fiction, began to compete with poetry in a process that, whilst gradual and to some extent masked by reprints of dead and living poets, nevertheless palpably encroached on the market for new verse.[69] Biography was amongst the prose forms that flourished in this context and thus participated in this general competition. But biographical prose also challenged new poetry in a unique sense, since much of it was literary biography and, more specifically, focused on the living poets.

'Lives' of the poets pervaded the periodical press, feeding a growing curiosity amongst readers about the private lives of literary men and women. Many of the new magazines carried series of biographical 'Portraits' or 'Sketches' of living or recently dead authors, including poets.[70] Other forms of biographical writing in newspapers and periodicals included obituary articles and miscellaneous memoirs and conversations, both genuine and fictionalized or semi-fictionalized.[71] As the notorious examples of the 'Cockney School' articles demonstrate, critical essays and reviews also became increasingly focused on the lives of their subjects. Some of this biographical writing was reverential, some judiciously critical, some satirical, and some nakedly defamatory, but

---

[68] Ibid. 28–30.

[69] St Clair, *The Reading Nation*, 414.

[70] See Higgins, *Romantic Genius and the Literary Magazine*, for the best discussion of these magazine series. I am indebted to his listing (163) of some of the following examples: [John Scott], 'Portraits of Authors', *Champion* (1814); 'Contemporary Authors', *Monthly Magazine* (1817–20); 'On Living Novelists', *NMM* (1820); 'Sketches of Living Authors', *London Magazine* (1820–1); [Leigh Hunt], 'Sketches of the Living Poets', *Examiner* (1821); William Hazlitt, 'The Spirits of the Age', *NMM* (5 pts., 1824) becoming *The Spirit of the Age* (1825); William Maginn, 'Humbugs of the Age', *John Bull Magazine* (1824); [F. D. Maurice], 'Sketches of Contemporary Authors', *Athenaeum* (1828); William Maginn, 'The Maclise Portrait Gallery of Illustrious Literary Characters', *Fraser's Magazine* (1830–8); [Alan Cunningham?], 'Living Literary Characters', *NMM* (1831); Alan Cunningham, 'Biographical and Critical History of the Literature of the last Fifty Years', *Athenaeum* (1833) (in book form 1834). The auto/biographical articles by De Quincey for *Tait's* (1833–41) follow this tradition of sketches of the living poets, in some respects, see Ch. 5.

[71] There were, e.g., numerous obituary articles on Byron, Shelley, Hemans, and Landon, some of which are discussed below (see Chs. 3–6). These were sometimes the basis of more extended memoirs in editions or published separately, e.g. Delta [David Macbeth Moir], Obituary essay on Hemans, *Blackwood's*, 38 (July 1835), 96–7, later expanded to form 'Biographical Memoir of the Late Mrs Hemans' in *Poetical Remains of the Late Mrs Hemans* (Edinburgh: William Blackwood & Sons; London: T. Cadell, 1836), pp. ix–xxxiii. The first major biography of Hemans, *CM*, was also derived from a series of articles by Chorely published in the *Athenaeum* (May–July 1835–6). For details see Susan J. Wolfson (ed.), *Felicia Hemans: Selected Poems, Letters, Reception Materials* (Princeton: Princeton University Press, 2000), 613. Examples of magazine memoirs and conversations included [Thomas Jefferson Hogg], 'Percy Bysshe Shelley at Oxford', *NMM* 34–5 (Jan.–Dec. 1832) and 'The History of Percy Bysshe Shelley's Expulsion from Oxford', ibid. 38 (May 1833), later incorporated into Hogg, *The Life of Percy Bysshe Shelley*, 4 vols. [only 2 pub.] (London: Edward Moxon, 1858); [Marguerite Gardiner, Lady Blessington], 'Journal of Conversations with Lord Byron, by the Countess of Blessington', *NMM* 35–9 (July 1832–Dec. 1833), later published as *Conversations of Lord Byron* (London: Henry Colburn, 1834).

whatever the tone, as more journals began to appear and the periodical press reached growing numbers of readers, these articles held the power to determine a poet's lifetime and posthumous reputation and readership. Whilst journals clearly capitalized on poets and other authors by selling their lives, they also provided a visible demonstration of the dependency of living poets on magazine biography as well as reviews, for their readership. At a time when the market value of new poetry was becoming uncertain, these periodical 'portraits' were an irritating reminder to poets of the popular currency of their lives over their works.

David Higgins has rightly stressed the little acknowledged importance of magazine biography at the period and has explored its various constructions of Romantic genius, as influenced by the target readerships and political and commercial rivalries of the magazines.[72] I will also be looking at biographical representations of the poets in the periodical press in later chapters, but, important as these were, we should not lose sight of other forms of publication, if we are to see the whole picture of literary biography in the marketplace at the period and its generic rivalry with poetry. Coleridge and Wordsworth found biography a threat some years before the expansion of the periodical press, and there were clearly popular forms of biography in book publishing too. Higgins finds that the magazines contained few lives of female poets compared to male.[73] Another benefit of casting our net more widely is that we discover a significant number of such lives in other publishing formats.

Single *Lives* of living or recently dead poets, in volume form, were less common than magazine biography in the period from 1800 to the early 1840s, but, even setting aside the *Lives* of Byron, to be discussed in the next chapter, there were important, full-length biographies of Cowper, Burns, Scott, Coleridge, Hannah More, Felicia Hemans, and Letitia Landon—some of which attracted great sales and publicity.[74] There were also numerous collective

[72] Higgins, *Romantic Genius and the Literary Magazine*.
[73] Ibid. 6.
[74] For the biographies of Cowper 1800–37, see Norma Russell, *A Bibliography of William Cowper to 1837* (Oxford: Clarendon Press, 1963), 241–61. See also e.g. in chronological order: [John Gibson Lockhart], *Life of Robert Burns*, vol. xxiii of Constable's Miscellany (Edinburgh: Constable, 1828); James Hogg, *The Domestic Manners and Private Life of Sir Walter Scott, with a Memoir of the Author* (New York: Harper and Brothers, 1834; repr. Glasgow: John Reid & Co., 1834); William Roberts, *Memoirs of the Life and Correspondence of Mrs Hannah More*, 4 vols. (2nd edn, London: R. B. Seeley and W. Burnside, 1834); *A Short Sketch of the Life of Mrs. Hemans: With Remarks on her Poetry; and Extracts* (London: James Paul, 1835); *CM*; Joseph Cottle, *Early Recollections, Chiefly Relating to the Late Samuel Taylor Coleridge, During his Long Residence in Bristol*, 2 vols. (London: Longman, Rees & Co. and Hamilton, Adams & Co., 1837); John Gibson Lockhart, *Memoirs of the Life of Sir Walter Scott*, 7 vols. (Edinburgh: Cadell, 1837–8); James Gilman, *The Life of Samuel Taylor Coleridge*, 2 vols. [only 1 pub.] (London: William Pickering, 1838); Henry Thompson, *The Life of Hannah More: With Notices of Her Sisters* (London: T. Cadell; Edinburgh: Blackwood, 1838); Laman Blanchard, *Life and Literary Remains of L. E. L.*, 2 vols. (London: Henry Colburn, 1841).

biographies of men and women, including male and female poets, dead and living, with other 'eminent' public figures.[75] Most significantly of all, perhaps, there were biographical editions. The coupling of a poet's works with his or her life and, often, letters, was a rising trend in publishing at the period. Wordsworth was alarmed at the way in which Currie's biographical edition of Burns, seemed to give precedence to the shocking aspects of a poet's life, over the poetry, but it was by no means alone in capitalizing on the life of a poet in this way. William Cowper's life became instantly marketable, following his death in 1800, both in biographies and biographical editions, igniting a debate between Evangelicals and their opponents, over the relationship between religious enthusiasm and mental illness.[76] One of the best-selling biographical editions of its day, William Hayley's three-volume *Life and Posthumous Writings of William Cowper* (1803), helped determine that Cowper's reputation was defined, first and foremost, by his controversial private life, rather than his works.[77] It was followed by numerous biographies and biographical editions. In the multi-volume editions published in the 1830s, by J. S. Memes (1834), the Revd T. S. Grimshawe (1835), and Robert Southey (1835–7), the life and letters of Cowper took up prime position and occupied half or more of the total number of volumes.[78]

As this suggests, during the 1830s, in particular, publishers were beginning to realize the commercial potential of the biographical edition as a way to maintain poets' sales. Indeed, the biographical preface, or 'introductory notice' of the life, became an almost obligatory, and often very substantial, part of any collected or

---

[75] Examples of collective literary biography, in volume form, containing 'Lives' of living female poets are given in Ch. 6. For male and female poets, see e.g. Henry F. Chorley, *The Authors of England: A Series of Medallion Portraits* (London: C. Tilt, 1838).

[76] See Russell, *A Bibliography of William Cowper*, 241 and see 244: 'In a letter to Hayley [Cowper's first, official biographer] on 5 July 1800, Lady Hesketh wrote that as administratrix of Cowper's estate, she was daily warding off applications from people who wanted to write Cowper's life.'

[77] William Hayley, *The Life and Posthumous Writings of William Cowper*, 3 vols. (London: J. Johnson, 1803–4) and several subsequent editions. For an indication of sales, see St Clair, *The Reading Nation*, 555. The publication in 1816 of Cowper's own, frank, account of his mental breakdown in his *Memoir*, naturally heightened biographical curiosity.

[78] See Russell, *A Bibliography of William Cowper*, 221–61; John S. Memes (ed.), *The Miscellaneous Works of William Cowper*, 3 vols. [i. *The Life and Letters of William Cowper*; ii. *Letters*; iii. *Poems*] (Edinburgh: Fraser and Co; London: Smith, Elder and Co.; Dublin: W. Curry, Jun. and Co., 1834). Memes's *Life*, pub. separately 1837. T. S. Grimshawe (ed.), *The Life and Works of William Cowper. His Life and Letters by William Hayley Esq. Now First Completed with an Introduction of Cowper's Private Correspondence*, 8 vols. [i–v contained the 'Life'] (London: Saunders and Otley, 1835); Robert Southey (ed.), *The Life and Works of William Cowper*, 15 vols. [i–iii contained the 'Life' and iv–vii the letters] (London: Baldwin and Cradock, 1835–7). See also John Johnson (ed.), *The Works of the Late William Cowper*, 10 vols. [iii contained 'A Sketch of his Life by his Kinsman' by Johnson] (London: Baldwin, Cradock and Joy, 1817); John Corry, *The Life of William Cowper* (London: B. Crosby and Co., 1803); and Thomas Taylor, *The Life of William Cowper Esq.* (London: Smith, Elder and Co., 1833).

selected edition of poetry.[79] Grimshawe's edition of Cowper sold 32,000 copies, and Southey's, lacking Grimshawe's appeal to the Evangelical readership, still managed around 6,000.[80] After the success of his seventeen-volume collected edition of Byron's *Works* (1832–3), prefaced by Thomas Moore's *Life*, the publisher John Murray planned a biographical edition of Crabbe, printing 7,000 copies of the first volume, which contained an original life of Crabbe, based on family letters, as compared to 5,000 of subsequent volumes, containing the poems. Eventually, 9,500 copies of the first volume were sold, as compared to 7,000 of each of the other volumes.[81] As we will see, the reputations of Byron, Shelley, and Hemans were also very largely determined by the *Life and Works* format in which they were brought to readers in the 1830s and for many years subsequently. In the biographical edition a competitive interdependency of poetry and biography became inscribed in the means of disseminating the idea of the 'Romantic poet'.

Biography was thus sold to readers in the 1820s and 1830s in a variety of forms, from the highest priced volumes—Moore's *Letters and Journals of Lord Byron*, or Croker's edition of Boswell, for instance—to middle-range and cheaper periodical and book publications.[82] Of course, as we might expect, some new ventures in biographical publishing were comparatively unsuccessful, and some

---

[79] See below, Ch. 3, for John Murray's marketing of Byron's poetry in biographical editions in the 1830s, and Ch. 4, for Mary Shelley's editions of P. B. Shelley in the 1820s and 1830s. See also e.g. Robert Southey (ed.), *Attempts in Verse, by John Jones, an Old Servant: with some Account of the Writer, written by Himself; and an Introductory Essay on the Lives and Works of our Uneducated Poets* (London: John Murray, 1831) [the 'Essay' includes biographical sections, interspersed with selections from the poetry of John Taylor, Stephen Duck, Ann Yearsley, and others]; Robert Southey (ed.), *Select Works of the British Poets, from Chaucer to Jonson, with Biographical Sketches* (London: Longman, Rees, Orme, Brown and Green, 1831) [pub. in order to reprint 'the elder poets, the fathers of our poetry' (p. iii), each selection was prefaced by a page of biography]; Thomas Medwin, *The Shelley Papers: Memoir of Percy Bysshe Shelley and Original Poems and Papers by Percy Bysshe Shelley. Now First Collected* (London: Whittaker, Treacher and Co., 1833); W.A.B. (ed.), *National Lyrics and Songs for Music by Felicia Hemans* [2nd edn., *With an Introductory Notice of her Life and Writings*] (Dublin: William Curry; London: Simpkin, Marshall & Co.; Edinburgh: Fraser & Co., 1836); Hemans, *Poetical Remains* (1836); *HM; Early Blossoms, a Collection of Poems Written between Eight and Fifteen Years of Age. By Felicia Dorothea Browne: Afterwards Mrs. Hemans, with a Life of the Authoress* (London: T. Allman, 1840); *The Poetical and Dramatic Works of Samuel Taylor Coleridge, with a Life of the Author* (London: John Thomas Cox, 1836).

[80] Russell, *Bibliography of William Cowper*, p. xvii.

[81] Erickson, *The Economy of Literary Form*, 150.

[82] Moore's book was originally sold at the very high price of 84 shillings; 1,050 of the initial print run of 1,750 were remaindered, but cheaper reprints kept it in print for most of the century, see St Clair, *The Reading Nation*, 621. James Boswell, *The Life of Samuel Johnson, LL.D. Including a Journal of a Tour to the Hebrides, A New Edition. With Numerous Additions and Notes, by John Wilson Croker, LL.D. F.R.S.*, 5 vols. (London: John Murray, 1831), sold at £3. Many of the cheap series that appeared from the late 1820s contained biography. Amongst the publications of Henry Brougham's Society for the Diffusion of Useful Knowledge was the *Biographical Dictionary*, a venture which foundered. Colburn and Bentley's *National Library* series also included biography— John Galt's *The Life of Lord Byron* (London: Henry Colburn and Richard Bentley; Edinburgh: Bell and Bradfute; Dublin: Cumming, 1830) was the first number in the series.

flourished, either immediately or in the longer term. Whilst acknowledging the mixed picture in relation to both poetry and biography in these decades, we can, nevertheless, see that new poetry was struggling to find an audience, whilst biography was suited to the new directions in publishing and reaching an increasingly wide audience through diverse avenues.

The careers of Robert Southey, poet, magazine essayist, and biographer, and the publisher Henry Colburn, suggest the comparative difficulties and opportunities offered by the different genres. Both show a commercially motivated decision to shift from poetry to biography. Southey, who could not earn enough money from poetry alone to support his family, relied on his work as an essayist in the periodical press between 1796 and 1834 to make his living.[83] But his most popular work was his *Life of Nelson* (1813). Its origins in a review for the *Quarterly Magazine*, it went into numerous editions and was one of the most successful biographies of the century.[84] Southey felt able to resign from the *Quarterly* in 1834, in order to concentrate on biography and biographical editions, of which he published several during his career.[85] This diversification of literary output made Southey an exception amongst poets in being able to earn his living by his writing. The move from poetry to biography is also visible in the career of one of the most innovative publishers of the period, Henry Colburn (1784/5–1855). Colburn was not only a publisher, but a retail bookseller, a library owner, and the proprietor of magazines, including the *New Monthly Magazine*, one of the best-selling of its day, with 5,000 subscribers at its peak in the early 1820s.[86] He was one of the first publishers to understand 'the mutual interest of the publisher, the lending library and the opinion-forming journal', and effectively used his diverse publications to promote each other, fully exploiting the potential of the new markets of the day.[87] He is most often mentioned in relation to the expansion of the market for fiction in the 1830s, and particularly as the publisher of the 'silver fork' novels of Bulwer Lytton and Disraeli, but his

---

[83] Southey, like other poets, increased the income from his poems by publishing them in newspapers before they came out in the much less lucrative book form. See St Clair, *The Reading Nation*, 158–9.

[84] Robert Southey, *The Life of Nelson*, 2 vols. (London: John Murray, 1813). The initial print run was 3,500. See St Clair, *The Reading Nation*, 555.

[85] Erickson, *The Economy of Literary Form*, 84–5. For Southey's biographical editions, see e.g. *The Remains of Henry Kirke White: With an Account of his Life*, 2 vols. (London: Vernor, Hood & Sharpe, 1807); *Attempts in Verse, by John Jones* (1831); *Select Works of the British Poets* (1831); *Horae Lyricae. Poems . . . by Isaac Watts. With a Memoir of the Author* (Sacred Classics, ix, London: 1834); and *The Life and Works of William Cowper* (1835–7).

[86] See John Sutherland, 'Henry Colburn, Publisher', *Publishing History*, 19 (1986), 59–84, and Veronica Melnyk, '"Half Fashion and Half Passion": The Life of Publisher Henry Colburn', unpub. PhD thesis, University of Birmingham, 2002. Colburn founded the *NMM* in 1814 and sold his share in 1845. Amongst other journals founded by Colburn were the *Literary Gazette* in 1817 and the *Athenaeum* in 1828.

[87] Sutherland, 'Henry Colburn', 80. Melnyk, '"Half Fashion and Half Passion"', 62, writes that Colburn 'is thought to have been the first publisher with a dedicated advertising department'.

list was, in fact, divided between fiction, 'Memoirs'—that is biography, autobiography, and letters—and travel. Of the 996 books Colburn published in his career, 527 were fiction, 207 were memoirs, and 141 were travel. Only 29 were poetry titles.[88] Between 1812 and 1820 when Colburn was the proprietor of Morgan's Library, he published travelogues and memoirs, many of them by aristocratic French exiles. During the 1820s, 1830s, and 1840s he published most of the early Byron biographies (some of them starting life in his *New Monthly Magazine*), as well as Hazlitt's *Table Talk* (1821), the *Memoirs* of Goethe (1824), Evelyn's *Memoirs* (1818), Pepys's *Diaries* (1825; 2nd edn. 1848), and the best-selling *Lives of the Queens of England* by Elizabeth and Agnes Strickland (1840–8).[89] He also brought out the most important fictionalized versions of the lives of Byron and Shelley: Lady Caroline Lamb's *Glenarvon* (1816), Mary Shelley's *The Last Man* (1826), and Disraeli's *Venetia* (1837). Amongst the seven copyrights Colburn considered most valuable and which he retained after his retirement, three were of biographical works.[90] Colburn's focus on aristocratic memoirs, and especially the life of Byron, clearly ties in with his interest in the 'silver fork' novels. He knew the selling power of aristocratic life, whether fictional, semi-fictional, or biographical, to the aspiring middle-class audience targeted by his various publications. Veronica Melnyk contrasts the reputation of John Murray, as a gentleman publisher, with Colburn's status as a '"trade"' publisher of increasingly 'populist' literature.[91] Yet, as we shall see, Murray also understood the selling power of Byron's life and that of literary biography more generally. In their different ways, the strategies of both Colburn and Murray, two of the most influential figures in publishing at this period, vividly demonstrate the rising power of biography, relative to poetry in the literary marketplace.

2.3 BRINGING THE POET HOME TO THE READER: THE DEFENCE OF BIOGRAPHY

The nature of biography, especially literary biography, its dangers and virtues, was discussed in numerous reviews and articles, biographical prefaces and private letters, and in the first full-length treatise on the subject, by James Stanfield, which appeared in 1813. Central to the debate was the issue of the reader's relationship to the biographical text. Many—including potential victims of

---

[88] Sutherland, 'Henry Colburn, Publisher', 79–81.
[89] Melnyk, '"Half Fashion and Half Passion"', 36 and 155–6; Sutherland, 'Henry Colburn, Publisher', 69. For his contribution to publishing Byron biography, see Melnyk, '"Half Fashion and Half Passion"', 201–8 and 218.
[90] They were his editions of Evelyn and Pepys, and the Stricklands' *Lives of the Queens of England*. See Melnyk, '"Half Fashion and Half Passion"', 171.
[91] Ibid. 20, 51.

biography and their supporters—shared the concerns of Coleridge and Wordsworth at the appetite of readers for Boswellian biography.[92] There was a
continuing strain of resistance to biography, on the grounds that it opened up
the private life of genius to the masses, but this was countered by a substantial
number of essays defending the genre for precisely the same reason. From widely
differing standpoints, commentators returned to certain themes in this defence.
Biography was celebrated for its peculiar authenticity, its power to re-create life.
It was valued, above all, for its ability to form an intimate relationship between
the reader and the subject. In the case of literary biography, it was this relationship, rather than that between the reader and the work, which was seen as
primary. In this section I will look at how biography was defended as the
means of bringing the reader into the domestic space of the subject and, thereby,
of bringing the subject home to the reader.

For some, biography was welcomed as a genre that extended educational
opportunity. As we have seen, Mary Hays presented it as a source of entertaining
enlightenment for women. William Godwin also envisaged biography as an
important means by which the new readerships could find access to education
and to their national, literary culture.[93] In his *Essay on . . . Biography*, James
Stanfield (1749–1824), an abolitionist and friend of Thomas Clarkson, assumed
the stance of an educator of the people, writing from a conviction of the 'utility'
of the genre as a means to understanding and thereby improving the moral
character of man.[94] By contrast to Coleridge, Stanfield welcomed the prospect of
the reader also becoming a writer of biography—his essay was partly a
manual for the aspiring biographer. He expressed some unease at the revelations
made by Rousseau and Boswell, and '[t]he rage for indiscriminate biographical
reading . . . indicating the frivolous taste of the present times', but the essay
stemmed from a profound belief in good biography as a discourse that might
educate through the intimate relationship it created between reader and subject.[95] Stanfield quoted a passage from the *Looker On*, celebrating biography's
power to awaken sympathetic feeling:

' . . . biography is studious of finding out the paths, which lead to our finest sensibilities; and
by acquainting us with the domestic transactions, introducing us to the private hours,

[92] e.g. [John Wilson], 'Observations on Mr Wordsworth's Letter Relative to a New Edition of
Burns' Works; By a Friend of Robert Burns', *Blackwood's Magazine*, 1/3 (June 1817), 261–6; [John
Wilson], 'Vindication of Mr Wordsworth's Letter to Mr Gray, on a New Edition of Burns' and
'Letter Occasioned by N's Vindication of Mr Wordsworth in Last Number', *Blackwood's*, 2 (Oct.
1817), 65–73 and 201–4. All three letters seem to have been by Wilson, taking up different
positions on Wordsworth's character and his *Letter*, but agreeing that his opinions on biography
were 'tolerably rational and judicious' ('Observations', 263). See Higgins, *Romantic Genius and the
Literary Magazine*, 92–3.
[93] See below, Ch. 4.
[94] Stanfield, *Essay on . . . Biography*, p. xiv. He was formerly a sailor on a slave boat and author of
Observations on a Guinea Voyage (1788).
[95] Stanfield, *Essay on . . . Biography*, 335.

and disclosing to us the secret propensities, enjoyments, and weaknesses of celebrated persons, increases our sympathy in proportion to our intimacy with the object held up to us'.[96]

His essay was a strong endorsement of the opened domestic space as universally improving.

Stanfield's essay, appearing before Wordsworth's *Letter* and the Byron scandal of 1816, was at a far remove from the smart, literary infighting of later debates on biography in the London and Edinburgh periodical press. The focus of discussion there in the 1820s and 1830s was on literary biography, including lives of the poets, and the tenor of much of this discussion was pointedly opposed to the views of Wordsworth. Hazlitt, who wrote with characteristic acuity on the subject, was to some extent torn between respect for the autonomy of the poet on the one hand and sympathy with the public desire for intimate relationship with their literary heroes, on the other. At one point in his essay on 'Spence's Anecdotes of Pope' (1820), he asserts that Pope's poetry stands immutable and impermeable to reports of the man himself, and in a later essay, 'On Reading New Books', he deplores the contemporary taste for setting up literary idols in order to tear them down:

What is the prevailing spirit of modern literature? To defame men of letters. What are the publications that succeed? Those that pretend to teach the public that the persons they have been accustomed unwittingly to look up to as the lights of the earth are no better than themselves, or a set of vagabonds or miscreants that should be hunted out of society?[97]

However, the essay on 'Spence's Anecdotes', his most extended discussion of biography, begins with a resounding defence of literary biography in which he adopts the reader's, rather than the subject's, point of view, and celebrates exactly the appetites that had so dispirited Coleridge and Wordsworth:

There is no species of composition, perhaps, so delightful as that which presents us with personal anecdotes of eminent men; and if its chief charm be in the gratification of our curiosity, it is a curiosity at least that has its origin in enthusiasm.... [we want] to look into the minute details, to detect incidental foibles, and to be satisfied what qualities they have in common with ourselves, as well as distinct from us . . .[98]

Where Wordsworth had defended the poet's privacy and projected his fantasy biography in the image of a tree beautified by a disguising veil of mist, Hazlitt identifies with the public appetite for clarity of vision. Using the analogy of visual portraiture, he voices the readers' demand to see the complete man—'the limbs, the drapery, the background', as well as the *heads* of great men'—and imagines spying on the poet at work in his study:

---

[96] Stanfield, *Essay on . . . Biography*, 131.
[97] Hazlitt, *Works*, xvi. 164; 'On Reading New Books', *NMM* (1827), Hazlitt, *Works*, xvii. 211.
[98] Hazlitt, *Works*, xvi. 152.

What would we not give to any modern Cornelius who would enable us to catch a glimpse of Pope through a glass door, leaning thoughtful on his hand, while composing the Rape of the Lock, or the Epistle of Eloisa[99]

His, and 'our', dream is to penetrate the domestic interior of genius—to see, to know, to touch, and even to take the poet home with us. Biography is a form of literary tourism and relic collection:

We like to visit the birth-place or burial-place of famous men, to mark down their birth-day, or the day on which they died. Cicero's villa, the tomb of Virgil, the house in which Shakespear was brought up, are objects of romantic interest, and of refined curiosity to the lovers of genius; and a poet's lock of hair, a *fac-simile* of his handwriting, an ink-stand, or a fragment of an old chair belonging to him, are treasured up as relics of literary devotion. These things are thus valued, only because they bring us into a sort of personal contact with such characters; vouch, as it were, for their reality, and convince us that they were living men, as well as mighty minds.

Hazlitt himself becomes anecdotal, relaying a story of the youthful Sir Joshua Reynolds who touched the hem of Pope's coat at a picture sale:

Who, in reading this account, does not extend his hand in involuntary sympathy, and rejoice at this unequivocal testimony and cheerful tribute of applause to living merit,—at this flattering foretaste which the elegant poet received of immortality?[100]

It is a living chain by which the reader, in imagination, also touches the poet's garment, acknowledging Pope's divinity, but also the humanity he holds in common with his worshippers. It is not enough to be a 'mighty mind', abstracted from the world inhabited by the reader. The poet only becomes *real* for the reader because biography establishes this 'living' relationship. The absence of great events in the lives of literary men, leaves us at greater liberty 'to explore their domestic habits.... In the intimacy of retirement, we enjoy with them "calm contemplation and poetic ease"'.[101] In literary biography,

We draw down genius from its air-built citadel in books and libraries, and make it our play-mate and our companion. We see how poets and philosophers 'live, converse, and behave,' like other men. We reduce theory to practice; we translate words into things, and books into men.[102]

Hazlitt responds to Wordsworth's view that the poet's works tell the reader all they need to know, by arguing that literary men are peculiarly suited to biography for the precise reason that their works do *not* tell us about their lives:

The difficulty of forming almost any inference at all from what men *write* to what they *are*, constitutes the chief value of the problem which the literary biographer undertakes to

---

[99] Ibid. 152–3.
[100] Ibid. 153.
[101] Ibid.
[102] Ibid. 153–4.

solve. . . . there is nothing to show that the writer of the Eloise to Abelard was a little, deformed person, or a Papist . . . [103]

Here biography's power to put the reader in contact with the physical presence of the poet exposes the Romantic conception of a perfect identity of author and work as a fiction. In this view, the poet does *not* author himself. The balance of power has shifted as the reader, previously stooping to touch the hem of Pope, discovers him to have been a 'little, deformed person'.

Hazlitt's emphasis on biography's communication of the living reality of the subject to the reader was amplified in Carlyle's 1832 review of Croker's edition of Boswell's *Life of Johnson* (1830). For Carlyle, the unique power of biography was to convey a 'Reality' that brought the dead back to life in an heroic resurrection—'they who are gone are still here; though hidden they are revealed, though dead they yet speak'.[104] Like Hazlitt, Southey, Mary Shelley, and many other biographers of the period, Carlyle had an ambivalent relationship to the genre. He was aware of its commercial potential, but also contemptuous of what he saw as the poorly written and opportunistic *Lives* daily pouring from the press.[105] His essays of the late 1820s and early 1830s tended to defend a rarely embodied biographical ideal rather than contemporary practice but, in so doing, eloquently responded to Wordsworth by asserting what was by then a reality of the marketplace: the power of the biographer over the poet.

For Carlyle, biography was a kind of ur-genre: '"History," it has been said, "is the essence of innumerable Biographies"' and fictions are nothing more than 'mimic Biographies'.[106] It was, for Carlyle, less a literary representation of life, than life itself:

Not only in the common Speech of men; but in all Art too, which is or should be the concentrated and conserved essence of what men can speak and show, Biography is almost the one thing needful.[107]

Biography, not poetry, speaks the real language of men, because it is the sign of the human presence within any work of art and of the biographer's '*open and loving heart*'.[108] Carlyle dissociates himself from the critic, who is interested only

[103] Hazlitt, *Works*, xvi. 154. See also Hazlitt, 'Lady Morgan's Life of Salvator' (1824), *Works*, xvi. 284–5: 'The great charm of biography consists in the individuality of the details, the familiar tone of the incidents, the bringing us acquainted with the persons of men whom we have formerly known only by their works or names.'

[104] Thomas Carlyle, 'Review of James Boswell's *The Life of Samuel Johnson LL.D.*, ed. John Wilson Croker, 5 vols. 1831, *Fraser's Magazine*, 27–8 (Apr.–May 1832), repr. as 'Biography', in *CME* iii. 44–135, see 75, 80. See also 77–8 on the retrieval of past time in Boswell's *Johnson*.

[105] See e.g. his letter to Thomas Murray (7 June 1819), in *The Collected Letters of Thomas and Jane Welsh Carlyle*, Duke-Edinburgh edn., gen. ed. Charles Richard Sanders (Durham NC: Duke University Press, 1970–), i. 181; and 'Jean Paul Friedrich Richter', *Edinburgh Review* (1827), in *CME* i. 1: '[R]ich as we are in Biography, a well-written Life is almost as rare as a well-spent one.'

[106] 'Biography', *CME* iii. 46, 48.

[107] Ibid. 45.

[108] Ibid. 57.

in the artistic product, and instead signals his allegiance to the reader, whose conversation is itself '*Biography* and *Autobiography* ', and who looks for the same in art:

Even in the highest works of Art, our interest, as the critics complain, is too apt to be strongly, or even mainly of a Biographic sort. In the Art we can nowise forget the Artist.[109]

This populist vision of cultural consumption entails hero worship—the reader's adulation of the biographical subject who, like Johnson, rises above the crowd to become 'the "Announcer of himself and of his Freedom"'.[110] But Carlyle's essays undermine the heroism of the poet-subject by representing him as wholly dependent on his biographer to create community with the reader. In what seems to be a pointed response to Wordsworth's *Letter*, he writes in 1830:

It has been said that no Poet is equal to his Poem, which saying is partially true; but, in a deeper sense, it may also be asserted, and with still greater truth, that no Poem is equal to its Poet. Now, it is Biography that first gives us both Poet and Poem, by the significance of the one elucidating and completing that of the other. That ideal outline of himself, which a man unconsciously shadows forth in his writings, and which, rightly deciphered, will be truer than any other representation of him, it is the task of the Biographer to fill-up into an actual coherent figure, and bring home to our experience, or at least our clear undoubting admiration, thereby to instruct and edify us in many ways.[111]

Wordsworth defended the poet's 'admirable edifice' of self-making, and cursed those who claimed its foundations were 'hollow', its frame 'unsound', but this is exactly the assumption underlying Carlyle's matter-of-fact statement that it is the biographer's job to complete the 'Poem' by making the outline of the poet into a fully substantiated reality. This biographical embodying of the 'outline' of the author brings the poet home to the reader, as a living person.[112] Far more emphatically than in Hazlitt's argument, this entails an explosion of the myth of poetic self-making. Not only does biography supersede autobiography—the poet's life is best told by others, rather than by himself—but the life is of more significance than the work.

It is a point Carlyle makes repeatedly in his essays from this period. In a review of Lockhart's *Life* of Burns, he describes Burns's works, great as they are, as 'no more than a poor mutilated fraction of what was in him; brief, broken glimpses of a genius that could never show itself complete', and praises Lockhart for giving the reader 'the whole man, as he looked and lived among his fellows'.[113] In a

---

[109] Ibid. 45. He does not, however, share Johnson's belief that all lives could make potentially interesting biographical subjects—see 86–90.

[110] Ibid. 90.

[111] 'Jean Paul Friedrich Richter', *Foreign Review* (1830), *CME* ii. 100–1.

[112] Compare Joseph Cottle, *Early Recollections* (1837), vol. i, pp. xvi, xix: he will show the poet in his 'home-dress' for '[t]he ultimate appeal is to the Reader'.

[113] 'Burns', *Edinburgh Review*, 96 (1828), in *CME* i. 266, 260.

passage that provides a rationale for the biographical edition, Carlyle dismisses Burns's poetry, except in so far as it is read as part of a larger life-story:

But to leave the mere literary character of Burns, which has already detained us too long. Far more interesting than any of his written works, as it appears to us, are his acted ones: the Life he willed and was fated to lead among his fellow-men. These Poems are but like little rhymed fragments scattered here and there in the grand unrhymed Romance of his earthly existence; and it is only when intercalated in this at their proper places, that they attain their full measure of significance.[114]

In similar vein, in his review of Croker's edition, he writes that all Johnson's works are inferior to Boswell's *Life*. Just as the life of Burns is a great prose poem, dwarfing his fragmentary rhymes, so Boswell's biography is a *'Heroic Poem'*, a *'Johnsoniad'* to which Johnson's works, already 'becoming obsolete for this generation', will in future be a mere 'Prolegomena and expository Scholia'.[115] The genre hierarchy, defended by Coleridge and Wordsworth, is inverted and the needs of the reader invoked as the impetus for a future resurgence of literary biography at the expense of its subjects' work. The literary biographer becomes, himself, both poet and poet-maker.

Carlyle's review of Croker's Boswell was merely the most forceful statement of a vision of biography that had already started to accumulate around this long-anticipated and highly publicized new edition. Croker's preface and the controversial reviews of Macaulay and Lockhart in 1831, followed by Carlyle's in 1832, inaugurated a decade of notable literary biographies with a bullish defence of the genre.[116] Despite his excoriating attack on Croker as editor, Macaulay, particularly, celebrated Boswell as having brought Johnson to the reader as a living 'companion' thereby eclipsing the importance of his dead corpus of writings for ever:

What a singular destiny has been that of this remarkable man! To be regarded in his own age as a classic, and in ours as a companion . . . to be more intimately known to posterity than other men are known to their contemporaries! . . . The reputation of those writings, which he probably expected to be immortal, is every day fading; while those peculiarities of manner, and that careless table-talk, the memory of which, he probably thought, would die with him, are likely to be remembered as long as the English language is spoken in any quarter of the globe.[117]

---

[114] *CME* i. 290–1.
[115] Ibid. iii. 110, 77.
[116] [Thomas Babbington Macaulay], Review of *The Life of Samuel Johnson . . . By John Wilson Croker*, *Edinburgh Review*, 107 (Sept. 1831), 1–38; [John Gibson Lockhart], Review of *The Life of Samuel Johnson . . . By John Wilson Croker*, *Quarterly Review*, 46 (Nov. 1831 and Jan. 1832), 1–46. In his preface, Croker, *Life of Samuel Johnson*, vol. i, p. v, referred to the offence taken by some of Boswell's contemporaries, as a thing far in the past and trumpeted his edition on the grounds of its entertainment-value.
[117] [Macaulay], Review of Croker, 38. See also 36 on the lively style of Johnson's letters as opposed to the dead pomposity of his written prose. Lockhart is more circumspect than Macaulay when it comes to the relative survival prospects of Boswell and Johnson's works. He also quotes Wordsworth's *Letter* respectfully (20–2), but disagrees with him on the unsuitability of authors as subjects for biography. He admires Boswell for making the reader feel they know Johnson (23–4)

Both Macaulay and Lockhart, like Carlyle after them, included their own biographical sketches of Johnson in their reviews. All three, alluding to his early poverty and his wanderings with Richard Savage, as recounted in the 1744 *Life of Mr. Richard Savage*, painted him as the tragic, Romantic poet, victim of the marketplace. Lockhart made an explicit comparison between Johnson and Burns in this context.[118] For Carlyle, as for Currie, Wordsworth, and others, Burns's life encapsulated the tragedy of the modern poet, struggling for economic independence. In all of these reviews, but most obviously in Carlyle's, the contrast between the heroic failure of the poet-subject and the triumph of the biographer, shows how literary biography had begun to inscribe its own market competition with poetry within its narrative of the poet's life. In the following chapters we will see how this competition evolved in practice, in the biographical afterlives of six major poets of the period.

and proclaims the superior reality of biography to fiction: 'what can the best character in any novel ever be, compared to a full-length of the reality of genius?' (11). See also Francis Jeffrey, Review of *Memoirs of the Life of the Right Honourable Sir James Mackintosh, Edinburgh Review*, 62 (Oct. 1835), 205–55, for a Johnsonian defence of the interest to readers of letters, journals, and other private writing of literary men.

[118] [Lockhart], Review of . . . Croker, 14–15.

3

The *Lives* of Byron

Byron's life and afterlives demonstrate the extent to which celebrity, the commodification of a personality, depends upon biography. There is little doubt that his fame today is constituted by a myth of the man, rather than by his work, but in his own lifetime and in the decade following his death, biography was already the linchpin of his reputation. It bound together the products of the Byron industry, not only the memoirs, conversations, anecdotes, fictional and semi-fictional representations of the poet, but the poetry itself, its editorial apparatus and its reviews, as well as portraits, artefacts, and other cultural manifestations of Byronism.[1] Unlike the other poets of his age, he did not have to die young or live to a venerable age to become the subject of a full-length biography—one was published when he was only 34.[2] When he did die, two years later, an unprecedented number of obituaries and memoirs followed, fuelled by the formidable selling power of his name.

Initially, of course, Byron was the author of his own celebrity. There has been much attention to the sophisticated manipulations by which he marketed himself, through his poetry and prose, his public posturing, and his efforts to control his visual image.[3] But Byron's control over his self-projections inevitably slipped away as reviewers, relatives, friends, enemies, and other self-appointed commentators capitalized on his life.[4] In an embodiment of Wordsworth's anxieties of 1816, the poet

---

[1] Bibliographies of this material include Samuel C. Chew, *Byron in England: His Fame and After-Fame* (1924; New York: Russell and Russell, 1965); Alex Alec-Smith, 'Appendix: Byron in Fiction. A List of Books', in Frances Wilson (ed.), *Byromania: Portraits of the Artist in Nineteenth- and Twentieth-Century Culture* (Basingstoke: Macmillan; New York: St Martin's Press, 1999), 221–6; and John Clubbe's survey of 19th-cent. Byron biography, 'George Gordon, Lord Byron', in Frank Jordan (ed.), *The English Romantic Poets: A Review of Research and Criticism*, 4th edn. (New York: Modern Language Association of America, 1985), 465–592.

[2] [John Watkins], *Memoirs of the Life and Writings of the Right Honourable Lord Byron with Anecdotes of some of his Contemporaries* (London: Henry Colburn, 1822).

[3] See e.g. Philip W. Martin, *Byron: A Poet Before His Public* (Cambridge: Cambridge University Press, 1982); Peter W. Graham, 'His Grand Show: Byron and the Myth of Mythmaking', in Wilson (ed.), *Byromania*, 24–42; Ghislaine McDayter, 'Conjuring Byron: Byromania, Literary Commodification and the Birth of Celebrity', ibid. 43–62; Christine Kenyon Jones (ed.), *Byron: The Image of the Poet* (Newark, Del.: University of Delaware Press/Rosemont Publishing and Printing Corp./Associated University Presses, 2008); Tom Mole, *Byron's Romantic Celebrity: Industrial Culture and the Hermeneutic of Intimacy* (Basingstoke: Palgrave Macmillan, 2007).

[4] Byron's own response to the flood of biographical speculation fluctuated, as the extent of public appropriation of his life become clear. See e.g. *BCH*, 6 on Byron's uneasy relationship to his

who made himself his own product, had, in the act of publication, become the product of others. On his death, with the destruction of his 'Memoirs' in John Murray's drawing room in Albemarle Street, readers were denied what may have been Byron's most intimate account of himself, and the market was opened up for biographers to supply these revelations on his behalf.[5] The autobiographical voice was appropriated by the biographical. Theodore Hook, for instance, composed an 'extract' from the 'Memoirs', entitled 'My Wedding Night', describing how Lady Byron had first 'turned herself away to the most remote verge [of the bed], and tightly enwrapped herself in the bed-clothes', but then succumbed to Byron's 'glowing, boiling passion'.[6] A procession of *Lives* filled the absence left by the 'Memoirs'. By the time the authoritative biography, Thomas Moore's *Letters and Journals of Lord Byron* (1830) appeared, the argument that an autobiographical poet, more than any other, requires a biographical approach, was put forward as uncontroversial:

What has been said of Petrarch, that 'his correspondence and verses together afford the progressive interest of a narrative in which the poet is always identified with the man,' will be found applicable, in a far greater degree, to Lord Byron, in whom the literary and the personal character were so closely interwoven, that to have left his works without the instructive commentary which his Life and Correspondence afford, would have been equally an injustice both to himself and to the world.[7]

Murray, Byron's publisher, was a prime mover in exploiting the market potential of biography. He purchased the rights for posthumous publication of the 'Memoirs' from Moore for 2,000 guineas and, although he approved their destruction in 1824, to protect Byron's reputation, he took full advantage of the opportunities for biography this created.[8] By the late 1820s and early 1830s, no doubt influenced by Colburn's success in marketing *Lives* of Byron, fictional-ized and otherwise, Murray's publishing decisions indicated a belief that Byron's life, rather than his works, would attract the largest numbers of new readers. His

audience after 1816; McDayter, 'Conjuring Byron', 48 on Byron's realization of 'his own relative insignificance in the construction of his public image'. On the other hand, he was an enthusiastic reader of literary biography and made his own journals, memoirs, and letters available to Moore, to form the basis of his posthumous memorialization. See Thomas Medwin, *Journal of the Conversations of Lord Byron. Noted During a Residence with his Lordship at Pisa, in the Years 1821 and 1822* (London: Henry Colburn, 1824), 196 on Byron's fondness for Johnson's *Lives of the Poets*. See also Leigh Hunt, *Lord Byron and Some of his Contemporaries; with Recollections of the Author's Life, and of his Visit to Italy* (London: Henry Colburn, 1828), 65 on his love of Boswell's *Life* of Johnson; and letter from Byron [to John Cam Hobhouse], 30 Sept. 1818, referring to Johnson's *Lives of the Poets* as 'the type of perfection', in *Byron's Letters and Journals*, ed. Leslie A. Marchand, 12 vols. (London: John Murray, 1973–82), vi. 72.

   [5] The destruction was discussed in newspapers in the days that followed. See *LLB*, 45.

   [6] [Theodore Hook], 'My Wedding Night; the Obnoxious Chapter in Lord Byron's Memoirs', *John Bull Magazine and Literary Recorder*, 1/1 (July 1824), 19.

   [7] *LJB*, vol. i, pp. vii–viii.

   [8] See *LLB*, 16. Murray also printed extracts from Byron's journal notebook in his newspaper *The Representative*. He tried and failed to persuade Hobhouse to make a selection of Byron's letters for publication.

confidence in the selling power of biography is demonstrated not just by the £4,000 fee he paid in order to secure the contract for Moore's *Letters and Journals*, but by his decision to market Byron's poetry to readers in the 1830s by repackaging it as biography.[9] He advertised his seventeen-volume edition of the collected works of 1832–3 as providing 'the clearest picture of the history of the man' yet to be put before the public and carried this out by devoting the first six volumes of the works to a reprint of Moore's biography.[10] The poetry was then presented in the form of a life story, chronologically ordered and appended with extensive notes deriving from the poet's private correspondence and from the personal testimonies of his friends. Murray assumed that readers would need the reassurance of a biographical narrative before they felt able to approach the verse. Thus, by encountering first the juvenilia,

the reader is enabled to take 'the river of his life' at its sources, and trace it gradually from the boyish regions of passionately tender friendships, innocent half-fanciful loves, and that vague melancholy which hangs over the first stirrings of ambition, until, widening and strengthening as it flows, it begins to appear discoloured with the bitter waters of thwarted affection and outraged pride. . . . every page of it [vol. vii] is in fact, when rightly understood, a chapter of the author's 'confessions;' and it is by contemplating these faithful records of the progress of his mind and feelings, in conjunction with those already presented in the prose notices of his life,—which mutually illustrate and confirm each other throughout,—that the reader can alone prepare himself for entering with full advantage on the first canto of Childe Harold.[11]

He targeted what he called 'a new generation' of readers, who would need help in understanding the poetry.[12] This included female readers, whose sensibilities he appealed to when he revealed that the manuscript of the original draft of 'Fare Thee Well!' 'confirms, and more than confirms, the account of the circumstances under which it was written. . . . It is blotted all over with the marks of tears'.[13] The approach was shrewd and the formula successful—more than 20,000 copies of the edition had been sold by 1833.[14] Having recognized, less

---

[9] See *LLB*, 262–97, for a detailed account of the negotiations with Moore. Moore originally planned to publish with Longmans and veered between them and Murray. Murray conclusively contracted Moore, by paying off the £3,000 owed to Longmans, together with an additional fee and making available his collection of Byron papers for Moore's use.

[10] *The Works of Lord Byron: With his Letters and Journals, and his Life, by Thomas Moore, Esq.*, 17 vols. [advertised in vol. i as 14 vols.] (London: John Murray, 1832–3), vol. vii, p. vi.

[11] Ibid., pp. vi–vii.

[12] Ibid., vol. viii, p. ix.

[13] Ibid., vol. x, p. vi. See *LLB*, 291: When Hobhouse told Murray that Jerdan disliked Moore's passages on Byron's religious scepticism, Murray replied: '"aye...well, let Lady Julia read the book and hear her opinion"'. Hobhouse took this 'to be a clever mode of letting me know the book is written for the women' (Hobhouse, 'Journals', 14 Jan. 1830).

[14] Chew, *Byron in England*, 240. In 1837 Murray brought out a 1-vol. edn. of Byron's *Works*, which repeated the formula of the 1832–3 edn., reproducing and augmenting the biographical footnotes. It was accompanied by a 1-vol. reprint of Moore's *Letters and Journals*, together with prose works by Lord Byron.

than a decade after the poet's death, that Byron's life had at least equalled his work in the public interest, Murray helped ensure that it became, in the long term, his major popular, cultural legacy.[15]

All *Lives* of the poets in the 1830s were in some measure responses to Byron biography—we will see this particularly in the case of Mary Shelley's memorialization of her husband. The biographical lens through which we view the Romantic poets is thus coloured distinctively by Byronism. This chapter looks at the first and most intense explosion of interest in the poet's life, between 1816 and the late 1830s. My discussion will build on existing studies of the cultural construction of 'Byron' in the nineteenth century and beyond, but its focus will be as much on what Byronism did for biography as on what biography did for Byronism.[16] In taking this approach I hope to go some way to countering what has tended to be a scant and, at best, lukewarm response to these early *Lives* of the poet amongst Byron scholars. Those who, like Doris Langley Moore, have looked for factual accuracy or a certain image of Byron, have unsurprisingly been disappointed, but even those seeking the broader context of these biographies' cultural significance have tended to be disapproving.[17] This has been especially true of reactions to the most influential of the early biographers, Thomas Moore. His narrative, in which the poet's letters and journals were embedded, has typically been dismissed as a dull setting for Byron's jewels.[18] Andrew Elfenbein argues that Moore's biography was the most important influence in the process by which Byron was recast by the Victorians:

while his Byron is not altogether respectable, his relentlessly conventional interpretation neutralized all the more shocking sides of Byron's character as the effects of 'genius'.... Moore's Byron embodies all the irregularities permitted to genius as they are judged through Moore's bland pieties. The sheer size of Moore's volume, along with his detailed research into Byron's life and reproduction of Byron's letters, gave his account of genius

---

[15] The biographical presentation of the poetry in the 17-vol. edn. was justified in words that echoed those in Moore's *Letters and Journals*, by arguing that Byron was a poetical autobiographer and should thus be read biographically. See *Works*, 17 vols., vol. vii, p. v. Andrew Elfenbein, in *Byron and the Victorians* (Cambridge: Cambridge University Press, 1995), 78, argues that the poet's letters produced for some readers 'an alternative canon even more interesting than Byron's poetry'.

[16] For the construction of 'Byron' and Byronism from the early 19th cent. onwards, see e.g. Chew, *Byron in England*; *LLB*; *BCH*; Elfenbein, *Byron*; Wilson (ed.), *Byromania*; James Soderholm, *Fantasy, Forgery, and the Byron Legend* (Lexington, Ky: University Press of Kentucky, 1996); Mole, *Byron's Romantic Celebrity*; and Kenyon Jones (ed.), *Byron*.

[17] Doris Langley Moore, in *LLB*, finds the majority of Byron's early biographers self-seeking, treacherous, and inaccurate. Only Moore's *Letters and Journals* meets with her approval.

[18] See e.g. Chew, *Byron in England*, 225, arguing that Moore's book is shallow and moralizing, its only merit being that it made the letters and journals of Byron public. Otherwise, '[t]he portrait produced is feeble and unconvincing....it is not a great biography'. See also Joseph W. Reed, *English Biography in the Early Nineteenth Century: 1801–1838* (1965; New Haven: Yale University Press, 1966), p. vii: Moore's biography is a 'glorious failure'.

an authority that no other account could match, but he used this authority to enclose Byron within the bounds of respectability.[19]

Elfenbein's analysis of Byron's Victorian reincarnations is astute, but his Romantic antipathy to the process of making Byron 'respectable' privileges the poetic over the biographical. From his perspective, a biographical discourse appealing to the middle-class reader, is inevitably demoted in relation to the aristocratic poetic—the 'conventional' a threatening subordinate to the creative.[20] What is described here as a process of enclosing Byron within the bounds of respectability, might be looked at differently—as, in the senses discussed in my introductory chapters, biography's mediation of the poet to the reading public, by means of its ideological domestication of genius.

Ghislaine McDayter writes that Byron's 'career will help elucidate not simply the birth of celebrity, and with it popular culture as we know it, but also a dramatic shift in the relations of production developing between authors, their works, and the reading public—a cultural event which marked the industrialisation of Romanticism'.[21] Biography was a key player in bringing about this shift. In this chapter I will reassess the biographical literature on Byron, especially in the years between 1816 and 1840, with particular attention to the most influential *Life*: Moore's *Letters and Journals*. My purpose is to look at the ways in which biography intervened in and competitively redefined the model of a poet's relationship with his readers by asserting its own powers as a domesticating form. The chapter starts by looking at how Byronism shifted attitudes to the ownership of private life and recharged the existing understanding of biography as a transgressive act. It moves on to explore the opposition between genius and domesticity as a central theme in *Lives* of Byron and then considers these texts as responses to contemporary perceptions of the relationship between the poet and his audience, examining the various strategies of biographical texts in creating intimacy between the reader and subject. The chapter finishes by discussing challenges to Byron's masculinity, especially by his female biographers.

The Separation scandal of 1816 was the seminal event for Byron biography and an important moment for biography more generally. After a year of increasingly unhappy married life, Lady Byron took their daughter Ada with her to her parents, and did not return.[22] Byron wrote two highly personal poems,

---

[19] Elfenbein, *Byron*, 79. He argues persuasively that 'Byron', as understood by the Victorians, constituted a sign of immaturity which they had to reject, hence 'a ritual of the Victorian authorial career in which writers repeatedly defined themselves against what they understood Byron to represent' (n.p.). He reads Carlyle's *Sartor Resartus* as a rewriting of Moore's *Letters and Journals*, with Teufelsdröckh as a redeemed Byron.

[20] See e.g. Elfenbein, *Byron*, 84–5 on the tendency of the 17-vol. edn. to package Byron 'as a respectable author by emphasizing niceties of textual and biographical observations and by downplaying his political and poetic radicalism'.

[21] McDayter, 'Conjuring Byron', 44.

[22] They were married on 2 Jan. 1815. Lady Byron left on 15 Jan. 1816.

responding to these events. 'Fare Thee Well!' was a sentimental expression of regret, addressed directly to his wife and containing apparently intimate details—'Would that breast were bared before thee | Where thy head so oft has lain'. 'A Sketch from Private Life' was a bitter satire on her maid, Mrs Clermont, who, he believed, had helped plot the escape, and whom he portrayed as a subversive interloper—'She dines from off the plate she lately wash'd'— ascending to become 'the Hecate of domestic hells'. Byron gave Murray permission to print fifty copies for private circulation, but the poems were quickly reprinted in the *Champion* newspaper as 'Lord Byron's Poems on His Own Domestic Circumstances' and then widely pirated, causing an immediate sensation and numerous responses in the press.[23] The reasons for the sensation were multiple and its effects far-reaching. A large measure of Byron's popularity was, of course, founded on readers' curiosity about his private life, something which he himself was already perceived to have encouraged, most notably in his equivocal prefaces to *Childe Harold*, I and II and *The Corsair*, which at once denied and affirmed the autobiographical basis of the poems.[24] But the publication of 'Fare Thee Well!' and 'A Sketch from Private Life' seemed to mark a new phase in Byron's willingness to display his private self to public view. The poems appeared to invite the reader to speculate, as never before, about his most intimate, domestic secrets, and especially about his sexual life, which, the rumours had it, included not only adultery but incest and sodomy.[25] The pamphlets and articles responding to the poems in 1816, repeatedly alluded to Byron's breach of his own privacy as an unprecedented act and, in the same breath, as a justification for their own extension of the boundaries of what was proper for public consumption—a now familiar defence of press intrusion into the lives of celebrities. His 'Sketch from Private Life', for instance, was parodied as 'A Sketch from Public Life', pointing critically to Byron's inappropriate conflation of the two, whilst conflating them itself.[26] Another writer accused Byron directly:

We were well enough disposed to treat you with distant respect, but you have courted and demanded our gaze. You have bared your bosom when no man entreated you; it is your

---

[23] *The Champion* (14 Apr. 1816). For accounts of the Separation literature and scandal see e.g. Chew, *Byron in England*, 19–26 and *LLB*, 162–6. I. R. Cruikshank's cartoon, 'The Separation, a Sketch from the Private Life of Lord Iron who Panegyrized his Wife, but Satirized her Confidante!!', depicted Byron at home, about to ascend the stairs with Mrs Mardyn, the actress, quoting 'Fare Thee Well!' at Lady Byron, Ada and Mrs Clermont as they leave the house. 'A Sketch from Private Life' lies between them on the carpet.

[24] See e.g. Francis Jeffrey's review of *Childe Harold*, I and II, Edinburgh Review, 19 (dated Feb. 1812, issued May 1812), in *BCH*, 38–42.

[25] These rumours began to circulate almost immediately as explanations for the Separation—see Fiona MacCarthy, *Byron: Life and Legend* (London: John Murray, 2002), 267–8.

[26] 'Tyro', *A Sketch from Public Life, and A Farewell: A Poem* (London: J. Hatchard, 1816). The title page parodies Byron's motto as 'Crede Judas'. The poem calls him '[t]he public slanderer of a private name' (6).

own fault if we have seen there not the scars of honourable wounds, but the festering blackness of a loathsome disease.[27]

A letter from 'John Bull', by John Gibson Lockhart, commented that 'when a man is really afflicted by a domestic calamity, it is by no means natural for him to make the public his confidant' but followed this up with allusions to his wife and child and his sexual adventures on the Continent.[28] As these examples suggest, the 'Poems on His Own Domestic Circumstances' had two major consequences for biography: they produced a shift towards a more aggressive culture of public access to private life and they ensured that the biographical exploration of domestic life became newly charged and newly marketable as a transgressive act.

3.1 THE OWNERSHIP OF PRIVATE LIFE

The debate on public right of access to private life, sparked off by the Separation literature, gathered pace at Byron's death, in the controversies surrounding his posthumous memorialization. Was the poet's private life his own, or did it belong to his biographers and their readers? Newspapers, journals, and biographies, especially in the period from 1824 to 1830, engaged in a battle between those, especially the biographers themselves, who asserted the public's right to know about Byron's private life and those, notably Hobhouse and Lady Byron, who defended its sanctity.[29] Some biographers equivocated about the propriety of this curiosity, but this was little more than lip service.[30] Their trajectory was relentlessly intrusive. One of the first posthumous biographies, Thomas Medwin's *Journal of the Conversations of Lord Byron* (1824) began by quoting, or possibly fabricating, Byron's opinion that '"[a] great poet belongs to no country; his works are public property, and his Memoirs the inheritance of the public"'. Medwin followed this up by describing the destruction of the 'Memoirs' as 'a manifest injustice . . . to the world', an 'evil' which he, in his biography, could 'endeavour to lessen, if not to remedy'.[31] The *Journal* was a bold statement in

---

[27] 'Presbyter Anglicanus', 'Letter to the Author of *Beppo*', *Blackwood's Magazine*, 3 (June 1818), see *BCH*, 127.

[28] *Letter to the Right Hon. Lord Byron* (London: William Wright, 1821), 62–3. See also *Poems on his Domestic Circumstances. By Lord Byron. I. Fare Thee Well! II. A Sketch from Private Life. With the Star of the Legion of Honour, and Other Poems. To Which is Prefixed, The Life of the Noble Author,* 11th edn. (London: R. Edwards, 1816), 7–8, where the anonymous author of the 'Life' regrets that the Separation 'is now unfortunately the subject of conversation from one extremity of the empire to another', but goes on to quote the newspaper gossip about 'a fascinating Actress' [Mrs Mardyn] who played a part in the marital discord.

[29] See Watkins, *Memoirs of . . . Byron*, 231, for the argument that Byron's life was already, in 1822, wholly exposed to public view.

[30] See e.g. ibid. 6 or John Galt, *The Life of Lord Byron* (London: Henry Colburn and Richard Bentley; Edinburgh: Bell and Bradfute; Dublin: Cumming, 1830), 186.

[31] Medwin, *Conversations*, p. v.

favour of public access and Hobhouse saw it as signalling a newly aggressive phase in biography, writing 'if no one dares to contradict these falsehoods what is to become of biography? What is to become of private life?'[32] Of course, whatever the point of view, the public debate already inscribed public ownership of Byron. The act of guarding Byron's privacy exposed it more seductively than ever, as Hobhouse and Lady Byron discovered when they went into print to challenge Byron's biographers. Hobhouse attacked Dallas's *Recollections* in the *Westminster Review*, as a cynical profit-making venture which, published on the day of Byron's funeral procession through London, was akin to bodysnatching.[33] He went on to refute Medwin's *Conversations*, point by point, in parallel columns headed: 'Mr. Medwin *makes* Lord Byron *say*' and 'The Fact', but in doing so, offered readers just what they wanted: an even more scrupulously authentic view of the private man. If Medwin's Byron described a lock of Napoleon's hair, given to him by his sister, as black, Hobhouse clarified, 'The *lock* of hair sent by Mrs. Leigh was just eight hairs, half an inch long, and all the hairs were either white or of a grisly grey'.[34] In castigating biography as relic-hunting on a grand scale, Hobhouse merely provided more relics. Lady Byron's efforts to curb biography were equally self-thwarting. In response to the first volume of Moore's *Letters and Journals*, she circulated a pamphlet which fuelled, as it censored, the public appetite for disclosures: 'Domestic details ought not to be intruded on the public attention; if, however, they *are* so intruded, the persons affected by them have a right to refute injurious charges'.[35] The fact of her having gone into print at all, together with the insights she gave into the part played by her parents and Mrs Clermont in the whole affair, and a hint from Dr Lushington on 'the circumstances' of the Separation, provoked another burst of public interest in the matters she wanted to bury.[36] When Moore reprinted Lady Byron's pamphlet in the appendix to the second volume of his *Letters and Journals*, the anti-biographical was decisively assimilated to the biographical.

The culture in which these biographies were produced, and which they themselves furthered, was one in which the poet's life had become the reader's property. Medwin's *Journal of the Conversations of Lord Byron* (1824), R. C. Dallas's *Recollections of the Life of Lord Byron* (1824), Hunt's *Lord Byron and Some of his Contemporaries* (1828), Moore's *Letters and Journals* (1830), and John

---

[32] *Journals* (13 Nov. 1824), quoted in *LLB*, 110.

[33] [John Cam Hobhouse], 'Dallas's "Recollections" and Medwin's "Conversations"', *Westminster Review*, 3/5 (Jan. 1825), 3.

[34] Ibid. 20 and 31.

[35] A. I. Noel Byron, *Remarks Occasioned by Mr. Moore's Notices of Lord Byron's Life* (London: Richard Taylor, [1830]), 3. At first privately printed, the pamphlet soon became widely available—see *LLB*, 312, 320–4.

[36] See *LLB*, 324–32 on the publicity generated by the pamphlet, including the press campaign waged on Lady Byron's behalf, against Thomas Moore, by Thomas Campbell in *NMM* (Apr. 1830). In the course of his defence, Campbell spread more rumours about Byron's relationship with his sister.

Galt's *The Life of Lord Byron* (1830) all produced public controversy as each pitted itself against its predecessors, claiming greater authority and authenticity than the last (Fig. 3.1).[37] Boswell, too, had opened his *Life of Johnson* by dismissing potential and actual rivals—first, and most respectfully, Johnson himself, who had failed to write his own life, then, more competitively, Sir John Hawkins. But there was nothing here approaching the passions and cut-throat marketing involved in the public quarrels between Byron's biographers in the 1820s and 1830s. As each biographer, in turn, fought out their individual claim over Byron's life, they cumulatively asserted the public claim as a given. The newly proprietary attitude amongst biographers to private life had lasting consequences for the empowerment of biography, marking a shift in attitude amongst biographers, their public and the publishing industry.

Legal efforts to stem the public consumption of private life had limited effect and simply served to return Byron's life to public ownership. Following a copyright dispute between R. C. Dallas and Hobhouse, over the publication of some of the poet's correspondence, the Lord Chancellor, Lord Eldon, passed a judgement, defining the right of the recipient of a letter to own it 'for the purpose of reading and keeping it' but not for purposes of publication and Dallas was forced to paraphrase the letters in his *Recollections*.[38] But the Dallas case, in the end, demonstrated biography's power to sidestep censorship. Despite all the efforts of Hobhouse, Dallas published an edition of the letters in France and they were quickly translated into English.[39] More significantly for the general reader in Britain, the publicity surrounding the case assumed and enacted public ownership of the correspondence. 'Lord Byron's Letters', in the *John Bull Magazine* for August 1824, reported, facetiously, on the injunction taken out against Dallas, mocking Hobhouse's motives as petty and self-serving. The article advertised several Byron letters for publication in *John Bull*, only awaiting Lord Eldon's judgement, and hinted at 'some very strange domestic scenes' in them, which would elucidate the mysteries in some of the poems including *Manfred*. Extracts from these letters appeared in the November issue and were presented in

---

[37] A. R. C. Dallas, who completed his father's biography of Byron, defended its veracity and authenticity by contrast to what he argued was Medwin's scandalmongering, baseless portrait of depravity—see R. C. Dallas, *Recollections of the Life of Lord Byron, from the year 1808 to the End of 1814; Exhibiting his Early Character and Opinions, Detailing the Progress of his Literary Career, and Including Various Unpublished Passages of his Works, taken from Authentic Documents in the Possession of the Author* (London: Charles Knight, 1824), 302–5. Moore and Hunt published satirical verses denouncing each others' efforts—see *LLB*, 282–3. Moore's *Letters and Journals* took its impetus in large part from the desire to rebuff Hunt and in it Moore repeatedly disparaged his memoirs—see e.g. *LJB* ii. 627: its 'utter and most deserved oblivion', 'that ungenerous book'. Galt, in turn, presented his biography as a corrective to Moore's portrait of Byron, characterized as 'too radiant and conciliatory' a likeness—see Galt, *Life of Lord Byron*, p. iv. See also [John Galt], 'Pot versus Kettle. Remarks on Mr. Hobhouse and Mr. Galt's Correspondence respecting Atrocities in the Life of Lord Byron', *Fraser's Magazine*, 2/2 (Dec. 1830), 533–42.

[38] See *LLB*, 88.

[39] See Dallas, *Recollections*, 'Preface' by A. R. C. Dallas.

THE AUTHOR OF A "LIFE OF BYRON."

Fig. 3.1. Daniel Maclise, '[John Galt] The Author of a "Life of Byron"', first pub. *Fraser's Magazine*, 2 (December 1830); repr. 1898. The bust of Byron stands on a pile of biographies of the poet by Galt, Moore, Hunt, Medwin and Dallas.

the same tone: 'Pretty lights and shadows of domestic life! We shall not print the still worse morceau on Lady Caroline Lamb'.[40] Dallas died just before the publication of his *Recollections*, but it appeared with a lengthy preface in which his son, the Revd A. R. C. Dallas, defiantly rehearsed the details of the copyright dispute. Despite his disapproval of Byron and of sensationalist biography, he produced an outspoken defence of the rights of the biographer. In response to the words of the injunction, that the publication of the letters would constitute ' "a breach of private confidence, and a violation of the rights of property" ', he defended his father's claim to the letters and distinguished between the terms 'private' and 'confidential', used interchangeably by Hobhouse and Hanson, in such a way as to define the private as available for public consumption:

The *private letters* of a *public* man are those in which, unrestrained by the *present* intention of publication to the world, he naturally and inartificially conveys his thoughts, senti-ments, and opinions to a friend. Can it be said that when a man's celebrity has raised him from his peculiar circle to belong to the unlimited one of all mankind, and when his death has made him the subject of history, and rendered the development of his character interesting to all the world, it is a breach of confidence to give to the world such *private* letters so written?

In this view, celebrity sanctioned and was, indeed, defined by public ownership of private life.[41] By the later 1830s J. Mitford was echoing Medwin—'[a] great poet['s] . . . works are public property, and his Memoirs the inheritance of the public'—this time as a self-evident truth, prefacing his semi-fictionalized and cheerfully bawdy account of Byron's 'Voluptuous Amours' and 'Secret Intrigues':

Everything connected with the life and character of so illustrious a bard as the late Lord Byron is public property. There can be no need of keeping either his frailties or his virtues from public view; there is no occasion to conceal names, when truth is held as the guide to all information.[42]

3.2 BIOGRAPHICAL TRANSGRESSIONS

Byron biography thrived on the fact that his poetry, the critical response to that poetry, the gossip circulating in high society, and, later, the efforts of such as Hobhouse and Lady Byron to prevent publicity, together enhanced the rhetoric of transgression which, as we have seen, had begun to define the biographical act

---

[40] 'Lord Byron's Letters', *John Bull Magazine and Literary Recorder*, 1/2 (Aug. 1824), 41–2; 'Lord Byron's Memoirs', ibid. 1/5 (Nov. 1824), 165; 'His Marriage', ibid. 165–6; 'His Departure', ibid. 166–7.

[41] Dallas, *Recollections*, pp. xxxiii, lxxxvi. Throughout the *Recollections* R. C. Dallas uses similar terms in expressing his regret at having to paraphrase rather than quote directly from Byron's correspondence.

[42] J.[ohn] Mitford, *The Private Life of Lord Byron* . . . (London: H. Smith, n.d. [1836?]), 3.

from around the 1780s. At every level, early Byron biography promoted itself by accentuating its function of disclosure. Readers of the first posthumous *Lives* were confronted with scattered asterisks, concealing and thus revealing indecent or actionable material—most famously in Moore's *Letters and Journals*, where they were liberally and provocatively deployed, but also in Dallas's *Recollections* and Medwin's *Conversations*. These biographies promised revelations: the mystery of Byron's character would be unfolded, including his true religious beliefs and, above all, the truth of his sexual life.[43] In the wake of the 'Poems on His Own Domestic Circumstances', the word 'domestic' itself, became newly charged and newly eroticized. One pamphlet of 1816 talked of him as having invited his critics

home to his closet, to feed and fatten on his domestic feuds;—to the private sanctuary of his domestic hours, to torture and misrepresent. . . . [the critic] lurks in his closet, watches his actions, perverts their meaning. . . he eagerly fastens on the first seeds of domestic disunion and hatches them into life . . .[44]

Byron's original epigraph for *Don Juan* was 'domestica facta', from Horace, translated by Byron as 'Common life'. Hobhouse persuaded him to abandon it because, as Peter Graham argues, following the Separation scandal, it would have been misinterpreted by the readers as '"domestic facts"' or '"Lord Byron's private relations"'.[45] The scandals surrounding the sexual revelations in *Lives* of Wollstonecraft, Burns, and Nelson formed a precedent, as we have seen, but, arguably, none carried the force of the disclosures of Byron biography.[46] It is not only that his domestic secrets were inherently more transgressive of moral codes. The crucial difference for contemporary commentators was Byron's status as a member of the hereditary aristocracy and thus the capacity of biography to cross lines of class in exposing his private life to the reading public.

The irritation of some modern critics at the nineteenth-century biographical embourgeoisification of Byron echoes the class outrage of his contemporaries. Looking back from the vantage point of 1831, Macaulay recognized that the condemnation of the poet's domestic conduct following the Separation scandal of 1816, implied the values of a middle-class readership. He was disgusted at what he saw as its hypocrisy in judging Byron, in 'one of its periodical fits of morality', showing that once in a while '[w]e must teach libertines, that the

---

[43] See e.g. J. W. Simmons, *An Inquiry into the Moral Character of Lord Byron* (London: John Cochran, 1826), 3: 'the mystery of his being remains still to be developed'.

[44] *A Narrative of the Circumstances which attended the Separation of Lord and Lady Byron; Remarks on his Domestic Conduct, and a complete refutation of the calumnies circulated by Public Writers* (London: R. Edwards, 1816), 4–5.

[45] Graham, 'His Grand Show', 33–4. See Hobhouse's *Diary* for 27 Dec. 1818, on *Don Juan*, I and II: 'the blasphemy and bawdry and the domestic facts overpower even the great genius it displays', quoted in *BCH*, 159.

[46] Byron biography continues to sell itself on new interpretations of his sexual relationships and sexuality of course. See e.g. MacCarthy, *Byron*, which foregrounds his homosexuality.

English people appreciate the importance of domestic ties'.[47] On Byron's death, his inner circle saw his biographers as social upstarts. Hobhouse referred to Medwin's *Conversations* as 'a scandalous breach of the first rules of society' and Augusta Leigh was irritated when William Parry, a former firemaster in the Navy, and author of *The Last Days of Lord Byron* (1825), visited her home: 'he is among the Biographers I fear—a most *vulgar rough Bearish* person'.[48] Hunt, particularly, was on the receiving end of attacks from those who saw him as a lowly interloper, with no sensitivity to the respect due to a Lord. Moore satirized Hunt's biography as a domestic invasion carried out with socially subversive intent:

> Next week will be published (as 'Lives' are the rage)
> The whole Reminiscences, wondrous and strange,
> Of a small puppy-dog, that once lived in the cage
> Of the late noble Lion at Exeter 'Change.
>
> .   .   .   .
>
> How that animal eats, how he snores, how he drinks,
> It is all noted down by this Boswell so small;
> And 'tis plain from each sentence, the puppy-dog thinks
> That the Lion was no such great things after all.
>
> .   .   .   .
>
> However, the book's a good book, being rich in
> Examples and warnings to Lions high-bred,
> How they suffer small mongrelly curs in their kitchen,
> Who'll feed on them living, and foul them when dead.[49]

Having been allowed a private view, Hunt's offence was to taint Byron with his own low breeding. A review of Galt's *Life of Byron* criticized Hunt as 'too much of a vulgar and conceited cockney' to write a good biography of Byron and also dismissed Moore as a social climber 'too fond of the crumbs that fall from the rich man's table'.[50]

The Johnsonian conception of the domestic space of biography as a meeting place for high and low had become newly contentious in the context of the expansion of the reading public. If Byron's private life was public property, it was the property of a broad spectrum of the middle classes, as well as the higher echelons.[51] This created inherent tensions within Byron biography. From one

[47] Thomas Babbington Macaulay, Review of Moore's *Letters and Journals*, *Edinburgh Review*, 53 (June 1831), in *BCH*, 298.

[48] Hobhouse, *Journals*, 3 Nov. 1824 and letter from Augusta Leigh, dated 2 Mar. 1825, quoted in *LLB*, 106, 169.

[49] 'The "Living Dog" and the "Dead Lion"', *The Times*, 10 Jan. 1828, ibid. 282. Hunt replied with 'The Giant and the Dwarf'.

[50] 'Galt's *Life of Byron*', *Fraser's Magazine*, 2/19 (Oct. 1830), 347.

[51] Elfenbein, *Byron*, 49, reminds us that the audience for 'Byron', as disseminated in various products, including biography, 'was less a monolithic middle class than a loose accumulation of lower gentry, wealthy farmers, tradesmen, ambitious artisans, professionals, and members of a

point of view, its revelations might provide a middle-class audience with a flattering fantasy of being part of the closed circle of the aristocracy.[52] But they could also, of course, confirm a sense of middle-class solidarity amongst readers *against* the values of their social superiors, as represented by Byron. Byron's aristocratic disregard for bourgeois, domestic life, added to his voluntary exile from the country, came to signify a betrayal of home and hearth extending naturally, to a betrayal of homeland. The reprint of 'Fare Thee Well! ' and 'A Sketch from Private Life' as 'Lord Byron's Poems on His Own Domestic Circumstances' in the *Champion* was accompanied by an editorial casting doubt on his patriotism.[53] Publishers such as Henry Colburn and the biographers themselves were alert to the advantages of exploiting this multiple betrayal of what were projected as the fundamental values of the readership. All of them capitalized on the vicarious pleasures offered by insight into the world of the aristocracy, but many were openly critical of this world. John Galt, siding with his readers rather than his subject, recalled how, observing Byron as a young man on board ship, during his first European tour, he felt that 'his lordship affected, as it seemed to me, more aristocracy than befitted his years, or the occasion. . . . Hobhouse, with more of the commoner, made himself one of the passengers at once; but Byron held himself aloof'. Later he identified '[t]he pride of rank' as 'one of the greatest weaknesses of Lord Byron'.[54] John Mitford, in the late 1830s, appealed to middle-class voyeurism, but also to disapproval of the aristocracy when he advertised his *Private Life of Lord Byron* as including '*Various Singular Anecdotes of Persons and Families of the highest Circles of Haut Ton . . . being an amusing and interesting Expose of Fashionable Frailties, Follies, and Debaucheries*'. But class was not the only respect in which biography appealed to its audience through an ambivalent critique of Byron. 'Byron' signified the undomesticated subject not only by virtue of his sexual transgressions and his aristocracy, but also his genius and his masculinity. It was the conjunction of these values that biography's ideological investment in the 'domestic' challenged.

variety of other groups'. These other groups, of course, included the aristocracy. The pricing of the biographical literature varied. The first edition of Moore's *Letters and Journals* was very costly—see St Clair, *The Reading Nation*, 621, but this was the exception. Colburn's prices were high, but affordable to the well-off middle classes, and other publications, e.g. in magazines and pamphlets, were less expensive. John Murray made efforts during the 1830s to make his subsequent editions of Moore's *Letters and Journals* more affordable. See St Clair, ibid. 590.

[52] See Elfenbein, *Byron*, 51.

[53] MacCarthy, *Byron*, 275. 'Tyro', *A Sketch from Public Life*, 7, charged the sentiments of 'A Sketch from Private Life' with being unBritish: 'A foreign taste and language may excuse | Detractions foreign to the British Muse'. 'Presbyter Anglicanus' linked his condemnation of the 'Poems on His Own Domestic Circumstances' to the lack of moral standards and patriotism in Byron's works: 'In all your writings, how little is there whose object it is to make us reverence virtue, or love our country!'—see *BCH*, 126.

[54] Galt, *Life of Lord Byron*, 60–1, 154.

3.3 GENIUS AND DOMESTIC LIFE

Byron biographies published in the 1820s and 1830s drew on a discourse of separate, gendered, spheres of public and private life in their narratives of his struggle to reconcile his aristocratic, masculine genius with his domestic affections. Repeatedly they represented the defining event of his life as the 'Separation'—the divorce of genius from domesticity. Whilst all these biographies capitalized on the glamour of Byronic genius, there were a variety of attitudes towards its perceived incompatibility with the mundane and, more especially, with the norms of a bourgeois marriage.

The first substantial biography, published by John Watkins in 1822, was the most unswervingly critical. Writing in the poet's lifetime, he had to base his account largely on the poetry. His thesis, running counter to his method, was that poetry and life did not mix: 'Poetry is an elegant art, but it ought not to be made the business of life'. Byron's mistake was to live as a poet, thereby outraging the quotidian world. Speaking as a self-appointed guardian of bourgeois morality and friend of 'social order', Watkins conflated the aristocratic elevation of his subject with the elevation of genius and deplored both as distancing Byron from 'common virtue and understanding'.[55] He argued that the poet's life confirmed the fundamental immorality of his work. His aristocratic affectations—the pet bear, the drinking cup made from a skull—were deplorable signs of misanthropy.[56] His behaviour towards his wife and child was shocking. His sexual conduct united the contempt of an aristocrat and a genius for 'ordinary' moral standards. He could not even be discreet in his infidelities, but brought his mistress, Mrs Mardyn, home to dinner:

> that man must have worked up his mind to a high pitch of contemptuous superiority over the ordinary principles by which the social relations are maintained in harmony, who can presume to bring depravity under his roof, and introduce vice to his table.[57]

Watkins's relentless condemnation of the poet for his abrogation of responsibility to ordinary—especially family—life was based on a contempt for poetry itself. The message was clear that the poet and his works should not and would not escape being judged by his private conduct. He presented his *Memoirs* as a warning to Byron to change his ways, to return home and devote his talents to 'utility'.[58]

---

[55] Watkins, *Memoirs of... Byron*, pp.175, vii and see 241: 'Instead of taking the straight and obvious course which every man of common virtue and understanding would have adopted in such an exigency [the Separation], this exalted genius soars into the clouds, and leaving his tenderest concerns on earth to be discussed in a printing-office, solaces his afflicted mind by composing pathetic and caustic verses ['Fare Thee Well!' and 'A Sketch from Private Life'].'

[56] Ibid. 86, 90.

[57] Ibid. 234. Watkins is wholly on Lady Byron's side in the Separation controversy.

[58] Ibid. 419 and 425.

For R. C. Dallas, in his *Recollections of the Life of Lord Byron* (1824) the cause was already lost. Looking back at the period at which he had been closely involved with Byron, he showed more affection and respect for him than Watkins, but also lamented the poet's disregard for conventional religious and domestic values. The *Recollections* included Dallas's avuncular letters to Byron exhorting him to temper the religious scepticism of his poetry and regret at his alienation from domestic life: '[a]s for domestic happiness he had no idea of it'. Dallas also recalled how he had tried and failed to persuade Byron of the value of family life:

> It was in vain for me to argue that the nursery, and a similarity of pursuits and enjoyments in early life, are the best foundations of friendship and love; and that to choose freely, the knowledge of home was as requisite as that of wider circles.[59]

There was a pervasive tone of disappointment here that Byron could not quite be as great a man as he was a genius and a suggestion of personal rejection, especially after the publication of *Childe Harold*, when Byron 'made himself his own god'. Dallas's attempt to save the better Byron before fame overtook him was, finally, presented as a tragic failure.[60]

Both Watkins and Dallas argued that Byron's genius should have been placed in the service of a more conventional life, represented especially in terms of duty to the family, understood as the location of a bourgeois ideal of social relations. Other biographers, whilst engaging in the same debate, gloried in the poet's elevation above the ordinary. Cosmo Gordon's *Life and Genius of Lord Byron* (1824), hastily compiled to take advantage of the demand for material on Byron following news of his death, was a prolonged, eulogistic obituary.[61] Responding to Watkins, Gordon celebrated Byron's genius for the very fact that it raised him above the common order of men: 'There is something in this sublime and solitary elevation of genius, which at once commands the admiration, nay almost the adoration of the unprejudiced mind'.[62] Byron was unique, he argued, exceptional as a poet and a hero and we should not judge his vices by ordinary standards. Just as rank determines how we judge an individual, so should genius. Middle-class standards were invoked only to be rejected by Gordon: 'the same measure which applies to a dull clerk or a posing lecturer, should not be applied to such a man as him'.[63] In keeping with this, he viewed the Separation merely as an opportunity for Byron to launch himself on a yet more glorious

---

[59] Dallas, *Recollections*, 62–3. He also remarks on Byron's disgust at female society, 61–2 and 245.

[60] Ibid. 331, 297–8.

[61] Cosmo Gordon, *Life and Genius of Lord Byron* (London: Knight and Lacey, 1824). News of the death reached England in mid-May 1824. Gordon's biography was published in June or July. See *LLB*, 59.

[62] Gordon, *Life and Genius*, 9.

[63] Ibid. 14.

stage of his career: 'the noble bard, ejected, as it were, from scenes which once had promised him the sweets of domestic peace, appeared again upon the wide world an accomplished candidate for more extended and imperishable renown'.[64] Where others had implied a criticism of Byron's masculine autonomy, Gordon celebrated his escape from domestic ties as a token of the aristocratic, masculine vigour of his genius.[65]

The most lengthy, subtle, and influential defence of Byron's undomesticated genius came from Thomas Moore. His book was a combined edition of Byron's letters and journals with a substantial biographical narrative supplied by Moore. A complex of problematic oppositions between public and private life ran throughout. On the one hand, he represented Byron's genius as masculine, autonomous, antipathetic to the mundane, social realities of the public 'world'. The poet was detached from the realm of ordinary things and other people, superior to an uncomprehending public.[66] On the other hand, Byron's genius was self-destructively worldly:

Born with strong affections and ardent passions, the world had, from first to last, too firm a hold on his sympathies to let imagination altogether usurp the place of reality.... His life, indeed, was one continued struggle between that instinct of genius, which was for ever drawing him back into the lonely laboratory of Self, and those impulses of passion, ambition, and vanity, which again hurried him off into the crowd, and entangled him in its interests; and though it may be granted that he would have been more purely and abstractedly the *poet*, had he been less thoroughly, in all his pursuits and propensities, the *man*, yet from this very mixture and alloy has it arisen that his pages bear so deeply the stamp of real life...[67]

This double aspect of Byron as, at once, withdrawn melancholic and social man, Childe Harold and Don Juan, was a motif within Moore's narrative, as it was within other biographies.[68] In Moore's view, Byron's worldly impulses were potentially fatal distractions from his poetic calling, but Moore managed to assert the masculinity both of the poet who, like Frankenstein, retreats to 'the lonely laboratory of Self', and of 'the *man*' whose 'strong affections and ardent passions', compensate for his 'vanity' in chasing after the crowd. This attempt to claim the compatibility of Byron's worldliness with his masculine poetic genius is

[64] Gordon, *Life and Genius*, 49.
[65] See e.g. ibid. 3 and appendices for the emphasis on Byron's heroic masculinity—esp. associated with his exploits in Greece.
[66] See e.g. *LJB* i. 60, on Byron's refusal to conform at school: 'the powers and movements of a mind like Byron's, which might well be allowed to take a privileged direction of its own'. See also *LJB* i. 211.
[67] *LJB* i. 592.
[68] See *LJB* i. 327n, where Moore notes that the original name for Childe Harold was 'Childe Burun', underlining Byron's 'intention of delineating himself in his hero'. He refers to Byron's life as 'his indefinite pilgrimage' (186) and to Byron at the period of his writing *Childe Harold* as 'the young pilgrim' (251). For Byron as a compound of Harold and Juan, see e.g. 253.

typical of Moore's narrative. But worldliness could be more easily assimilated to genius than domesticity. From the opening of his first volume, Moore also stressed Byron's desire for, yet alienation from, the feminine, domestic sphere. The 'dearth of all home endearments' in his childhood was identified as the source of a lifelong 'agony' of unfulfilled affection.[69] Rejected by his mother and lacking, as yet, the 'softening' influence of a sister's love, Byron's untamed feelings vented themselves on 'boyish friendships' at school and thereafter, if at all, on a series of unhappy infatuations with women which culminated in a disastrous marriage.[70] Moore was clear that the lack of domestic harmony in Byron's life was the primary cause of his personal unhappiness, but he justified this suffering on the grounds that domestic life was wholly incompatible with greatness—the man may flourish in the bosom of his family, but the poet will wither. Indeed, Moore argued a poet's inability to tolerate the nurturing environment of the home was an index of his genius:

A more genial and fostering introduction into life, while it would doubtless have softened and disciplined his mind, might have impaired its vigour; and the same influences that would have diffused smoothness and happiness over his life might have been fatal to its glory.[71]

In passages such as this, Byron's masculine autonomy, free from the softening effects of the domestic sphere, was celebrated, albeit with some equivocations.

The antagonism between genius and domestic life was most directly discussed, of course, when Moore took on the subject of Byron's marriage. In these important passages, forming the grand finale to volume i of the *Letters and Journals*, Moore defended Byron from public censure by arguing that, in the matter of his relationship with his wife, his actions as a man were justified by his needs as a poet. Far from being undermined by the marriage's failure, Byron's place with the world's greatest poets was confirmed by it. He was in good company:

rarely, if ever, have men of the higher order of genius shown themselves fitted for the calm affections and comforts that form the cement of domestic life . . . [Poets from Homer to Byron] have been, in their several degrees, restless and solitary spirits, with minds wrapped up, like silk-worms, in their own tasks, either strangers, or rebels, to domestic ties . . .[72]

As the cocoon image suggests, poetic greatness, as Moore defined it, demonstrates 'an unsocial and detaching tendency', and

It is, indeed, in the very nature and essence of genius to be for ever occupied intensely with Self, as the great centre and source of its strength. . . . To this power of self-concentration, by which alone all the other powers of genius are made available, there

---

[69] Ibid. 178, 176.
[70] Ibid. 177–8, and see 43. See also 93, women 'were, from first to last, the ruling star of his destiny'.
[71] Ibid. 324.
[72] Ibid. 589, 591.

is, of course, no such disturbing and fatal enemy as those sympathies and affections that draw the mind out actively towards others . . .[73]

This poetic 'power of self-concentration' was gendered masculine throughout. It was represented as both vulnerable to and able to define itself against the feminine, domestic realm, associated by Moore with the affective, the social, and the mundane—imagination 'tends to wean the man of genius from actual life'.[74] The great poet was, for Moore, a man engaged in solitary conquest, not a child, nursed by home comforts. The sight of a poet tamed by domesticity may be delightful but

it is not thus smoothly or amiably immortality has been ever struggled for, or won. The poet thus circumstanced may be popular, may be loved; for the happiness of himself and those linked with him he is in the right road,—but not for greatness . . .[75]

Moore articulated his position on the conflict between genius and domestic life at greater length than any other contemporary biographer, but Medwin and Hunt, before him, and Lady Blessington and Mitford after him, all intervened in the debate by representing Byron, whether tragically, critically, or comically, as a man unable to stoop to normal social relationships and especially to family life. Medwin's Byron was caught between contempt for domestic life and longing for it, but the tendency of this biography was to find his failure tragic—the volume ends by quoting lines from an 'Ode to the Memory of Lord Byron': 'Domestic joy he nobly sacrificed, | To shun the path of pleasure was his doom— | These for heroic dangers he despised; | Then Greece, the land of heroes, be his tomb!'[76] The tendency of Hunt's *Life*, as we shall see, was more critical of the poet's aristocratic aloofness from ordinary life and (possibly motivated, in part, by the belief that Byron had slighted Hunt's own family), of the poet's shortcomings on the domestic front.[77] For Hunt, Byron's central character trait was 'an indulgence of his self-will and self-love' and a commensurate lack of concern for the happiness of others. Crucially, he was unable to form proper relationships with women: 'Fare Thee Well! ' was insincere: 'I do not believe that he ever had the good-fortune of knowing what real love is', 'no woman could have loved him

---

[73] *LJB* i. 589, 591.

[74] Ibid. 590.

[75] Ibid. 592.

[76] Medwin, *Conversations*, 345. Medwin represents Byron as having little respect for his wife and a general contempt for women (71–2). His appendix reprints Hobhouse's 'Some Account of Lord Byron's Residence in Greece' which characterizes Byron as 'one satiated and disgusted with the formality, hypocrisy, and sameness of daily life' (299). But he also argues that Byron's central sadness was the failure of his marriage: 'All the tender and endearing ties of social and domestic life rudely torn asunder, he has been wandering on from place to place, without finding any to rest in' (108).

[77] See *LLB*, 402–3; Hunt may have seen Byron's letter to Mary Shelley in which he commented that the Hunt children were 'dirtier and more mischievous than Yahoos. What they can't destroy with their filth they will with their fingers. . . . Poor Hunt with his six little blackguards'. Hunt's brother had also seen a letter in which, according to Mary Shelley, Byron had made the *Liberal* look like 'a work of charity—a kind of subscription for Hunt's family'.

long'.[78] By the late 1830s, when Mitford published *The Private Life of Lord Byron*, Moore's argument on the incompatibility of genius and domestic life had become a cliché, available for comic treatment, in a narrative with the structure of a pornographic novel, consisting almost entirely of brief sexual encounters, in which Byron, Juan-like, both succumbs to the female domestic embrace and perpetually eludes it. Byron could have been tamed by the love of a woman 'to their mutual happiness and his domestic comfort; but then the world would have lost one of the finest writers that ever breathed the stern voice of morality through the ever-changing medium of Ovidean verse'.[79]

In its thematic concern with the poet's relationship to domestic life, Byron biography, along with other *Lives* of the poets in the 1820s and 1830s, formed an active arena of debate on the separate spheres and, more particularly, the issue of the social responsibilities of genius that preoccupied poets, reviewers, and others at the period. But the ideological engagement with domestic life that shaped biography, extended these debates in distinctive ways. Although Byron's biographers took various perspectives on the issue of the conflict between aristocratic, masculine genius and a middle-class ideal of domesticity, they all employed biography as a medium within which the poet *was* domesticated—that is, on the most literal level, seen at home, with family and friends, represented, first and foremost, as a private man, and thereby brought home to the reader. This set up a fundamental tension in texts such as Moore's which argued for the divergence of genius and domesticity, whilst demonstrating their interdependence at every level. Biography invited readers to stand in awe of Byron's aristocratic, masculine genius, but, by positioning them as members of his intimate, social circle, encouraged a fantasy of familiarity. In so doing this genre made an important intervention in the wider debates of the period on the nature of a poet's relationship to his audience, but also created a powerful relationship, itself, with the new readerships of the day. Before returning to the biographies, to see how they did this, I want to glance at the reception of Byron's poetry, especially after 1816, since the public debate over the poet and his audience is an important context for understanding the biographical literature that followed. Byron and his reviewers together redefined the relationship between a poet and his public, but biography also played an important part in this and was, I would argue, the ultimate beneficiary.

3.4 THE PROMISE OF INTIMACY:
BYRON AND HIS READERS

Following the 'Poems on His Own Domestic Circumstances', the publication of *Childe Harold*, III later in 1816, with its address to Ada, seemed to confirm

---

[78] Hunt, *Lord Byron*, 77, 7, and 25. See also 41.
[79] Mitford, *The Private Life of Lord Byron*, 40.

Byron's impulse to self-revelation, and produced reviews which focused with renewed intensity on what was perceived as the poet's cultivation of an unprecedentedly personal relationship with his readers.[80] In 1818, reviewing *Childe Harold*, IV, Scott wrote that,

since the time of Cowper he has been the first poet who, either in his own person, or covered by no very thick disguise, has directly appeared before the public, an actual living man expressing his own sentiments, thoughts, hopes and fears. Almost all the poets of our day, who have possessed a considerable portion of public attention, are personally little known to the reader. . . . Childe Harold appeared—we must not say in the character of *the* author—but certainly in that of a real existing person, with whose feelings as such the public were disposed to associate those of Lord Byron. . . . it is certain that no little power over the public attention was gained from their being identified.[81]

In the same year John Wilson compared Byron and Rousseau as writers with 'an intense sensibility of passion' whereby they had won an unusually sympathetic relationship with their readers, but above all as writers whose power 'lies in the continual embodying of the individual character—it might almost be said, of the very person of the writer. . . . We feel as if we had transiently met such beings in real life'. Their works were living portraits, 'images, pictures, busts of their living selves' and, in Byron's case, '[t]here is felt to be between him and the public mind, a stronger personal bond than ever linked its movements to any other living poet'.[82] An obituary in *The Examiner* summed up his appeal as that of a personal friendship: 'Every reader of his immortal writings is, at the least, an acquaintance—often an ardent and sympathising friend', and on hearing of his death, Carlyle recorded in his journal the same fantasy: 'I dreamed of seeing him and knowing him'.[83]

By emphasizing the reader's affective relationship with Byron in this way, the reviews feminized the reader, sometimes projecting the relationship as erotic or domestic.[84] Wilson, for instance, talked of the apparently 'private and confidential communications' of Rousseau and Byron, personal confessions experienced

---

[80] See Elfenbein, *Byron*, 53 ff. for discussion of this relationship as delineated by the reviews. See *BCH*, 109, for Francis Jeffrey's comment, of the Childe Harold of Canto III, 'There is a dreadful tone of sincerity . . . the author has at last spoken out in his own person, and unbosomed his griefs a great deal too freely to his readers, the offence now would be to entertain a doubt of their reality'; and see ibid. 86, for Sir Walter Scott's statement in his review of *Childe Harold*, III (1816), *Quarterly Review*, 16 (dated Oct. 1817; issued Feb. 1817), that 'it becomes impossible for us to divide Lord Byron from his poetry'.

[81] Sir Walter Scott, Review of *Childe Harold*, IV, *Quarterly Review*, 19 (dated Apr. 1818; issued Sept. 1818), in *BCH*, 138.

[82] John Wilson, Review of *Childe Harold*, IV, *Edinburgh Review*, 30 (dated June 1818; issued Sept. 1818), in *BCH*, 147–8 and 153.

[83] Obituary quoted in Sir Cosmo Gordon, *Life and Genius of Lord Byron*, 71. Thomas Carlyle, letter to Jane Baillie Welsh (19 May 1824), in *The Collected Letters of Thomas and Jane Welsh Carlyle*, Duke-Edinburgh edn., gen. ed. Charles Richard Sanders (Durham, NC: Duke University Press, 1970-), iii. 68.

[84] See Elfenbein, *Byron*, 60.

as 'secrets whispered to chosen ears'—'we feel as if chosen out from a crowd of lovers'.[85] In a more mocking vein Lockhart wrote (anonymously) of the gullibility of young, female readers. In spite of Beppo and Don Juan,

every boarding-school in the empire still contains many devout believers in the amazing misery of the black-haired, high-browed, blue-eyed, bare-throated, Lord Byron. How melancholy you look in the prints!... Now, tell me, Mrs. Goddard, now tell me, Miss Price, now tell me, dear Harriet Smith, and dear, dear, Mrs. Elton, do tell me, is not this just the very look, that one would have fancied for Childe Harold?... Perhaps her *Ladyship* was in the wrong after all.—I am sure if I had married such a man, I would have borne with all his little eccentricities...[86]

The fantasy of friendship becomes, in this satirical account, a dream of marriage. But the suggestion here, of course, is that such fantasies are baseless and doomed to betrayal. Even as critics marvelled at Byron's production of a new intimacy between poet and reader in *Childe Harold*, they had in mind the Separation.

Already in Scott's review of 1818, Byron's intimate, personal relationship with the reader was acknowledged to be inauthentic: 'Childe Harold may not be, nor do we believe he is, Lord Byron's very self, but he is Lord Byron's picture, sketched by Lord Byron himself'.[87] Later, the poet's insincerity or theatricality became a mantra of criticism, repeated, not only by Lockhart, but by Carlyle, Macaulay, and Henry Taylor amongst others. It was a deception of the reader who had entered a sympathetic relationship in good faith only to find that the emotional contact was a sham. Lockhart's point was that the reader taken in by such 'humbug' must be as naïve as a boarding-school girl. Carlyle argued that, with the exception of *Don Juan*, 'the only work where he showed himself, in any measure, as he was', his poetry was a performance: 'To our minds there is... something which we should call theatrical, false, affected, in every one of these otherwise so powerful pieces'.[88] Macaulay thought Byron himself had been confused: 'How far the character in which he exhibited himself was genuine, and how far theatrical, would probably have puzzled himself to say' and Taylor criticized Byron's work as misanthropic poetry of effect rather than content.[89] Exclusion of the reader from genuine, affective sympathy with the poet was identified as a prime cause of Byron's perceived decline in popularity in the 1830s.[90]

---

[85] *BCH*, 149–50.

[86] [John Gibson Lockhart], *Letter to the Right Hon. Lord Byron. By John Bull* (1821), see *BCH*, 182–3.

[87] Ibid. 138.

[88] Thomas Carlyle, 'Burns' (1828), *CME*, i. 269. See also Carlyle's letter to Macvey Napier (28 Apr. 1832): 'all had a certain falsehood, a brawling theatrical insincere character', Carlyle, *Letters*, vi. 149.

[89] Macaulay (1831), *BCH*, 315. Henry Taylor, Preface to *Philip Van Artevelde* (1834), *BCH*, 325–9.

[90] See Carlyle, *Letters*, vi. 148–9: 'In my mind Byron has been sinking at an accelerated rate, for the last ten years, and has now reached a very low level.... His fame has been very great, but I see not how it is to endure'; and Taylor, Preface (1834): his poetry is declining 'in popular estimation'

The pattern whereby Byron promised intimacy only to withdraw it was also described by his reviewers in terms of the social chasm which existed between the poet and his readers. Hazlitt famously identified the poet's rank as the heart of a problematic relationship with his readers. Already, in 1821, he wrote of 'the retiring ebb of that over-whelming tide of popularity' as a result of Byron's aristocratic contempt for his readers—a feeling which could soon '"become mutual"'.[91] In 1825 he returned to the theme, contrasting him, unfavourably, with Scott. Byron

> is, in a striking degree, the creature of his own will. He holds no communion with his kind; but stands alone, without mate or fellow—
>
> > 'As if a man were author of himself,
> > And owned no other kin.'
>
> He is like a solitary peak, all access to which is cut off not more by elevation than distance.... He exists not by sympathy, but by antipathy.... Perhaps the chief cause of most of Lord Byron's errors is, that, he is that anomaly in letters and in society, a Noble Poet.[92]

Hazlitt linked elevation of birth explicitly with the arrogance of the self-creating genius and both with a lack of human sympathy. Reviewers at the other end of the political spectrum from Hazlitt also worried about the poet's relationship with his audience. Scott, for instance, drew attention to the inequality of the relationship in *Childe Harold*, where the reader is invited to be familiar with 'a superior being', who apparently disdains him, and despises 'the ordinary sources of happiness ... the pleasures which captivate others'.[93]

Concern was widely expressed in the press for the damage being done to the moral and religious welfare of Byron's readers, by this aristocratic genius, especially following the publication of *Don Juan*, I and II (1819) and *Cain* (1821), but often this anxiety was focused on Byron's representation of women and was directed specifically at his female readers.[94] An article in *Blackwood's* in 1819, for instance, worried about the effect of *Don Juan* on 'the public mind'. It poured 'scorn upon every element of good or noble nature in the hearts of his readers. Love—honour—patriotism—religion, are mentioned only to be scoffed at and derided', but it was the lack of chivalry to the female sex in his poetry and

---

and is part of a more general decadence in poetry: 'The poetry of the day, whilst it is greatly inferior in quality, continues to be like his in kind. It consists of little more than a poetical diction, an arrangement of words implying a sensitive state of mind ... merely symbols or types of feelings', *BCH*, 329.

[91] 'Pope, Lord Byron, and Mr. Bowles', *London Magazine* (1821), in *The Complete Works of William Hazlitt*, ed. P. P. Howe, 21 vols. (London: Dent, 1930–4), xix. 64–5.

[92] 'Lord Byron', from *The Spirit of the Age* (1825), in Hazlitt, *Works*, xi. 69 and 77.

[93] *BCH*, 139.

[94] See ibid. 7–9. Byron felt in 1822 and 1823 that the relationship between himself and the public was one of mutual hatred. The calls for greater moral responsibility were also heard earlier however—see e.g. Jeffrey (1816), ibid. 102–3: 'a great poet is necessarily a Moral Teacher'. Byron could do better with his heroes: he is too fond of their sins. His misanthropy is also damaging.

especially his satire on Lady Byron in *Don Juan*, which tainted all his poetry retrospectively.[95] The poet was figured as a false suitor—a man who courted the female reader only to corrupt and reject her, with potentially wide-reaching social consequences. A sermon by the Revd Styles, inscribed 'To the Youth of the Congregation of Holland Chapel' in 1824, condemned Byron for targeting young female readers, poisoning their minds and thereby spreading corruption through the nation. A spirit of 'infidelity' pervaded his life and works, which were consequently 'destructive of all the sympathies, tendernesses, and ties of social nature, and therefore subversive of thrones, altars, household amities, and heartfelt joys'.[96] Byron's central crime was to seduce his female readers from their domestic duties. The 'arch fiend' began with 'female character' and so did Byron: 'Let the sex be unfitted for the discharge of domestic duties—let modesty, truth, and delicacy, and hallowed love, be rooted out of their nature, and the cement of society is gone':

If a man . . . would demoralize a nation; and thus prepare it for revolution and ruin let him begin at the source; let him debase the character of woman. . . . empires are composed of families, and their stability or weakness depends upon the firmness or the laxity of the bonds which hold together the domestic circle. If domestic life be robbed of its peaceful felicities, if the blessed relation of husband and wife, of son and daughter, cease to be relations of principle and virtue—if they become only the cold compact of necessity, or the sport of selfishness and passion—what is likely to be the doom of the community![97]

Here we see displayed the full implications of the middle-class investment in the domestic ideal, as Styles extends Byron's personal, domestic failure to the betrayal of his female readers and thereby of his nation.

The major full-length biographies published between the early 1820s and the late 1830s intervened in and extended these debates. It was not simply the Byronic cult of personality that opened the way for biography, but the ambiguous nature of his relationship with his readers, as projected in his poetry and discussed in the periodical press and elsewhere. The poet who was, at once, intimate and withdrawn, a domestic familiar and exotic, aristocratic genius, provided his public with a simultaneous experience of identification and alienation. Byron's biographers capitalized on this paradox of familiarity and distance by stressing the gulf that had

---

[95] 'Remarks on Don Juan', *Blackwood's Magazine* (Aug. 1819)—see *BCH*, 167–8. The article may have been by Wilson or Lockhart. It enraged Byron, who responded in 'Observations upon an Article in *Blackwood's Magazine*', which was unpublished in Byron's lifetime, but printed by Murray in the 17-vol. edition of Byron's *Works*, xv.

[96] Revd John Styles, D.D., *Lord Byron's Works Viewed in Connexion with Christianity, and the Obligations of Social Life: A Sermon, Delivered at Holland Chapel, Kennington, July 4th, 1824* (London: Knight and Lacey, 1824), 6. Styles's title page epigraph is a quotation from Coleridge: 'That they are calculated to call forth severe reprobation from good men, is not the worst feature of such poems. Their moral deformity is aggravated in proportion to the pleasure which they are capable of affording to vindictive, turbulent, and unprincipled readers.'

[97] Ibid. 24.

opened up between poet and reader in order to claim, in various ways, a mediating
role. If Byron was perceived, increasingly, to have shunned the reader or failed to
serve the reader's interests, biography could bring them back together, re-establishing the bond that he had broken and developing the relationship to new levels of
intimacy. Biography was a major influence—arguably the major influence—in
sustaining the model of Byronic genius as aristocratic, masculine, and autonomous,
but it also existed in a critical and competitive relationship with that model. Even
those *Lives* which were explicitly opposed to the vision of the domesticated poet,
were engaged in a process of bringing him back home to the reader. Moore's *Letters
and Journals*, which did most to argue for the unapproachable autonomy of Byron's
genius, did most to reclaim him for his audience. In the remainder of this chapter
I will explore in more detail the ways in which these biographies re-established and
developed a domestic intimacy between Byron and the reader, and the implications
of this, both for the vision of the Romantic poet they handed down, and for
biography as a genre.

3.5 THE EXPERIENCE OF INTIMACY:
EARLY BYRON BIOGRAPHY

Overwhelmingly, the biographies published between 1824 and 1840 were written
in the first person, by those who had known Byron. This is a significant phenomenon, suggesting that the market demand was above all for an intimate vision.
Almost without exception, biographers opened by advertising their special closeness
to the man. R. C. Dallas, for instance, began with an explanation of his family
connection to Byron. A. R. C. Dallas, his son, also underlined the point in his
introduction, being careful to mention his father's 'intimacy' and 'frequent correspondence' with Byron between 1808 and 1814, and referring scathingly to the way
in which 'all Lord Byron's *monthly* friends prostitute the word *intimacy*'.[98] Medwin,
to the annoyance of Hobhouse and others, announced that his *Conversations* were
the record of 'a period of many months' familiar intercourse', and later quoted
Byron as saying: 'I believe you know more of me than any one else'.[99] William Parry
carefully outlined his credentials as trusted servant:

During the last two months of his existence, there was no person in whom he placed more
confidence than in me. I was employed by him to carry his designs into execution: I was
intrusted with the management of his funds, and made the depository of his wishes.
I lived under the same roof with him, was his confidential agent, and was honoured by
being made his companion.[100]

---

[98] Dallas, *Recollections*, vol. iv, p.lxviii.
[99] *Conversations*, iii. 226.
[100] Preface to Parry's, *The Last Days of Lord Byron* (1825), quoted in *LLB*, 171.

Hunt, in his preface, spoke of 'my intimacy with Lord Byron', and Moore capped all these claims in his biography where he basked in displays of intimacy with a man portrayed as only truly known to a small circle of friends: 'From the time of our first meeting, there seldom elapsed a day that Lord Byron and I did not see each other; and our acquaintance ripened into intimacy and friendship with a rapidity of which I have seldom known an example'.[101]

We have seen this emphasis on the intimate relationship between biographer and subject already in the theory of Johnson and the practice of Boswell, but Byronism gave it a new charge. This was not only because of the transgressive glamour which surrounded disclosures of his private life. Almost all his early biographers sought to rediscover the closeness that had seemed to exist between the poet and his public, but that had turned out to be illusory.[102] Unlike Boswell, they acted as mediators of their subject to an audience they projected as in danger of becoming alienated by his works, if left to stand alone. They simultaneously capitalized on and competed with Byron's original bond with the reader, restoring and enhancing the reader's erotic fantasy of familiarity with the poet. They did this not only by seeking out every possible detail of his personal history and domestic relationships—with his mother, sister, friends, servants, wife, lovers, and daughters—but by means of characteristic motifs and styles. In order to demonstrate the methods by which Byron biography created intimacy between subject and reader, I will focus on three important techniques: the trope of the poet's home, the eyewitness portrait, and intimate forms of address, including the use of private documents and informal style and structure.

The poet's home became a significant motif in Byron biography, as in *Lives* of the poets more generally at the period. Descriptions of Byron at home and detailed accounts by visitors to Newstead Abbey were commonly included in the early *Lives*.[103] The memoirs by Medwin and Hunt gave prolonged accounts of their experiences as Byron's house guests, and those by Moore and Lady Blessington also stressed their daily, domestic contact with the poet. As we have seen, for Johnson and Boswell, the ideal biographer was one who had cohabited with his subject and the insight granted to the reader into his home signified the

---

[101] Hunt, *Lord Byron*, p. iv. *LJB* i. 322. See also Moore's inclusion of letters from Byron expressing his pride in their friendship.
[102] Elfenbein, *Byron*, 53, argues that 'Byron's career generated a model of success whereby the book trade responded to the mass market's anonymity by offering readers a simulacrum of intimacy'. His analysis, however, concentrates, principally, on the periodical reviews, ignoring the particular sense in which the biographical text offers intimacy. Mole, *Byron's Romantic Celebrity*, p. xiv, identifies 'the hermeneutic of intimacy' as 'the reading paradigm that characterises celebrity culture' and investigates it in relation to Byron's poetry.
[103] e.g. [Alexander Kilgour], *Anecdotes of Lord Byron from Authentic Sources; with Remarks Illustrative of his Connection with the Principal Literary Characters of the Present Day* (London: Knight and Lacey; Aberdeen: W. Gordon, A. Stevenson, D. Wylie and L. Smith, 1825), pp. vi–x, gives a detailed description of interior and grounds of Newstead Abbey, including an account by Walpole. See also Galt, *Life of Lord Byron*, 365–72 for accounts of Newstead Abbey by Lake, Walpole, and from the *London Literary Gazette* (1828).

authenticity of insight into the subject himself. Boswell was an important model
for Byron's biographers. Even when not living under the same roof as the poet,
they tended to emphasize their achievement of daily contact with him. This was,
in part, biography as an extension of literary tourism. It was one of the products
by which 'Byron' was quite literally domesticated in the sense of being made the
subject of artefacts designed and marketed for consumption within the homes of
the British middle classes. His lyrics were adapted as parlour songs; editions of his
poetry, engraved portraits, and scenes from his life were designed to be collected
and displayed in the home; and Finden's *Illustrations of the Life and Works of Lord
Byron* were used to decorate a Spode dinner service.[104] The early *Lives* of Byron,
which, besides their function as textual mementoes, often contained collectable
engravings—portraits, landscapes, facsimile manuscripts, and so on—answered
the same demand for memorabilia, to be acquired, pored over, and displayed.
As the reader was invited into the home of the poet in these biographies, so
they introduced him into the middle-class reader's home. In these biographies,
the entry into Byron's house was an erotically charged moment—his home the
location of his sexual relationships and alleged sexual crimes. The pleasure of
intimate insight was compounded of alienation and recognition—his home life
showed that Byron was different from the reader, but also the same. We have
seen how, for Wordsworth, the domestic space was a figure for the embattled
autonomy of genius, threatened by biography and its readers. Byron's biographers represented the poet's house in such a way as to make it the rightful
property of the reading public, welcoming them in, exploiting the voyeuristic
pleasures of intimate insight into his domestic circumstances.

Medwin's *Conversations* opened cannily with his attempt to gain access to
Byron's residence—the Lanfranchi Palace in Pisa. He began by stressing Byron's
distance from his own (and by extension the reader's) social orbit, describing the
poet's entourage of 'seven servants, five carriages, nine horses, a monkey, a bulldog and a mastiff, two cats, three pea-fowls and some hens', adding '(I do not
know whether I have classed them in order of rank,)'. The joke cuts both ways.
Medwin deflates Byron's aristocratic pretensions, but he also adopts the reader's
position as a bourgeois tourist, gawping at this splendidly individual 'travelling
equipage'.[105] The keynote to Medwin's description of the visit is Byron's
aristocracy, which forms around him a wall as impenetrable to outsiders as the
Lanfranchi Palace itself. The biographer can only gain entry through the offices
of a fellow poet and member of Byron's intimate circle—Shelley—who is also
Medwin's relation and schoolfriend. As he is led inside the palace by Shelley, so
Medwin leads the reader:

'It is one of those marble piles that seem built for eternity, whilst the family whose name it
bears no longer exists,' said Shelley, as we entered a hall that seemed built for giants.

---

[104] Elfenbein, *Byron*, 80–3.   [105] *Conversations*, 1.

'I remember the lines in the Inferno,' said I: 'a Lanfranchi was one of the persecutors of Ugolino.' 'The same,' answered Shelley[106]

The exchange adds to the sense of Byron's alienation from the common man—he is associated with a decadent and cruel aristocracy and is a genius great enough to inhabit a house built for 'giants' immortalized by Dante. But the pair have still to encounter him in person. The hallway is forbidding and the stairs guarded by an English bulldog. He knows Shelley, growls, and lets them pass. At last they arrive at the inner sanctum:

we found his Lordship writing. His reception was frank and kind; he took me cordially by the hand and said:

'You are a relation and schoolfellow of Shelley's—we do not meet as strangers—you must allow me to continue my letter on account of the post. Here's something for you to read, Shelley, (giving him part of his MS. of 'Heaven and Earth;') tell me what you think of it'.[107]

It is a rush of intimacy: the poet, in his private chambers, extends his hand and greets Medwin as a friend. The giant shrinks to a human scale, the legend becomes a real man, the social barriers fall and the reader comes into contact with Byron at his least forbidding and most concerned for the response of his audience. Medwin comments, a little later, that 'the familiar ease of his conversation soon made me perfectly at home in his society'.[108] This is precisely the effect that his account of the entry into Byron's residence aims to create for the reader. It is a fantasy of the literary tourist who miraculously transforms into the writer's valued companion.

In *Lord Byron and Some of His Contemporaries*, Hunt, like Medwin, introduced the reader to an intimate relationship with Byron by breaching the walls of his houses, but here, in the least reverent of all early biographies of Byron, such intimacy was more pointedly demystifying and socially levelling. The tone is set when, in a reversal of Medwin's opening, it is Byron who first visits Hunt—in prison, and then in Hunt's modest rooms in Paddington.[109] Hunt's perspective is far from deferential: Byron, 'I thought, took a pleasure in my room, as contrasted with the splendour of his great house. He had too much reason to do so. His domestic troubles were just about to become public'.[110] When Hunt and his family become Byron's guests in Italy, there is always trouble behind the splendid facades of Byron's houses. The first one is at Monte Nero: 'the hottest-looking house I ever saw. Not content with having a red wash over it, the red was

---

[106] Ibid. 2. See Dante, *Inferno*, Canto XXXIII.

[107] *Conversations*, 11–12.

[108] Ibid. 14.

[109] Hunt and his brother were imprisoned for two years in 1813, charged with libelling the Prince Regent. Hunt's cell was relatively comfortable and had wallpaper with roses on it (a fact he does not mention in the *Journal*). He received many celebrated visitors, sympathetic to his cause.

[110] *Lord Byron*, 4.

the most unseasonable of all reds, a salmon colour. Think of this, flaring over the country in a hot Italian sun!' The colour is not only vulgar and unsettlingly exotic, it is indicative of sexual impropriety and social mayhem going on inside. Hunt is taken into the interior to find the Countess Guiccioli, scarlet like the house: 'Her face was flushed, her eyes lit up, and her hair . . . looking as if it streamed in disorder'.[111] He has arrived in the aftermath of a quarrel amongst the servants, during which the Countess's brother has been stabbed. The angry servant, in the red hat of a sans-culotte, waits outside to stab anyone who dares come out: 'the house was in a state of blockade; the nobility and gentry of the interior all kept in a state of impossibility by a rascally footman'. Hunt feels that he has stepped into a scene from *The Mysteries of Udolpho*: 'Everything was new, foreign, and violent. There was the lady, flushed and dishevelled, exclaiming against the "*scelerato*," the young Count, wounded and threatening; the assassin, waiting for us with his knife; and last, not least, in the novelty, my English friend, metamorphosed, round-looking and jacketed, trying to damp all this fire with his cool tones, and an air of voluptuous indolence'.[112] It is a comic vignette, a Gillray cartoon, or a farcical scene from *Don Juan*, which gives the reader a behind-the-scenes view exposing the poet as ludicrously unable to control the disorder of his household. He is a man emasculated, an aristocrat deposed, a victim of his own domestic neglect. When Hunt moves into the Lanfranchi Palace in Pisa, the tone shifts since now it is the biographer and his family who suffer from this neglect. Byron gives them the ground floor, but Hunt is far from grateful—he makes it clear that it was common to share houses in this way in Italy and Byron was not, himself, using this floor in any case. Their furniture is plain and cheap.[113] Hunt again offers detailed insights into Byron's daily routines in Pisa—and here they are, by contrast with the farcical scenes at Monte Nero, quietly drawn, deliberately mundane:

Our manner of life was this. Lord Byron, who used to sit up at night, writing Don Juan (which he did under the influence of gin and water), rose late in the morning. He breakfasted; read; lounged about, singing an air, generally out of Rossini, and in a swaggering style, though in a voice at once small and veiled; then took a bath, and was dressed; and coming downstairs, was heard, still singing, in the court-yard, out of which the garden ascended at the back of the house. The servants at the same time brought out two or three chairs. My study, a little room in a corner, with an orange-tree peeping in at the window, looked upon this court-yard. I was generally at my writing when he came down, and either acknowledged his presence by getting up and saying something from the window, or he called out 'Leontius!' and came halting up to the window with some joke, or other challenge to conversation. (Readers of good sense will do me the justice of discerning where any thing is spoken of in a tone of objection, and where it is only brought in as requisite to the truth of the picture.)[114]

[111] *Lord Byron*, 9.   [112] Ibid. 10–11.
[113] Ibid. 14–15.   [114] Ibid. 37–8.

The details accumulate to give the reader a genuine sense of being, like Hunt, Byron's house guest, knowing and even seeing Byron—Hunt proceeds to describe his dress, 'a nankin jacket, with white waistcoat and trousers, and a cap, either velvet or linen, with a shade to it'.[115] But he remains a relatively cold-eyed observer of his host's aristocratic airs. He carefully distinguishes himself from the poet, who composes at night on gin and water, where he works more wholesomely in the morning at his desk next to an orange tree. He displays the 'truth' of his own picture, by contrast, to Byron's inflated behaviour. Byron is swaggeringly masculine, but Hunt suggests something artificial here—his voice is 'small and veiled'. His joking approach to his guest—'Leontius!'—suggests a gratifying intimacy, but is part of the whole, exaggerated performance. Even at his most private Byron is an actor. Hunt has penetrated the poet's inner sanctum, but will still, like Byron's reading public, come up against the impenetrable facade of his posturing.

Hunt's theme in his memoir is Byron's failure, ultimately, to establish close relationships with friends and even with lovers. He goes on to describe the Countess Guiccioli, who joins Byron for breakfast, 'her sleek tresses descending', and at this point an engraving of her is inserted in the text, depicting her with flowing locks, diaphanous shawl, and décolletage. Hunt describes her with flattering quotations from Chaucer and Dryden, but adds that, although she had a good nose, she was not very intelligent. She 'was a kind of buxom parlour-border, compressing herself artificially into dignity and elegance, and fancying that she walked, in the eyes of the whole world, a heroine by the side of a poet'.[116] The description, of course, reflects on Byron himself, suggesting fakery in terms of class, affection, and even genius. He was too mercurial to form intimate relations with women, Hunt tells us—a fact that is ominous for his readers.[117] Hunt's practice as a biographer exposes the failure—and ostentatiously compensates for it.

As these passages show, Hunt enhanced his inside view of Byron's homes, with detailed, eyewitness portraits of his personal appearance and that of members of his circle. This was common practice in the early *Lives* of Byron. Biography compensated for his last withdrawal from his readers—his death—by re-creating the physical presence of the author through descriptions of his body, his clothes, his movement, his speech. When, in 1818, John Wilson described the works of Rousseau and Byron as 'images, pictures, busts of their living selves' he drew attention to the readers' desire to possess the body of the poet, both figuratively, through their works, and literally in the case of Byron, whose portrait—in engravings, busts, and other forms—was, of course, widely collected.[118] The

---

[115] Ibid. 38.
[116] Ibid. 38–40.
[117] Ibid. 41.
[118] Wilson (1818), in *BCH*, 147–8. For a full treatment of Byron portraiture, see Christine Kenyon Jones (ed.), *Byron: The Image of the Poet.*

pen portraits of Byron in posthumous memoirs capitalized on this sense of loss felt in the aftermath of the poet's death. They supplied an absence and vied to bring the poet back to the reader more vividly than he had ever been present to them in his lifetime. Biographers stressed the eyewitness authenticity of their verbal portraits and foregrounded the illuminating detail of the poet's physical presence—better still, physical contact between biographer and poet. The anonymous 'Personal Character of Lord Byron' (1824), for instance, promised a more complete vision than ever before: 'I am quite sure that, after a perusal of the following paper, the reader will be able to see Lord Byron, mind and all, "in his habit as he lived:" '.[119] Dallas highlighted the moment when Byron, coming from giving his maiden speech in the House of Lords, shook his hand:

I had an umbrella in my right hand, not expecting that he would put out his hand to me—in my haste to take it when offered, I had advanced my left hand—'What,' said he, 'give your friend your left hand upon such an occasion?' I showed the cause, and immediately changing the umbrella to the other hand, I gave him my right hand, which he shook and pressed warmly.[120]

The minute detail with which Dallas describes this exchange draws the reader in to the culminating moment of affective sympathy—the warm touch of the poet. The tendency of these biographical portraits towards the prosaic, individual detail went counter to the dicta of Reynolds on portrait painting, still influential in the 1820s and 1830s and was, as several of the biographers pointed out, a notable departure from the idealized visual images of the poet in circulation in his lifetime. Medwin prefaces his portrait of Byron by remarking that 'Thorwaldsen's bust is too thin-necked and young. . . . None of the engravings gave me the least idea of him' and Hunt compares his appearance when he first knew him to the Phillips portrait, but stresses the changes over time: 'I hardly knew him, he was grown so fat'.[121] They both imply that their biographical portraits will allow the reader to see Byron, for the first time, as he truly was.

As with the descriptions of Byron at home, so with the portraits of his physical self, the biographer's mediation of Byron to the reader always involves a tension between distance and familiarity, as the reader is invited, at once, to stand back in awe and to find common ground. The balance between the ideal and the real Byron, spirit and flesh is always present, if variously weighted. Medwin and Lady Blessington, both of whom produce lengthy physical descriptions in the first pages of their memoirs, portray the poet as a thorough compound of the godlike and the human. For Medwin, he is like Milton—but only because 'he barely escaped being short and thick'. He is like Caesar, in being

---

[119] 'Personal Character of Lord Byron', *London Magazine* (Oct. 1824), 337. He begins by asserting that the author 'has had unusual opportunities of observing the extraordinary habits, feelings, and opinions of the inspired and noble Poet'.
[120] Dallas, *Recollections*, 204.
[121] Medwin, *Conversations*, 12; Hunt, *Lord Byron*, 4, 9.

on the way to baldness. He has 'Grecian beauty', but 'mustachios, which were not sufficiently dark to be becoming'. His eyes had the fire of inspiration, but 'were placed too near his nose . . . and one was rather smaller than the other'. He has a Grecian upper lip and expressive, but odd-shaped eyes—his nose was 'a little *too thick*'.[122] The figure of bathos becomes a characteristic feature of portraits of the poets in biographies of the period. The art of sinking is a token of authenticity—a language of witness, directed to a readership eager for relics, the more mundane the better, by which Byron's fleshly existence can be verified and, in imagination, restored.[123] This is most acutely apparent in the eyewitness accounts of the poet's death.

Byron's deathbed scene was usually narrated as a redemption—whether it was the poet as domestic repentant—his final words, 'My wife! My child! My sister!'— or hero of Greek independence—his last cry 'Greece!'[124] The immortal spirit soared forth, but this was accompanied, and countered, by detailed descriptions of his body in its decline. In the death scenes, biographies made their own, distinctive, contribution to the narrative of Byron's poetic decline from spirit to flesh—from *Childe Harold* to *Don Juan*—that was also present in reviews. The voluminous appendices to Medwin's biography, for instance, including Greek funeral orations, formed, from one point of view, a triumphant finale to the life of the poet, but also dwelt to a disturbing extent on the perishability of his body. The account of Byron's servant, William Fletcher, included there, gave the minutiae of the sickbed: 'Though rather feverish during the night, his lordship slept pretty well, but complained in the morning of a pain in his bones and a head-ache. . . . I prepared a little arrow-root, of which he took three or four spoonfuls, saying it was very good, but could take no more'.[125] This was followed by a response from Dr Bruno, one of the attending physicians, who disputed Fletcher's version of events and attempted to vindicate himself from blame as having contributed to the poet's death. Bruno's autopsy notes formed part of the documentation: 'On opening the body of Lord Byron; the bones of the head were found extremely hard, exhibiting no appearance of suture, like the cranium of an octogenarian. . . . The *dura mater* was so firmly attached to the internal parietes of the cranium, that the reiterated attempts of two strong men were insufficient to detach it'.[126] The head of the poet, like his home, is opened up, the mind reduced to matter, capable of handling—if, even here, resisting the ultimate invasion.

---

[122] Medwin, *Conversations*, 13 and see *Lady Blessington's Conversations of Lord Byron*, ed. Ernest J. Lovell (Princeton: Princeton University Press, 1969), 5–6.

[123] Mourners after his death reputedly bought bottles of the fluid in which his body was embalmed.

[124] The last words as reported, respectively, by Byron's servant, William Fletcher, as quoted in Hobhouse's obituary article, 'Lord Byron in Greece', *Westminster Review* (July 1824), repr. in Medwin, *Conversations*, 298–329, see 329; and by M. Spiridion Tricoupi, in his funeral oration, given in Messolonghi on 10 Apr. 1824, ibid. 342.

[125] Ibid. 326.

[126] Ibid. 333.

Such fleshly detail was a way in which the reader could have and hold the poet by vicariously witnessing, touching, even entering his body, recognizing it as familiarly human. As such it both drew on the glamour of genius and effectively demystified it—ironizing the narrative of immortality with one of perishability. The spirit might outlive the flesh, but, then again, as several reviewers had suggested, it might not.[127] His tendency to corpulence, for example, frequently mentioned by his biographers, became a token of his mortality, his worldliness, his effeminacy—all ways in which he departed from the ideal of the transcendent, masculine genius. Captain Roberts wrote that Byron was 'grossly corpulent', 'vulgarly fat', his face 'pallid and fleshy, and . . . closely shaved up to the ears, giving his visage an unmanly and unbecoming appearance', and Hunt that 'his person was very handsome, though terminating in lameness, and tending to fat and effeminacy', so that he was taken for a woman in the Levant.[128] The satirical tone of some of these biographical portraits contained an appeal to the middle-class public. Hunt's portraits of Byron, as we have seen, took his aristocratic airs as an object of ridicule. In a passage which enraged Byron's circle, he pictured him as socially awkward and lacking in 'self-possession': 'he hummed and hawed, and looked confused, on very trivial occasions'.[129] The Countess Guiccioli, described by Hunt as 'a kind of buxom parlour boarder', is a fitting consort for this déclassé Byron.

Moore, in reaction to Hunt, sought to assimilate his subject's fleshly defects to an ideal of physical perfection consistent with the construction of Byron as heroic, masculine genius which informed his narrative. He tried to belittle the importance of Byron's deformed foot as 'trifling' and argued that it was an incentive to heroic achievement.[130] Later Moore provided a catalogue of features, some of which are unflattering—a small head, a narrow forehead, a 'rather thickly shaped' nose, but tried, again, to make each defect a token of Byron's uniqueness: the extraordinary proportions of the head, the height of the forehead, the handsome nose. He concluded that he had given in his portrait 'as good an idea perhaps as it is in the power of mere words to convey', implying that Byron's body was, like his genius, beyond language.[131] Of course, as these examples demonstrate, in the very act of sublimating Byron's human defects, Moore made them vividly present throughout his narrative. His effort to give a picture of Boswellian completeness in his biography also, inevitably, led to the inclusion

---

[127] See e.g. Wilson (1818), in *BCH*, 151–2. See also Macaulay (1831), ibid. 316, where he argues that much of Byron's poetry will die with the man. Macaulay, reviewing Moore's biography here, was evidently unimpressed by its chances of keeping the poet alive. By contrast, see Gordon, *Life and Genius of Lord Byron*, 4 on biography as a life-preserver: his biography was written 'to gratify . . . the wish that the bard had been as immortal as his writings; that his body had been of the same indestructible matter as his mind'.

[128] Quoted in *LLB*, 491. Hunt, *Lord Byron*, 87–8 and 90.

[129] Hunt, *Lord Byron*, 4, 26.

[130] *LJB* i. 94.

[131] Ibid. ii. 799.

of numerous details which humanized the poet. He dwells on Byron's 'fear of becoming, what he was naturally inclined to be, enormously fat' and quotes a witness to the fact that, in the summer of 1806, Byron appeared 'a fat bashful boy, with his hair combed straight over his forehead'.[132] But, above all, of course, Moore's biography quoted extensively from Byron's own letters and journals, in which the poet was his own best subverter, positing and puncturing the myth of disembodied genius at every turn, repeatedly inserting his imperfect, fleshly presence into the narrative. Byron's self-deflating, sometimes camp discussions of his own bodily functions and failings continually countered Moore's portrait of heroic genius: 'I get thinner, being now below 11 stone considerably. . . . [I have] *pared off* a sufficient quantity of flesh to enable me to slip into "an eel skin," and vie with the slim beaux of modern times'.[133] As Moore's connecting narrative strove to assimilate Byron's body to an ideal of genius, so Byron's letters underlined their ironic disparity.

Whatever their explicit position on the responsibility of genius to domestic life, in so far as they invited the reader into his home and granted an eyewitness vision of the body of the poet, early biographers of Byron 'domesticated' the poet. But an ideological commitment to the domestic was already implicit in the languages of intimacy employed in these texts. Only a small proportion of most of the early *Lives* of Byron was devoted to formal, third-person, chronological narrative. Typically they were a bricolage of fragmented, first-person narrative, in a mixture of modes including letters, journals, and conversations. Moore's biography was dominated by Byron's letters and journals. Medwin and Lady Blessington represented Byron almost entirely by means of extracts from his conversations with them, and Hunt largely so. The selling power of such access to Byron's private utterance and writings was clear. It established biography as the means by which the lost relationship of poet and reader could be restored and, indeed, taken to a new level. The conversations and letters appeared to quote the very words of the man at his least guarded, giving the illusion of direct contact. In conversing with Medwin or Lady Blessington, Byron was also conversing with the reader; and in most of the biographies, but especially Moore's, the reader became the vicarious recipient of Byron's most private correspondence. Both Medwin and Lady Blessington kept their interventions in the reported conversation to a minimum, thus allowing space for the reader to enter and receive, for instance, a first-hand insight into Byron's feelings about his marriage and separation or trivia about his diet ('"My digestion is weak; I am too bilious," said he, "to eat more than once a-day, and generally live on vegetables"').[134] Both also presented Byron as an inveterate

---

[132] Ibid. i. 93–4, 65.
[133] Ibid. 115–16.
[134] Medwin, *Conversations*, 14.

gossip, only too willing to divulge the secrets of his private life.[135] There was nothing the reader couldn't know, seemingly, direct from the poet's mouth.

Within the broad designation of memoir, the early, full-length Byron biographies typically comprised a loose and even fragmented collection of personal testimony—relics of the great man. It was common, for instance, to find in them voluminous appendices with documents by other writers and witnesses, including obituaries, biographical articles, reviews, letters, and poems. The effect could be akin to that of a scrapbook. One of the most fragmented, Alexander Kilgour's *Anecdotes of Lord Byron* (1825), was prefaced by an introduction giving a brief overview of Byron's life, but otherwise consisted entirely of a string of anecdotes selected to amuse, with little or no connecting narrative or sense of chronology. There was a slightly stronger narrative thread in the conversational memoirs of Medwin, Hunt, and Lady Blessington, produced by the trajectory of the biographer's relationship with the poet, but only slightly. These, too, were disjointed and anecdotal. Biographers drew attention to this as a way of extending the atmosphere of informality, but also as proof of the authenticity of their witness. The main body of Medwin's *Conversations*, for instance, is a loose sequence of daily encounters with Byron which, as the biographer readily admits, is in some ways monotonous, commonplace, deliberately mundane.[136] The anecdotes culled from Byron's conversation are not drawn together by a commentary and thus have a kind of inconsequentiality. The effect is of a total record, unsifted, every remark a valuable relic to be preserved. Medwin advertised the unfinished nature of his book as a sign of its truth: 'My sketch will be an imperfect and a rough one, it is true, but it will be from the life'.[137] Hunt, too, was unashamedly informal, drawing attention to his conversational style and digressive narrative structure.[138] Moore's narrative, introducing and commenting on Byron's letters and journals, was more formal in structure and style and more polished than that of any of his fellow biographers, but it, too, projected its own compendious mundanity as artlessly sincere. It has been castigated as stiff and dull by contrast with the brilliance of the letters, but Moore makes no attempt to compete with Byron's self-subverting wit. Indeed, from the title page onwards, he positions his narrative as subordinate, indeed, almost incidental to Byron's, whose own words, in his letters and journals, will form 'the liveliest and best records' of his life.[139]

Of course, Moore and his fellow biographers were far from artless and readers who found each biographer challenging the veracity of the last, might also have

---

[135] See e.g. Medwin, *Conversations*, 36 ff. for Byron's completely frank account of his feelings for his wife. Medwin presents him as someone who will tell anything to anyone. For Lady Blessington on Byron as a gossip, see Julian North, 'Self-Possession and Gender in Romantic Literary Biography', in Arthur Bradley and Alan Rawes (eds.), *Romantic Biography* (Aldershot: Ashgate, 2003), 129–31.

[136] Medwin, *Conversations*, 21.

[137] Ibid. p. iv.

[138] Hunt, *Lord Byron*, 13, 92.

[139] Ibid. 40.

questioned the possibility of authentic witness. But, in advertising their contribution in this way, Byron's biographers were defining a distinct area of operation
for biography. In reproducing his letters and conversations, they capitalized on
the informal intimacy of Byron's own epistolary style, but, at the same time, they
claimed a more sincere language than the poet himself was able to achieve. They
elaborated on the criticism of the reviews that Byron was theatrical, a chameleon
performer whose words the reader could not trust.[140] Moore described Byron's
character as a series of performances—his self-conscious projection of a mercurial
personality, shifting between extremes of melancholy and humour, self-will
and self-denial, debauchery and romantic love, meanness and generosity.[141]
He referred admiringly to 'the unparalleled versatility of his genius...those
quick, chameleon-like changes of which his character...was capable', but also
repeatedly warned the reader not to trust the poet's self-descriptions—his 'self-
portraiture...must be taken with a due portion of...allowance for exaggera-
tion', from his youth he was an actor.[142] Having said that Byron's letters will
form 'the liveliest and best records' of his life, Moore suggested the incapacity,
not only of Byron, but of poets in general, for true biography. He elevated poetry
above prose, but he also pointed to poetry's limitations. Thus, he commented on
the 'Poems on His Own Domestic Circumstances' that its title

carried with it a sufficient exposure of the utter unfitness of such themes for rhyme. It is,
indeed, only in those emotions and passions, of which imagination forms a predominant
ingredient,—such as love, in its first dreams, before reality has come to imbody [*sic*] or
dispel them, or sorrow, in its wane, when beginning to pass away from the heart into
the fancy—that poetry ought ever to be employed as an interpreter of feeling. For the
expression of all those immediate affections and disquietudes that have their root in the
actual realities of life, the art of the poet, from the very circumstance of its being an art, as
well as from the coloured form in which it is accustomed to transmit impressions, cannot
be otherwise than a medium as false as it is feeble.[143]

The antitheses here are those that have been present throughout Moore's connecting narrative between the poetic transfiguration of feeling into art, on the one
hand, and its domestic embodiment in 'the actual realities of life' on the other.
But in this passage it emerges strikingly that, in defining the strength of poetry,
Moore also identifies its weaknesses, and that where poetry is a 'false' and 'feeble'

---

[140] See e.g. Hunt, *Lord Byron*, 90, on the insincerity of his conversation, 'all quip and crank', and
111 on 'Fare Thee Well!': 'He sat down to *imagine* what a husband might say, who had recently
loved his wife, to a wife who had really loved him; and he said it so well, that one regrets he had not
been encouraged when younger to feel the genuine passion'. See also ibid. 118: 'Lord Byron was
always acting, even when he capriciously spoke the truth'. Contrast Hunt's epigraph from
Montaigne for protestations of biographical truthfulness and see e.g. 123 for a demonstration of
the value he sets on authenticity.
[141] See e.g. *LJB* i. 393, 430; and ii. 650, 783.
[142] Ibid. ii. 648; and i. 68, 79.
[143] Ibid. i. 664–5.

medium, biography is true and powerful. All that is defined by Moore as unpoetic is precisely the material of the Boswellian biographer. Moore thus defines his role as biographer as being lower than that of the poet, but indispensable to it. Adopting a stance of reliable sincerity, he sets himself up in opposition to his decentred subject's inauthentic self. Like Boswell, he concluded his biography by remarking on the 'plurality' of his subject's selves and implying that it is the biographer's task to find a 'pivot' to the character.[144] But he differed from either Johnson or Boswell by defining biographical discourse as counterpoetic. Boswell had pointed out that Johnson did not have enough 'persevering diligence' to write his own life, but he was nevertheless flatteringly sure that, if it had been written, it would have been 'probably ... the most perfect example of biography that was ever exhibited'.[145] Moore, by contrast, justified any departures from 'the exact letter' of Byron's 'injunctions' upon him as his biographer by arguing that there were 'no hands in which his character could have been less safe than his own'.[146]

   Moore was careful to ally himself with his readers. He argued that Byron was only 'seen in his true colours' by 'those who had got, as it were, behind the scenes of his fame', and he sold his biography on its promise to take the reader behind closed doors into the intimate, personal circle.[147] Introducing selections from Byron's 'Journal' of 1813, for example, he promised that, despite omissions, there would be enough here

to enlarge still further the view we have opened into the interior of the poet's life and habits, and to indulge harmlessly that taste, as general as it is natural, which leads us to contemplate with pleasure a great mind in its undress, and to rejoice in the discovery, so consoling to human pride, that even the mightiest, in their moments of ease and weakness, resemble ourselves.[148]

The pronouns signal Moore's complicity with his readership. Where, for Coleridge and Wordsworth, the biographer invades and violates the hearth and home, Moore takes the public on a tour of the great man's private apartments to discover that, seen from this perspective, he may be like them, after all. Unlike Coleridge or Wordsworth, Moore does not stand aloof here from the reader's curiosity, but is sympathetic to it, as harmless, natural, common to all. If we look back at his apparent ideological commitment to a model of genius as necessarily undomesticated, rising above the petty cares of married life, we can see a fundamental conflict at the heart of his biography. Whilst the *Letters and Journals* promoted a conception of genius as masculine, heroic, autonomous, and capitalized on the glamour of the poet's

---

[144] *LJB* ii. 783, 782. Unlike Boswell, he finds that pivot 'almost wholly wanting' (i. 782).
[145] *Boswell's Life of Samuel Johnson*, ed. George Birkbeck Hill and L. F. Powell, 6 vols. (Oxford: Oxford University Press, 1934–50), i. 25.
[146] *LJB* ii. 807.
[147] Ibid. i. 393.
[148] Ibid. 435.

distance from the reader's experience, it directed the interest of the readers else-where: to the private, domestic space, where they could form an intimate relation-ship with Byron, not as a poet, but as a man.

3.6 THE FEMININE EYE

Marlon Ross reads Moore's defence of Byron's undomesticated genius as part of a more widespread, embattled gendering of poetic genius as masculine, in the wake of the popular success of female poets:

> By denying the role of domesticity in a poet's life, Moore hopes to bolster the strength of the poet within culture. He hopes both to assert that poetry is a true manly enterprise and to repress the function of the 'feminine' in poetry's progress, to diminish the reality of a 'profession' that has become increasingly domesticated, an activity that seemingly has been taken over by blushing maidens, timid spinsters, and busy matrons reading poetry and even writing it in the comfort of their homes, rather than by courageous warring men on the figurative fields of battle.[149]

For all the reasons suggested above, the gendering of poetic genius by Moore and other biographers was more ambiguous than this suggests. The promotion of Byron's masculine strength as a poet could not remain untouched by the fact that these narratives questioned his masculinity in other ways. The very fact that all Byron's biographers, including Moore, made the issue of Byron's domestic circumstances central to their narratives, in itself challenged his autonomous, aristocratic, masculinity. The detail of the texts everywhere furthered this chal-lenge. In common with other biographers, Moore witnessed Byron's famed 'mobility' partly in terms of gender. He included, for instance, a description contributed by Mary Shelley, in which she recalled that his ceaselessly changing expressions moved painfully between feminine 'softness'—the '"affectionate eagerness kindling in his eyes, and dimpling his lips into something more sweet than a smile"'—and masculine hardness: '"I have seen him look absolutely ugly—I have seen him look so hard and cold, that you must hate him"'.[150] In Mitford's account Byron has curling auburn hair which 'fell over his bosom', long eye lashes, fair skin, and 'feminine' features. He is mistaken for a woman by the old Count Gamba.[151] His sexuality was represented ambiguously by Moore, for the most passionate love letters he reproduced were those from the poet to his biographer.[152] Moore argued that Byron wasn't suited to married life and,

---

[149] Marlon B. Ross, *The Contours of Masculine Desire: Romanticism and the Rise of Women's Poetry* (New York: Oxford University Press, 1989), 20.
[150] *LJB* ii. 799.
[151] Mitford, *The Private Life of Lord Byron*, 44, 152.
[152] See e.g. *LJB* i. 411–34.

through these letters and the depiction of his intimacy with Byron, projected himself, instead, as Byron's truest wife.

Moore may have wanted to repress 'the function of the "feminine" in poetry's progress', but he and others asserted it within the progress of biography. Successive biographers viewed Byron critically through a feminine eye. Hunt adopted the viewpoint of his own wife. He presented her reading of the poet's character as more perceptive than his own, as well as more hostile: 'I saw nothing at first but single-hearted and agreeable qualities in Lord Byron. My wife, with the quicker eyes of a woman, was inclined to doubt them'. He later came to agree with her. Mrs Hunt ruthlessly demystifies genius. She thinks the portrait by Harlowe made him look like 'a great school-boy, who had had a plain bun given him, instead of a plum one'. She cannot communicate with the poet, the families remain separate, and Hunt and Byron suffer 'diminished cordiality'.[153] His wife's vision of the poet is vindicated, as we have seen, by the biography as a whole. Appropriately, Hunt took as his frontispiece, an engraving of his wife's paper cut profile of Byron, seated, informally, with hat, riding boots, and whip, instead of one of the official portraits more commonly in use. Entitled 'Lord Byron as he appeared after his daily ride at Pisa & Genoa', it was a visual token not only of the biographer's insight into the quotidian private life of his subject, but also of his uxorious perspective (Fig. 3.2).

Some of the most interesting challenges to Byron's masculine genius came from his female biographers. In her *Conversations of Lord Byron*, Lady Blessington constructed a persona for herself, as Byron's interlocutor, which was caustically deflating, comically juxtaposing the poetic genius and the fleshly man. She allowed what were represented as his words to dominate the conversation, but her chosen form advertised her control—the authenticity of Byron's contribution was immediately, and rightly, questioned. She foregrounded the conflict between his poetry and his domestic life, his relationships with Lady Byron, Ada, and the Countess Guiccioli, and his opinion of female genius. There was no simplistic sense of sisterhood here. She was complicit, for instance, in Byron's mockery of Madame de Staël, and her competition with Byron led her, generally, to emulate him as well as to assert her difference. But she created a distinctively feminine voice in her exploitation of gossip's subversive potential and in her open criticisms of Byron's masculine blindness to female experience:

Men are capable of making great sacrifices, who are not willing to make the lesser ones, on which so much of the happiness of life depends. The great sacrifices are seldom called for, but the minor ones are in daily requisition; and the making them with cheerfulness and grace enhances their value, and banishes from the domestic circle the various misunderstandings, discussions, and coldnesses, that arise to embitter existence, where a little self-denial might have kept them off.[154]

---

[153] Hunt, *Lord Byron*, 2, 27, 26.
[154] *Conversations*, ed. Lovell, 123–4.

Fig. 3.2. Marianne Leigh Hunt, 'Lord Byron as he appeared after his daily ride at Pisa & Genoa', frontispiece engraving of papercut profile, in Leigh Hunt, *Lord Byron and Some of his Contemporaries* (London: Henry Colburn, 1828).

Lady Blessington follows this reminder of the significance of quotidian, domestic life to women with a conciliatory address to men: 'study her [woman's] happiness, and you insure your own', but her vision of Byron's failed marriage nevertheless pointedly revised Moore's, from a female perspective.[155]

[155] Ibid. 124. For a fuller discussion of Lady Blessington's *Conversations*, see North, 'Self-Possession and Gender in Romantic Literary Biography'.

Later in the century, Byron's former mistress, Theresa, the Countess Guiccioli produced a lengthy memoir, *My Recollections of Lord Byron* (1869), in which she unashamedly eulogized the poet in a sentimental rhetoric clearly intended to appeal to the feminine sympathies of her readers.[156] Her biography offered a direct riposte to Moore, arguing that poets could lead perfectly happy domestic lives:

We hear constantly repeated—because it was once said—that men of great genius are less capable than ordinary individuals of experiencing calm affections and of settling down in to those easy habits which help to cement domestic life. By dint of repeating it has become an axiom. But on what grounds is it founded? Because these privileged beings give themselves to studies requiring solitude . . . because, their mental riches being greater, they are more independent of the outer world and the intellectual resources of their fellow creatures . . . does it therefore necessarily follow that the goodness and sensibility of their hearts are blunted?

To create a harmonious relationship, the wife simply needed to indulge 'these privileged beings' in their need for solitary retirement from the 'tiresome' world of 'ordinary persons'. If poets had famously been unhappy at home, it was only because they had chosen wives who were not prepared to make these sacrifices. Dante would have been happy with Beatrice, and Byron with Theresa.[157] In keeping with the role of conciliatory wife, Guiccioli wrote her biography as a series of excuses for the personality defects with which Byron had been charged— irritability, mobility, misanthropy, pride, vanity. This argument and approach would seem to assert the feminine point of view within biography but only as subordinate to and supportive of masculine poetic genius, traditionally conceived. Yet Guiccioli's biography cumulatively undermined this model of genius by thoroughly feminizing Byron. She signalled the key to Byron's character as 'goodness', admitting that this is a difficult quality to represent. Her effort throughout was, accordingly, to erase his defects and produce the opposite of everything he had formerly been characterized by. The 'Byron' she produced was a saintly, would-be Catholic, who preferred his Bible to all other reading and wished for a happy, respectable marriage.[158] He seemed to be surrounded by a 'kind of supernatural light . . . like a halo'.[159] Her chapters, including one on Byron's 'modesty', reshaped the poet so that he became the pious heroine of an exemplary female *Life*.

The following year Harriet Beecher Stowe published her *Lady Byron Vindicated* (1870).[160] It was in part a response to Guiccioli's attack on Lady Byron and

---

[156] Theresa Countess Guiccioli, *My Recollections of Lord Byron and those of Eye-Witnesses of his Life*, new edn., trans. [from the French by] Hubert E. H. Jerningham (London: Richard Bentley, 1869).

[157] Ibid. 386–7.

[158] She quotes him as saying, just before leaving for Greece, that if only he could have married her ' "we should have been cited, I am certain, as samples of conjugal happiness, and our retired domestic life would have made us respectable!" ' (ibid. 388–9).

[159] Ibid. 44.

[160] Harriet Beecher Stowe, *Lady Byron Vindicated: A History of the Byron Controversy from its beginning in 1816 to the Present Time* (London: Sampson, Low, Son, and Marston, 1870); see also Stowe, 'The True Story of Lady Byron's Life', *Macmillan's Magazine*, 20 (Sept. 1869), 377–96.

countered her sentimental indulgence of the poet, with an outspokenly feminist, forensic defence of his widow. Stowe addressed her readers as 'my sisters' and set out to retrieve the story of the poet's chief female victim, extending this as a protest against the mistreatment of women in marriage more generally.[161] His crime against Lady Byron was made explicit, sensationally, for the first time in print. Guiccioli had, with apparent naïvety, praised Byron's love for his daughter and his sister in the same breath, wrapping both in a golden glow: 'His tenderness for his child, and for his sister was like a ray of sunshine which lit up his whole heart'.[162] Stowe, by contrast, stated in plain terms: '"He was guilty of incest with his sister!"'[163] Thus, in a reversal of Guiccioli's book, Lady Byron became the sainted heroine of this memoir, not Lord Byron, who was presented as having martyred her by violating the most fundamental taboos of family life. Stowe also replied to Moore (described as a sycophantic 'gilder' of Byron's sins) by defending domestic respectability as a woman's right and sought to reconfer it on Lady Byron's memory.[164] Susan Wolstenholme argues that, in the *Vindication*, Lady Byron is created as a heroic mother figure, with whom Stowe identifies, their joint mission being to save Byron's soul.[165] But this would be to read the *Vindication* as having a similar effect, in the last analysis, to Guiccioli's memoir. James Soderholm is nearer the mark in describing the *Vindication* as 'a work that hurled Byron into a lake of fire and canonized his wife'.[166] It is a late Victorian judgement on the irresponsibility of the Romantic poet, but also a feminist apotheosis.

The history of Byron biography powerfully suggests the feminization of a genre. It is interesting that, from 1816 to 1870 and beyond, his reputation stood or fell, within biography, by his relationships with women. The public interest in Byron's life was, from the beginning, attached to an appetite to know more about his wife and mistresses, and the numerous twentieth-century biographies of Arabella, Ada, Augusta, and his many female amours were an early example of what has become a more general marketing ploy in biography—to capitalize on the life of the famous male subject by bringing out *Lives* of his female associates.[167] This phenomenon, which has also, of course, been linked, latterly, to the rise of feminist historiography, is partly attributable to publishers' consciousness of the female audience for biography. Biography today often judges the public

---

[161] Stowe, *Lady Byron Vindicated*, 269 and see e.g. 78–9.

[162] Guiccioli, *My Recollections of Lord Byron*, 171.

[163] Stowe, *Lady Byron Vindicated*, 155.

[164] Ibid. 64. Stowe reminds her readers that Lady Byron had been called a whore in the press.

[165] Susan Wolstenholme, 'Voice of the Voiceless: Harriet Beecher Stowe and the Byron Controversy', *American Literary Realism*, 19/2 (Winter 1987), 48–65.

[166] Soderholm, *Fantasy, Forgery*, 101.

[167] Of the numerous *Lives* of Byron's female relatives and lovers, see e.g. Malcolm Elwin, *Lord Byron's Wife* (London: Macdonald, 1962); and Margot Strickland, *The Byron Women* (London: Peter Owen, 1974). Other examples of this phenomenon include e.g. Norma Clarke, *Dr Johnson's Women* (London: Hambledon and London, 2000).

performance of men and women by their private lives and particularly by their sexual relationships. Byron biography, from its inception, was presented in this way, sometimes in a crudely sensationalist fashion, but much of it attempted a more thoughtfully critical account of masculine genius. Byronism produced and was produced by a biographical literature which reshaped the figure of 'the poet' by mediating it to the middle-class reader. The myth of transcendence and masculine strength was present, and sometimes dominant in these *Lives*, but always in tension with the search for intimate relationship. Together these created a highly successful biographical paradigm. As we shall see in the next chapter, this paradigm was also present in nineteenth-century *Lives* of Percy Shelley, but engendered a biographical afterlife quite different from Byron's, although at least as controversial.

4
Biography and the Shelleys

Victorian biographies of Percy Bysshe Shelley have been profoundly influential in shaping academic and popular conceptions of 'the Romantic poet'. This has long been acknowledged, but usually as a matter for regret. Mary Shelley's editions of her husband's *Posthumous Poems* (1824) and *Poetical Works* (1839), with their biographical prefaces and notes, and after them Lady Shelley's *Shelley Memorials* (1859) have been regarded as especially culpable in disseminating a hagiographic construction of Shelley as a man of angelic goodness, beauty, and unworldliness, his poetry, like its creator, pure and ethereal. From Leigh Hunt and Thomas Medwin in the 1820s and 1830s, to Thomas Jefferson Hogg, Edward Trelawny, and Edward Dowden, in the mid- to late Victorian period, all the major biographers have been associated with the promotion of this 'Shelley myth', as false as it is seductive. Biography has been placed at the centre of the effort to defuse the threat of Shelley as a religious, political, and sexual dissident, and to project a 'declawed' or 'virtually depoliticized' figure, marketable to middle-class readers.[1] The myth has been seen as having had disastrous consequences for his critical reputation—the poet of resistance was tamed and reinvented as an author of beautiful lyrics in Victorian criticism, becoming, in Arnold's famous phrase: "'a beautiful *and ineffectual* angel, beating in the void his luminous wings in vain'".[2] Mark Kipperman has argued that this version of Shelley and, by extension, a particular archetype of the Romantic poet, became institutionalized in universities and institutions of higher education in the 1880s and 1890s as part of the evolving academic discipline of English literature.[3] The famous attacks on Shelley's poetry by T. S. Eliot and F. R. Leavis in the 1930s were one damaging consequence. For Eliot, his poetry was tainted by immature, confused, and repugnant ideas.[4] For Leavis, it was vain, intellectually vacuous,

---

[1] Mark Kipperman, 'Absorbing a Revolution: Shelley Becomes a Romantic, 1889–1903', *Nineteenth-Century Literature*, 47/2 (Sept. 1992), 190; and Neil Fraistat, 'Illegitimate Shelley: Radical Piracy and the Textual Edition as Cultural Performance', *PMLA* 109/3 (May 1994), 410.
[2] Matthew Arnold, 'Shelley' [Review of Edward Dowden, *The Life of Percy Bysshe Shelley*], *Nineteenth Century* (Jan. 1888), in R. H. Super (ed.), *The Complete Prose Works of Matthew Arnold*, 11 vols. (Ann Arbor: University of Michigan Press, 1960–77), xi. *The Last Word*, 327. Arnold is quoting his own description of Shelley from his essay on 'Byron' (1881).
[3] Kipperman, 'Absorbing a Revolution'.
[4] T. S. Eliot, 'Shelley and Keats', in *The Use of Poetry and the Use of Criticism: Studies in the Relation of Criticism to Poetry in England* (1933; London: Faber and Faber, 2nd edn. 1964), 87–102.

and, again, immature.[5] Kipperman is one in a series of critics since the 1970s who have suggested that Shelley's Victorian biographers were ultimately responsible for these views and that their legacy was thus nothing less than a severely etiolated understanding of Romanticism.[6]

It is the nature of a myth, of course, to be a simplification of its sources. Arnold admitted that his angelic Shelley was based on a wilfully selective reading of the biographical literature available to him, and the tendency towards ideologically driven caricature of nineteenth-century *Lives* of Shelley has been persistent. The biographies have been dismissed by critics asserting Shelley's radical credentials as pandering to the middle-class reader, and have been deplored as a feminizing form by those who are keen to defend the masculine vigour of his genius. In 1845 Engels commented that the bourgeoisie owned 'only castrated editions' of Shelley and Byron, 'family editions, cut down in accordance with the hypocritical morality of to-day'.[7] Echoing Engels's twin anxieties—of gentrification and feminization—Timothy Webb defended Shelley in 1977 by arguing that the biographical literature had produced 'castrations of the real Shelley', images of him as 'a sexless angel', which allowed 'drawing-room readers' to ignore the challenging intellectual content of his poetry.[8] In 1998 Jerrold Hogle, replicating the figure of emasculation, wrote of the struggle in criticism to ' "make Shelley whole" ' in the wake of those, including Mary Shelley and Hogg, 'who would turn him into the ethereal "pure poet" safe for developing middle-class tastes'.[9]

The 'Shelley myth', as characterized here, was a 'domestication' of genius in a thoroughly negative sense—an 'appropriation and containment' whereby he was reshaped into 'a harbinger of mid-Victorian Liberalism'.[10] Yet the processes of this

---

[5] F. R. Leavis, 'Shelley', in *Revaluation: Tradition and Development in English Poetry* (1936; London: Chatto and Windus, 1962), 203–40. Leavis's view of Shelley owes much to Arnold's essay.

[6] See also Timothy Webb, *Shelley: A Voice Not Understood* (Manchester: Manchester University Press, 1977); Stuart Curran, 'Percy Bysshe Shelley', in Frank Jordan (ed.), *The English Romantic Poets: A Review of Research and Criticism*, 4 edn. (New York: Modern Language Association of America, 1985), 606–7; Karsten Klejs Engelberg, *The Making of the Shelley Myth: An Annotated Bibliography of Criticism of Percy Bysshe Shelley 1822–1860* (London: Mansell; Westport, Conn.: Meckler, 1988); Fraistat, 'Illegitimate Shelley'; and Jerrold E. Hogle, 'Percy Bysshe Shelley', in Michael O'Neill (ed.), *Literature of the Romantic Period: A Bibliographical Guide* (Oxford: Clarendon Press, 1998), 118–42. Kipperman, following Engelberg, argues that 'the Victorian obsession with the poet's life' produces 'the myth of a poet either ludicrously incapable, criminally irresponsible, or gloriously and ineffably transcendent' (189).

[7] Friedrich Engels, *The Condition of the Working-Class in England in 1844*, trans. Florence Kelley Wischnewetzky (1st English edn. 1892; London: George Allen & Unwin Ltd., 1936), 240. The word 'castrated' is replaced by 'ruthlessly expurgated' in Engels, *The Condition of the Working Class in England*, ed. and trans. W. O. Henderson and W. H. Chaloner (Oxford: Basil Blackwell, 1971), 273.

[8] Webb, *Shelley*, 17, 23, 25. Compare Leavis, 'Shelley', 211, 207: it is a poetry of 'high-pitched emotions' in which there is 'an absence of something', and see Julian North, ' "I change but I cannot die": The Metamorphoses of P. B. Shelley', in Carla Dente et al. (eds), *Proteus: The Language of Metamorphosis*, Studies in European Cultural Transition, 26, gen. eds. Martin Stannard and Greg Walker (Aldershot: Ashgate, 2005), 165–71.

[9] Hogle, 'Percy Bysshe Shelley', 118.

[10] Kipperman, 'Absorbing a Revolution', 191. He refers to G. H. Lewes's essay for the *Westminster Review* (1841), arguing that part of Lewes's intention was 'to win Mary Shelley's approval of himself as her husband's official biographer . . . it seems he even had completed such a manuscript (never published) by 1839' (ibid.).

domestication were both more conflicted than this suggests and of some significance in relation to the competitive interdependency of poetry and literary biography at the period. Dowden's biography has been described by Kipperman as part of a movement in Victorian criticism to detach Shelley's revolutionary ideals 'from any political or historical context'.[11] Yet, whilst Dowden is openly critical of Shelley's radicalism, his 'life and times' approach in fact contextualizes the poet's politics— his Godwinian sympathies and his political activism in Ireland, for example—in great detail. If we look at the biographical literature itself rather than using it to argue for a particular reading of Shelley's poetry, we see that the defensive softening of Shelley's political radicalism could coexist with its promotion, or with a recognition of its incompatibility with mid-century Liberalism. Michael O'Neill has pointed out the radical affiliations of John Hunt who published Mary Shelley's edition of the *Posthumous Poems* (1824), containing in its preface the seminal memoir of Shelley, and to the political content of many of the poems she included in her edition.[12] Leigh Hunt's essay on Shelley, published in 1828, described him as an angel, but not in Arnold's terms—his face was 'seraphical' like 'the angel whom Milton describes as holding a reed "tipt with fire"', poised to ignite social revolution.[13] Later Peacock, imagining what Shelley would have become had he lived on to 1860, pictured a man refusing to assimilate. Like Volney, he would have looked 'on the world from his windows without taking part in its turmoils' and, on his death, would have had one word inscribed on his tomb besides his name and dates, '"DÉSILLUSIONÉ"'.[14]

Biographers certainly glossed over the difficult details of Shelley's marriages and other sexual relationships, but again this was only part of the story.[15] Hogg stressed

---

[11] Kipperman, 'Absorbing a Revolution', 201. See also 192–3 and 202–4. Dowden's 'fascination with Shelley was directed not merely at producing an objective biography, but more at normalizing his politics and revising its revolutionary threat' (203).

[12] Michael O'Neill, ' "Trying to make it as good as I can": Mary Shelley's Editing of Shelley's Poetry and Prose', *Romanticism*, 3/2 (1997), 193–4.

[13] Hunt, *Lord Byron and Some of his Contemporaries; with Recollections of the Author's Life, and of his Visit to Italy* (London: Henry Colburn, 1828), 174–5. *Paradise Lost*, vi. 579–80, in fact, describes ranks of angels in Satan's army, about to light their cannons and devastate the troops of Michael and Gabriel. Hunt later aligns Shelley with 'the reformers and innovators of old, the Hampdens, the Miltons, and the Sydneys' (228), but also situates him in a more disturbingly contemporary revolutionary context when he relays, as an example of Shelley's heroic benevolence, an anecdote in which the poet warns an uncharitable gentleman that he will have his house burnt down by the poor 'if ever a convulsion comes to this country' (187–8n.).

[14] Thomas Love Peacock, 'Memoirs of Percy Bysshe Shelley', 1st pub. *Fraser's Magazine* (1858–60), repr. in H. F. B. Brett-Smith and C. E. Jones (eds,) *The Works of Thomas Love Peacock*, Halliford Edition, viii. *Essays, Memoirs, Letters and Unfinished Novels* (London: Constable and Co. Ltd.; New York: Gabriel Wells, 1934), 131.

[15] All the major biographers stressed Shelley's moral and sexual purity. Hunt, *Lord Byron*, argued that Shelley's domestic misfortunes were not his fault and presented him as the victim of Lord Eldon's ruling against Shelley's custody of the children of his first marriage, following his wife's suicide. Hunt also denied accusations of his sexual misconduct, including the charge that Shelley kept a 'seraglio' (191). See also Lady [Jane] Shelley (ed.), *Shelley Memorials: From Authentic Sources. To Which is Added An Essay on Christianity, by Percy Bysshe Shelley; now First Printed* (London: Smith, Elder & Co., 1859), presenting the first marriage as 'unfortunate' (21) and maintaining that

Shelley's sexual purity, but also his attractiveness to women and was on the point of detailing the scandalous end of his first marriage and the beginning of the relationship with Mary Godwin when publication was halted by Lady Jane Shelley.[16] Although sympathetic to Shelley, Peacock made it clear that his first marriage had not ended by mutual consent and that he had abandoned Harriet for an adulterous relationship. Mary Shelley's editions, unsurprisingly, passed over the first marriage and the circumstances under which her own relationship with Shelley started, but, as we shall see, she also countered her defence of Shelley's private virtues with a critical recognition of his capacity to abrogate domestic responsibility.[17] All Shelley's biographers glamorized an angelic or eccentric other-worldliness in the poet and thereby made his views and behaviour more palatable for their readers. Yet they rarely validated his other-worldliness in an unqualified sense. They created, instead, an effective tension between the ethereal poet and the earthbound biographer, capable of bringing the angel into the orbit of their readers. In so doing the biographical literature intervened vigorously, if ambivalently, in the critical debate on Shelley's responsibility to audience, so that he became an important focal point for biography's self-definition as a genre that promoted and questioned the figure of the 'Romantic poet' and claimed its own, superior attention to the needs of the readerships of the day.

The final section of this chapter will look briefly at the contributions of Trelawny, Hogg, Lady Jane Shelley, and Edward Dowden to the biographical representation of Shelley, but the main body of the argument will focus on Mary Shelley's posthumous construction of her husband in the context of her professional commitment to biography as a genre. My discussion is indebted here to some fine scholarship on her editions of Shelley's work, but will differ from previous approaches in reading them, first and foremost, as biographical productions, in the context of the marketing and practice of literary biography from the early 1800s and, more particularly, of Mary Shelley's own career as a biographer.[18] She is both the key player, if often named the chief culprit, in forming Shelley's posthumous reputation, and a neglected figure in the history of literary biography. I will look at

---

Shelley had nothing to do with Harriet's suicide (65–6). Again she stressed the injustice of Lord Eldon's decision (75).

[16] Thomas Jefferson Hogg, *The Life of Percy Bysshe Shelley*, 4 vols. [only 2 pub.] (London: Edward Moxon, 1858).

[17] There is evidence that she intended to confront the subject of his life with Harriet in the full-length biography she planned but never published. See *MWSJ*, 445 n.

[18] See esp. Mary Favret, 'Mary Shelley's Sympathy and Irony: The Editor and her Corpus', in Audrey A. Fisch, Anne K. Mellor, and Esther H. Schor (eds.), *The Other Mary Shelley: Beyond Frankenstein* (New York: Oxford University Press, 1993), 17–38; Susan J. Wolfson, 'Editorial Privilege: Mary Shelley and Percy Shelley's Audiences', ibid. 39–72. Fraistat, 'Illegitimate Shelley'; and O'Neill, '"Trying to make it as good as I can"'. None of these reads the editions as biography, nor makes links between them and the rest of Mary Shelley's biographical output.

how her fragmented memorials of Shelley, influenced by radical and feminist traditions in biography, became increasingly critical of the poet for placing himself beyond the reach of his readers. In so doing I will consider the relationship between her editions and her popular, encyclopaedia biographies—an area of her writing which has only relatively recently begun to attract much critical attention.[19] The chapter is entitled 'Biography and the Shelleys' because it looks at the intertwining of two very different literary careers, each, to some extent, determining the other.

After Shelley's death, in 1822, his reputation was disseminated amongst Victorian, middle-class readers first and foremost through biographical editions. From 1821, pirated editions of *Queen Mab*, had led to a following amongst readers of the radical press, but otherwise his poetry was not widely known in his lifetime.[20] Mary Shelley's editions of his poetry and prose changed the situation by making his works, published and unpublished, more generally available, but also by tying them to the story of his life.[21] Her 1824 edition of the *Posthumous Poems* was prefaced by a sketch of Shelley's life and last days.[22] Her father-in-law, Sir Timothy Shelley, objected and *Posthumous Poems* had to be withdrawn soon after publication.[23] When, in the late 1830s, she requested permission for a new edition, Sir Timothy agreed, but on condition that no memoir be attached—'Sir Tim forbids biography'.[24] Nevertheless, when her edition of the *Poetical Works*

[19] The publication of *LL* represents the major advance, making available the substantial proportion of her biographical work. Recent work on Mary Shelley as a biographer includes Lia Guerra, 'Mary Shelley's Contributions to Lardner's *Cabinet Cyclopaedia: Lives of the Most Eminent Literary and Scientific Men of Italy*', in Laura Bandiera and Diego Saglia (eds.), *British Romanticism and Italian Literature: Translating, Reviewing, Rewriting* (Amsterdam: Rodopi, 2005), 221–35; Greg Kucich, 'Mary Shelley's *Lives* and the Reengendering of History', in Betty T. Bennett and Stuart Curran (eds.), *Mary Shelley in Her Times* (Baltimore: Johns Hopkins University Press, 2000), 198–213; and Lucy Morrison, 'Writing the Self in Others' Lives: Mary Shelley's Biographies of Madame Roland and Madame de Staël', *Keats-Shelley Journal*, 53 (2004), 127–51.

[20] See Fraistat, 'Illegitimate Shelley', for radical piracies of Shelley and his working-class readership in the 1820s and 1830s. For the publishing history of *Queen Mab* and Shelley's other poems, including sales figures, and for his place in 'the radical canon, 1820s onwards', see William St Clair *The Reading Nation in the Romantic Period* (Cambridge: Cambridge University Press, 2004), 317–22, 336–7, 649–51, and 679–82. St Clair comments that Shelley's books of poetry, apart from *Queen Mab*, 'had by the time of the poet's death, ceased to be available at all. Most of them, whose first and only edition had consisted of 750 copies or less, had lain in the warehouse, been remaindered, or sent for trunk lining' (320).

[21] See *PPS*, *PWS*, and *ELS*. Between 1824 and 1839, there were at least five unauthorized editions of Shelley's poems, based on Mary Shelley's—see Charles H. Taylor, *The Early Collected Editions of Shelley's Poems: A Study in the History and Transmission of the Printed Text* (New Haven: Yale University Press, 1958), 11–33. By 1887 there were at least fourteen memoirs of Shelley—see Newman I. White, 'The Beautiful Angel and his Biographers', in Frank Jordan (ed.), *The English Romantic Poets: A Review of Research and Criticism*, 3rd edn. (New York: Modern Language Association of America, 1972), 74.

[22] This prefatory 'Life' was of great importance to Mary Shelley. When Leigh Hunt, who was originally commissioned to write the biographical 'Notice', failed to deliver, she wrote 'it would break my heart if the book should appear without it' (*MWSL* i. 404).

[23] Ibid. 444.

[24] Ibid. ii. 299 n. and 301.

appeared in 1839, the biographical content was enhanced. In this, Mary Shelley's most substantial published contribution to the memorialization of her husband, she arranged his poems as a chronological narrative, with a preface and over a hundred pages of explanatory notes charting his life story from the age of 18, when he wrote *Queen Mab*, to his death. She also reprinted the 1824 Preface.[25]

These publications, together with her edition of Shelley's prose, *Essays, Letters from Abroad* (1840 [1839]), shaped his work biographically, in lieu of the full-length memoir Mary Shelley had always wanted to write. A few months after Shelley's death, she was already planning a biography.[26] Her unpublished manuscript 'Life of Shelley', probably dating from 1823, was her earliest attempt. It is a brief, fragmentary account, of eleven written pages, comprising some episodes at his family home, Fieldplace, sketches of his time at Eton (1805–10), an effort to articulate her own role as his biographer and some reflections on Shelley's character.[27] Her revisions suggest that she expected it to form the basis of a published biography. There is evidence that she still intended, in the early 1840s, to produce a complete *Life*, and although this aim was never realized, her editions, together with the memoirs of Medwin Hunt and Hogg, framed Shelley's poetry biographically for the reading public in the 1820s and 1830s and beyond.[28]

In many respects it is surprising that Mary Shelley decided to present her husband's work in this way. There were good reasons not to. Her repeated circumventions of her father-in-law's objections were economically risky for herself and her son, since they were dependent on his allowance and his permission to publish Shelley's work. She also jeopardized her husband's reputation and her own by venturing into memoir, in which the scandals of his life and the sexual irregularities of their relationship would inevitably be brought once more to the attention of the public. The consequences of William Godwin's *Memoirs* of Mary Wollstonecraft for her posthumous reputation were a personal reminder to Mary Shelley of the damage that could be done by publishing intimate recollections. Her letters reveal her own fear of the publicity that would come from being a named—or even an unnamed—presence in a Shelley

---

[25] See *PWS* iv. 237–40.

[26] Shelley drowned on 8 July 1822. See *MWSL* i. 252, for evidence that she was already thinking of writing his life on *c*.27 Aug. See also *MWSJ* pp. xxii, 417 n., and 444–5. She drew on her journals for the biographical notes for *PWS*—see *MWSJ* p. xix.

[27] The title is not hers. For a facsimile, transcription, and detailed commentary, see *A Facsimile and Full transcript of Bodleian MS. Shelley adds.c.5*, ed. Alan M. Weinberg, 22/2 of *The Bodleian Shelley Manuscripts. A Facsimile Edition, with Full Transcripts and Scholarly Apparatus*, gen. ed. Donald H. Reiman (New York: Garland Publishing Inc., 1997), 267–87. A transcript is also in *LL* iv. 220–6. The 'Life' was 1st pub. in edited extracts in Hogg's *Life of...Shelley*, i. See Elizabeth Nitchie, 'Shelley at Eton: Mary Shelley vs. Jefferson Hogg', *Keats-Shelley Memorial Bulletin*, 11(1960), 48–54, for Hogg's alterations.

[28] *MWSJ*, 445 n. It seems that she also wanted her journals to survive as a memorial, supplementing her prefaces and notes—see ibid., p. xix.

biography, and her sensitivity to the capacity of biography, within the contemporary marketplace, to defame its subjects, especially when female.[29] In this light we have to ask why she persisted, as she did, with the biographical framing of her editions. In part it can be explained as a consequence of the culture of defamatory, biographical criticism in the periodical press, of which Shelley, like Byron and Keats, was a victim.[30] His atheism, radical politics, sexual transgressions, and his first wife's alleged prostitution, her suicide, and the ensuing custody battle for his children were all cited as grounds for criticism of him as a man and a poet in the literary reviews in his lifetime.[31] The decisions of Mary Shelley, Hunt, and Hogg to mount biographical defences of Shelley were, to some extent, simply responses in kind—part of the familiar trap whereby the guardians of privacy become instruments of publicity. Yet, there are a number of other contexts for Mary Shelley's decision that illuminate her conception of biography and her construction of Shelley.

4.1 MARY SHELLEY AS A BIOGRAPHER

In the 1820s and 1830s, when she published her editions, Mary Shelley was forging a career not only as a novelist but as a biographer. She was a lifelong practitioner of biography. Some of her earliest unpublished writings were fragmentary, manuscript lives of Theseus and Cyrus, taken from Plutarch, and in 1814 she began but did not finish a biography of the French Girondist and novelist Jean Baptiste Louvet de Couvray.[32] As well as the editions of Shelley, she published a biographical essay on Madame d'Houtetôt (1823) and a brief

---

[29] See e.g. *MSWL* ii. 72, on the prospect of appearing in Trelawny's *Life* of Shelley. See also e.g. *MWSL* i. 476; and ii. 168–9, asking Leigh Hunt and Lady Blessington to remove references to Claire Clairmont from their accounts of Shelley and Byron. She feared for Clairmont's marriage prospects and for her own reputation, by association, and expressed a personal sense of relief when Lady Blessington agreed to her request: 'I am thankful to her as I would thank someone who had been threatening me with a stiletto, and then spared me. . . . He who steals my purse | steals trash [*Othello*, III. iii. 150] To employ the language of Shakespeare, but he who publishes on the subject of myself, does me a far greater injury'.

[30] See e.g. the notorious review by John Taylor Coleridge of *Laon and Cythna (The Revolt of Islam)* in the *Quarterly Review* (Apr. 1819), repr. in Newman Ivey White (ed.), *The Unextinguished Hearth: Shelley and His Contemporary Critics* (1938; New York: Octagon Books, 1966), 133–42. Coleridge dropped dark hints about Shelley's private life and accused him of 'shamefully dissolute' conduct (137), 'low pride . . . cold selfishness . . . unmanly cruelty' (142). Leigh Hunt responded in the *Examiner* (Sept.–Oct. 1819), deploring these allusions to Shelley's private life—see White, *Unextinguished Hearth*, 143–50.

[31] See e.g. review of *Queen Mab*, *Literary Gazette* (19 May 1821), ibid. 56n.: 'We declare against receiving our social impulses from a destroyer of every social virtue; our moral creed, from an incestuous wretch; or our religion, from an atheist.'

[32] 'The Theseus Fragment', *LL* iv. 203–4; 'The Cyrus Fragment', ibid. 205–8. The most likely date of composition for both is *c*.1815, when she read Plutarch's *Parallel Lives*. She finished reading Jean Baptiste Louvet de Couvret's memoirs on 12 Nov. 1814, and began writing his life on the same day—see *MWSJ*, 44. The manuscript is now lost.

'Memoirs of William Godwin' (1831).[33] After his death in 1836, she started a full-length memoir of her father.[34] Her major published work as a biographer was the extensive series of literary *Lives* of *The Most Eminent Literary and Scientific Men*, of Italy, Spain, Portugal, and France, which she published in five volumes of Dionysius Lardner's *Cabinet Cyclopaedia* between 1835 and 1839.[35] She also projected, but never wrote, full-length *Lives* of Mahomet, Josephine, Madame de Staël, and collective biographies of the English philosophers and of celebrated women.[36] Her reading-lists, journal entries, and letters attest to the fact that biography, autobiography, and memoirs were amongst her own and Percy Shelley's favourite reading matter.[37] Her own life was written about almost before she had begun to live it. Godwin's *Memoirs* of Mary Wollstonecraft, concluding with the narrative of her birth, made her a famous biographical subject at the age of 1. She continued, in her adulthood, to appear as a minor player, in memoirs of her husband and their circle, as well as making important contributions to these texts.[38]

This life of life-writing is vital in understanding the inception and nature of the Shelley editions. Biography represented many things for Mary Shelley other than a threat. It was the means to bring high culture to a popular audience; a genre attuned to communicating her understanding of the relationship between public and private life; a discourse which offered a unique sense of the reality of the subject; and a commercially viable form. Her conception of the genre and its potential was shaped in each of these respects by other biographers, including William Godwin, Mary Hays, and others working in the tradition of female, collective *Lives*, and by Byron's early biographers, especially Thomas Moore.

Godwin encouraged her projected lives of the English philosophers and of celebrated women and, through his own work, was also an important influence on her conception and practice of biography. He offered her a radicalized model of literary biography as a means of broadening access to education. In his *Life of Geoffrey Chaucer* (1803) he had made bold claims for the genre as a means to

---

[33] 'Madame d'Houtetôt', *The Liberal. Verse and Prose from the South*, 2/3 (1823), 67–83; 'Memoirs of William Godwin', in William Godwin, *Caleb Williams* (Standard Novels, no. 2; London: Henry Colburn and Richard Bentley; Edinburgh: Bell & Bradfute; Dublin: Cuming, 1831), pp. iii–xiii. Both repr. in *The Novels and Selected Works of Mary Shelley*, gen. ed. Nora Crook, with Pamela Clemit, introd. Betty T. Bennett, 8 vols. (London: William Pickering, 1996).

[34] 'Life of William Godwin', in *LL* iv. 3–113. See ibid., pp. xiii–xxvii for a detailed account of the composition and MS.

[35] See *LL* i–iii.

[36] See *MWSL*, vol. ii, p. xv.

[37] For the Shelleys' reading list, see *MWSJ*, 631–84. See also e.g. *MWSL* ii. 223 on Boswell's *Life of Johnson*, 'the most amusing book in the world'. She has read it 'I am sure ten times—& hope to read it many more'.

[38] See e.g. *MWSL* ii. 87 for correspondence with Cyrus Redding on his 'Memoir of Percy Bysshe Shelley' in *Poetical Works of Coleridge, Shelley, and Keats* (Paris: Galignani, 1829), pp. v–xi. Her contributions to Moore's *Letters and Journals* and the help she offered other biographers are discussed below.

establishing national high culture on a wider base.[39] He argued in his Preface that Chaucer, as the father of English poetry and the English language, must be brought to all readers, not merely to the select few who already knew the poet through his works. His biography aimed at 'enabling the reader, who might shrink from the labour of mastering the phraseology of Chaucer, to do justice to his illustrious countryman'. He wanted to produce a new kind of 'popular' history for '[a]ntiquities have too generally been regarded as the province of men of cold tempers and sterile imaginations'.[40] Godwin's method was to produce a monumentally detailed 'life and times' biography. At every stage of the chronological narrative, he contextualized Chaucer's life within the history of his culture and society.[41] This bringing together of private and public life was part of his radical, popularizing agenda—his belief that the national culture involved all readers. At the same time, Godwin simply aimed, as he put it in his Preface, to make the reader 'feel for the instant as if he had lived with Chaucer'.[42]

This last phrase, inviting the reader to cohabitation with greatness, struck a chord with Mary Shelley and, together with his claim that through biography he could interpret a hitherto obscure poetic language for the reader, had special relevance to her Shelley editions. Her biographical practice, especially in the 1830s, shows that she kept faith with his vision of biography's educative power. In forging a career for herself as a professional writer in the 1820s and 1830s she had taken advantage of publishing contexts which aimed to unite accessibility and cultural capital.[43] Her work for Lardner's *Cabinet Cyclopaedia* in the mid- to late 1830s placed her at the heart of a biographical project intended to extend the audience for high culture. Nora Crook describes the *Cyclopaedia* as one of 'the many series which arose during the 1820s and 30s in response to the so-called March of Mind'. Like other self-improvement literature, it was aimed at the general reader, especially from the new middle-classes and 'the aspiring skilled artisan class'.[44] The *Cyclopaedia* also had Godwinian links—John Williams

[39] William Godwin, *Life of Geoffrey Chaucer, The Early English Poet: Including Memoirs of his near Friend and Kinsman, John of Gaunt, Duke of Lancaster: With Sketches of the Manners, Opinions, Arts and Literature of England in the Fourteenth Century*, 2 vols. (London: Richard Phillips, 1803). Percy and Mary Shelley read Godwin's biography in 1815.

[40] Godwin, *Life of Geoffrey Chaucer*, 2nd edn., 4 vols. (London: Richard Phillips, 1804), vol. i, pp. v, ix.

[41] See ibid., p. vi: 'The full and complete life of a poet would include an extensive survey of the manners, the opinions, the arts and the literature, of the age in which the poet lived. This is the only way in which we can become truly acquainted with the history of his mind, and the causes which made him what he was.'

[42] Ibid., p. xi.

[43] See John Williams, *Mary Shelley: A Literary Life* (Basingstoke: Macmillan, 2000), 129, on her work for *The Keepsake* and other such journals and magazines.

[44] *LL*, vol. i, p. xix and see Johanna M. Smith, *Mary Shelley* (Twayne's English Authors Series, 526; New York: Twayne Publishers; London: Prentice Hall International, 1996), 130–1: Lardner's *Cyclopaedia* was advertised as aiming 'to "stimulate the diffusion of knowledge" to the "general reader" by making the arts and sciences "attractive" and "universally intelligible," but he also

points out that, to write *The History of England*, Lardner chose Sir James
Mackintosh, a former member of Godwin's circle, made an honourary French
citizen in 1792, and the author of the *Vindiciae Gallicae* (1791). Williams makes
a case for Lardner's project as more than implicitly radical in its popularizing
agenda and allies it to 'the radical French encyclopaedic tradition of the eighteenth-century *philosophes*'.[45] Although the political affiliations of both the
French *Encyclopédie* and Lardner's *Cyclopaedia* were more complex and diverse
than Williams suggests, Lardner's project had in common with its more famous
French forebear a reforming purpose in its aim of a national, popular educational
programme and, within individual articles, a tendency to question social and
political institutions and to promote social change.[46] Mary Shelley's work for the
Cyclopaedia shared these progressive aims. As in her biographical essays on
Godwin, also from the 1830s, she engaged sympathetically with radical political
views, but at the same time signalled her allegiances to a different age of peaceful
agitation for social and political reform.[47] Lisa Vargo argues that, although she
'was not a doctrinaire republican', in her French *Lives* she engaged 'directly with
Enlightened and Revolutionary France as the child of Wollstonecraft and Godwin'. Her choice of Condorcet, Mirabeau, Madame Roland, and Madame de
Staël, represented 'a concerted attempt to dissociate the early ideals of the French
Revolution from its subsequent extremism and state-authorised bloodshed'.[48]
But Godwin's most significant influence on his daughter's biographical practice
was his 'life and times' approach, for the connection between the personal and
the political and, more generally, the private and public life of her subjects,
became not only a method, but a central theme of her essays. The Shelley
editions were different in many respects from the *Cyclopaedia* project, but her
work for Lardner has an important bearing on them, as we shall see, in relation to
her conception of the audience for biography, its popularizing power as an
instrument of high culture, and her commitment to the responsibility of public
to private life.

Mary Shelley's practice as a biographer was also directly influenced by the
tradition of female, collective biography discussed in Chapter 1. She knew and
admired the work of Mary Hays, the woman who introduced Godwin and
Wollstonecraft. She had also read George Stewarton's *Female Revolutionary*

---

intended to "inculcate sound principles" and "raise the tone of the public mind"'. It comprised 133
volumes (1829–1846), cloth-bound, at 6 shillings each.

[45] Williams, *Mary Shelley*, 165.

[46] For the political complexity of the *Encyclopédie; ou, Dictionnaire raisonné des sciences, des arts et
des métiers* (1751–72), ed. Denis Diderot and Jean Le Rond d'Alembert, see John W. Yolton, Roy
Porter, et al. (eds.), *The Blackwell Companion to the Enlightenment* (1991; Oxford: Blackwell, 1995),
145–50.

[47] See Smith, *Mary Shelley*, 123. For her reformist sympathies in the Lardner *Lives*, see e.g. *LL*
iii. 323, her reference to 'the excess of labour and poor living to which the inferior classes in our
manufacturing towns are subject'.

[48] *LL*, vol. ii, pp. xlvi–xlvii.

Plutarch.[49] Her Lardner contributions included *Lives* of literary women inter-
polated within a much more extensive series of essays on men, under the title
Eminent Literary and Scientific Men.[50] She was the only contributor to include
female subjects. Her anonymity meant that she disguised her gender under the
cloak of an assumed masculinity in a way that Mary Hays and other female
biographers did not, and, unlike them, did not explicitly target a female audience. Yet the *Cyclopaedia* was aimed at female as well as male readers. As Nora
Crook notes, 'its Prospectus anticipated a place in "the drawing room and the
boudoir"'.[51] Mary Shelley's action in introducing lives of women into the series
showed her appealing to this audience and demonstrated her belief in the equal
standing of female genius—something she makes explicit, for instance, in the
opening of her essay on 'Madame de Sévigné'.[52] Her female *Lives* could also be as
radical as Hays's in their concern for the improvement of women's social as well
as cultural standing.[53] Greg Kucich argues that they are examples of feminist
historiography and constitute one of her 'most substantial interventions in the
gender ideologies of her time'. Like other feminist historiographers before her,
including Wollstonecraft and Hays, she not only brought women into history
but altered 'the fundamental structures of historical representation in patriarchal
versions of the past' so that 'the individualized story of the human subject'
resurfaced in opposition to the 'totalizing inclination' of conventional historiography. She thereby furthered 'the kind of cultural extension of emotional
sympathies she had always promoted as the model of healthy personal and social
relations'.[54] Her practice here was in keeping with the continuing focus of
collective female biography on domestic virtue in relation to public life, and its
enactment in the educational agenda of these publications. We have seen how

---

[49] Mary Hays was a close friend of her parents. Mary Shelley wrote to her in 1836 on Godwin's
death: 'your name is of course familiar to me as one of those women whose talents do honor to our
sex', *MWSL* ii. 270. For Mary Shelley's reading of Stewarton in 1814, see *MWSJ*, 679. Both Hays's
and Stewarton's 'Lives' of Madame Roland are important contexts for reading Mary Shelley's
Lardner essay on the same subject.

[50] The female lives she included were those of 'Vittoria Colonna', *Eminent Literary and Scientific
Men of Italy, Spain, and Portugal,* ii (1835); 'Madame de Sévigné', *Eminent Literary and Scientific
Men of France,* i (1838); 'Madame Roland' and 'Madame de Staël', *Eminent Literary and Scientific
Men of France,* ii (1839).

[51] *LL*, vol. i, pp. xx.

[52] See *LL* iii. 93: 'We could not omit a name so highly honourable to her country as that of
madame de Sévigné, in a series of biography whose intent is to give an account of the persons whose
genius has adorned the world.'

[53] See Smith, *Mary Shelley*, 122, on her earlier life of 'Madame D'Houtetôt': 'As often in Mary
Shelley's biographies, the life of a "woman of talent" becomes a vehicle for criticizing cultural
systems injurious to women'—here 'the "heartlessness" of French marriage customs'. Such concerns
are also very much present in the Lardner lives. See e.g. 'Madame Roland', *LL* iii. 435, for Mary
Shelley's approval of her subject's rejection of the 'shackles' of marriage for social position alone. In
'Rousseau', ibid. 330, she protests that '[i]t is not to-day that we have learnt, that it is not true, that
when a woman loses one virtue she loses all'.

[54] Kucich, 'Mary Shelley's *Lives*', 199, 201–2, 210. Kucich also notes that this 'redemptive
"sympathy," [is] usually expressed within domestic communities' (211).

Mary Hays in the early 1800s sought to contribute to the general advancement of female intellect, by encouraging women to educate themselves through biography. This aim only strengthened in the 1830s and 1840s, in the context of the market for self-improving literature.[55] The interactions of domestic and public life so central to female collective biography and its investment in the reader, exerted their influence on Mary Shelley's *Cyclopaedia* essays and on her biographical shaping of Shelley.

Mary Shelley was highly attuned to the literary marketplace and made efforts to take advantage of the current vogue for literary *Lives*, especially in the wake of Byronism. She was forced to supplement her allowance through her writing and her letters demonstrate her daily struggles as a professional author. Fiction was her primary means, but biography became, especially in the 1830s, an important second string. She was herself involved in the Byron industry—after 1824 she was regularly consulted by his biographers, asking her to look over their manuscripts and contribute letters and other information. Her sensitivity to biographers' violations of private life was partly a product of this experience, but so was her interest in the opportunities presented by biography for both author and subject. When Medwin wanted her to look over the manuscript of his *Conversations of Lord Byron*, which included a ten-page footnote sketching Shelley's life, she refused to cooperate on the grounds that 'Years ago "When a man died the worms ate him.{"}—Now a new set of worms feed on the carcase of the scandal that he leaves behind him & grow fat upon the world's love of tittle tattle—I will not be numbered among them'.[56] There was disgust at the parasitical biographer here, but also awareness that, in the post-Byron world, literary biography might represent a good career move for a writer and a guaranteed audience for both author and subject.[57] By the 1830s, the marketing of Byron was a significant factor in her decision to develop the biographical edition as a means of selling Shelley.

Although she refused to be associated with Medwin's *Conversations*, Mary Shelley played a major part as a collaborator with Moore in his *Letters and Journals of Lord Byron*, by supplying materials for his book, and soliciting others

[55] See e.g. Mrs [Anne Katharine] Elwood, *Memoirs of the Literary Ladies of England, from the Commencement of the Last Century*, 2 vols. (London: Henry Colburn, 1843), vol. i, pp. v–vi, where biography is presented as a pleasurable means of female education.
[56] *MWSL* i. 453. The quotation is from *As You Like It*, IV. i. 110. Elsewhere she admits, if playfully, to liking biographical scandal—see *MWSL* i. 506. Thomas Medwin, *Journal of the Conversations of Lord Byron. Noted During a Residence with his Lordship at Pisa, in the Years 1821 and 1822* (London: Henry Colburn, 1824) and his *The Shelley Papers. Memoir of Percy Bysshe Shelley and Original Poems and Papers by Percy Bysshe Shelley. Now First Collected* (London: Whittaker, Treacher and Co., 1833), were widely condemned as the works of an inaccurate, money-grubbing opportunist. Medwin first announced his *Conversations* to Mary Shelley in July 1824, a few weeks after the appearance of *PPS* in early June. The *Conversations* were published in Oct.
[57] See *MWSL* i. 447: Medwin is publishing his account of Shelley for 'yellow coin' (he received £500 from Colburn—see ibid. 439n.).

to do the same.[58] She also contributed footnotes to Murray's seventeen-volume edition of the works of Byron, prefaced by Moore's *Letters and Journals* (1832–3).[59] Medwin's book, for her and others, had represented the dangerous power of biography, as inaccurate gossip, but she viewed Moore's as a model of biographical practice. She praised him for his '*tact*' but, above all, it was his ability to bring Byron home to her as a living presence and thereby to make her like him again, that attracted her:

the Lord Byron I find there is our Lord Byron . . . I live with him again in these pages— getting reconciled (as I used in his lifetime) to those waywardnesses which annoyed me when he was away, through the delightful & buoyant tone of his conversation and manners.[60]

'I live with him again'—she echoes Godwin's hope for the readers of his *Life of Chaucer*. In reading Moore she enters into a harmonious, domestic relationship with the poet. Murray's edition of the works of Byron attracted her because it placed the poetry within a biographical narrative which traced the work back to the authentic, living emotions of the man:

The feelings which gave rise to each poem, are so dwelt on in the Letters in Mr Moore's Life—that there seems nothing left to say on that subject.—and by printing the poems in a Chronological order, you force on the readers apprehension his state of mind when he wrote them. . . . The depth of passion, nursed in solitude—and wild romantic scenery which breathes in his poems to Thirza—Who she was I do not know—I believe a cousin—at any rate she was a real person *decidedly*—and his feelings of misery on her death most real'.[61]

The letter from which this comes is, itself, a mini-biography of Byron by Mary Shelley—a sketch linking life and works: 'I have thus run through his works, to shew you what I think and know of the periods of their composition and the moods of mind in which they were written'.[62] This might be a description of her own editorial method in the 1839 *Poetical Works.* and it is clear that her edition was not only deeply influenced by Moore's *Letters and Journals* of Byron, but directly modelled on Murray's edition of Byron's *Works*, with its biographical prefaces and footnotes.[63] In these memorials to Byron Mary Shelley found the same desire to communicate the 'real', living presence of the subject to a wide

[58] She started helping Thomas Moore in July 1824. See *MWSL* i. 437. See also ibid., vol. ii, p. xv, *MWSJ*, 108 and Paula R. Feldman, 'Mary Shelley and the Genesis of Moore's *Life* of Byron', *Studies in English Literature 1500–1900*, 20/4 (1980), 611–20.
[59] *The Works of Lord Byron: With his Letters and Journals and his Life, by Thomas Moore Esq.*, 17 vols. [advertised in vol. i as 14 vols.] (London: John Murray, 1832–3). See *MWSL* ii. 159.
[60] Ibid. 101–2.
[61] Ibid. 162–3.
[62] Ibid. 164.
[63] See ibid. 105, 113 for her attempts to take advantage of Murray's interest in biography by proposing to write *Lives* of Madame de Staël and Mahomet for him in 1830. He did not take up her offers.

audience that she had seen in Godwin and Hays, but this time she also found examples of how a biographical approach could enhance a contemporary poet's posthumous reputation and accrue commercial success. The terms in which she praised them are significant, for Moore and Murray demonstrated the power of biography to create an intimate, affective relationship between the poet and his readers, bringing him home as a man. This was what she had, herself, been aiming for with her 'Lives' of Shelley in the 1820s and what she continued to develop in 1839. But Shelley was not Byron. The nature of the public construction of Shelley's genius at the time of his death, shaped his widow's biographical response in distinctive ways.

4.2 MAKING SHELLEY 'BELOVED': THE POET AND HIS READERS

We have seen how Byron was portrayed by the reviews in his lifetime as a poet who had established a uniquely personal bond between himself and his readership only to betray it. Shelley, by contrast, was represented as wilfully denying such a relationship from the outset. The keynote of reviews, whether favourable or not, and whether from the right or the left, was that his was a poetry of obscurity and abstraction, a deliberate flight from the world: 'He deals too much with abstractions and high imaginings—and forgets the world to which he writes, and by whom he must expect to be read'; Shelley has three styles, 'one which can be generally understood; another which can be understood only by the author; and a third which is absolutely and intrinsically unintelligible'; 'the work cannot possibly become popular'.[64] The last comment was from Leigh Hunt, one of Shelley's staunchest defenders, who argued in 1818 that although *The Revolt of Islam* was 'full of humanity . . . it certainly does not go the best way to work of appealing to it, because it does not appeal to it through the medium of its common knowledges'.[65] Hunt took the same position ten years later in his posthumous memoir of the poet, where he defended the humanity of Shelley's vision but admitted that much of the poetry would never gain a wide readership. His consolation was that Shelley would have ' "fit audience though few" . . . and it is these audiences that go and settle the world'.[66]

Mary Shelley's editions and the other nineteenth-century biographies of Shelley were all, in a variety of ways, responses to the sense that he had signally

---

[64] White (ed.), *The Unextinguished Hearth*, 206, 240–1 and 124. The comments come from *The Independent, a London Literary and Political Review* (Feb. 1817); [W. S. Walker], *Quarterly Review* (Oct. 1821); and [Leigh Hunt], *The Examiner* (Feb. 1818).

[65] White (ed.), *The Unextinguished Hearth*, 123.

[66] Hunt, *Lord Byron*, 209, responding angrily to Hazlitt's review of *PPS* in the *Edinburgh Review* (July 1824).

rejected the Byronic appeal to the reader. On the one hand Mary Shelley replicated the image of Shelley projected by the more favourable reviews, as a being abstracted from reality and by that token permitted to transcend the understandings of the public at large. On the other, she echoed some of the concern at his apparent disregard for the reader. The debate was most openly articulated in the preface and notes to her edition of the 1839 *Poetical Works* in her influential division of Shelley's poetry into two classes: the first comprising poems that are 'purely imaginative' and the second 'those which sprung from the emotions of his heart'.[67] Mary Shelley grouped amongst the first, purely imaginative class 'Adonais', 'The Triumph of Life', and, pre-eminently, 'The Witch of Atlas' in which 'he gave the reins to his fancy, and luxuriated in every idea as it rose'—it is 'wildly fanciful, full of brilliant imagery, and discarding human interest and passion'.[68] Such poems, she argued, do not aim to communicate but are wilfully mysterious, showing 'a clinging to the subtler inner spirit, rather than to the outward form—a curious and metaphysical anatomy of human passion and perception. . . . His imagination has been termed too brilliant, his thoughts too subtle. He loved to idealise reality; and this is a taste shared by few'.[69] His acute sensibility led him to retreat from the world of other people into poetry as a means of self-protection: 'he delivered up his soul to poetry, and felt happy when he sheltered himself from the influence of human sympathies, in the wildest regions of fancy'.[70] By contrast, the second class of poetry, springing from the poet's heart, 'speaks to the many'—'to emotions common to us all', especially to love, and is therefore 'the more popular'.[71] She names his greatest achievement as a work of this kind: *The Cenci*, a drama inspired by sympathy with the sufferings of the historical characters whose story he tells and achieving, unlike most of his other poetry, '[u]niversal approbation'. Significantly, it is a success Shelley himself did not wish to repeat: 'the bent of his mind went the other way'.[72]

As Susan Wolfson has argued, there is an ambivalent 'poetics of audience' in the editions.[73] Mary Shelley's Preface to the *Posthumous Poems* shows conflicting representations of Shelley as poet of the people, of a small coterie of friends, and of another element altogether, a bright track in the memory of his friends and his

---

[67] *PWS*, vol. i, p. x. Her division was directly influenced by Hazlitt's review of *PPS* and Hunt's reply. Hazlitt had criticized the idealist tendencies of Shelley's poetry, describing it with tropes of vacuousness and absence, and accused him of having 'no deference for the opinions of others, too little sympathy with their feelings'—see *The Complete Works of William Hazlitt*, ed. P. P. Howe, 21 vols. (London: Dent, 1930–4), xvi, 267. Hunt, *Lord Byron*, 210, divided Shelley's poetry into two classes, one exemplified by the 'The Witch of Atlas', which would appeal to the few, the other, more popular strain represented by the dramatic poems where 'the spiritual part of him is invested with ordinary flesh and blood'. Mary Shelley's division followed exactly the same lines.

[68] *PWS*, vol. i, p. x; and iv. 51.

[69] Ibid., vol. i, pp. x–xii.

[70] Ibid., p. xii.

[71] Ibid., pp. xiii, x.

[72] Ibid. ii. 279–80.

[73] Wolfson, 'Editorial Privilege', 45.

widow. In the 1839 *Poetical Works* she identifies herself at times with the 'few' who will appreciate Shelley's purely imaginative poetry, but assumes that her readers will belong to the 'many' who are alienated by such poetry and, on balance, it is their perspective that she tends to adopt. In her note on Poems of 1820 she recalls Shelley's lack of interest in making his poetry popular as a subject of dispute between herself and her husband: 'The surpassing excellence of the Cenci had made me greatly desire that Shelley should increase his popularity, by adopting subjects that would more suit the popular taste, than a poem conceived in the abstract and dreamy spirit of the Witch of Atlas'.[74] She had remonstrated with him in the belief that 'public applause' would not only have enhanced her husband's fame and poetic powers but also his personal happiness, and that lack of public sympathy 'took away a portion of the ardour that ought to have sustained him while writing'. Shelley would not be swayed, but she affirms that 'Even now I believe that I was in the right'.[75]

The division identified here in Shelley's poetry, and Mary Shelley's ambivalent position in relation to it, were replicated in her approach as his biographer. In part she validated the idea of pure poetry by abstracting and sanctifying the poet. In the letters immediately following Shelley's death she described herself, in terms which echo 'Alastor', as one questing after an immortal being—she feels 'as poets have described those loved by superhuman creatures & then deserted by them— Impatient, despairing—& resting only on the moment when he will return to me'.[76] In the 1823 'Life of Shelley', again, she is 'the chosen mate of a ceslestial spirit' [*sic*] and in the 1824 Preface to *Posthumous Poems*: 'To his friends his loss is irremediable: the wise, the brave, the gentle, is gone for ever! He is to them as a bright vision, whose radiant track, left behind in the memory, is worth all the realities that society can afford'.[77] Again she alludes to Shelley's description of the youthful poet in 'Alastor'—'Gentle, brave, and generous' (l.58)—and, in eulogizing his heroic transcendence over social realities, ignores the poem's critique of his rejection of human love in favour of a solitary quest for the ideal. Shelley's elevation above the concerns of ordinary mortals is here a mark of his eternal life—'his unearthly and elevated nature is a pledge of the continuation of his being'.[78] The Preface to the 1839 *Poetical Works* opens in only slightly more muted terms: 'Whatever faults he had, ought to find extenuation among his fellows, since they proved him to be human; without them, the exalted nature of his soul would have raised him to something divine'.[79] On the other hand, Mary Shelley wanted to make all three of her editions popular and was not satisfied

---

[74] *PWS* iv. 51. She is offering an explanation here of the stanzas prefacing 'The Witch of Atlas' in which Shelley alludes to this dispute.
[75] Ibid. 51–2, 51.
[76] *MWSL* i. 264, to Jane Williams (18 Sept. 1822). See also *MWSJ*, 434 (5 Oct. 1822).
[77] *LL* iv. 226; *PPS*, p. iv.
[78] *PPS*, p. vii.
[79] *PWS*, vol. i, p. viii.

with an ethereal Shelley, far beyond the reach of his public.[80] The Preface to the *Poetical Works* expresses a tension between the desire to withhold Shelley from the audience—'I abstain from any remark on the occurrences of his private life; except inasmuch as the passions which they engendered, inspired his poetry'—and to create a sense of intimate relationship: 'The qualities that struck any one newly introduced to Shelley, were, first, a gentle and cordial goodness that animated his intercourse with warm affection, and helpful sympathy'.[81] In her unpublished 'Life' of 1823, she conceived of her role as Shelley's earthly representative, a priestess whose duty was to make him beloved to others: 'Methinks my calling is high. I am to justify His ways; I am to make him beloved to all prosterity [*sic*]'.[82] Her 1824 Preface put this into practice by displaying him, pre-eminently, as a deserving object for his readers' affections. Shelley, she admits, was in his lifetime 'personally known to few', but her Preface, written by one who knew him better than any other, will remedy the situation.[83] She places him at the centre of a small, loving community of family and friends—her 'only consolation' following his death 'was in the praise and earnest love that each voice bestowed and each countenance demonstrated for him we had lost', '[n]o man was ever more devoted than he, to the endeavour of making those around him happy; no man ever possessed friends more unfeignedly attached to him'.[84] Mary Shelley thus attempts to elicit the sympathies of readers for Shelley and his works, by making them part of his private, domestic community. This community is even more strongly there in 1839, with the presentation of the *Poetical Works* as family memoir, authored by the grieving widow, and 'Affectionate Mother' of his son, to whom the edition is dedicated.[85] Her preface to this edition invites the readers to sympathize with the family's loss, assuring them that 'his place among those who knew him intimately, has never been filled up', he cheered their lives 'with his sympathy and love'.[86]

Mary Shelley's determination to make Shelley 'beloved' shows her awareness of a literary marketplace where readers had begun to conceive of their relationship with writers—especially Byron—as a personal intimacy with a living body. An important part of her effort to rehabilitate Shelley in her editions was therefore the attempt to bring him back as a bodily presence. The theme of reanimation, of course, runs throughout her fiction—most famously in *Franken-stein*, but also in her short stories, 'Valerius. The Reanimated Roman', composed

---

[80] *MWSL* i. 411, to Hunt (9 Feb. [1824]), where she responds to Hunt's suggestion that they delay publication of *PPS* for a year, that she wants to catch the ebbing tide of Shelley's 'celebrity even popularity'. See also ibid. 430 and ii. 326 for evidence that she also wanted *ELS* to be popular.
[81] *PWS*, vol. i, pp. vii–viii.
[82] *LL* iv. 226.
[83] *PPS*, iii.
[84] Ibid., pp. vii, iv.
[85] The dedication reads: 'to Percy Florence Shelley, The Poetical Works of his Illustrious Father are dedicated, by his Affectionate Mother, Mary Wollstonecraft Shelley'. See also title page of *PWS*, vol. i: 'The Poetical Works of Percy Bysshe Shelley. Edited by Mrs. Shelley'.
[86] *PWS*, vol. i, p. xv.

in 1819 and 'Roger Dodsworth: The Reanimated Englishman' (1826). Susan Wolfson has argued that Mary Shelley conceived of her work as Shelley's editor—gathering her materials to restore a fragmented poetic corpus to wholeness, not wishing to 'mutilate' the texts—as analogous to Frankenstein's reanimation of the dead.[87] I would argue that her conception of her editorial work should be seen as part of her understanding of biography as the reconstitution of the physical presence of the dead. As she wrote in a letter, objecting to the brief 'Memoir' of Shelley produced for Cyrus Redding's *Galignani* edition:

I should have written it in a different style. . . . It is a mere outline & is as communicative as a skeleton can be—about as like the <original> truth as the skeleton resembles the 'tower of flesh' of which it is the beams & rafters[88]

The ideal memoir is figured as Shelley's resurrected body. We have seen her delight, on reading Moore's *Letters and Journals*, in feeling that Byron's living presence was restored—'I live with him again in these pages'. This compares with Carlyle's celebration of Boswell's uncanny ability to reanimate the ghosts of the past by retrieving their substance, making a lost '*Reality*' present to the reader in visible and audible form: 'they who are gone are still here; though hidden they are revealed, though dead they yet speak'.[89] Yet Mary Shelley was also conscious of the effects on Byron's reputation of the intensive marketing of images, visual and verbal, of his body.[90] She modelled her practice on Moore's *Life* and Murray's biographical edition of Byron, but at the same time she, like Hunt, was determined to distinguish Shelley—as spirit—from Byron—as flesh.[91] To make Shelley beloved, the public must be made to feel his physical presence, but to bring his body too vividly before them would be to risk comparison with Byron.

Mary Shelley garners her readers' sympathies by continual reference to Shelley's suffering flesh. His physical ailments—ophthalmia, pulmonary abscesses, 'internal irritability'—form a motif of her prefaces and notes.[92] Yet, significantly, although she included an engraved portrait in the 1839 *Poetical Works* (Fig. 4.1), she almost completely avoided portraying Shelley's external appearance—a striking omission in the context of contemporary fashions in literary biography.

---

[87] Wolfson, 'Editorial Privilege', 47–50.

[88] *MWSL* ii. 87.

[89] Review of John Wilson Croker's edition of James Boswell's *Life of Samuel Johnson*, *Fraser's Magazine* (1832), *CME* iii. 78, 80.

[90] It is notable that the material she supplied for Moore's *Letters and Journals* include a detailed description of Byron's appearance, but none of Shelley's—see *LJB* ii. 799.

[91] Both were responding to Medwin, *Conversations and Shelley Papers*, where Shelley's affinities with Byron were accentuated. Hunt, *Lord Byron*, defended Shelley by presenting him as Byron's opposite. Mary Shelley followed this pattern in e.g. *PWS*, i. 375, where she noted that in the summer of 1816 Shelley's 'genius was checked by association with another poet [Byron], whose nature was utterly dissimilar to his own', although Byron had for a while been influenced by Shelley's 'more abstract and etherealised inspiration'.

[92] *PWS*, vol. i, p. xiv. See also 377, 140 and ii. 129–30.

Fig. 4.1. Engraved portrait of Percy Shelley 'From an Original Picture in the Possession of Mrs. Shelley', frontispiece to *The Poetical Works of Percy Bysshe Shelley. Edited by Mrs Shelley*, 4 vols. (London: Edward Moxon, 1839).

The closest we get to a sense of what he looked like is another evocation of his triumph over the suffering body: 'you read his sufferings in his attenuated frame, while you perceived the mastery he held over them in his animated countenance and brilliant eyes'.[93] She assures her readers at one point that '[t]o see him was to love him' but instead of supplying a description, she slides past the visible and into a defensive tropological substitution: 'his presence, like Ithuriel's spear, was alone sufficient to disclose the falsehood of the tale, which his enemies whispered in the ear of the ignorant world'.[94] This metaphorical evocation of Shelley's physical presence is her preferred technique in the *Poetical Works* where the poetry is figured as an extension of the poet's own living body. The Preface opens by announcing her intention of 'detailing the history' of his poems, 'as they sprung, living and warm, from his heart and brain'.[95] Shelley's personal beliefs 'breathe throughout his poetry'. They were 'the features that marked' his favourite works.[96] His interests in natural philosophy and chemistry 'gave truth and vivacity to his descriptions'.[97] She speaks of 'the solemn spirit which breathes throughout' 'Alastor', a poem which 'was the out-pouring of his own emotions, embodied in the purest form he could conceive'.[98] This figurative use of Shelley's body in Mary Shelley's editions distinguishes them from Byron biographies with their vivid passages of biographical portraiture. Arguably, her evasion of direct description of Shelley's physical appearance works against her desire to introduce him to the reader as a man. Nevertheless she strives to create such a relationship—whether by assuring the reader of his capacity for affection, invoking his suffering body, or figuring his poems as flesh. The next section looks at how, in this process, Mary Shelley pitted biography against poetry.

4.3 A CONTEST OF GENRES

Mary Favret has explained Mary Shelley's efforts to garner sympathy for Shelley in her editions, as a self-promoting critique of Shelley's poetry and even of poetry as a genre. In the *Poetical Works* her prose mediates between the reader and Shelley's poetry, encouraging us to sympathize with the poetry, but, in so doing, signalling its 'inadequacy'—its inherent failure to gain the readers' sympathies for itself.[99]

On the one hand, Percy Shelley is rendered more sympathetic—more tangible, more pitiable—through her notes; the poet's work then becomes more accessible. On the other

---

[93] *PWS*, vol. i, p. xiv.
[94] *PPS*, p. iv.
[95] *PWS*, vol. i, p. vii.
[96] Ibid. pp. ix–x.
[97] Ibid. 103.
[98] Ibid. 141–2.
[99] Favret, 'Mary Shelley's Sympathy and Irony', 31.

hand, the implication grows throughout the notes that the editor *needs to* bring the poet and poetry down to earth, *needs to* draw them within the circle of our sympathies, because poet and poetry are innately unsympathetic and inaccessible.[100]

Mary Shelley's edition thus 'becomes a contest between a poetic corpus and a prose body. Which is livelier?'[101] Favret suggests that it is Mary Shelley's 'prose body'—her preface and notes. Because the poet and the poetry, as Mary Shelley represents them, are, respectively, transcendent and 'inaccessible', they are dependent on her offices to establish communication with the reader. This she does, not merely by focusing on the material contexts for the production of Shelley's poetry, but by figuring it as a living body, tied to the history of his physical ailments.[102] The solicitation of the readers' sympathies by such methods is, itself, a critical and self-validating strategy:

> her method successfully alienates the poet and his practice from the reading public while it reinforces her own literary practice. . . . The notes locate 'truth' and 'reality' apart from poetic imagination; they are found instead in human relationship, lived experience, dialogue, and the human body—all of which she detaches from poetry. . . . Elevating the poet above the demands of 'hard reality,' Mary Shelley simultaneously establishes poetry as an exercise in vanity: beautiful but ineffective, spiritualized but out of touch with the world.[103]

There are several problems with Favret's argument. It overrides the ambivalence of Mary Shelley's position in relation to 'purely imaginative' poetry and the fact that she believed that Shelley could make poetry engage with the real and with the sympathies of a wider audience when he wanted to.[104] More seriously, it misreads the nature of the contest of genres inscribed in the editions. Favret suggests that Mary Shelley materializes the immaterial Shelley in the *Poetical Works* in a way that is typical of nineteenth-century women writers' response to Romantic ideological privileging of the figural and the transcendent over the literal and the immanent. Mary Shelley's avoidance of literal description of Shelley's body creates problems for this line of argument, but there is also the further question of how Favret understands the prefaces and notes to the *Poetical Works* in generic terms. Conventionally enough she chooses to read them as fiction.[105] Mary Shelley's edition, she argues, promotes fiction at the expense of

---

[100] Ibid. 19.
[101] Ibid. 22.
[102] Ibid. 23.
[103] Ibid. 27.
[104] See *PWS*, vol. i, p. xv, where Mary Shelley claims that his poetry has already effected social change: 'his influence over mankind, though slow in growth, is fast augmenting, and in the ameliorations that have taken place in the political state of his country, we may trace in part the operation of his arduous struggles'.
[105] See e.g. Favret, 'Mary Shelley's Sympathy and Irony', 18, *PWS* is the product 'of an experienced writer of fiction'. At times Favret acknowledges the generic indeterminacy of the prefaces and notes—she veers between calling the notes simply 'prose' (19), 'prose fiction' (18), 'the various modes of prose fiction' (19), 'biography' (27), and (referring to the note to Poems of

poetry: '[i]t is a novelist's reality to which she draws her readers'.[106] In this
reading, Mary Shelley's edition suggests that it is the woman novelist and not the
Romantic poet who has 'an immediate social and ideological influence', and it is
in these terms that the *Poetical Works* 'sets in motion a profound reevaluation of
gender and genre' which 'models the definition of genres for the rest of the
nineteenth century'.[107]

Of course fictional techniques come into play in the notes to the *Poetical
Works*, but, for all the reasons so far discussed, her editions must be seen in the
context of her biographical rather than her fictional work. Her difficulties with
these notes are precisely because they are auto/biographical and not fictional:

> My task becomes inexpressibly painful as the year draws near that which sealed our
> earthly fate. . . . I feel that I am incapable of putting on paper the history of those times.
> The heart of the man, abhorred of the poet,
>
> > Who could peep and botanize upon his mother's grave,
>
> does not appear to me less inexplicably framed than that of one who can dissect and probe
> past woes, and repeat to the public ear the groans drawn from them in the throes of their
> agony.[108]

Already in the manuscript 'Life' of 1823 we find Mary Shelley defining her role
as a biographer in competition with Shelley's as a poet:

> By his works he has raised himself to that well deserved height that must make him the
> wonder & glory of future ages. But his private life would remain unknown & many of his
> most excellent qualities sleep with his beloved ashes if I did not fulfil the task of recording
> them.[109]

Shelley's works have elevated him to glory, but they have not communicated his
private life to the world. As his widow biographer, guardian of his 'beloved
ashes', Mary Shelley implies that she has a power that, as a poet, he does not. This
perception, complicated by collaborative and self-effacing strategies, survives into
her editions where poetry is dependent on the offices of the biographer.[110] It is
no coincidence that the work she praises as Shelley's greatest achievement in

---

1822), 'a progressively explicit performance of fiction writing' demonstrating 'the various
techniques of editor, biographer, novelist . . . and poet' (32), but she is clear that fiction is the
dominant genre.

[106] Favret, 'Mary Shelley's Sympathy and Irony', 27.
[107] Ibid. 19.
[108] *PWS* iv. 149.
[109] *LL* iv. 225–6.
[110] Mary Poovey, *The Proper Lady and the Woman Writer: Ideology as Style in the Works of Mary
Wollstonecraft, Mary Shelley, and Jane Austen* (Chicago: University of Chicago Press, 1984), 143–71,
reads her career as shaped by the conflict between Romantic ambition and feminine self-effacement.
Clearly, the difficulties of memoir for her, as Shelley's widow, accentuate these tensions. This is
particularly obvious in the 1823 'Life'. Wolfson, 'Editorial Privilege', 49, draws attention to 'the
considerable authority, at times co-creation, that her editing involved'. This relationship of 'co-
creation' is presented by Wolfson as conciliatory rather than competitive.

popular poetry is *The Cenci*. She reveals that Shelley had initially proposed that she take on the subject and that it was, in effect, a semi-collaborative project. It is also a poem that mirrors her own work as his biographer. Just as she is trying to bring him to life as a sympathetic presence in her edition, so his drama was inspired by sympathy for the dead and the desire to resurrect 'passions, so long cold in the tomb'.[111]

In her Preface to *Essays, Letters from Abroad*, she presents the selected prose writings of the poet as having been remade by her into biography. The contest between biography and poetry is clear:

These volumes have long been due to the public; they form an important portion of all that was left by Shelley, whence those who did not know him may form a juster estimate of his virtues and his genius than has hitherto been done.

We find, in the verse of a poet, 'the record of the best and happiest moments of the best and happiest minds.' [*A Defence of Poetry*] But this is not enough—we desire to know the man.[112]

Mary Shelley rejects a universalized, poetic language as falsely ameliorating. It is not enough to find generalized poetic emotions—readers will want to know the man, with the intimacy that only biography can establish. In a passage that shows, again, her affinities with Carlyle, she writes:

We desire to learn how much of the sensibility and imagination that animates his poetry was founded on heartfelt passion, and purity, and elevation of character; whether the pathos and the fire emanated from transitory inspiration and a power of weaving words touchingly; or whether the poet acknowledged the might of his art in his inmost soul; and whether his nerves thrilled to the touch of generous emotion. Led by such curiosity, how many volumes have been filled with the life of the Scottish plough-boy and the English peer; we welcome with delight every fact which proves that the patriotism and tenderness expressed in the songs of Burns, sprung from a noble and gentle heart; and we pore over each letter that we expect will testify that the melancholy and the unbridled passion that darkens Byron's verse, flowed from a soul devoured by a keen susceptibility to intensest love, and indignant broodings over the injuries done and suffered by man. Let the lovers of Shelley's poetry—of his aspirations for a brotherhood of love, his tender bewailings springing from a too sensitive spirit—his sympathy with woe, his adoration of beauty, as expressed in his poetry, turn to these pages to gather proof of sincerity, and to become acquainted with the form that such gentle sympathies and lofty aspirations wore in private life.[113]

Here Mary Shelley allies her edition of Shelley's prose with popular *Lives* of Burns and Byron and represents the biographical as necessary to the poetic by virtue of its fundamental difference to it. The difference is seen in terms both of the popular appeal of biography and of the nature of the reality which the biographer has as her object. Her description of the power of Burns and Byron biographies purifies the two most scandalous literary lives of the age, but she also

---

[111] *PWS* ii. 274.   [112] *ELS*, vol. i, p. v.   [113] Ibid., pp. v–vi.

identifies her own tastes with the desire, the 'curiosity', the 'delight' of the reading public who 'pore' over documents searching for intimate revelations. Only by means of biography's capacity to trace the poetic emotion to the man, will the reader be assured that the affections which are apparently present in the poetry are actually so. Only biographies of Burns, Byron, and now Shelley can offer true testimony to the public that their poetry is not mere 'transitory inspiration and a power of weaving words touchingly'. Poetry is dependent on biography to generate this popularity on its behalf because biography offers the reader a distinct kind of reality. Where the poet deals in imagination, the biographer deals in empirical evidence—'proof'.

She comments in 1839, after describing Shelley's visits to the cottages of the poor in Marlow and his consequent attack of opthalmia, that 'this minute and active sympathy with his fellow-creatures gives a thousand-fold interest to his speculations, and stamps with reality his pleadings for the human race'.[114] Biography gives the stamp of reality to poetry. It is a figure to which she recurs to describe what is, for her, the peculiarly literal sense in which writing Shelley's life is a life-giving activity: 'I have . . . the liveliest recollection of all that was done and said during the period of my knowing him. Every impression is as clear as if stamped yesterday'.[115] The specifically counter-imaginative realism of biography was distinct in her mind from fiction. As she told Edward Moxon, whilst composing her *Cyclopaedia Lives*, she thought she was much better at this kind of writing than at 'romancing'.[116] Her emphasis on the unique capacity of biography to communicate the 'real' man finds its nearest parallel in Carlyle's celebrations of Boswell's *Life of Johnson* in 1832: 'Strange power of *Reality*! . . . Do but consider that it is *true*, that it did in very deed occur!'[117]

In Mary Shelley's editions, it is biographical prose, not fictional, which defines itself against the poetic by competitively mediating the poet to his public. The distinction is important partly because it challenges the dominance of prose fiction as the focus of Mary Shelley studies, but more so because, if, as Mary Favret argues, the *Poetical Works* set 'in motion a profound reevaluation of gender and genre' which modelled 'the definition of genres for the rest of the nineteenth century', we should recognize the role of biography in bringing this about.[118]

---

[114] *PWS* i. 377.

[115] Ibid., p. xvi.

[116] Quoted in Miranda Seymour, *Mary Shelley* (London: John Murray, 2000), 434.

[117] *CME* iii. 56. Mary Shelley knew and corresponded with Carlyle. She took her motto for *ELS* from his *Wilhelm Meister*. It expresses the importance of knowing the true history of the 'inner man'. See *MSWL* ii. 329 n.

[118] Favret, 'Mary Shelley's Sympathy and Irony', 19.

4.4 THE LARDNER *LIVES*

Mary Shelley's biographical practice domesticated genius in the sense of working to establish an intimate, affective relationship between the poet and the public. In this respect she might be compared to Moore and other biographers of Byron, but in her case this was shaped by a sophisticated awareness of the gendering of private and public life and an ideological commitment to the domestic affections as the foundation of genius. This was, of course, also a central concern of her fiction, which has been read as producing a feminine critique of masculine Romanticism—a critique in which her vision of domestic life played a central part.[119] Critics have explored the complexity of her understanding of the domestic as it is played out in her fictional texts and have latterly focused on her doubts there about the efficacy of the domestic affections in producing a new, feminized world order.[120] Her emotional investment in a feminine ideal of domestic life is ironized by the tragic vision of her fictional work and her increasing disillusion with the redemptive power of the family. But domesticity, gender, and genius are also central issues within her biographical writing. Her encyclopaedia *Lives* of Madame Roland, Madame de Staël, and Rousseau, all of which appeared in the second volume of the *Eminent Literary and Scientific Men of France* (1839), in Lardner's *Cyclopaedia*, show this most clearly. They describe the ways that male and female writers have responded to the conflicts between private and public life and suggest that, regardless of gender, the writer must strive to find a healthy relationship between the two. In this respect, as in others, the *Cyclopaedia* essays provide an important context for reading her 'Lives' of Shelley.

Madame Roland and Madame de Staël are represented by Mary Shelley as great women who managed the balancing of private and public life with differing degrees of success. We have seen how the anti-Jacobin biographer Stewarton had used Madame Roland as an example of 'how easily a domestic rebel is transformed into a political conspirator', but for Mary Shelley, as for Mary Hays before her, her heroism is defined by her ability to extend her domestic affections into the public sphere as, not merely a professional writer, but a

---

[119] Ann Mellor, in *Mary Shelley: Her Life, her Fiction, her Monsters* (London: Methuen, 1988), argued that her fiction was informed by an ethic of care and equality, grounded in the trope of 'a mutually supportive, gender free family' (44). For Mellor, domestic ideology within these texts thus constituted a challenge to 'the dominant romantic and patriarchal ideologies of her day' (p. xii).

[120] See e.g. Kate Ferguson Ellis, 'Subversive Surfaces: The Limits of Domestic Affection in Mary Shelley's Later Fiction', in Fisch et al. (eds.), *The Other Mary Shelley*, 220–34. Ellis interprets *Frankenstein* as an indictment of the kind of domestic affection which is confined to the socially isolated domestic unit. Smith, *Mary Shelley*, 92–118, agrees with Ellis that the Frankenstein family is less than ideal, partly because of 'the constraining effects of domestic affection' (41). The family, in fact, produces Victor's rejection of the domestic affections in favour of masculine ambition.

political activist.[121] Her 'enthusiasm' and usefulness as a wife becomes 'enthusiasm' and 'usefulness on a grand scale' to her country.[122] Her maternal nurturing
as demonstrated, privately, in her loving care for her daughter and then for her
fellow prisoners expands to include parenting the freedom of the nation as a
whole. De Staël's life is similarly framed as a negotiation between family life and
public ambition, but she is less successful than Madame Roland in marrying the
two. Exposed by her mother to the public eye from an early age: 'this extraordinary woman imbibed, as it were with her mother's milk, a taste for society and
display'.[123] Her taste for display eventually produces a self-indulgent, 'Byronic'
melancholy in her novels, rather than what the reader needs, the lesson of 'moral
courage'.[124] Her interventions in politics are equally imperfect—marred by an
instinct towards self-aggrandizement. Yet Mary Shelley makes the point that the
'instant interchange with others' gained in salon society was the lifeblood of her
genius and the means by which she was able to achieve her full potential.[125] She
also, wistfully, contrasts de Staël's situation with the typically alienated relationship between the contemporary writer and his or her readers in England—'How
seldom, how very seldom, does an English author hear one word of real
sympathy or admiration!'[126] In Mary Shelley's ideal domestic paradigm of the
author/reader relationship, the sympathy of her public sends de Staël back to her
own family: 'The praises she received developed also the feelings of her heart. She
passionately loved her parents and her friends'.[127] It is a model of openness to
public sympathy which the 'life and times' method of Mary Shelley's *Lives* itself
attempts by making constant connections between the private and the public, the
subject's personal life and her genius whether displayed in the literary or political
world at large.

De Staël falters when she follows a masculine poetic (Byronic) model of genius
and the Lardner *Lives* show Mary Shelley making an outright attack on masculine, heroic creativity as self-indulgent and socially divisive. Her principal target
here is Rousseau, who is presented as a case study in the malign social consequences of self-absorbed genius. Rousseau and Voltaire (another of her subjects)
were contrasting characters, she argues in her opening paragraph, but they shared
one quality in common:

---

[121] [G. L. Stewarton], *The Female Revolutionary Plutarch*, 3 vols. (London: John Murray, 1806),
iii. 394. See also Mary Hays, 'Madame Roland', in *Female Biography; or Memoirs of Illustrious and
Celebrated Women, of all Ages and Countries, Alphabetically Arranged*, 6 vols. (London: Richard
Phillips, 1803), vi. 103–311.
[122] *LL* iii. 438, 443.
[123] Ibid. 459.
[124] Ibid. 480, 493.
[125] Ibid. 459.
[126] Ibid. 463.
[127] Ibid. 459.

It is difficult to know what to call it. In ordinary men it would be named egotism, or vanity. It is that lively and intimate apprehension of their own individuality, sensations, and being, which appears to be one of the elements of that order of minds which feel impelled to express their thoughts and disseminate their views and opinions through the medium of writing;—men of imagination, and eloquence, and mental energy. This quality is good as long as it renders an author diligent, earnest, and sincere; it is evil when it deprives him of the power of justly appreciating his powers and position, and causes him to fancy himself the centre, as it were, of the universe. Rousseau was its victim; it was exaggerated till his mind became diseased; and one false idea becoming fixed and absorbing, a sort of madness ensued.[128]

Mary Shelley was not alone, of course, in attributing self-absorption, solipsism, and eventual monomania to Rousseau. The charge of self-indulgence had long been made in Britain against the author of the *Confessions*. Burke and other anti-Jacobin commentators linked his confessional mode with his republican politics and represented his autobiographical 'vanity' as a root-cause of the French Revolution.[129] But her reading of Rousseau's life is distinguished from Burke's and others' by identifying egotism as an issue relating primarily to the relationship between domestic and public life.

She presents Rousseau as the product of an oppressive patriarchal family. The consequence of this early injustice was that he became a self-deluded dreamer who could not create successful relationships in adult life. After his failure with Madame de Warens, he formed a catastrophic liaison with a mistress, who, although faithful to him, was 'ignorant', 'illiterate', and 'wanting in common understanding'.[130] Because in France it was considered a disgrace for a mistress to bear children, he sent his five infants, one after another, to a foundling hospital. The unsuitable match with Thérèse and, even more, the disastrous abrogation of duty to his children are, for Mary Shelley, unforgivable errors. She returns to the theme of Rousseau's abandonment of his children obsessively in the rest of the essay. About halfway through she signals her intention to bring the matter to a close—'We now dismiss this subject.... it is too painful to dwell further upon'—but a few sentences further on has recurred to it and continues to create crescendos of outrage on the subject throughout the remainder of the article.[131] The basis of her indignation is Rousseau's cruelty in leaving his children to suffer neglect or even death, but worst of all, in placing them in the 'public care' of a Parisian foundling hospital, thereby ensuring that they feel 'the burden, ever weighing at the heart, that they have not inherited the commonest

[128] Ibid. 320.
[129] See Julian North, 'Autobiography as Self-Indulgence: De Quincey and his Reviewers', in Vincent Newey and Philip Shaw (eds.), *Mortal Pages, Literary Lives: Studies in Nineteenth-Century Autobiography* (Aldershot: Scolar Press, 1996), 63.
[130] *LL* iii. 334.
[131] Ibid. 335. See James O'Rourke, ' "Nothing more unnatural": Mary Shelley's Revision of Rousseau', *English Literary History*, 56/3 (Fall 1989), 546.

right of humanity, a parent's care'. As she argues later, '[o]ur first duty is to render those to whom we give birth, wise, virtuous, and happy, as far as in us lies. Rousseau failed in this.'[132]

James O'Rourke rightly pointed to this portrayal of Rousseau as suggesting that he was an important model for the character of Victor Frankenstein, who also, of course, abandons his offspring to the variable mercies of public care.[133] As in the novel, so in her 'Life' of Rousseau Mary Shelley links this abrogation of parental responsibility with a particular brand of genius. At first she expresses surprise that his genius did not prevent him from acting in this way, but it soon becomes apparent that it was precisely what led him to do so. His neglect of parental care is consistent with his eventual monomania and suicide—both the extreme products of the independence of spirit upon which his genius is founded. He is 'short-sighted'—unable to empathize with others, including even his own children.[134] The essay concludes with a passionate indictment of the domestic consequences of this independent genius which sets a self-absorbed life of the imagination before social duty:

Rousseau had passed his existence in romantic reveries. This abstraction of mind always engenders an indolence that concentrates the mind in self, and hates to be intruded upon by outward circumstances. Pride and indolence conjoined, created the independence of spirit for which he took praise to himself. Independence is of two sorts. When we sacrifice our pleasures and our tastes to preserve the dear privilege of not deferring our principles and feelings to others, we foster an exalted virtue; but the independence that finds duty an unwelcome clog—that regards the first claims of our fellow-creatures as injurious and intolerable, and that casts off the affections as troublesome shackles—is one of the greatest errors that the human heart can nourish; and such was the independence to which Rousseau aspired when he neglected the first duty of man by abandoning his children.[135]

The passage does not make a necessary link between Rousseau's sex and the gender of his genius but, in one angry outburst, she links masculine ambition with an innate absence of domestic affection in men—Rousseau's behaviour 'shows . . . that a father is not to be trusted for natural instincts towards his offspring; for the mother wept'.[136] The abrogation of domestic responsibility extends, with disastrous consequences, to the public sphere, as we see from her musings on what might have happened if Rousseau had not sent his children to the foundling home:

Brought up in virtue and honour, as a man of his talents ought to have brought up his offspring,—or genius were a vainer gift even than it is,—these children might have clustered round him in his days of desolation, have cheered his house with smiles, and been a help and support in his age. He would not have felt friendless, nor been driven to

---

132   *LL* iii. 335, 334, 335.
133   O'Rourke, '"Nothing more unnatural"'.
134   *LL* iii. 335.
135   Ibid. 365.
136   Ibid. 334.

suicide by the sense of abandonment and treachery. He indeed sowed the wind, and reaped the whirlwind. France was on the eve of a sanguinary revolution. The social state of things was about wholly to change. Who knows of what use Rousseau's sons might have been to check barbarous outrages, to teach justice, or display fortitude?[137]

The domestic affections are not only the means to sustain the personal happiness of genius, they are, for good or ill, the basis of the happiness of society at large.[138] Had his sons been nurtured in a loving family home the whole course of the French Revolution might have been changed. They would not only have returned their parents' affection, but have extended it in lives as peacemakers on the public stage. Mary Shelley thereby sidesteps the topic which interests Burke and other commentators, of the importance of Rousseau's *writings* in instigating the French Revolution, and nominates as his most significant contribution in determining the course of history his failure to be a good father to his boys. As her comment on the vanity of genius suggests, literary achievement pales before the importance of domestic relationships—her own province as the biographer who has rejected 'romancing' in favour of 'truth'.

Mary Shelley's 'Life' of Rousseau provides an interesting gloss on *Frankenstein*, but, read alongside her essays on Madame Roland and Madame de Staël, it is also an important context for her edition of Shelley's *Poetical Works*, which she was preparing at the same period as her *Cyclopaedia* articles. The Lardner *Lives* may be read as her most fully articulated biographical critique of genius abstracted from domestic responsibility and, by extension, holding itself aloof from the needs of the reader, but in her fragmented attempts to narrate the life of her husband, from the early 1820s onwards, this critique was also surfacing, more gradually and more problematically.

4.5 SHELLEY'S DOMESTIC AFFECTIONS

In her earliest 'Life' of 1823, there was as yet no sign of a disjuncture between Shelley's genius and his capacity for domestic affections—indeed, these were represented as the basis of his unique powers. In telling the story of his adolescence and schooldays, Mary Shelley dwelt on his alienation from his father and his recourse to alternative communities of domestic nurturing—a surrogate family of servants and friends, with Dr Lind as his benevolent father figure.[139] Only inspired by Lind and with the help of the servants could he continue his

---

[137] Ibid. 335.

[138] See ibid. 337: 'Let us advance civilisation to its highest pitch, or retrograde to its origin,—and let both bring freedom from political and social slavery; but in all let us hold fast by the affections: the cultivation of these ought to be the scope of every teacher of morality, every well-wisher to the improvement of the human race'.

[139] See *LL* iv. 220, where she reports Shelley as saying: '"I owe that man far—oh! far more than I owe my father—he loved me & I shall never forget our long talks where he breathed the spirit of the kindest tolerance & the purest wisdom."'

pursuit of his 'self sought studies' of the occult sciences, Chemistry and Natural Philosophy.[140] At school, he was alienated once more by a patriarchal community. Mary Shelley included a diatribe against schoolmasters for their failure to nurture: 'Affection does not enter in the head master[']s code of laws'. They govern by law, fear, and 'the rod' rather than by reason, affection, and 'gentle remonstrance'. The schoolmaster's proper role should have been maternal: 'his heart & soul . . . engaged in forming perfect human beings from the little embryo's [*sic*] placed under his care'.[141] But Shelley was not treated in this way and as a result defied school discipline to continue his own studies, escaping from his tutor's house at midnight to stand over a stream, drink from a skull, and chant spells to raise a ghost. As at his father's house, the basis of his resistance to the oppressive patriarchy of school was in his capacity to create alternative relationships by which his 'passionate' nature was sustained—'he formed several sincere friendships . . . he was adored by his equals'.[142] His refusal to obey, at Eton and in future life, was not a destructive insistence on autonomy:

The bad man follows his own will governed by none—the good person whose mind is yet deeply imbued by independance [*sic*] is to be led, even as an infant to the mother's breast—by affection & reason. And S—— from the sensibility of his nature, & the forwardness of his understanding was peculiarly susceptible of both these modes of government.[143]

Here Mary Shelley postulated an independence of mind which, unlike Rousseau's in her later essay, was childlike in its dependency on feminine affection and reason. Her husband's genius was '[t]amed by affection but unconquered by blows'.[144] The masculine independence of his genius was governable within a family, presided over by maternal love. Where Moore in 1830, despite opening up Byron's domestic interior, argued that masculine genius needs to reject the domestic world, Mary Shelley in 1823 showed the reverse to be true. She represented Shelley's alienation from patriarchal communities, at home and at school, as the very stamp of his genius. She was clearly anxious to defend her husband from the imputation of lawlessness, but she also defended his reputation as 'the future opponant [*sic*] of superstition & tyranny'.[145] He rightly refused to submit to 'that law of a public school denominated *fagging*'—a law which Mary Shelley represented as encouraging tyranny in the older boys and slavishness in the younger. He 'would never obey—and this incapacity of his part was the cause of whatever persecutions might attend him both at school & in his future life'.[146]

---

[140] *LL* iv. 221.
[141] Ibid. 224.
[142] Ibid. 220.
[143] Ibid. 223.
[144] Ibid. 224.
[145] Ibid. 222.
[146] Ibid. 223.

This was not a 'declawed' or 'de-politicized' Shelley, but a feminized vision of radical resistance.

In the 1824 Preface to his *Posthumous Poems* a disparity between Shelley's poetic world, as she represented it, and her concerns as a biographer started to emerge. We see her beginning to dwell on his preference for solitude. She summarizes his life as 'spent in the contemplation of nature, in arduous study, or in acts of kindness and affection', but her narrative shows much more of his solitary contemplation of nature and private study than of his philanthropic social interactions.[147] His family background and schooldays are absent in this account, and his affective life is shown, rather, as the product of a Wordsworthian fostering in nature: 'the varied phoenomena [*sic*] of heaven and earth filled him with deep emotion. . . . In the wild but beautiful Bay of Spezzia [*sic*], the winds and waves which he loved became his playmates'.[148] His poetry is the product of solitude: 'At night, when the unclouded moon shone on the calm sea, he often went alone in his little shallop to the rocky caves that bordered it, and sitting beneath their shelter wrote the "Triumph of Life"'.[149] Such images subscribe to a lyrical vision of heroic creativity, but she also notes, in a voice of wifely anxiety, that this behaviour was damaging to his health and spirits.[150] In describing their 'lonely' life on the shores of the Bay of Spezia, she reiterates his enjoyment of solitude, but again, and this time more pointedly, does not include herself in the emotion:

the refined pleasure which he felt in the companionship of a few selected friends, our entire sequestration from the rest of the world, all contributed to render this period of his life one of continued enjoyment. I am convinced that the two months we passed there were the happiest he had ever known: his health even rapidly improved, and he was never better than when I last saw him, full of spirits and joy, embark for Leghorn. . . . I was to have accompanied him, but illness confined me to my room, and thus put the seal on my misfortune.[151]

The connection between solitude and ill health is also present here, but this time it is Mary who suffers. Her husband's expedition is in the company of one of their 'few selected friends', John Williams, to help another, Leigh Hunt, while Mary waits at home with Jane Williams:

We waited for them in vain; the sea by its restless moaning seemed to desire to inform us of what we would not learn:—but a veil may well be drawn over such misery. The real

---

[147] *PPS*, p. iv.
[148] Ibid., p. v.
[149] Ibid., p. vi.
[150] See ibid., p. v: 'Ill health and continual pain preyed upon his powers, and the solitude in which we lived, particularly on our first arrival in Italy, although congenial to his feelings, must frequently have weighed upon his spirits'.
[151] Ibid., p. vi.

anguish of these moments transcended all the fictions that the most glowing imagination ever pourtrayed: our seclusion, the savage nature of the inhabitants of the surrounding villages, and our immediate vicinity to the troubled sea, combined to embue with strange horror our days of uncertainty. The truth was at last known,—a truth that made our loved and lovely Italy appear a tomb, its sky a pall.[152]

The lyrical surface of the narrative is momentarily disrupted by being figured as a veil behind which her distress, here inexpressible, is concealed. The Platonic veil is, of course, one of Shelley's own favourite metaphors for the appearances of the world, behind which lies a reality only dimly apprehended by the poetic imagination, but Mary Shelley rewrites it as a veil of mourning, concealing a 'real anguish' beyond the powers of even 'the most glowing imagination' to re-create.

In 1824, her account of their secluded life together in Italy hinted at the ease with which the poet's choice of a select society of friends might phase into a self-destructive preference for solitude and suggested a link between social isolation and the destruction of domestic happiness. By 1839, in *The Poetical Works*, the tensions between the domesticating voice of the biographer and an intransigent subject had become more noticeable. In her discussion there of the division between his purely imaginative and popular poetry, the conflicts that lurked in the Preface to *Posthumous Poems* between the representation of the poet as social and as solitary came out into the open. Now Mary Shelley conceded Shelley's preference for poetry as a retreat into self rather than as an engagement with others and made it central to her narrative of his life. The 1839 Preface and notes began to suggest affinities between Shelley and the Rousseau who 'passed his existence in romantic reveries'—an 'abstraction of mind' which had unhappy consequences for his women, his children, and, eventually for the world at large.

As we have seen, the title page of the four-volume *Poetical Works* presented the edition, from the outset, as a family concern and Mary Shelley's own role as editor was, at once, respectfully and sympathetically domestic—the reverential widow of the 'illustrious' poet and loving mother to his son. In her note on Poems of 1818 she reproaches herself for her failure in wifely sympathy at a time of need in Shelley's life. If there was a failure here, the loving adulation of the Preface and notes implicitly supply the deficiency and, in so doing, also construct her relationship to Shelley as one of deferential, wifely service. In the *Poetical Works* she represents her notes to Shelley's poems as the office of the wife who bows to her husband's genius.[153] Yet the role of widow vied with a less deferential domestic persona. By 1839, when Mary Shelley was 42, she adopted the position of the mother who was, at once, indulgent to and wiser than the poet who died at the age of 29. The representation of Shelley as immature was one of her major strategies in mediating his controversial views to her audience, and was often repeated by other biographers of Shelley. It was one, influential, manifestation of

---

[152] *PPS*, pp. vi–vii.   [153] See *PWS* iii. 162; vol. i, p. xvi.

the more widespread Victorian construction of the Romantic poet and the Romantic age as perpetually youthful: a way of reconciling readers to controversial political, social, sexual, and religious views by consigning them to the past. The Preface prepares the reader to bear in mind Shelley's youthfulness as an excuse for the excesses of his poetry:

A wise friend once wrote to Shelley, 'You are still very young, and in certain essential respects you do not yet sufficiently perceive that you are so.' It is seldom that the young know what youth is till they have got beyond its period; and time was not given him to attain this knowledge. It must be remembered that there is the stamp of such inexperience on all he wrote; he had not completed his nine and twentieth year when he died. The calm of middle life did not add the seal of the virtues which adorn maturity to those generated by the vehement spirit of youth.[154]

Her readers, looking back from the age of reform, are asked to indulge the poet as they would a child, but also, implicitly, to acknowledge the superior wisdom of his middle-aged editor and biographer whose self-reproachful voice as his widow is here transformed into a lofty authority beyond that of the poet himself. In her note to his most controversial poem, *Queen Mab*, she takes his immaturity as the main basis of her defence of his 'peculiar views'.[155] She is the powerful mother, in touch with the contemporary audience, he the disempowered child, who needs to be introduced and explained. From an adopted position of maternal wisdom and experience she, albeit indulgently, distances herself from the dreamy abstractions of pure poetry:

The luxury of imagination, which sought nothing beyond itself, as a child burthens itself with spring flowers, thinking of no use beyond the enjoyment of gathering them, often showed itself in his verses: they will be only appreciated by minds who have resemblance to his own; and the mystic subtlety of many of his thoughts will meet the same fate.[156]

The poet, childlike, is attracted to an ephemeral beauty. The flowers are uprooted and not destined, unless by his mother, to be placed in water. She, not he, will anthologize his poems and give them life.

In 1839, as in 1823 and 1824, Mary Shelley strove to portray a man who, like Madame Roland, reconciled private and public life, domestic affections and love of mankind. But the strains in her argument begin to tell in the *Poetical Works* and, as the notes proceed, Shelley becomes more akin to her portrayal of Rousseau. The strains are particularly visible in her descriptions of Shelley's domestic arrangements. In the note to 'The Revolt of Islam', she tells us that '[a]s a poet, his intellect and compositions were powerfully influenced by exterior circumstances,

---

[154] *PWS*, vol. i, pp. xiii–xiv.
[155] Ibid. 100. See ibid. 97, the poem embodies 'the speculations of his boyish days'. She laments that in our society 'no false step is so irretrievable as one made in early youth' (99). Shelley himself decided he was too young to publish it at the time it was written (96).
[156] *PWS*, vol. i, pp. xii–xiii.

and especially by his place of abode'.[157] The progress of the poetry is marked by a series of moves between houses—we are informed, for instance, that 'Alastor' was composed while he was living in a house at Bishopgate Heath, on the borders of Windsor Forest, the 'Hymn to Intellectual Beauty' while they were living on the shores of Lake Geneva, 'The Revolt of Islam' in Marlow, Buckinghamshire, and 'Prometheus Unbound' while at I Capuccini, a villa lent to them by Byron.[158] Shelley flits from address to address and, through this catalogue of houses, she focuses increasingly critically on the male poet's relationship to domestic life.

He is not shown writing at home in the first few notes, but eager to escape out of doors to compose in the woods, and on the rivers, lakes, seas which abut his residences and for which they are chosen. In the 1824 Preface Mary Shelley had noted that in England he 'made his study and reading-room of the shadowed copse, the stream, the lake and the waterfall' and in Italy 'he made his home under the Pisan hills, their roofless recesses harboured him as he composed "The Witch of Atlas," "Adonais" and "Hellas"'.[159] In 1839 his creativity as a poet is also associated with his eagerness to escape the family home—to make his house of nature. 'In 1816 he again visited Switzerland, and rented a house on the banks of the lake of Geneva; and many a day, in cloud or sunshine, was passed alone in his boat. . . . The majestic aspect of nature ministered such thoughts as he afterwards enwove in verse'.[160] His family life indoors, including Mary Shelley's own cohabitation with him, is typically shadowy in these notes. Her former self and their children are marginal, although significant, presences in all her accounts of Shelley. Their marginality is partly Mary Shelley's modest effacement of delicate private matters, but it also suggests the way in which Shelley's life as a poet is beyond the reach of ordinary domestic affections.

His love of solitude takes on a darker significance in 1839 than it had done in 1824:

We lived in utter solitude—and such is not the nurse of cheerfulness. . . . the society of the enlightened, the witty, and the wise, enables us to forget ourselves by making us the sharers of the thoughts of others.[161]

Even within the family home Shelley seeks out solitary spaces—studies removed as far as possible from his wife and children. At I Capuccini he chooses to work in a summer house at the end of the garden.[162] At the Villa Valsovano he spends his time writing in a glazed terrace at the top of the house—an 'airy cell' which

looked out on a wide prospect of fertile country, and commanded a view of the near sea. The storms that sometimes varied our day showed themselves most picturesquely as they were

---

[157] *PWS* i. 375.
[158] Ibid. 140–1 and 375–6. Ibid. iii. 160.
[159] *PPS*, p. v.
[160] *PWS* i. 375.
[161] Ibid. iii. 162–3.
[162] Ibid. 160.

driven across the ocean; sometimes the dark lurid clouds dipped towards the waves, and became water-spouts, that churned up the waters beneath. . . . At other times the dazzling sunlight and heat made it almost intolerable to every other; but Shelley basked in both . . .[163]

The poet luxuriates in an element of his own, surveying the natural landscape from on high, away from all social contact. Mary Shelley's descriptions of I Capuccini and the Villa Valsovano are both juxtaposed with accounts of the deaths of their children, William and Clara, whilst living there. She relates these deaths tersely and, startlingly, as incidental to the main thread of her narrative—which is to describe the environment within which Shelley's poetry was composed. The grief of the father, vividly evoked elsewhere in the notes, is all but suppressed at this point, as is her own, and displaced by descriptions of the view from Shelley's study.[164] The reality of family life—and death—is occluded in pure poetry and Mary Shelley here collaborates in this suppression.[165] She almost writes the children out of her domestic life with Shelley, but not quite. Their almost absence produces a disquieting irony, much sadder and more complex than the angry accusations levelled at Rousseau for his parental neglect. But as the notes proceed the irony deepens. The crisis point is reached in the final note, on poems of 1822 and Shelley's death scene.

Shelley's premature and dramatic death abroad was, of course, an important factor in shaping his reputation and the narrative trajectories of his biographies.[166] Hunt's memoir of 1828 concluded with his own and Trelawny's vivid narratives of the death at sea and of the funeral pyre and Medwin's *Shelley Papers* (1833) culminated in a powerful description of his solitary journey to Casa Magni in the aftermath of the drowning. Mary Shelley's *Posthumous Poems* framed her prefatory memoir as a memorial to the dead and this was still the tone of the 1839 editions. The Preface and notes to the *Poetical Works* moved inexorably towards the drowning, as the defining event of his life, predicted and even willed through his actions and his poetry.[167] Subsequent biographies echoed this pattern and forecast his end in proleptic motifs of sailing.[168] The life

---

[163] Ibid. ii. 275–6.

[164] See e.g. ibid. iii. 207 where we learn of Shelley's 'burning love' for his children and his sufferings when they were taken away from him, either by the Lord Chancellor's decree or by death.

[165] Her figures of the body hint that his passions and his poetry are another kind of children to him. See e.g. ibid., vol. i, p. vii: 'those productions, as they sprung, living and warm, from his heart and brain. I abstain from any remark on the occurrences of his private life; except, inasmuch as the passions they engendered, inspired his poetry.'

[166] The best discussion of the death scenes in *Lives* of Shelley and the other Romantic poets is Samantha Matthews, *Poetical Remains: Poets' Graves, Bodies, and Books in the Nineteenth Century* (Oxford: Oxford University Press, 2004). Matthews shows how lingering descriptions of death and burial fed a public desire for relic worship. See also Richard Holmes, 'Death and Destiny', *Guardian*, Review section (24 Jan. 2004), 4.

[167] 'Adonais' was read by Mary Shelley, Medwin, and all Victorian biographers thereafter as a prophecy of Shelley's own end.

[168] The many anecdotes of Shelley's fondness for sailing paper boats were repeated by most of his Victorian biographers in a way that suggested his eventual fate.

was thus presented as inevitably cut short. This was an important factor in making Shelley palatable. The death foretold endowed his life and works with pathos and invited sympathy, but it also sanctified his unworldliness. He was always meant for another element. Too good for the earth, he was a spirit, and a poet, in waiting for immortality. It allowed biographers from Mary Shelley onwards to represent his work as an unformed beginning rather than a mature reflection.[169] These implications are all present in Mary Shelley's narrative of the final weeks of Shelley's life in the long, concluding 'Note on Poems Written in 1822'.[170] Here, nearly twenty years after the catastrophe, she makes an anguished return to the train of events that led to her husband's death. In so doing she plays out the differences between female biographer and male poet in a vivid account of their last family home, Casa Magni, near the village of San Terenzo.

As ever, Shelley chooses the house, not for its intrinsic merits, but for its surroundings. It is in a remote and beautiful situation and, above all, near the sea—in the Bay of Spezia. Shelley and his friend Williams, both enthusiasts 'for adventure and manly exercises', are waiting for delivery of 'the fatal boat' from Genoa.[171] They then sail to Pisa, drowning on the return journey. Shelley's love of boats and sailing, on any river, lake, or sea available, has been a motif of the notes, heavy with elegiac portent. His need to be on water is proof for Mary Shelley of his feyness, his existence already within an element other than human. As the notes on 'Alastor' and 'The Revolt of Islam' suggest, it is also literally and figuratively associated with poetic creativity as a solitary journey away from the earthly, the real, the social. Shelley's sailing trips threaten to re-enact the quest narratives of 'Alastor' and 'Adonais', where the poet-heroes travel away from the disappointments of earthly life towards glorious transcendence in a lonely shallop.[172] Casa Magni, isolated, surrounded by natural beauty, the point of embarkation for the last sailing, is, like Shelley's other Italian villas, a figure in Mary Shelley's narrative, for the subordination of the domestic affections to a particular brand of poetic ambition—that associated by her in her preface with the 'purely imaginative' class of poetry. The only difference is that now this desire for transcendence has become a death wish—in Casa Magni 'the sea came up to the door' and sometimes 'the howling wind swept round our exposed house, and the sea roared unremittingly, so that we almost fancied ourselves on board ship'.[173]

---

[169] Holmes, 'Death and Destiny', 6, still takes this perspective, asking what might have been had Shelley lived—he 'would surely have become involved with the Great Reform Bill of 1832'.

[170] *PWS* iv. 225–36.

[171] Ibid. 227, 230.

[172] See ibid. 236 where Mary Shelley quotes the last stanza of 'Adonais' as her conclusion to this note, 'my spirit's bark is driven, | Far from the shore, far from the trembling throng'. Wolfson, 'Editorial Privilege', 61–2 discusses this and Mary Shelley's own elegiac poem, also included in the note.

[173] *PWS* iv. 210.

Shelley's impatience to sail leads to his choosing inadequate accommodation for the two families:

Shelley and his friend went to Spezzia [*sic*] to seek for houses for us. Not one was to be found at all suitable; however, a trifle such as not finding a house could not stop Shelley; the one found was to serve for all. It was unfurnished; we sent our furniture by sea, and with a good deal of precipitation, arising from his impatience, made our removal.[174]

Again the purely imaginative genius is childlike—not yet domesticated. Casa Magni is not a family house governed by rational affections, it is a playhouse. Mary Shelley describes Shelley and his friend as boyish in their boating enthusiasm. In her maternal voice of hindsight she quotes Williams's comment on seeing the boat arrive: '"we have now a perfect plaything for the summer"' and adds, portentously, 'It is thus that short-sighted mortals welcome death'.[175] Yet she includes herself in this temporary folly: 'Living on the sea-shore, the ocean became as a plaything: as a child may sport with a lighted stick, till a spark inflames a forest and spreads destruction over all, so did we fearlessly and blindly tamper with danger, and make a game of the terrors of ocean [*sic*]'.[176] Spring flowers become firesticks and the self-absorption of the childlike poet is indicted as both destructive of the self and of the wider community. All of them are led by the poet into a regressive state, described here as a savage madness—and we think here of the extremities of self-absorption that led to the 'madness' of Rousseau.[177] The owner of the estate on which Casa Magni is situated 'was insane' and had left his crumbling mansion unfinished, the olive trees rooted out and a hillside of forest trees—a plantation which, although to the English taste, was regarded by the Italians as 'a glaring symptom of a very decided madness'.[178]

The natives were wilder than the place. Our near neighbours, of Sant 'Arenzo, were more like savages than any people I ever before saw. Many a night they passed on the beach, singing or rather howling, the women dancing about among the waves that broke at their feet, the men leaning against the rocks and joining in their loud wild chorus. We could get no provisions nearer than Sarzana, at a distance of three miles and a half off, with the torrent of the Magra between; and even there the supply was very deficient. Had we been wrecked on an island of the South Seas, we could scarcely have felt ourselves further from civilisation and comfort; but where the sun shines the latter becomes an unnecessary luxury, and we had enough society among ourselves. Yet I confess housekeeping became rather a toilsome task, especially as I was suffering in my health, and could not exert myself actively.[179]

---

[174] Ibid. 228.
[175] Ibid. 230–1.
[176] Ibid. 232.
[177] *LL* iii. 320.
[178] *PWS* iv. 228.
[179] Ibid. 229–30.

The house continues to be a site of conflict between the literal and the figurative, gender and genre. Her conception of the domestic, as a woman and as her husband's biographer, depends upon an interchange of private and public—the family and the wider community. Casa Magni's isolation from the social forces of 'civilisation and comfort' rewrites the domestic space as a masculine regression into pure poetry. Mary Shelley rallies momentarily, arguing that the two families were society enough, but quickly reverts to her sense of exile in her own home. Casa Magni is poetic, but she allies herself with mundane realities—of shopping, housekeeping, and health. The savage landscape, beloved of the poet, prevents the gathering of supplies. To the eye of the female biographer, the house of poetry is beautiful—'[t]he scene was indeed of unimaginable beauty'—but also crazy and alien.[180]

Shelley and Williams sail. The heat intensifies as does her presentiment of evil, but her grasp on the real is slipping away under the spell of pure poetry:

The beauty of the place seemed unearthly in its excess: the distance we were at from all signs of civilization, the sea at our feet, its murmurs or its roaring for ever in our ears,—all these things led the mind to brood over strange thoughts, and, lifting it from every-day life, caused it to be familiar with the unreal. A sort of spell surrounded us, and each day, as the voyagers did not return, we grew restless and disquieted, and yet, strange to say, we were not fearful of the most apparent danger.

The spell snapped, it was all over ...[181]

She luxuriates in the unreal but registers its social isolation and its deceptiveness as fatal. As throughout this final note, she veers between poetic lyricism and biographic realism, the one associated with the causes of Shelley's death, the other with its effects. Her lyricism engages sympathetically with the poetic unreal, but she allies herself, albeit bitterly, with biographical reality. Once the spell snaps, her prose confronts the detail of the mundane practicalities which the widows—she and Jane Williams—have to deal with. She dwells on the disposal of the remains, and the dreamlike world of Casa Magni is suddenly opened up to the wider social community as she negotiates with the Italian authorities aided by 'the kind and unwearied exertions of Mr. Dawkins, our Chargé d'Affaires at Florence' and 'the zeal of Trelawny'. She also includes physical details of the cremation which almost brutally bring Shelley back to his body, back to earth. The burning of Shelley on the beach was not witnessed by her, nor is it directly described, but her account of Trelawny's singed hands displaces the imagined effects of the flames on the poet's flesh and does her duty as a biographer in gratifying the voyeuristic reader's curiosity:

It was a fearful task: he stood before us at last, his hands scorched and blistered by the flames of the funeral pyre, and by touching the burnt relics as he placed them in the

----

[180] *PWS* iv. 229.   [181] Ibid. 233.

receptacles prepared for the purpose; and there, in compass of that small case, was gathered all that remained on earth of him whose genius and virtue were a crown of glory to the world—whose love had been the source of happiness, peace, and good,—to be buried with him.[182]

The poet is encompassed in his casket, and although Mary Shelley eulogizes his genius and virtues and his capacity for love, her tragic irony seems to extend, surprisingly, in the last phrase, to the thought that these have, in fact, died with him.

The final paragraphs of the note attempt to imitate Shelley's own poetic transfiguration of the poet's death into eternal life, but the attempt is interrupted by the realism of the biographer, who breaks through in an open expression of dissatisfaction with the poetic sublimation of the real. She finishes by quoting two stanzas from 'Adonais': one, describing Keats's tomb at the cemetery in Rome, and reapplying the lines to Shelley's, in the same cemetery, the second prophesying his own death as a reunion with 'the Eternal'. But between the two stanzas she interjects, in her own voice:

Could sorrow for the lost, and shuddering anguish at the vacancy left behind, be soothed by poetic imaginations, there was something in Shelley's fate to mitigate pangs, which yet, alas! could not be so mitigated; for hard reality brings too miserably home to the mourner, all that is lost of happiness, all of lonely unsolaced struggle that remains. Still though dreams and hues of poetry cannot blunt grief, it invests his fate with a sublime fitness, which those less nearly allied may regard with complacency.[183]

The self-absorbed house of poetry has in the end destroyed domestic happiness and Mary Shelley represents herself as left reluctantly in the house of 'hard reality'. It is a bleak biographical credo, but it is a serious indictment of the 'dreams and hues of poetry'. '[P]oetic imaginations' may provide aesthetically pleasing sublimations of grief but cannot reach out to the grieving widow to offer genuine consolation. Biography, on the other hand, perhaps can—and we remember here her first impulse on Shelley's death, recorded in her *Journals*: 'I shall write his life—& thus occupy myself in the only manner from which I can derive consolation'.[184] But Mary Shelley does not write biography only to console herself. Her edition has argued that the public will not be satisfied for long by poetry that leaves 'hard reality' behind. Her practice as Shelley's editor demonstrates a belief that biography will compensate—that, in bringing Shelley's human presence before them, she can stimulate the affections of the public in a way that purely imaginative poetry cannot.

---

[182] Ibid. 234.
[183] Ibid. 235.
[184] *MWSJ*, 444–5 (17 Nov. 1822).

4.6 AIR AND EARTH: MARY SHELLEY'S LEGACY

Mary Shelley's portrait of her husband remains elusive, curiously sketchy, compared with the flesh and blood presence of Boswell's Johnson, Moore's Byron, De Quincey's Wordsworth, or indeed, almost any male subject of the popular literary biographies of her day. Her conception of biography's 'stamp of reality' bears comparison, as we have seen, to Carlyle's praise of Boswell's *Life of Johnson*, but she does not share Carlyle's love of the warts-and-all image as a sign of the humanity of the poet ('The purfly, sand-blind lubber and blubber, with his open mouth, and face of bruised honeycomb; yet already dominant, imperial, irresistible!').[185] The difficulty for her of broaching Shelley's private life in public forces her to aim at the seemingly impossible paradox of an intimate portrait without the private dimension.[186] The emotional centre of her memorials is displaced from Shelley himself to her own response to him, as the grieving widow. The flavour of her prefaces and notes is thus quite different to that of Moore's Byron, but she created a highly successful biographical formula none-theless, for the declared absence at the centre of her editions challenged others to step in and supply the deficiency. She had made Shelley's suffering body a theme and used figures of the body to convince her readers of the humanity of Shelley's poetic vision. Other biographers, including Trelawny and Hogg, made the same essential argument, but with the extra force gathered from the fact that they, unlike Mary Shelley, gave detailed pen portraits of the poet as well as dramatizing his conversation. In their accounts the poet's body was vividly realized and became a testament to his sincerity and a proof that his idealism could issue in sympathy and benevolent actions. At the same time, the biographical embodi-ment of a poet who had come to be identified to a unique degree with the transcendence of spirit over flesh was an activity rich in ironic and critical potential.

In his *Records of Shelley, Byron and the Author* (1878), expanded from his original *Recollections of the Last Days of Shelley and Byron* (1858), Trelawny described Shelley on first sighting as only partly corporeal—'a pair of glittering eyes' in the darkness, a spirit figure '[s]wiftly gliding in' and, just as quickly, vanishing.[187] But, in the tradition of early Byron biographers, he positioned himself as eyewitness to genius in the flesh: 'I was on the most intimate terms with both [Shelley and Byron], and saw them almost every day'.[188] Biography,

---

[185] *CME* iii. 93.

[186] See e.g. *MWSL* ii. 221, persuading Maria Gisborne to surrender her letters from Shelley for publication in the edition: 'You know how I shrink from all *private* detail for the public—but Shelley's letters are beautifully written, & everything *private* could be omitted'.

[187] Edward John Trelawny, *Records of Shelley, Byron, and the Author*, ed. David Wright (1973; 2nd edn., Harmondsworth: Penguin, 1982), 67.

[188] Ibid. 50.

Trelawny argued, had too often been 'like unrolling an Egyptian mummy, wrapped in countless cerecloths and containing nothing but dry bones'.[189] He would give readers Shelley's flesh and, as if to underline the fact, he tells us that he often saw Shelley 'in a state of nudity, and he always reminded me of a young Indian, strong-limbed and vigorous'.[190] Trelawny's descriptions of Shelley's appearance were in part an attempt to attract the reader's sympathies. The poet's artless, feminine face and gawky figure, with its ill-fitting clothes, were indicative of his youthful naïvety and of the mismatch between the public perception of him as a satanic influence and the reality of his well-meaning, if unworldly, benevolence.[191] Yet Trelawny's embodiment of Shelley was also blatantly sensationalizing. The biography, which began with a poet hovering between flesh and spirit, ended with a blow by blow account of the rotting corpse on the beach at Viareggio. An appendix added in 1878 but professing to be the eyewitness notes taken in 1822, recorded: 'I was paralysed with the sharp and thrilling noise a spade made in coming in direct contact with the skull. . . . The legs had both separated at the knee-joints, the bones of the thigh projecting; the hands were likewise parted at the wrists; the skull, for the scalp was off, was of a dingy hue, and the face entirely destroyed and fleshless'.[192] The grotesque corporality of this vision of the poet asserted Trelawny's credentials as his earth-bound biographer and the right of the reader to experience the humanity of the poet.

The most vivid, developed, and complex biographical portrait of Shelley in the Victorian period was by Hogg. His series of essays, 'Percy Bysshe Shelley at Oxford', were first published in the *New Monthly Magazine* in 1832 and later incorporated wholesale into his much expanded *Life of Shelley* (1858), commissioned by Lady Jane Shelley, who gave Hogg access to the family papers, but withdrew her support after the publication of the first two volumes, in protest against his editorial alterations to the letters and other documents she had supplied.[193] These freedoms with his primary materials as well as his self-serving suppression of his own youthful radicalism and the true nature of his relationship with Harriet Westbrook, have all placed Hogg's biography under suspicion.[194] At the same time he has been accused of being in thrall to the estate and

[189] Ibid. 49.
[190] Ibid. 51–2.
[191] Ibid. 67.
[192] Ibid. 302.
[193] [Thomas Jefferson Hogg], 'Percy Bysshe Shelley at Oxford', *NMM*, 34–5 (Jan.–Dec. 1832) and 'The History of Percy Bysshe Shelley's Expulsion from Oxford', *NMM*, 38 (May 1833); revised as *The Life of Percy Bysshe Shelley*, 4 vols. [only 2 pub.] (London: Edward Moxon, 1858). For Lady Shelley's objections, see her *Shelley Memorials*, pp. vii–ix.
[194] See David Higgins, *Romantic Genius and the Literary Magazine: Biography, Celebrity and Politics* (Abingdon: Routledge, 2005), 80: 'Hogg greatly understates his friend's youthful radicalism and totally conceals his own'.

producing a sentimentalized account of Shelley.[195] The Preface to the 1858 *Life* certainly pays homage to the myth of the angelic Shelley but Hogg's biography, as a whole, is considerably more acerbic than this suggests.[196] As Hogg was careful to point out in his Preface, Mary Shelley had encouraged his original essays and facilitated their publication in the *New Monthly Magazine*.[197] He started his Preface with extracts from her 1823 'Life' of Shelley, and presented his biography almost as if it were the one the widow herself was prevented from writing. His account of Shelley, by contrast to hers, contains a fully realized, physical embodiment of the poet, within a detailed, chronological narrative of the period of their friendship, but his sceptical response to Romantic genius and his conception of his role as Shelley's biographer show that Hogg was, in many senses, her heir.

In the *New Monthly Magazine* essays of 1832, Hogg, like Mary Shelley in 1839, infused his retrospective with the superiority of hindsight. He distanced himself from Shelley's creed: '"Above all things, Liberty!"'. He was 'half right', but his beliefs were the product of his youth and the Revolutionary times in which he lived.[198] He portrayed his subject, from the perspective of wisdom and common sense, as childlike, naïve, eccentric, even an idiot savant. Shelley's intellectual enthusiasms at Oxford are represented as unique, charming, invigorating, but also slightly unbalanced. He is a benign Frankenstein, his experiments endearingly amateurish, resulting in little more than burns in the carpet, holes he enlarges by tripping over them.[199] He eats with the messiness of a child—his chair surrounded by a ring of crumbs on the carpet. His rooms in University College, in an image of his unformed but fertile mind, are a 'primeval chaos'.[200] His generosity of spirit and of intention is unquestioned but Hogg's anecdotes also stress Shelley's naïvety as the product of an aristocratic aloofness from the reality of ordinary, working life. The poet, a stranger to more mundane ways of making, marvels as he watches a brick being formed or a coat mended: 'had the tailor consumed the new blue coat in one of his crucibles, and suddenly raised it, by magical incantation, a fresh and purple Phoenix from the ashes, his admiration could hardly have been more vivid'.[201] He startles a mother on Magdalen Bridge, when he asks: '"Will your baby tell us anything about pre-existence, Madam?"'[202] He leaves a working-class family bemused when he takes their

---

[195] See e.g. Hogle, 'Percy Bysshe Shelley', 118.

[196] In the Preface to his 1858 *Life* Hogg eulogized Shelley effusively and revealed that Bulwer, the editor of the *NMM*, had prevented him from expressing the full measure of his enthusiasm for the poet in his original essays.

[197] *The Life of Percy Bysshe Shelley, by Thomas Jefferson Hogg, with an Introduction by Professor Edward Dowden* (London: George Routledge and Sons; New York: Edward Dutton, 1906), 5.

[198] *NMM* 35/142 (Oct. 1832), 321.

[199] Ibid. 34/134 (Feb. 1832), 139.

[200] Ibid. 137.

[201] Ibid. 35/142 (Oct. 1832), 328.

[202] Ibid. 35/144 (Dec. 1832), 509.

daughter under his wing and begs food for her from a neighbouring cottage. Before we read such anecdotes as outright critiques of Shelley's aristocratic unworldliness, we should recognize the extent to which, in the 1832 essays, Hogg emphasizes his capacity for individual acts of benevolence.[203] We should also note that Hogg himself demonstrates a hearty contempt for the lack of imagination of the common crowd. However, in the sections added to the full-length biography of 1858, his sympathies with Shelley wore thinner and he began to define his own role, as biographer, as explicitly antithetical to the poetic.

The 1858 narrative frames the original essays, with an account of Shelley's life before and after Oxford, up to his first meeting with Mary Godwin, and is quite largely autobiographical. To some extent Hogg takes on the role of Shelley's doppelgänger in the narrative. He notes that they were inseparable at Oxford and he later enjoys the fact that he is sometimes mistaken for his friend.[204] He also follows him and (more particularly) his wife around the country whenever he has the opportunity. Yet he also insists on their differences. He openly states his political divergence from Shelley, portraying himself as Tory and even suggesting, with considerable dishonesty, that he was already a Tory in 1810.[205] Above all he presents himself in his post-Oxford life, as 'of the earth, earthy', a steady, hard-working student of law, prosaic, practical, solvent. Shelley by contrast is 'of the heaven, heavenly', pursuing wild schemes, rather than steady employment, existing in a world of the imagination, hopelessly impractical and dependent on Hogg, amongst others, for his financial security.[206] Like Mary Shelley, who had mothered her husband in the 1839 *Poetical Works*, Hogg, in 1858 represents himself, by contrast to his friend, as able to change and mature. Hogg, unlike Shelley, moves beyond the intellectual playground of Oxford and forges ahead in the real world. The oppositions come to a head in a passage where Hogg writes of Shelley as

fugitive, volatile; he evaporated like ether, his nature being ethereal; he suddenly escaped, like some fragrant essence; evanescent as a quintessence. He was a lovely, a graceful image, but fading, vanishing speedily from our sight, being portrayed in flying colours. He was a climber, a creeper, an elegant, beautiful, odoriferous parasitical plant; he could not support himself; he must be tied up fast to something of a firmer texture, harder and more rigid than his own, pliant, yielding structure; to some person of a less flexible formation: he always required a prop. In order to write the history of his fragile, unconnected, interrupted life, it is necessary to describe that of some ordinary everyday person with whom he was familiar, and to introduce the real subject of the history, whenever a transitory glimpse of him can be caught.

---

[203] See Higgins, *Romantic Genius*, 79.
[204] *Life of . . . Shelley* (1858; repr. 1906), 469.
[205] Ibid. 13.
[206] Ibid. 435.

In exhibiting a phantasmagoria, a magic lantern, a spectrum of prismatic colours, a solar microscope; the white sheet, the screen of blank paper, the whitened wall claim no merit, no share in the beauty of the exhibition, yet are these indispensable adjuncts in order to display wonderful, beauteous, or striking phenomena.[207]

Hogg is justifying his auto/biographical approach here on the grounds that Shelley's ethereal, fleeting presence and the 'fragile, unconnected, interrupted' quality of his life, make him a uniquely elusive biographical subject. They need to be given substance, stability, and coherence by means of Hogg's own story, which is the record of a solid, 'ordinary every-day person'. He presents himself as the prosaic antithesis to Shelley's poetic genius, and thus his best chronicler—the white wall upon which the creature of imagination is projected—the spine around which the fugitive spirit entwines itself. It is a passage that suggests the affinities between his approach as a biographer and Mary Shelley's in her editions. Both style themselves as representatives of the real, mediating the creature of imagination to an audience otherwise likely to feel baffled if not alienated.

Hogg's homage to Mary Shelley was lost on the family. Lady Jane Shelley published her *Shelley Memorials* (1859) as an angry retort to his biography. Her book was presented as a family memoir, a sequel to Mary Shelley's editions of 1824 and 1839. Although Lady Jane Shelley expressed more sympathy with the poet's radicalism than has been acknowledged, she reshaped his religious and political views, to appeal to the liberal, reformist sympathies of her readers.[208] As a result she has been seen as the most hagiographic and anodyne of Shelley's biographers.[209] Yet critics have overlooked the fact that the *Shelley Memorials* are a memoir of two lives, and two literary careers—Percy's and Mary's. Lady Jane draws heavily on Mary Shelley's 'Life' of 1823, her editions, and her letters and journals. Her Shelley is very much the same as her mother-in-law's, a youthful idealist, drawn inexorably to his death (the first edition of her *Memorials* has its commemorative function underlined not only by the title, but the frontispiece engraving of Shelley's tomb in Rome). The joint memorial celebrates Mary's supportive role in their marriage and her softening influence in leading him to found his resistance to political and social abuses in domestic affections, rather than anger. The marriage is represented as his domestic salvation: 'Evil might be without; but by his hearth were sympathy, and encouragement, and love'.[210] When Lady Shelley comes to the poet's death, she does not stop there, but

---

[207] *Life of ... Shelley* (1858; repr. 1906), 302–3.

[208] She approves the friendship with Hunt, praises a letter from Shelley defending *The Revolt of Islam* as 'a remarkable specimen of the courage with which he defied conventional opinions' (ibid. 81) and has no sympathy for the censorship of *Swell Foot the Tyrant* by the Society for the Suppression of Vice (133).

[209] See e.g. Ian Hamilton, *Keepers of the Flame: Literary Estates and the Rise of Biography* (London: Pimlico/Random House, 1992), 131–43.

[210] Lady Shelley, *Shelley Memorials*, 73.

continues with a chapter on Mary's life and work, as a widow, followed by extracts from Mary's Private Journal. These pages celebrate Mary's life as a heroic struggle against grief, isolation, and financial hardship and her career as a professional novelist, editor, and biographer as part of this heroism. As bread-winner for her son and ageing father, 'she worked incessantly with her pen, and met her liabilities by the fruits of her literary industry'.[211] Lady Shelley holds her up as an example of moral courage, hard work, and personal, if not public, commitment to liberal causes, including women's rights, quoting a now famous passage from the Journals: 'If I have never written to vindicate the Rights of Women, I have ever befriended women when oppressed'.[212] Gradually some-thing approaching an ironic contrast builds between Mary Shelley's life and work and those of her dead husband. Where he promised, she performed. She is, above all, the survivor. As in Mary Shelley's 1839 *Poetical Works*, so in Lady Shelley's *Memorials*, the biographer sustains and outlives the poet. Hers is the model of authorship that endures.[213]

In 1886 Edward Dowden produced the first full-scale biography of Shelley. His monumental, scholarly *Life* was written with the cooperation of Lady and Percy Shelley who gave him access to the archive of Shelley papers held at Boscombe Manor. The result was that Mary Shelley continued to preside over the construction of her husband's posthumous reputation, for, as Dowden acknowledged, her records of their life together, in her journal and unpublished correspondence, formed his most important source for the years from 1814.[214] Her legacy was also seen in Dowden's vision of Shelley's life as a journey away from the early radicalism and idealism towards a Wordsworthian poetry of human sympathy and engagement with 'actual events and living men and women'.[215] He charted this journey very largely in terms of Shelley's relation-ships with women, commenting, for instance, on the breakdown of the first marriage, that Harriet could not be expected to 'dwell for ever in a golden mist of liberty, equality, and fraternity, feeding on roots and fruits, and sipping distilled water'.[216] Dowden advocated a model of marriage in which 'a wiser, tenderer affection, clarified from the grossness of spurious idealizings and vain hopes, may root itself in earth and rise towards the upper airs'.[217] He argued that, on the whole, Shelley's marriage to Mary offered this balance. It was 'a serviceable education for Shelley's sympathies, bringing them close to reality, and helping

---

[211] Ibid. 222.

[212] Ibid. 250.

[213] See also Edward Dowden, *The Life of Percy Shelley*, 2 vols. (London: Kegan Paul, Trench & Co., 1886), ii. 472: 'It was well for him that she [MWS] recognized realities of life as deserving of consideration which were matters of indifference to him.'

[214] See ibid. vol. i, pp. v–vi. He also draws extensively on Hogg, but only after pointing out that Mary Shelley vouched for Hogg's truthfulness.

[215] Ibid. ii. 506. See also i. 159–60; and ii. 382, 468–9.

[216] Ibid. i. 403.

[217] Ibid. 404.

to mature his mind'.[218] As this suggests, Dowden throughout his book shows a sensitive and sympathetic interest in the situation of the women in Shelley's life and a preference for the feminine pragmatic over the masculine poetic. In the final chapter, as the doom gathers, Shelley persuades Jane Williams and her children to go sailing with him. With the boat sinking under them, Shelley

> with brightening face exclaimed joyfully, 'Now let us together solve the great mystery.' Preferring the colours inwrought upon 'the painted veil which men call life,' Jane, with feminine adroitness, beguiled her uncanny oarsman to thoughts of the shore.[219]

The anecdote nicely captures what Dowden demonstrates throughout the biography—the poet's dependency on redeeming, female common sense—but it also, of course, foreshadows his final and fatal voyage away from domestic salvation.

The conservatism of Victorian Shelley biographies was far from blandly mystifying, despite the fact that twentieth-century critics, irritated by their reshaping of his radicalism, have represented it in this way. We should not underestimate the service of these biographies to Shelley's works in terms of drawing in a wider readership by means of a sentimentalized myth of the angel poet. At the same time, the nineteenth-century biographical embodiment of Shelley retained its critical edge in the wake of Mary Shelley's editions, questioning the appeal, to contemporary audiences, of the myth it helped create. In 1974 Richard Holmes began his *Shelley: The Pursuit* by disavowing what he characterized as the disembodied Shelley of Trelawny and Maurois, '[t]hat fluttering apparition is not to be found here, where a darker and more earthly, crueller and more capable figure moves with swift pace through a bizarre though sometimes astonishingly beautiful landscape'.[220] But even this 'more earthly . . . figure' invokes the youthful hero of 'Alastor', on his narcissistic quest for a visionary love that transcends the merely human. Holmes's claim to give us the real Shelley relies on the same ironic coupling of ethereal spirit and living man, air and earth, that was the basis of Mary Shelley's biographical editions—as it was for all subsequent *Lives* of the poet. As a biographical paradigm, the writer in pursuit of a disembodied subject proved lastingly successful. It was, of course, a version of the Romantic quest narrative itself—it is for good reason that 'Alastor' reverberates through all these *Lives* of Shelley—but a version in which the bystanders in the poetic quest also found a voice.

[218] Dowden, *The Life of Percy Shelley*, ii. 468.
[219] Ibid. 503.
[220] Richard Holmes, *Shelley: The Pursuit* (London: Weidenfeld and Nicolson, 1974; Penguin Books, 1987), p. ix.

5

De Quincey and the Lake Poets

'Do you know De Quincey?'. . . .

'Yes, sir,' said Southey, with extraordinary animosity, 'and if you have opportunity, I'll thank you to tell him he is one of the greatest scoundrels living!' I laughed lightly, said I had myself little acquaintance with the man, and could not wish to recommend myself by that message. Southey's face, as I looked at it, was become of slate colour, the eyes glancing, the attitude rigid, the figure altogether a picture of Rhadamanthine rage,—that is, rage conscious to itself of being just . . . 'I have told Hartley Coleridge,' said he, 'that he ought to take a strong cudgel, proceed straight to Edinburgh, and give De Quincey, publicly in the streets there, a sound beating—as a calumniator, cowardly spy, traitor, base betrayer of the hospitable social hearth, for one thing!'[1]

De Quincey's biographical essays on Coleridge, produced for *Tait's Edinburgh Magazine* (1834–5), soon after the poet's death, provoked collective outrage from friends and family.[2] Wordsworth tried and failed to have publication halted, writing that '[t]his notice is, in most points, relating to Mr C's personal *Character*, highly offensive, and utterly unworthy of a Person holding the rank of a Gentleman in english [*sic*] society'. De Quincey had 'abused' Coleridge's confidence in him and 'perverted the communications made to him', it was an 'obnoxious publication', a 'false' and 'injurious' account.[3] There were similar reactions to De Quincey's portrait of Wordsworth when it appeared in the five essays entitled 'Lake Reminiscences', published in *Tait's* in 1839.[4] This time

---

[1] Thomas Carlyle, report of a conversation with Robert Southey *c*.1836–7, in James Anthony Froude, (ed)., *Reminiscences by Thomas Carlyle*, 2 vols. (London: Longmans, Green and Co., 1881), ii. 315–16.

[2] 'Samuel Taylor Coleridge. By the English Opium-Eater', *Tait's*, 1/8 (Sept. 1834), 509–20; 1/9 (Oct. 1834), 588–96; 1/10 (Nov. 1834), 685–90; 2/13 (Jan. 1835), 3–10. The last part promised a concluding instalment, which never materialized.

[3] Letter to Joseph Henry Green [mid-Sept. 1834], in *The Letters of William and Dorothy Wordsworth*, ed. E. de Selincourt, *The Later Years*, pt. 2, *1829–1834*, 2nd rev. edn., ed. Alan G. Hill (Oxford: Clarendon Press, 1979), 740. See also Dora Wordsworth: 'poor Hartley says he will "give it him" & I do hope he will . . . Aunt Sara [Hutchinson] burns with indignation against the little Monster—whom she never liked over well', and Coleridge's daughter Sara: 'We have been much hurt with our former friend, Mr. De Quincey . . . for publishing so many personal details respecting my parents in *Tait's Magazine*', quoted in Grevel Lindop, *The Opium-Eater: A Life of Thomas De Quincey* (London: J. M. Dent and Sons, 1981), 315–16.

[4] 'Lake Reminiscences, from 1807 to 1830, by the English Opium-Eater', *Tait's*, 6/61 (Jan. 1839), 1–12; 6/62 (Feb. 1839), 90–103; 6/64 (Apr. 1839), 246–54; 6/67 (July 1839), 453–64; 6/68 (Aug. 1839), 513–17. The first three 'Reminiscences' were subtitled 'William

Hartley Coleridge went on the offensive: '[t]he fellow cannot even let Mrs. Wordsworth's squint alone!...I should not be very unwilling to pitch the Opium-Eater into this lake!'[5] Wordsworth himself claimed later that he had 'never read a word of his infamous production nor ever shall....A man who can set such an example, I hold to be a pest in society, and one of the most worthless of mankind'.[6]

De Quincey embodied all that Coleridge and Wordsworth most feared from the biographer. His essays on them formed part of the long-running series 'Sketches of Life and Manners; from the Autobiography of an English Opium-Eater', which ran in *Tait's* between 1834 and 1841.[7] Auto/biographical in character, the series contained portraits of many contemporary literary figures, including the Lake Poets and their circle, and was a calculated popular success.[8] His portraits of the poets, in the manner of gossip, claimed their private lives for public consumption.[9] The protests of the Wordsworth circle registered their disturbance at this exposure by translating the personal betrayal of the biographer into social subversion on a grand scale. De Quincey was described as not merely a false friend, but a fifth columnist, an unEnglish 'spy', a 'traitor' to his country and his class. The only punishment fitting for the writer who has dragged the private life of genius out into the open was public humiliation—a dunking in the lake or, better, a beating on the streets of Edinburgh. But the most telling phrase comes at the end of Southey's diatribe where he branded De Quincey 'betrayer of the hospitable social hearth'. It was, of course, a quite literal betrayal of hospitality—De Quincey's essays on Coleridge, Wordsworth, and Southey were partly based on his experiences as a guest in their family homes and, on one level, Southey simply expressed, on behalf of his dead friend, a sense of outrage

Wordsworth', followed by 'William Wordsworth and Robert Southey' and 'Southey, Wordsworth and Coleridge'.

[5] Quoted in Lindop, *The Opium-Eater*, 333.
[6] Written in the margin of Barron Field's MS 'Life' of Wordsworth, quoted in John E. Jordan, *De Quincey to Wordsworth: A Biography of a Relationship, with the Letters of Thomas De Quincey to the Wordsworth Family* (Berkeley and Los Angeles: University of California Press, 1962), 347.
[7] 'Samuel Taylor Coleridge' and the 'Lake Reminiscences' were closely related to De Quincey's 25-part series 'Sketches of Life and Manners; from the Autobiography of an English Opium-Eater', *Tait's* (Feb. 1834–Feb. 1841). For a detailed account of the relationship see my headnote in *DQW* xi. 41–2.
[8] J. G. Bertram, *Some Memories of Books, Authors and Events* (Westminster: A. Constable, 1893), 62, recorded that '[t]he publisher of *Tait* entertained a high opinion of De Quincey's abilities as a contributor.... For the numbers of *Tait* containing his sketches there was usually a brisk demand'.
[9] There was some disapproval of his gossiping style from reviewers. See e.g. [Julius Hare], 'Samuel Taylor Coleridge and the English Opium-Eater', *British Magazine*, 7 (1835), 15–27; and Harriet Martineau, Obituary of De Quincey (1859), in *Biographical Sketches. 1852–1875*, new edn. (London: Macmillan, 1893), 416, condemning his 'malicious gossip, virulent and base'. See also [George Gilfillan], 'Miscellaneous', *The Critic*, 2 (1854), 157 and 'Thomas De Quincey and his Works', *Westminster Review*, 5 NS (Apr. 1854), 532, regretting the gossip about the Wordsworth family.

on reading De Quincey's revelations of his former host's plagiarism, his opium habit, and the unhappiness of his marriage. But the treacherous desecration of the hearth and home also echoed figures of domestic invasion and violation which, as we have seen, lay at the heart of discussions of biography at the period, and which were central to Wordsworth's and Coleridge's own, earlier, antagonistic responses to the genre.

Part of the shock was that Coleridge and Wordsworth were being treated like Byron or Shelley in these articles, despite the fact that, unlike the younger poets, neither was cut off in their radical and controversial prime. By the mid-1830s Coleridge had, apparently, left his creative years as a poet far behind him and was revered by many as a philosophic sage. Wordsworth was beginning to achieve the fame and respectability that had long eluded him. After many years of poor sales, his public standing was growing (to be confirmed by an honorary degree from Oxford in 1839, followed by the Poet Laureateship in 1843).[10] An important element in Wordsworth's reputation, by strict contrast to Byron or Shelley, was his close association with the poetry of domestic life and his celebration of domestic affections. Felicia Hemans wrote enthusiastically of him in 1826 as 'the true *Poet of Home,* and of all the lofty feelings which have their root in the soil of home affections'.[11] Four years later, staying at Rydal Mount as Wordsworth's guest, she pictured him as the living refutation of Moore's theory that genius and domestic happiness were incompatible.[12]

Despite these differences from their more flamboyant contemporaries, Coleridge and Wordsworth were caught up in the relentless marketing of poets' lives. Biography had already played a part in establishing their reputations, the process starting with personal references in reviews and articles in the magazines.[13] Both had become the objects of literary tourism—the enactment of biographical consumption. Ensconced in Dr Gilman's house at Highgate, Coleridge received a trail of visitors hoping to experience his famous powers of conversation. Wordsworth's house in the Lakes had been a place of pilgrimage for devotees—such as Hemans—from the early 1830s. For both, this syndrome, so indicative of the cultural climate of the 1830s, whereby a passion for the works of a writer expressed itself in a wish to enter their home, was a warning of things to come. In the five years following Coleridge's death, a succession of biographical

[10] See Stephen Gill, *Wordsworth and the Victorians* (Oxford: Clarendon Press, 1998).
[11] Letter to Maria Jane Jewsbury, quoted in Susan J. Wolfson (ed)., *Felicia Hemans: Selected Poems, Letters, Reception Materials* (Princeton: Princeton University Press, 2000), 492. Wolfson notes that Jewsbury had published a poem 'The Poet's Home', 'about Wordsworth's residence at Rydal Mount' (493 n.).
[12] Letter to John Lodge (1830), in Wolfson (ed.), *Felicia Hemans,* 504. See below, Chapter 6.
[13] See e.g. [John Wilson], 'Letters from the Lakes', *Blackwood's Magazine* (Jan. and Mar. 1819). See David Higgins, *Romantic Genius and the Literary Magazine. Biography, Celebrity and Politics* (Abingdon: Routledge, 2005), 95–101 on these and Wilson's many articles on Wordsworth for *Blackwood's* between 1817 and 1825.

publications appeared, some capitalizing on the publicity given to Coleridge's opium habit by De Quincey.[14] Others aimed at damage limitation. H. N. Coleridge's *Specimens of the Table Talk of the Late Samuel Taylor Coleridge* (1835) responded critically to De Quincey, but the family continued to see biography as a means to keep Coleridge's reputation alive and produced further biographical editions of his works in the 1840s and 1850s.[15] As we have seen, even Wordsworth, despite his qualms, temporarily co-operated with Barron Field, his would-be biographer, in his lifetime. After his death, Christopher Wordsworth's *Memoirs* (1851) became an important adjunct to *The Prelude* (1850).[16] It was followed by numerous Victorian biographical editions and full-length biographies, including a three-volume *Life* by William Knight, published in 1889 to accompany the first fully annotated edition of the *Works*.[17]

Broadly speaking, the effect of this body of literature, together with the critical reception of Wordsworth's and Coleridge's writing, over the course of the century, was to consolidate their respectability. There were persistent doubts about Coleridge's private morality, centring on opium and the issue of his alleged plagiarisms, but by the late Victorian period he was regarded, in the words of J. R. De J. Jackson: 'as a major poet, a major thinker, and as a respectable if unfortunate man'.[18] Stephen Gill's evidence suggests that the Victorians shaped Wordsworth into a moral and spiritual guide, celebrating his domestic virtues and softening his early radicalism, to produce the only Romantic poet 'whose *life* was as exemplary as his *work*'—as Mrs Humphry Ward put it in 1891: '"a *respectable* genius"'.[19] Jackson and Gill base their evidence on a variety of sources, including personal testimony and reviews as well as biographical literature, but the more detailed picture of these writers' Victorian domestication in biography remains to be drawn. There were critical hints even in seemingly hagiographic accounts. Edward Dowden's essay 'Coleridge as a Poet', published in 1889, described his life as a domestic idyll: 'He lived with his own thoughts and fancies

[14] See [T. Allsop (ed.)], *Letters, Conversations and Recollections of Coleridge*, 2 vols (London: Edward Moxon, 1836); James Gilman, *The Life of Samuel Taylor Coleridge* [advertised as 2 vols.; only 1 pub.] (London: William Pickering, 1838); and Joseph Cottle, *Early Recollections, Chiefly Relating to the Late Samuel Taylor Coleridge, During his Long Residence in Bristol*, 2 vols. (London: Longman, Rees & Co. and Hamilton, Adams & Co., 1837).

[15] H. N. Coleridge, *Specimens of the Table Talk of the Late Samuel Taylor Coleridge*, 2 vols. (London: John Murray, 1835). See also [H. N. Coleridge and Sara Coleridge (eds.)], *Biographia Literaria* [with a 'Biographical Supplement', including thirty-three of Coleridge's letters], 2 vols. (London: William Pickering, 1847); and [Derwent and Sara Coleridge (eds.)], *The Poetical and Dramatic Works of S. T. Coleridge. With a Memoir* (Boston: Little, Brown, 1854).

[16] Christopher Wordsworth, *Memoirs of William Wordsworth, Poet-Laureate, D. C. L.*, 2 vols. (London: Edward Moxon, 1851).

[17] William Knight, *The Life of William Wordsworth*, 3 vols. (Edinburgh: William Paterson, 1889). See Gill, *Wordsworth and the Victorians*, 206–34.

[18] J. R. De J. Jackson (ed.), *Coleridge. The Critical Heritage*, 2 vols. (London: Routledge, 1970–91), ii. 18. For Coleridge's plagiarisms, see 'Samuel Taylor Coleridge', *DQW* x. 289–93.

[19] Gill, *Wordsworth and the Victorians*, 234.

in dell or on upland, his affections twined themselves around the beloved inmates of his cottage and cherished friends'. But Dowden also alluded to the unhappiness of his marriage, to the 'lack of real characterisation' in his portraits of Sara, and to the absence of 'distinctive personality' in Christabel or any other of his female figures.[20] Other Victorian 'Lives' showed the persistence of De Quincey's satirical edge.[21] Trelawny's 1858 vision of Wordsworth, quoted at the opening of my Introduction, gives us one example of a less than reverential mid-century portrait. Carlyle, in the same year, pictured Coleridge as a Romantic 'Magus, girt in mystery and enigma', but also a 'flabby and irresolute' man, shuffling 'in corkscrew fashion' through the garden at Highgate. This description applied the full ironic force of Boswellian solidity to the sublime insubstantiality of Romantic genius, drawing the reader into a relationship with a poet who had the capacity to converse for two hours, 'his face radiant and moist, and communicate no meaning whatsoever to any individual of his hearers'.[22]

De Quincey's contribution to the afterlives of Coleridge and Wordsworth constituted an unusually witty, ambivalent, and critical response to these writers and to the figure of the Romantic poet. By contrast to much of the material we have looked at so far, his essays have become part of the critical canon of nineteenth-century prose and are hardly in need of rescuing. This chapter, rather, aims to shed new light on this body of work by reading it in the context of the development of biography at the period and of De Quincey's career as a magazine biographer. I begin by considering the issue of the auto/biographical relationship—a theme touched on at several points so far, but of particular relevance to De Quincey's writing and to his critical reputation. This is followed by a discussion of the influence of *Tait's Magazine* in shaping his vision of biography and his portraits of the Lake Poets in the 1830s. Here I will be examining his attitudes to the expansion of the readership and of the magazine readership more particularly, and looking at the ways in which he frames his biographical discourse as gossip. The detailed readings of the essays, which follow, will explore his distinctive, biographical challenge to the ideology of autonomous, masculine genius.

5.1 DE QUINCEY AS AUTO/BIOGRAPHER

Most of the biographical writing we have looked at so far contains a more or less spectral autobiographical presence, but the nature of De Quincey's work and

[20] Jackson (ed.), *Coleridge: The Critical Heritage*, ii. 180–1.
[21] William Michael Rossetti's biographical preface to the 1870 Moxon edn. of Wordsworth's *Works* drew on De Quincey to controversial effect—see Gill, *Wordsworth and the Victorians*, 90.
[22] Carlyle, *The Life of John Sterling* (1851), *The Works of Thomas Carlyle*, Centenary Edition, ed. H.D. Traill, 30 vols. (1st edn., London: Chapman and Hall, 1896–7; repr. New York: Charles Scribner's Sons, n.d.), xi. 53–6.

his critical reception highlight the question of the auto/biographical relationship. He was most celebrated in his own lifetime, as he is today, as the author of an autobiography. His first substantial publication, the 'Confessions of an English Opium Eater' (1821) launched a long career writing for the periodical press.[23] It was the first part of an autobiographical project which continued, sporadically, in his magazine publications of the 1830s, 1840s, and 1850s, culminating in his revised *Confessions* of 1856.[24] Yet he also showed a lifelong commitment to literary biography. One of the first works he planned was a series of 'Lives of the Poets', modelled on Johnson's.[25] This failed to come to fruition, but during his career he chronicled the lives of numerous writers, including Hannah More, Charles Lamb, Elizabeth Smith, Shakespeare, Milton, Pope, and others besides the Lake Poets.[26] He often reviewed literary biography, sometimes as a pretext for his own biographical narratives, and his posthumous works include a substantial essay on biography.[27] De Quincey's writing demonstrates the full, fluid spectrum of biographical narrative positions. At one extreme he wrote confessional autobiography, carefully defining his genre for the reader as he did so.[28] At the other, he produced biography with little or no autobiographical presence, such as the *Lives* written in the 1830s for the *Encyclopaedia Britannica*. Between these polarities came the 'Sketches of Life and Manners', which moved sinuously between a variety of different biographical modes, including confessional autobiography, memoir, and biographical narratives from which the

---

[23] 'Confessions of an English Opium-Eater', *London Magazine*, 4/21 (Sept. 1821), 292–312 and 4/22 (Oct. 1821), 323–79 [repr. London: Taylor and Hessey, 1822].

[24] See 'Sketches of Life and Manners', *Tait's* (1834–41); 'Suspiria de Profundis', *Blackwood's Magazine* (Mar.–July 1845) and 'The English Mail Coach', *Blackwood's Magazine* (Oct.–Dec. 1849). The revised and considerably expanded *Confessions* appeared in 1856 in De Quincey's own collected edn., *Selections Grave and Gay*, 14 vols. (Edinburgh and London: James Hogg and Sons, 1853–60), v. See *DQW* x, xi, xv, xvi and ii.

[25] The series was planned for the *Westmoreland Gazette* in 1818. See Charles Pollitt, *De Quincey's Editorship of the Westmoreland Gazette* (Kendal: Atkinson and Pollitt, 1890), 70.

[26] See 'Mrs Hannah More', *Tait's* (Dec. 1833), *DQW* ix. 323–57; 'Sketches of Life and Manners', *DQW* x–xi; articles on Goethe, Pope, Schiller, and Shakespeare for the *Encyclopaedia Britannica*, 7th edn. (1838–9; reissued 1842), *DQW* xiii. 217–333; and essay on Milton, 1st pub. as a pamphlet in Charles Knight's *Gallery of Portraits* (1832), repr. in *Distinguished Men of Modern Times*, 4 vols. issued 'under the superintendence of the Society for the Diffusion of Useful Knowledge' (London: Charles Knight, 1838), ii. 288–305, in *DQW* viii. 209–20.

[27] 'Some Thoughts on Biography' (1841), 1st pub. in *The Posthumous Works of Thomas De Quincey*, ed. A. H. Japp, 2 vols. (London: Heinemann, 1891), i. 100–24, in *DQW* xxi. 25–38. Reviews of literary biography include 'Anecdotage, No. 1. Miss Hawkins's Anecdotes' [Review of Laetitia Matilda Hawkins, *Anecdotes, Biographical Sketches, and Memoirs*, i (London: F. C. and J. Rivington, 1822)], *London Magazine* (Mar. 1823), in *DQW* iii. 100–13; 'Notes on Gilfillan's "Gallery of Literary Portraits"' [Review of George Gilfillan, *A Gallery of Literary Portraits* (1845)], *Tait's* (Nov.–Dec. 1845; Jan. and Apr. 1846), in *DQW* xv. 260–310; 'Final Memorials of Charles Lamb' [Review of Thomas Noon Talfourd, *Final Memorials of Charles Lamb*, 2 vols. (1848)], *North British Review* (Nov. 1848), in *DQW* xvi. 365–97; and 'Coleridge and Opium-Eating' [Review of James Gilman, *The Life of Samuel Taylor Coleridge*, i (1838)], *Blackwood's* (Jan. 1845), in *DQW* xv. 102–25.

[28] See e.g. opening paragraphs of the *Confessions*, in *DQW* ii. 9–10.

autobiographical voice was temporarily excluded. The generic fluidity of these essays is suggested by De Quincey's own attempts to classify them. He referred to them as 'memorials of my own life', but he also compared them to Johnson's *Lives of the Poets.*[29] The first instalment of the 'Sketches' was typical of De Quincey's style in shifting between biography, memoir, and impassioned autobiography, interspersed with small disquisitions on an eclectic range of subjects—historical, linguistic, philosophical.[30] As the 'Sketches' proceeded, the biographical content increased in relation to the autobiographical. At the end of the tenth instalment De Quincey announced that he intended in subsequent essays to focus on what he saw of the 'literati', philosophers and poets of his time.[31] From this point until the end of the series, memoir and literary biography dominated.

The biographical aspect of De Quincey's work has been comparatively ignored by critics whose interest, until recently, has been overwhelmingly in his autobiographical voice and more especially in the areas of his writing deemed most akin to Wordsworthian, poetic autobiography. Virginia Woolf, influentially, celebrated De Quincey as an autobiographer.[32] She acknowledged that he wrote in a variety of genres including 'biographies and confessions and memoirs', but argued that his true and best subject was himself: 'He was a born autobiographer' and 'prose writer though he is, it is for his poetry that we read him and not for his prose'.[33] She described the 'Sketches' as an autobiographical work structured poetically by impressionistic moments of impassioned self-revelation, 'the solemnity of a splendid summer's day . . . the sound of hooves on the far-away high road, the sound of words like "palm", the sound of that "solemn wind, the saddest that ear ever heard"', and swept aside everything not contained in these heightened moments as anomalous, bathetic, mere connective tissue.[34] She wished that such heightened moments of self-revelation could be extracted from the surrounding prose. Woolf's was a high-handedly selective vision of De Quincey, but proved a seductive one. Later critics, from J. Hillis Miller to John Barrell, in their different ways, took her approach to its logical extreme by reading the totality of his works as seamless autobiography, and the dominant impulse in twentieth-century readings of De Quincey was to poeticize the oeuvre in order to recreate the work as a single, autobiographical expression.[35]

---

[29] *DQW* x. 212–13.
[30] Ibid. 3–26.
[31] Ibid. 178–9.
[32] See Woolf, 'Impassioned Prose', *Times Literary Supplement* (16 Sept. 1926), 601–2; and 'De Quincey's Autobiography', in *The Common Reader*, 2nd ser. (London: Hogarth Press, 1932), 132–9.
[33] 'Impassioned Prose', *The Essays of Virginia Woolf*, ed. Andrew McNeillie, 4 vols. (London: The Hogarth Press, 1986–1994), iv. *1925–1928* (1994), 361, 365, 361.
[34] Ibid. 365.
[35] J. Hillis Miller, *The Disappearance of God: Five Nineteenth-Century Writers* (1963; Cambridge, Mass.: Belknap Press of Harvard University Press, 1979); and John Barrell, *The Infection of Thomas*

Even Annette Wheeler Cafarelli, whose subject was Romantic prose and De Quincey as a literary biographer, situated his conception and practice of biography firmly in the context of Wordsworthian poetic autobiography:

> The visionary 'passages of life' that Wordsworth names 'spots of time' (1805 *Prelude*, XI: 257–78) reappear in the emblematic anecdotes of biography which suddenly and unexpectedly throw human character into brilliant illumination. . . . De Quincey's embrace of a discursive, fragmentary, and 'extempore' style adopted the Wordsworthian aesthetic of recreating the spontaneous overflow of powerful feeling . . .[36]

The impulse to read De Quincey in this way, as a Wordsworthian, poetic autobiographer, is a powerful illustration of the more general Romantic tendency in criticism to marginalize biography in favour of autobiography. It also ignores the highly ambivalent response in De Quincey's writing to the Wordsworthian, autobiographical voice.

In common with other writers of the period, including, of course, Wordsworth himself, De Quincey was conscious of the newness of writing autobiographically—and the need for self-justifying and self-defensive strategies when launching on this experiment. The allusions to Rousseau in the title and opening of the *Confessions of an English Opium-Eater* were a rhetorical display of anxiety.[37] De Quincey was here imitating Rousseau's own, earlier apologia for his focus on self at the beginning of his *Confessions* but it is noticeable that, as the *Confessions of an English Opium-Eater* proceeded, it was Wordsworth's as yet unpublished poetic autobiography, later to become *The Prelude*, that became the main focus of De Quincey's ambivalence. De Quincey was one of a handful of people to have read this poem in manuscript and the *Confessions* is thoroughly indebted to it, but his self-projection as a gentleman scholar, formed and blighted in an artificial paradise of opium, and on the streets of London, also operates as an ironic commentary on the poem.[38] Despite its darker strains, De Quincey reads *The Prelude* as a sublimely confident act of self-making by a poet sustained by divine providence speaking in and through nature. Wordsworth constructs the ability of the poet to make the world his home as a trope of heroic

---

De Quincey: A Psychopathology of Imperialism (New Haven: Yale University Press, 1991). See also Elizabeth Bruss, *Autobiographical Acts: The Changing Situation of a Literary Genre* (Baltimore: Johns Hopkins University Press, 1976), 18, 93, 96, for a reading of De Quincey's autobiographical practice as enacting a split between the impassioned prose 'lyric', with a 'transcendental subject', in e.g. 'Suspiria de Profundis', and autobiography as the objective record of an individual life, in e.g. the 'Sketches'. Bruss, like Woolf, values the poetic mode. For a more extended discussion of these responses to De Quincey, see Julian North, *De Quincey Reviewed: Thomas De Quincey's Critical Reception, 1821–1994* (Columbia, SC: Camden House, 1997).

[36] Annette Wheeler Cafarelli, *Prose in the Age of Poets: Romanticism and Biographical Narrative from Johnson to De Quincey* (Philadelphia: University of Pennsylvania Press, 1990), 161–2.

[37] See *DQW* ii. 9 where he argues that the impulse to self-revelation is French, not English.

[38] De Quincey read either MS A or B (both 1805–6) before the corrections added by Wordsworth to MS A and designated A^2 by de Selincourt. For further details of De Quincey's knowledge and use of *The Prelude* before its publication, see my headnote in *DQW* xi. 42–3.

autonomy: 'Now I am free, enfranchised and at large, | May fix my habitation where I will. | What dwelling shall receive me, in what vale | Shall be my harbour, underneath what grove | Shall I take up my home, and what sweet stream | Shall with its murmurs lull me to my rest?' (i. 9–14). By contrast, homelessness in De Quincey's autobiography is a sign of his lack of power to determine himself as he would wish, as a result of family pressure and economic necessity. Running away from boarding school, he becomes a vagrant whose failure to make the world his home is presented as an index of his humanity. In London, he inhabits an empty house in Greek Street, as the last of a succession of squatting tenants—a disreputable lawyer, an abandoned girl, his motley surrogate family:

in common with the rats, I sate rent free. . . . I had as large a choice of apartments in a London mansion as I could possibly desire. Except the Blue-beard room, which the poor child believed to be haunted, all others, from the attics to the cellars, were at our service; 'the world was all before us;' and we pitched our tent for the night in any spot we chose.[39]

The quotations, adapted from Milton's *Paradise Lost*, XII cast De Quincey and the girl as the fallen Adam and Eve, entering the world 'with wandering steps and slow', but there is a further irony here, of course, in the concealed reference to the opening of *The Prelude* where Wordsworth splendidly recasts Milton's lines in order to declare his autobiographical power: 'The earth is all before me—with a heart | Joyous, nor scared at its own liberty, | I look about, and should the guide I chuse | Be nothing better than a wandering cloud | I cannot miss my way' (i.15–19). De Quincey's relocation of the lines within an urban, Gothic interior which he shares in a common bond of suffering with an abandoned girl, suggests his exclusion from Wordsworth's autobiographical act but also the socially exclusive nature of that act. The *Confessions* as a whole reworks Wordsworth's poem in such a way as to present De Quincey as an autobiographer who, unlike his model, has retained his ability to communicate with others—he portrays himself as the true friend of the people (the humble folk of Wales and London) and especially of women—the London prostitutes, whom Wordsworth gazes at with mingled pity and revulsion.[40]

Whilst De Quincey's theory and practice of 'impassioned prose' were deeply influenced by Wordsworth, it was a less straightforward relationship than Cafarelli and others have suggested.[41] To read De Quincey's biographical prose through Wordsworth, emphasizing its affinities with *The Prelude*, the spontaneous overflow of feeling, the passions of the heart, ignores the important differences between the two writers—differences which were intimately tied to their

[39] *DQW* ii. 24.
[40] See Prelude, VII.
[41] See e.g. D. D. Devlin, *De Quincey, Wordsworth and the Art of Prose* (London: Macmillan, 1983), 24: 'It is a sign of De Quincey's greatness that his individual talent was not extinguished by the mighty wind of Wordsworth's genius, but burned more brightly because of it.'

contrasting career trajectories. As enacted both in the *Confessions* and the 'Lake Reminiscences', the Oedipal struggle with Wordsworth to some extent replicated a familiar pattern in the work of second-generation Romantic poets. The ironic commentaries of Shelley's 'Alastor' or Keats's *Endymion* on the solipsism of Wordsworthian autobiography, for example.[42] Yet the context of the critique makes an important difference. It is significant that in the *Confessions* De Quincey parodies a poem as yet unpublished, available only to a coterie readership, in a prose autobiography which is, by contrast, a sensationally self-publicizing piece, successfully aiming to bring his name to as wide a section as possible of the burgeoning magazine readership of the day. De Quincey's attitude to the contemporary readership clearly needs to be distinguished from Wordsworth's. His ironic stance on the conception of the self-creating writer develops subsequently within criticism and auto/biography that is always the product of a professional prose writer, making his way in the contemporary literary marketplace.

5.2 DE QUINCEY AND THE READER

De Quincey held a deeply divided attitude to the expansion of the readership. On the one hand he seems to have been wary and even sometimes contemptuous of the tide of new readers for whom he wrote. Lucy Newlyn has gone so far as to place him at the centre of the Romantic 'anxiety of reception' and Cian Duffy has argued that his criticism is influenced by his fear of the rise of the novel, allied to the growth in numbers of middle-class readers, whom he regarded as a 'revolutionary social insurgency', threatening the literature of 'Power'.[43] For De Quincey, if the author submitted to this audience, it was in an act of 'treachery', akin to that in his childhood dream of 'lying down before the lion', a betrayal of 'the aristocracy of "Power" to the reading "mob"'.[44] These critics are, again, allying De Quincey with Wordsworth and certainly we can see a close relationship between the two authors' conceptions of the literature of 'Power', a quality that both suggest is beyond the capacities of the popular readership to appreciate.[45] Yet De Quincey is always

---

[42] See Marilyn Butler, 'Satire and the Images of Self in the Romantic Period: The Long Tradition of Hazlitt's *Liber Amoris*', *Yearbook of English Studies*, 14 (1984), 209–25.

[43] Lucy Newlyn, *Reading, Writing, and Romanticism: The Anxiety of Reception* (Oxford: Oxford University Press, 2000), 45–8; Cian Duffy, '"His *Canaille* of an Audience": Thomas De Quincey and the Revolution in Reading', *Studies in Romanticism*, 44/1 (2005), 8. In fact, De Quincey defended the novel as a popular form in 1823, and in 1848 included it in the category of the literature of 'Power'—see *DQW* xvi. 338.

[44] Duffy, '"His *Canaille* of an Audience"', 20–1. Duffy's most convincing evidence is from De Quincey's 'The Life and Adventures of Oliver Goldsmith', *North British Review* (1848), *DQW* xvi. 309–31.

[45] See De Quincey's 'Letters to a Young Man Whose Education has been Neglected' (1823): 'All, that is literature, seeks to communicate power; all, that is not literature, to communicate knowledge', *DQW* iii. 71. His second important statement on the literature of power came in 'The

more ambivalent than Wordsworth on this issue and his writing displays a contradictory strain which shows a sympathetic response to the new readerships and a canny grasp of the fact that his living depended upon the ability to adapt his writing to their needs.[46] John Whale has discussed his creation of a magazine persona, working with and against the author/reader relationship as constructed in the *London Magazine* and *Blackwood's*; and Robert Morrison and David Higgins have shown how he shaped his political and critical views according to the radical, reforming ethos of *Tait's Edinburgh Magazine*.[47] Like Mary Shelley, he embraced the growing, popular appetite for literary biography and contributed to publications aimed at the new readerships—not only the literary magazines, but also the *Encyclopaedia Britannica* and two of Charles Knight's publications under the aegis of the Society for the Diffusion of Useful Knowledge.[48] His biographical practice altered markedly according to his vehicle. The *Encyclopaedia Britannica* as national, cultural monument, necessitated a distinct kind of popular biography from that demanded by the magazines and he clearly judged that Knight's *Gallery of Portraits* did too. It is striking how, in his *Lives* of Pope, Shakespeare, and Milton for these publications, he limited his incursions into his subjects' private and personal lives and elevated them as national icons for popular admiration. He took up the position of an objective, revisionary biographer, pitting his *Lives* of the poets against those which preceded them, especially Johnson's, in order to dismiss defamatory material—pronouncing the relationship between Pope and Martha Blount 'innocent', dismissing Shakespeare's alleged theft of a deer, and defending Milton's patriotism.[49] In Shakespeare's case he celebrated the ability of genius to transcend the domestic sphere—the Bard's sexual transgression and the unhappiness of his marriage were not his, but his wife's sins, and his unhappy domestic situation, which led him away from home and so initiated his glorious career, was posterity's luck rather than Shakespeare's failing.[50] Conscious of a duty to national culture, De Quincey was at his least exposing, most reverential in these popular literary *Lives*. They are not without humour, but make a show of expelling gossip as the currency of other biographers. The approach contrasts markedly with his style when writing, as he more commonly does, for the magazines.

Works of Alexander Pope' (1848), *DQW* xvi. 335–8. For Wordsworth's conception of 'Power', see 'Essay Supplementary to the Preface' (1815), *PWW* iii. 62–84.

[46] See Julian North, 'Wooing the Reader: De Quincey, Wordsworth and Women in *Tait's Edinburgh Magazine*', in Robert Morrison and Daniel Sanjiv Roberts (eds.), *Thomas De Quincey: New Theoretical and Critical Directions* (New York: Routledge, 2008), 99–121, for a fuller discussion of the differences between Wordsworth's and De Quincey's understanding of Power in relation to the reader.

[47] See John C. Whale, ' "In a Stranger's Ear": De Quincey's Polite Magazine Context', in Robert Lance Snyder (ed.), *Thomas De Quincey: Bicentenary Studies* (Norman, Okla.: University of Oklahoma Press, 1985), 35–53; Robert Morrison, 'Red De Quincey', *Wordsworth Circle*, 29/2 (1998), 131–6; Higgins, *Romantic Genius and the Literary Magazine*, 85–9.

[48] See n. 26, above.

[49] See *DQW* xiii. 270, 317–18, and viii. 213.

[50] *DQW*, xiii. 314.

John Whale situates De Quincey's relationship with his magazine readership in the context of the aim of *Blackwood's*, the *London Magazine*, and other early nineteenth-century periodicals to maintain the exclusive aura of the coterie whilst appealing to a popular audience.[51] To this end many of the magazines cultivated a style which offered both the cachet of a gentlemanly education and the informality and entertainment of intimate address. It was a fine balance and one which De Quincey showed considerable success in achieving, especially in his biographical articles. His *Lives* of contemporary writers offered the reader a cultural education, but in combination with the confiding tone of the literary auto/biographer—the eyewitness account of genius. One tactic in producing this relationship with the reader was De Quincey's self-consciously gossiping style. To some extent, of course, his essays on Pope, Milton, and Shakespeare deploy gossip simply by repeating defamatory rumours in order publicly to cast them out of court, but in his magazine articles the public dissemination of private lives is presented as an allowable indulgence for his readers. In his introduction to a *Blackwood's Magazine* essay, 'The Last Days of Kant' (1827), adapted from the German of Wasianski, he argued that

> biographical gossip . . . and ungentlemanly scrutiny into a man's private life, though not what a man of honour would choose to *write*, may be *read* without blame; and, where a great man is the subject, sometimes with advantage.[52]

In practice, as a magazine biographer, De Quincey had no scruples about allowing himself to write in this way. In this particular essay, for example, he claimed that he hardly knew 'how to excuse Mr Wasianski for kneeling at the bed-side of his dying friend, to record, with the accuracy of a short-hand reporter, the last flutter of his [Kant's] pulse'.[53] But his own narrative was heavily dependent upon Wasianski's— the gossip of Kant's amanuensis, who spread beyond the confines of the home, for public consumption, painful and sometimes ludicrous details of the daily rituals and physical and mental degeneration of his friend—relaying his bedtime and breakfast eccentricities, his homemade garters, his delusions and nightmares, and finally, despite his professed qualms, a minute by minute account of his dying breaths. De Quincey's sensitivity to audience, his desire to appeal to the public and his gossiping style were nowhere more apparent than in his auto/biographical 'Sketches', and especially his articles on the Lake Poets, written for *Tait's Edinburgh Magazine.*

5.3   *TAIT'S EDINBURGH MAGAZINE*

At its inception, a month before the Reform Bill of 1832, *Tait's* was a radical, Benthamite journal, which had proclaimed its 'liberal principles' and promised

---

[51] Whale, ' "In a Stranger's Ear" '.
[52] *DQW* vi. 75 (my italics).
[53] Ibid.

to bring to a popular audience 'more matured discussion of public affairs than can be expected in the daily and weekly journals'.[54] William Tait's prospectus advertised his journal as one concerned with the social and political welfare of the people. His concern would be with 'whatever appears calculated to extend the liberties, to advance the interests, or to improve the condition of mankind'. His 'one grand object was 'the good of THE PEOPLE'.[55] Competition with the *Westminster Review* meant that, in February 1834, *Tait's* reduced its price from the already low 2*s. 6d.* to 1*s.*, becoming the first of the shilling monthlies. The magazine's audience was thereby extended to include not only middle-class readers but literate artisans.[56] Equally significantly for De Quincey, the ethos of *Tait's* was shaped by the involvement, unique at the time for a national monthly journal, of a female editor, the novelist, critic, and journalist Christian Johnstone. Johnstone had worked on the magazine from its beginnings, but took over as active editor and as a major contributor from 1834 to 1846.[57] She continued William Tait's efforts to make this a journal of the people, but shifted the balance of articles from the political to the literary and introduced a distinctive focus on women's issues.[58] Throughout her articles and those of fellow contributors, there was a strong interest in the female perspective and a feminist advocacy of reform in the social, political and legal position of women.[59] As Alexis Easley has shown, for Johnstone, 'the question of how to promote social justice for the working classes was inextricably linked to the problem of how to empower women within literary and political realms'.[60] She published work by Harriet Martineau, Catherine Gore, Eliza Lynn Linton,

---

[54] William Tait's pre-launch 'Prospectus', as quoted in W. E. Houghton, E. R. Houghton, and J. H. Singerland (eds.), *The Wellesley Index to Victorian Periodicals 1824–1900*, 5 vols. (Toronto: University of Toronto Press, 1987), iv. 475.

[55] Ibid.

[56] See ibid. 478 and Michael Hyde, 'The Role of "Our Scottish Readers" in the History of *Tait's Edinburgh Magazine*', *Victorian Periodicals Review*, 14/4 (Winter, 1981), 135–40.

[57] See Houghton et al. (eds.), *Wellesley Index*, iv. 478–9.

[58] See ibid. 478, her editorship coincided with a change in format to what she described as the '"cheap *People's size*"'. See also Alexis Easley, *First-Person Anonymous: Women Writers and Victorian Print Media, 1830–1870* (Aldershot: Ashgate, 2004), 65 for Johnstone's commitment to encouraging working-class readers—her 'definition of reformist journalism was premised on the idea that positive social change would result if the literary tastes of the general public were improved'.

[59] See e.g. Christian Johnstone, 'Mrs Postans' Cutch; or, Random Sketches of Western India', *Tait's*, 6/61 (Jan. 1839), 32, '[w]hen Mrs Postans laments the hard fate of the Cutchee matrons, and their daily drudgery, is she aware, that not much better is that of the women, in a similar condition, in England and Ireland, if, as we fully believe, their menial toils do not greatly exceed those of their simple-minded sisters of the East?' See also the polemical feminism of her 'Mrs Jameson's Winter Studies and Summer Rambles in Canada', *Tait's*, 6/62 (Feb. 1839), 69–81; and 'Lady Morgan's "Woman and her Master"', *Tait's*, 7/78 (June 1840), 390–7. For feminist arguments in contributions by other women writers, see e.g. 'M. L. G.' [Mary Leman Grimstone], 'Men and Women', *Tait's*, 1/2 (Mar, 1834), 101–3, arguing, within a reformist political context, for female education and for the opening of civil offices to women.

[60] Easley, *First-Person Anonymous*, 71.

Mary Russell Mitford, Amelia Opie, and Mary Howitt, amongst others.[61] In her editorials, her short reviews contained in the monthly 'Literary Register', and in longer articles and reviews she was able to showcase women's writing and to discuss female genius and the condition of women more generally.[62] Whilst she sometimes assumed a female audience in her writing—as did other writers for the magazine—she worked within a community of writers and readers that she and fellow contributors typically constructed as male.[63] Nevertheless, as Easley demonstrates, Johnstone's anonymity as editor of and writer for the magazine allowed the question of the gender-perspective of the journal to remain open:

> During the 1830s, *Tait's* became a multi-layered text, capable of being read by multiple audiences from diverse class- and gender-based perspectives, while at the same time maintaining its identity as a reformist periodical aimed primarily at middle-class men. Reading with and against the grain, readers could uncover explicit and implicit dialogues over class and gender that both confirmed and challenged the dominance of men as writers and editors in the discourse on social reform.[64]

This is an important if little-recognized context for reading De Quincey's essays on the Lake Poets. He continued to publish in the Tory *Blackwood's*, but his new connection with *Tait's* from 1833 meant that he was, at the same time, producing material for a radical journal whose reformist agenda was based on actively courting a broad-based audience in terms of class and gender. As Robert Morrison has suggested, working for *Tait's* gave him the opportunity to moderate his Tory politics and to vent 'the compassionate and rebellious side of his political ideology'.[65] It turned his thoughts towards the particular readership he was addressing and to the opportunities presented by the expanding literary marketplace more generally. The 'Sketches' and, within this series, 'Samuel Taylor Coleridge' and the 'Lake Reminiscences' were characterized by an awareness of the reader-constituency addressed by the magazine.[66] De Quincey wrote with the aim of attracting a broad audience with a wide spectrum of educational

---

[61] Women contributors increased from *c.*19–37 per cent under her editorship—see Easley, *First-Person Anonymous*, 69.

[62] See e. g. Johnstone, 'The Duchess D'Abrantès and the Countess of Blessington', *Tait's*, 1/3 (Apr. 1834), 208, 'In the present month we owe all our entertainment, and the greater part of our instruction, to female pens—to Miss Edgeworth, Miss Martineau, Miss Stickney, Mary Howitt, and, lastly, to the rarely gifted authoress of THE HAMILTONS—Mrs. Gore.'

[63] See Easley, *First-Person Anonymous*, 69. For the assumption of a female readership, see e.g. Thomas Onwhyn ['Peter Paul Palette'], 'The Green Lane—No. 1', *Tait's*, 7/78 (June 1840), 341, 'Gentle reader! (and if that thou art *fair* as well as gentle, so much the better, the more glad shall we be of thy company,) is it asking too much of thy good nature to request the loan of thine arm for a brief space, whilst we take a pleasant ramble together . . . ?'

[64] Easley, *First-Person Anonymous*, 72.

[65] Morrison, 'Red De Quincey', 134.

[66] There are one or two signs, in these essays, of distrust of the poorly educated reader, e.g. *DQW* x. 189 on the 'poor stall women' of Paris, reading Voltaire and Rousseau, with no improvement to their minds, yet this comes after a complaint against literary men who exclude '[o]rdinary people' by their superior airs, see ibid. 187.

backgrounds. When the 'Sketches' were originally projected as a series for the *London Magazine* in the early 1820s, he already imagined them as answering the needs of a readership seeking not just entertainment, but education—he would give 'a special attention', he said 'to communicate in every No. some knowledge that the reader is likely to value'.[67] As composed for *Tait's*, the early 'Sketches', particularly, with their disquisitions on Oxford University and the philosophy of Kant, were clearly still directed at this kind of audience. His own persona, as projected in the essays, contributed to his stance as educator of the populace. In the *Confessions* he had stressed his social mobility, as a bourgeois gentleman who, chameleon-like, adapted to all walks of life, and was as capable of conversing and sympathizing with the aristocracy as with the street-child or common prostitute. The 'Sketches' showed him moving between bourgeois, aristocratic, and intellectual circles. There was an element of appeal here to an aspirational middle-class audience, with tales of his schoolboy friendship with 'Lord W—— [Westport]' and his encounter with the King—but he also tells his readers how, on coming to manhood, he renounced this hierarchical world as one in which he would always be an outsider, for a life of 'Peace, liberty to think, solitude'.[68] He enters the republic of letters, significantly, not as a writer, but as a reader. The 'Sketches' and 'Reminiscences' describe De Quincey's formative years, not as the preparation for creative genius, but as the Odyssey of a reader, journeying from his childhood browsing in his father's library, to his life-changing encounters with the works of Kant, Coleridge, and Wordsworth, and especially, of course, '"the ray of a new morning"' that dawned after opening *Lyrical Ballads*.[69] In these episodes De Quincey was vaunting his exceptional powers, suggesting that, having mastered Greek, German philosophy, and, above all, recognized the genius of Wordsworth so precociously, his unique range of knowledge and critical acumen fitted him to instruct the aspirational readership of *Tait's*.[70] But the exceptional reader is a less distant figure than the exceptional writer. Scattered comments suggest a conscious effort by De Quincey to signal support for a democratization of reading. Early on in the series he argues strongly for public right of access to national copyright libraries and suggests that even he had benefited from being introduced to great literature in more accessible forms.[71] The first of his many allusions to his unique insight into Wordsworth's genius follows a recollection of having come to a knowledge of eighteenth-century poetry, as a young man,

---

[67] Letter to J. A. Hessey (Apr. 1822), *DQW*, vol. x, p. xiii.
[68] Ibid. 211.
[69] Ibid. 287.
[70] See De Quincey's 'Diary' of 1803, *DQW* i. 12–69, for the importance of reading in his life at this period and for his catholic tastes.
[71] *DQW* x. 34–5.

through those pleasant miscellanies, half gossip, half criticism—such as Warton's *Essay on Pope*, Boswell's *Johnson*, Mathias's *Pursuits of Literature*, and many scores beside of the same indeterminate class—a class, however, which do a real service to literature, by diffusing an indirect knowledge of fine writers in their most effective passages, where else, in a direct shape, it would often never extend.[72]

De Quincey's self-projection as friend of the popular readership is central to his vision as a biographer and, as we shall see, particularly to his essays on Wordsworth.

His working relationship with Johnstone, and his awareness of the prominence she was giving to women's writing and gender issues in the magazine, also appears to have had a distinct influence on the content of his articles for *Tait's*.[73] The influence of Johnstone's editorial policies is seen in the theme of female authorship that is present throughout these essays and in the later 'Sketches'. As well as his portraits of the male Lake Poets, the 'Sketches' and 'Lake Reminiscences' include accounts of his meetings with Hannah More and Mary Lamb, the first biographical portrait of Dorothy Wordsworth, and an extended account of the life of Elizabeth Smith.[74] De Quincey scattered his articles with numerous, enthusiastic allusions to female authors including Mary Wollstonecraft, Susan Ferrier, Frances Trollope, Mary Mitford, Joanna Baillie, Elizabeth Hamilton, Mrs Inchbald, Sophia and Harriet Lee, Ann Radcliffe and Christian Johnstone herself.[75] He also mentioned his encounters with a number of other literary ladies—Mrs Green ('the Saracen's Head'), with whom he and the Wordsworths dine, the novelist Margaret Cullen, and her sister Mrs Millar, and the 'ladies of Llangollen', Sarah Ponsonby and Lady Eleanor Butler.[76] The inclusion of this material, in itself, suggests his efforts to appeal to the female readership courted by Johnstone. By following her editorial policy with regard to women's writing, his decision to place his sketches of the male Lake Poets besides portraits of the literary women of the Lakes also countered an exclusively masculine conception

---

[72] *DQW* x. 145.

[73] For evidence that he admired her work, see *DQW* ix. 107–8. See also letter from De Quincey to John Johnstone [her husband], 22 Sept. 1827 (Pierpont Morgan, MS MA3007), referring to 'the great pleasure with which I have lately read *Elizabeth De Bruce* [by Christian Johnstone, 1827], an admirable work, and in my judgement by many degrees superior to the novels of Miss Ferrier—of which so many fine things are said'. I am grateful to Barry Symonds for drawing my attention to this letter.

[74] See 'Mrs. Hannah More', Tait's (Dec. 1833), in *DQW* ix. 323–57 and 'Sketches of Life and Manners', *Tait's* (Aug. 1840), in *DQW* xi. 238–43. For Mary Lamb, in 'Recollections of Charles Lamb', see *Tait's* (Apr. 1838), in *DQW* x. 239–41. For the portrait of Dorothy Wordsworth, intertwined with that of William Wordsworth, see 'Lake Reminiscences', *Tait's* (Jan., Feb., and Apr. 1839), in *DQW* xi. 52–108. For the biographical sketch of Elizabeth Smith (1776–1806), oriental scholar and linguist, author of *Vocabulary, Hebrew, Arabic, and Persian* (1814), see 'Sketches', *Tait's* (June 1840), in *DQW* xi. 209–19. The account of Elizabeth Smith is largely derived from a biographical edition of her work by Henrietta Maria Bowdler.

[75] See *DQW* x. 205; xi. 56, 102–3, 105–7, 217; x. 100; xi. 257–8, 107–8.

[76] *DQW* xi. 168–71, 184–91, 213.

of genius and implied that male and female genius were deserving of comparable attention. His recollections of Wordsworth were in practice a joint memoir of the poet and his sister. He wrote of Dorothy Wordsworth, very much in the Johnstone style, that she 'would have merited a separate notice in any biographical dictionary of our times, had there even been no William Wordsworth in existence'.[77]

Johnstone was also an important influence in encouraging De Quincey's revelations of domestic life and his gossiping style. She valued literature which took a feminine perspective on private life and was no prude when it came to biographical revelations. Whilst she concurred with the widespread disapproval of Lady Blessington's biographical gossip, in her review of a *Life of Mrs Siddons*, she wished that the author had not 'fancied himself bound, in biographic decorum, or social propriety, to suppress' material.[78] She was a supportive editor to De Quincey and, no doubt with an eye to increasing her readership, she defended his autonomy as a critic and biographer after objections from the Revd William Shepherd to the truthfulness of the portraits of himself, James Currie (the biographer of Burns), and Mr Roscoe in one of De Quincey's 'Sketches'.[79] The *Tait's* context thus encouraged De Quincey to develop a gossiping style which appealed to a broad band of the literate public and more particularly to the female reader. The issues of readership and gender were linked in De Quincey's articles on the Lake Poets where, as we shall see, the relations of the male poet to his female, domestic, and literary communities become a crucial index of his ability to reach out to his audience.

5.4 THE DOMESTICATION OF COLERIDGE AND WORDSWORTH

All the evidence suggests that 'Samuel Taylor Coleridge' and the 'Lake Reminiscences' were inspired by De Quincey's profound reverence for the work of Coleridge and Wordsworth, but it would also be true to say that there are few literary biographies so determined to dispel the mythology of genius to which they contribute. De Quincey, conscious throughout his work of the antagonism

---

[77] Ibid. 108.
[78] See Johnstone, 'The Duchess D'Abrantès and the Countess of Blessington', 204–6 and 'Life of Mrs. Siddons. By Thomas Campbell Esq.', *Tait's*, 1/7 (Aug. 1834), 467–9, immediately preceding De Quincey's 'Sketches' for that month.
[79] See Christian Johnstone, 'Mr De Quincey, and the Literary Society of Liverpool in 1801', *Tait's*, 4/41 (May 1837), 337–40. She also allowed De Quincey, against William Tait's wishes, to protest in print that he had not been given adequate time to correct his proofs for one of the 'Sketches'—see letter from William Tait to Christian Johnstone (22 Aug. 1840), National Library of Scotland MS 1670, fos 74/5 and 73; and reply from Christian Johnstone, dated the same day, NLS MS 1670, fos. 71/72.

of opposites, was here resolutely ambivalent—hyperbole and bathos were his favoured rhetorical devices. Both Coleridge and Wordsworth were represented as 'original' minds, transcending the merely human, yet the method of these essays was to bring them down to earth and back to their human responsibilities.[80] An important part of this was, as in 'The Last Days of Kant', a literal domestication. Coleridge is first encountered just outside the home of his current host and Wordsworth emerging from his own home.[81] Both then invite De Quincey inside. The private, domestic setting, rather than the public context for their lives, continues to be De Quincey's focus. The poet's home is a central theme and trope of both sequences of essays, as De Quincey invades the inner sanctum of closet and library, to expose the poet's private life to the world. As we have seen, Wordsworth's 'Essays Upon Epitaphs' had argued that memorials of the dead should allow the life to remain mysterious and intact, detail erased, particulars subsumed into the general, imperfections into the ideal. In 'Some Thoughts on Biography' De Quincey agreed that this is appropriate for epitaph, but also argued that the funeral sermon was an excellent place for speaking frankly of the dead.[82] His biographies of the newly deceased Coleridge and the still living Wordsworth showed no signs of adhering to Wordsworth's view of biographical decorum. Both Wordsworth and Coleridge were introduced as disembodied presences, tracked down, embodied, and observed in detail amongst their immediate family and friends. The genius was thus placed within a private context, relocated within the human, fleshly realm and judged according to his intimate social relations.

De Quincey begins each of the essay sequences by recounting how, as a young man, he journeyed gradually towards his heroes, pursuing Coleridge, but, in Wordsworth's case, avoiding a meeting: 'the very image of Wordsworth, as I prefigured it to my own planet-struck eye, crushed my faculties as before Elijah or St Paul'.[83] He trembles in anticipation, mindful that, as Coleridge believes, the inevitable consequence of seeing an apparition will be death. The moment when Wordsworth, hitherto known only through his works, is finally made flesh is both climactic and, inevitably, bathetic: 'I heard a step, a voice, and, like a flash of lightning, I saw the figure emerge of a tallish man, who held out his hand, and saluted me with the most cordial manner, and the warmest expression of friendly welcome that it is possible to imagine'.[84] De Quincey continues to ironize the sublime by sinking to the mundane in the narratives which follow his first encounters with the two poets. He does so, in part, by dwelling on the details of the physical presence of each man and, as in much of the biographical

---

[80] See 'Samuel Taylor Coleridge', *DQW* x. 287 and 'William Wordsworth', ibid. xi. 44.
[81] See *DQW* x. 294–5 and xi. 49–50.
[82] *DQW* xxi. 27.
[83] Ibid. xi. 45.
[84] Ibid. 50.

literature on Byron, intercutting aspects drawn from the iconography of genius with an unsparing scrutiny of his subject's fleshly imperfections:

In height he [Coleridge] might seem to be about five feet eight; (he was, in reality, about an inch and a half taller, but his figure was of an order which drowns the height;) his person was broad and full, and tended even to corpulence; his complexion was fair, though not what painters technically style fair, because it was associated with black hair; his eyes were large and soft in their expression; and it was from the peculiar appearance of haze or dreaminess, which mixed with their light, that I recognized my object.[85]

Coleridge is tall, but not tall, fair but not fair, a visionary, but also a Falstaffian figure, his height drowned by his width. His fleshiness suggests an essential moral weakness: his sensual self-indulgence, which has led to errors De Quincey will later dwell on—his disastrous lack of judgement in his choice of a wife—'he had gone too far in his attentions to Miss F——, for any honourable retreat'—and, of course, his opium addiction.[86] Wordsworth's body, too, becomes a *paysage moralisé*. De Quincey gives a minute account of his skin tone, hair colour, shape of the head and features, with reference to portraits by Haydon, Carruthers and others.[87] He creates the literary equivalent of an engraving in one of the gallery of portraits of the great poets, popular in the magazines of the period—dwelling, for instance, on the resemblance between Wordsworth and an engraving of Milton, at the front of Jonathan Richardson's notes on *Paradise Lost*.[88] But the portrait of Wordsworth etched by De Quincey is not, like an engraved frontispiece, allowed to remain frozen for posterity. De Quincey begins his discussion of Wordsworth's appearance by taking issue with a reviewer who 'in noticing some recent collection of literary portraits, gives it as his opinion that Charles Lamb's head was the finest amongst them. This remark may have been justified by the engraved portraits; but, certainly, the critic would have cancelled it if he had seen the original heads'.[89] De Quincey's method through this description of Wordsworth is, as here, to turn from the static visual record to the living presence. The fleshly details create an iconic portrait, but they also show a man in *motion*—both through time as he ages (prematurely), and through space, as he walks ("like a cade").[90] His figure, observed in its entirety as he moves, reveals that he 'was, upon the whole, not a well-made man', his legs were poorly shaped:

A sculptor would certainly have disapproved of their contour. But the worst part of Wordsworth's person was the bust: there was a narrowness and a droop about the

---

[85] Ibid. x. 295.
[86] Ibid. 302.
[87] See Ibid. xi. 54–61.
[88] Ibid. 58–61.
[89] Ibid. 54.
[90] Ibid. 56.

shoulders which became striking, and had an effect of meanness when brought into close juxtaposition with a figure of a most statuesque order.[91]

The literary biographer's art, as De Quincey conceives it, draws on but is distinct from that of the engraver or the sculptor. Wordsworth, seen through his biographer's eyes, will not quite do as the subject for a heroic statue and, as with Coleridge, his physical defects are, of course, indicative of moral failings— his 'meanness' to De Quincey and others, which, as we shall see, lies at the heart of the 'Lake Reminiscences'—the fact that, when he walks in his cade-like way, he edges his companions off the path.[92]

As he admits, much of De Quincey's material on Wordsworth's physical appearance and personal habits is the stuff of gossip. He excuses himself on the grounds that, as interest in Wordsworth's poetry grows, so will interest in the poet. De Quincey dissociates himself from gossip in his persona as a scholar concerned with Wordsworth's '*intellectual characteristics*', but at the same time allows that it is a vital resource for the community of readers in understanding the poet and, in fact, a sign of genius—it is only another token of Shakespeare's enduring power that we should want to raise the curtain on his 'daily life'.[93] His argument, as a scholar, also serves his purposes as a gossip of course, since any detail can be shown by the biographer to be related to the poet's intellectual life—from mean shoulders to cade-like walk. In practice, both 'Samuel Talyor Coleridge' and the 'Lake Reminiscences' are like gossip, too, in being constructed from oral anecdote. The opening pages of 'Samuel Taylor Coleridge' build a picture of the subject by means of the gossip of others. In several passages De Quincey represents himself gleaning rumours from friends and neighbours. Thus on Wordsworth:

(for he always preserved a mysterious silence on the subject of that 'Lucy,' repeatedly alluded to or apostrophized in his poems, and I have heard, from gossiping people about Hawkeshead, some snatches of tragical story, which, after all, might be an idle semi-fable, improved out of slight materials)—let this matter have been as it might—at all events he made, what for him turns out, a happy marriage.[94]

Without giving anything concrete away, in the manner of the local gossips he consorts with, he manages to assure his readers that Wordsworth's marriage was happy, whilst giving them every reason to believe that it was not.

In 'Samuel Taylor Coleridge', De Quincey admits that his style is 'desultory and unpremeditated', 'almost *extempore*'.[95] It is, in part, a way of communicating

---

[91] *DQW* xi. 55. Virginia Woolf conveniently ignores such passages when she writes, in *The Common Reader*, 137, that De Quincey's 'portraits have the flowing contours, the statuesque poses, the undifferentiated features of Scott's heroes and heroines'.

[92] See *DQW*, xi. 55–6 and 73: 'I do not conceive that Wordsworth could have been an amiable boy; he was austere and unsocial, I have reason to think, in his habits; not generous; and, above all, not self-denying.'

[93] Ibid. 62.

[94] Ibid. 95.

[95] Ibid. x. 338.

his feelings about Coleridge in an immediate and unaffected manner and, in part, a journalistic necessity, due to the exigencies of the press:

Hence it had occured to the writer as a judicious principle, to create a sort of merit out of his own necessity; and rather to seek after the graces which belong to the epistolary form, or to other modes of composition professedly careless, than after those which grow out of preconceived biographies, which, having originally settled their plan upon a regular foundation, are able to pursue a course of orderly development, such as *his* slight sketch had voluntarily renounced from the beginning.[96]

Cafarelli interprets De Quincey's self-confessedly 'wandering narrative' as deriving from a Wordsworthian poetics of spontaneity, but here we have an alternative model—the 'careless' mode of private correspondence, of conversational rather than monumental prose biography.[97] The idea of the 'preconceived' biography built on 'a regular foundation', refers back to an earlier passage in the essay, where he differentiates between the conversation of 'the reading men in manufacturing towns', demonstrating 'unaffected good sense . . . elasticity and *freshness* of mind', and 'open expression of character', and that of leisured literary men 'who stand in awe of their own reputation' so that their words are studied, artificial, and self-concealing—they are careful never to say anything 'not properly planned and chiselled, to build into the general architecture of an artificial reputation'.[98] He is setting up a distinction here between biography as conversation and as monument—the former having the virtues of open self-expression and appealing to readers who are partially educated but eager for the means to further their self-improvement; the latter being self-protective, closed, frozen in the outmoded decorum of a classically educated elite. This description of his conversational style and the style itself, anecdotal, digressive, ironic, seem a pointed response to Wordsworth's conception of sincere epitaph as selective, spare, lapidary inscription and to the ideology of genius sanctified in this vision. It also challenges Coleridge's ideal of biography as dignified public record, and his horror at the graffiti-like, informal discourse of modern biographical productions. In 'Samuel Taylor Coleridge' De Quincey further specifies that challenge by implying a contrast between Coleridge's sublime conversational digressions and his own 'wandering narrative'. Where Coleridge's digressions are represented as manifesting the poet's splendid obliviousness to his audience, who quickly lose the thread of his rambling monologues, De Quincey displays his concern for the reader, by exposing his own wanderings to view and demystifying the transitions of his essay.[99] He displays the biographer's awareness that his readers need to be included in a conversation rather than subjected to a monologue.

---

[96] Ibid. 338–9.
[97] Ibid. 305. See Cafarelli, *Prose in the Age of Poets*, 161–2.
[98] *DQW* x. 295–6.
[99] See e.g. ibid. 296 where De Quincey writes that he is one of few who can see the circular pattern of Coleridge's discourses: 'Long before this coming-round commenced, most people had

The audience mentioned above is of 'reading men', but De Quincey's gossiping mode sometimes appeals more directly to a female readership. In describing Wordsworth's physical defects, for instance, he takes up a feminine subject position. He notes that Wordsworth's

> legs were pointedly condemned by all the female connoisseurs in legs that I ever heard lecture upon that topic. . . . useful, as they have proved themselves, the Wordsworthian legs were certainly not ornamental; and it was really a pity, as I agreed with a lady in thinking, that he had not another pair for evening dress parties—when no boots lend their friendly aid to masque our imperfections from the eyes of female rigorists—the *elegantes formarum spectatrices.*[100]

The style parodies the gossip column of a ladies magazine, and in so doing ridicules the feminine reduction of the great poet to the apparent trivia of physique and fashion. But, as De Quincey ridicules this style, so, of course, he adopts it and he goes on to relay, as anecdotal evidence, one of the occasions when just such a confidence was made to him by Dorothy Wordsworth—the woman of all women best placed to judge her brother by his genius rather than his figure. De Quincey and Dorothy are out walking. Wordsworth and his friend, Mr J———, 'a fine towering figure, six feet high, massy and columnar in his proportions' are walking ahead of them:

> Miss Wordsworth and myself being in the rear; and from the nature of the conversation which then prevailed in our front rank, something or other about money, devises, buying and selling, we of the rear-guard thought it requisite to preserve this arrangement for a space of three miles or more; during which time, at intervals, Miss W—— would exclaim, in a tone of vexation, 'Is it possible?—can that be William? How very mean he looks!' and could not conceal a mortification that seemed really painful, until I, for my part, could not forbear laughing outright at the serious interest which she carried into this trifle. She was, however, right as regarded the mere visual judgment.[101]

De Quincey and Dorothy are united in walking apart from and behind the great poet and his 'columnar' companion who talk of masculine topics, excluding both. In response the rearguard takes a feminine perspective to mock the 'front rank', gossiping about the back view of the great man.[102] De Quincey laughs at Dorothy's judgement and claims that the criticism is only right on a superficial level. However, he identifies himself with her in this passage and, as we have seen, his own prolonged description of Wordsworth's appearance suggests that the poet's 'meanness' is, in fact, more than merely skin deep. The scene encapsulates the ambivalences of De Quincey's stance as literary biographer throughout the

lost him, and naturally enough supposed that he had lost himself.' Contrast De Quincey, e.g. ibid. 305, 'to resume the thread of my wandering narrative'.

[100] *DQW* xi. 55.
[101] Ibid. 55–6.
[102] See also ibid. 98, where De Quincey recalls Dorothy mentioning William's nervous breakdown to him 'in a whispering tone, and (as if ashamed of it)'.

essays on Coleridge and Wordsworth. He reveres and emulates the masculine genius, but at the same time he always walks one step behind. To be biographer to the great man is to be second best, but, as De Quincey presents it, there are advantages in this position. Gossip is a discourse which unites a community of readers rather than acting to exclude them. In so doing it undermines masculine autonomy by making the private public, representing the poet as not self-created but the creation of others.

The essays on Coleridge and Wordsworth have much in common, but also show important differences of theme and approach. In the following sections I read them separately in order to display some of the distinctive, many-layered ambivalences of each portrait of the man of genius.

5.5 COLERIDGE

'Samuel Taylor Coleridge' begins by appearing to subscribe to the poet's ability to create himself and thereby the world around him:

> It was, I think, in the month of August, but certainly in the summer season, and certainly in the year 1807, that I first saw this illustrious man, the largest and most spacious intellect, the subtlest and the most comprehensive, in my judgment, that has yet existed amongst men. My knowledge of him as a man of most original genius began about the year 1799.[103]

From the essay's first sentences, Coleridge is hallowed as not only, apparently, divinely self-engendering, but, as co-author of *Lyrical Ballads*, the creator of whole new worlds in which his first readers, De Quincey and Professor Wilson, have been awakened, an unlikely Adam and Eve: 'I found in these poems "the ray of a new morning", and an absolute revelation of untrodden worlds, teeming with power and beauty, as yet unsuspected amongst men'.[104] Yet we cannot go even so far as this into the essay before admitting how the suggestions of Miltonic sublimity, already pointing to a poetic forefather, are oddly compromised by De Quincey's intrusive presence—the interposition of the phrase 'in my judgment' interrupts what otherwise promises to be an assertion of universal acclaim. Likewise, De Quincey cannot mention the appearance of *Lyrical Ballads* except in relation to his own response to it, although this is done with a characteristically self-promoting pretence at self-effacement: 'It would be directing the reader's attention too much to myself, if I were to linger upon this, the greatest event in the unfolding of my own mind'.[105] This is neither autobiography nor biography, but auto/biography, where the biographer has two, competing subjects: himself

---

[103] Ibid. x. 287.
[104] Ibid.
[105] Ibid.

and Coleridge, who are both child and father to each other. De Quincey presents himself as Coleridge's creation, but also as his creator. Where each of Johnson's *Lives of the Poets* typically begin with the subject's date and place of birth, De Quincey's subject is born, not in 1772, but at the moment he first meets his biographer—his conception is some years previously at the time when De Quincey first reads his poetry. These events are presented as the moments of the biographer's own first awakening, but the implication is also that his subject only comes to life at the point when he first comes into De Quincey's orbit.[106] The meeting between biographer and subject is not merely the first, but the pivotal event of the essay, a primal scene to which we are repeatedly returned. The opening of the essay culminates in the encounter, where the hitherto disembodied Coleridge is climactically made flesh and named by his biographer.[107] The narrative thereafter is presented as the biographer's meditation following that encounter. A chronological account of Coleridge's life starts here, but it is written as the creation of De Quincey's mind—a 'wandering' narrative, as we have seen, mapped out mentally as he walks the 40 miles back to Bristol on the evening of first setting eyes on Coleridge, and circling back again to the first encounter—the third time this event is recurred to in the essay. Subsequently the chronology continues, intermittently, but again with emphasis on those parts of it wherein De Quincey has, himself, been directly involved— the London lecture series, and the meetings between himself and the poet in the Lakes in 1809 and 1810.

The relationship between biographer and subject is represented throughout the essay as one of mutual dependency. De Quincey, like others after him, writes biography as a quest narrative, the biographer engaged in an inner and outer pursuit of his subject.[108] He draws attention to the likeness of himself and Coleridge—both reading the same authors, both procrastinators, both opium-eaters—and it is always open to question whether the biographer is taking on the image of his subject or vice versa. He claims, for instance, to have 'read for thirty years in the same track as Coleridge,—that track in which few of any age will ever follow us', but the order of precedence is uncertain—earlier in the essay De Quincey represents himself as the originator and Coleridge as belated: 'he had for some time applied his whole mind to metaphysics and psychology,— which happened to be my own absorbing pursuit'.[109] As De Quincey pursues Coleridge, through the villages of England, to the Lakes and to London, the biographer's life is not only emotionally but materially linked to his subject's, but De Quincey is careful to demonstrate his own power to return the favour by

---

[106] See also the first sentence of the 'Lake Reminiscences': 'In 1807 it was, at the beginning of winter, that I first saw William Wordsworth', *DQW* xi. 43.

[107] *DQW* x. 295.

[108] See e.g. A. J. A. Symons, *The Quest for Corvo* (London: Cassell, 1934) and Richard Holmes, *Shelley: The Pursuit* (London: Weidenfeld and Nicolson, 1974).

[109] *DQW* x. 293, 288.

revealing himself, for example, as Coleridge's secret financial benefactor and his amanuensis—placing marked passages in his hand to sustain his crumbling lecture series.[110]

His account of the mutually dependent relationship between biographer and subject mocks both. His pursuit of the anonymous authors of *Lyrical Ballads* is a parody of the heroic quest narratives of Romantic poetry, the hyperbole always threatening to deflate. Wordsworth and Coleridge are figured as illusive, female objects of his desire—as a young man he did not speak of either to others, in the same way that a 'lover' would shrink 'from giving up the name of his beloved to the coarse license of a Bacchanalian party'. His wish to know their identities was 'self-baffled' by dread at hearing their hallowed names profaned. There is a comic flight and pursuit as the biographer stalks his subject—Coleridge, De Quincey learns, has gone to Malta: 'I began to inquire about the best route to Malta; but, as any route at that time promised an inside place in a French prison, I reconciled myself to waiting'.[111] Temporarily thwarted by history, De Quincey bides his time until 'at last, happening to visit a relative at the Bristol Hot-wells, in the summer of 1807, I had the pleasure to hear that Mr. Coleridge was not only once more upon English ground, but within 40 and odd miles of my own station. In that same hour I mounted and bent my way to the south'. But he arrives at Mr Poole's at Nether Stowey just too late—the poet has already left for Lord Egmont's house and is now possibly 'on the wing to another friend's in the town of Bridgewater'.[112] The self-directed irony here shows De Quincey's awareness of the vulnerability of the literary biographer in relation to an ideology of genius which privileges originality—being there first—but also defends his inevitable belatedness. De Quincey's quest for Coleridge reveals that, although the subject appears to be always one step ahead of his biographer, he too is belated—his chaotic schedule the result of his habit of procrastination. The distinction between them is Coleridge's obliviousness to his position.

During the pursuit of Coleridge, action is suspended whilst De Quincey awaits an opportunity for meeting the poet. In the interim he talks with Mr Poole about their mutual friend. This is the moment when De Quincey decisively reveals what has been a spectre lurking in the narrative from its start: that Coleridge is not, after all, self-created, but a plagiarist. Mr Poole asks De Quincey's opinion on the originality of the interpretation given by Coleridge to Pythagoras' doctrine 'that a man might as well, for the wickedness of the thing, eat his own grandmother as meddle with beans'. De Quincey confirms that Coleridge has plagiarized a German author who argues that what Pythagoras intends us to understand by this is 'abstain from public affairs as you would from parricide'. De Quincey has been granted a tempting authority over the poet here

[110] See ibid. 304 and 321.
[111] Ibid. 287–8.
[112] Ibid. 288.

by Poole and does not pass up the opportunity to kill Coleridge with compli-
ments: 'if it should appear that Coleridge has robbed him [the German], be
assured that he has done the scamp too much honour'. He then goes on to detail
several more instances of Coleridge's plagiarism since spotted by himself as a way,
he says disingenuously, 'to forestal [*sic*] . . . other discoverers who would make a
more unfriendly use of the discovery'.[113] Again we find De Quincey trying to
arrive first, before the detractors of Coleridge in this case, and, in a sense, before
Coleridge himself, in proving that he has been to the poet's sources already. The
catalogue of thefts undermines the essay's initial claim of Coleridge's 'most
original genius', especially since what is being exposed here is not so much
particular plagiarisms, as the myth of creative autonomy itself.[114] He argues
that all poets will have debts to 'the great fathers of poetry' (although the first
author mentioned by De Quincey in his list of Coleridge's borrowings is a female
poet—Frederica Brun).[115] Coleridge and Wordsworth borrow from Milton who,
in turn, has borrowed from other poets. In arguing that to steal from Milton is 'as
impossible as to appropriate, or sequester to a private use, some "bright particular
star"', De Quincey merely confirms the impossibility of the self-creating genius.

Whilst Coleridge pretends to be self-created, he is, in fact, dependent on those
around him—on his poetic forerunners and contemporaries, his readers and
disciples such as Professor Wilson and De Quincey himself, and his family, and
friends, all of whom support him in a spirit of domestic nurturing. De Quincey
quotes from 'Resolution and Independence' to illustrate Coleridge's good fortune in receiving care from others, where he gave none for himself and comments
that '[f]ast as one friend dropped off, another, and another, succeeded: perpetual
relays were laid along his path in life, of judicious and zealous supporters;
who comforted his days, and smoothed the pillow for his declining age'.[116]
The 'perpetual relays' of friends are a structuring presence in De Quincey's
narrative—we hear of Mr Poole, Lord Egmont, and others who put him up as
a house guest for indefinite periods—but, as Coleridge moves from one house to
the next, so a disquieting sense grows of the poet's failure to acknowledge his debt
to those who support him. His 'domestication' with Basil Montagu in London
ends badly when the poet ignores his host's banishment of alcohol from his house
and invites a friend in to drink wine.[117] Unable to see beyond his own desire,
Coleridge not only fails to acknowledge what he owes to his host, but, by
disrupting the household from within, usurps his host's authority and even,
by setting himself up as the host, his identity. It is one of a series of embedded
narratives in the essay where De Quincey exposes the myth of the autonomous

---

[113] *DQW* x. 289–90.
[114] Ibid. 287.
[115] Ibid. 290. It would be wrong to make too much of this—De Quincey is clear that this is the
least important of the thefts (the others are all from male writers).
[116] Ibid. 336–7.
[117] Ibid. 333.

genius through an image of the appropriation of domestic space. In so doing he rewrites one of the most famous of all literary biographies—Johnson's *An Account of the Life of Mr. Richard Savage* (1744).

In Johnson's *Life of Savage*, the story of the writer compelled to author his own life is told as a fable of homelessness and the desire for a home. Johnson represents Savage's decision to become a writer as forced upon him by the fact that he is cruelly illegitimated by his parents: 'He was therefore obliged to seek some other Means of Support, and having no Profession, became, by Necessity, an Author'.[118] Having no name, Savage has to make one for himself. His search takes him to his supposed mother's house, where he lingers outside in the dark, but is thrown out when he tries to gain entry. Johnson comments that 'I know not whether he ever had, for three Months together, a settled Habitation, in which he could claim a Right of Residence' and Savage's life is represented throughout the essay as a series of moves between houses which he tries to transform into homes— the 'mean Houses' and 'Cellars' which he inhabits when penniless and the houses of a succession of patrons, each of whose hospitality he violates by behaving as owner rather than as guest.[119] When Lord Tyrconnel takes him in, Johnson's Savage, like De Quincey's Coleridge after him, chooses to 'assume the Government of the House', this time by ordering his host's butler 'to set the best Wine in the Cellar before his Company, who often drank till they forgot the Respect due to the House in which they were entertained'.[120] At the same time as he treats his patron's home as his own, he complains of the necessity of dependency—he laments 'the Misery of living at the Tables of other Men, which was his Fate from the Beginning to the End of his Life'.[121] Thus, Savage 'scarcely ever found a Stranger, whom he did not leave a Friend; but it must likewise be added, that he had not often a Friend long, without obliging him to become a Stranger'.[122] Johnson's wry symmetry suggests that Savage should have made the best of his position by submitting more graciously to his patrons' authority. His homelessness is not, in itself, heroic in Johnson's eyes, but an occasion for ironic reflection on the disparity between the material condition of the man and the magnitude of his works: 'On a Bulk, in a Cellar, or in a Glass-house among Thieves and Beggars, was to be found the Author of the *Wanderer*, the Man of exalted Sentiments, extensive Views and curious Observations'.[123]

De Quincey admired Johnson's *Life of Savage* and his account of his own vagrancy in Wales and London in the *Confessions* is in part a Romantic reading of the earlier biography, alluding to Johnson's lyrical accounts of Savage's

---

[118] Samuel Johnson, *Life of Savage*, ed. Clarence Tracy (Oxford: Clarendon Press, 1971), 12.
[119] Ibid. 52.
[120] Ibid. 59–60.
[121] Ibid. 52.
[122] Ibid. 60.
[123] Ibid. 97.

homelessness and recasting them as an ironically heroic self-authoring. Yet De Quincey also believed that Savage was 'the vilest of swindlers', 'an impostor who would now be sent to the tread-mill', who had hoodwinked Johnson into believing and abetting a 'monstrous libel' in persuading him that Lady Maccles-field was his mother.[124] In fulminating against Savage, De Quincey takes on what John Barrell has rightly identified as a characteristic role as defender of womanhood against male aggression. Savage 'had no legal claims upon her, consequently no pretence for molesting her in her dwelling-house', '[s]he, unhappily, as a woman banished without hope from all good society by her early misconduct as a wife (but, let it not be forgotten, a neglected wife), had nobody to speak a word on her behalf'.[125] Even had Savage's claim been true, he deserved to be ejected from her house as 'a disorderly reprobate'.[126] He was neither a gentleman, nor a genius as Johnson thought, in fact his work is unreadable.[127]

De Quincey's Coleridge is in many ways a recasting of Johnson's Savage. We can see this in the parallels between the narratives of their lives as a catalogue of moves between the houses of patrons, violating hospitality as they go, but the terms in which De Quincey excoriates Savage and his works are strong and seem, at first sight, in stark contrast to the reverential descriptions of Coleridge and his genius. Yet, if Savage is a criminal 'impostor', then, as De Quincey makes clear, so is Coleridge—not only a cuckoo in the nest, but a plagiarist, a thief of others' intellectual property. It is significant that De Quincey's ire is roused repeatedly in his work by Savage's attempts to insinuate himself into his 'mother's' home, for here what De Quincey reads as Savage's appropriation of a false identity, is enacted as a sexual violation. If we return to his essays on Coleridge, we will see in a sequence of emblematic moments in the narrative, that the violation of the domestic as a sexual act is also De Quincey's central figure here for the delusion of the masculine genius in believing that he can author himself.

Two of these emblematic moments contain figures of a violation of the domestic that relate to Coleridge's plagiarism. The first passage draws an analogy between the poet's kleptomania and the compulsion of some millionaires to commit petty theft:

With the riches of El Dorado lying about him, he would condescend to filch a handful of gold from any man whose purse he fancied; and in fact reproduced in a new form, applying itself to intellectual wealth, that maniacal propensity which is sometimes well known to attack enormous proprietors and *millionaires* for acts of petty larceny. The last Duke of Anc— could not abstain from exercising his furtive mania upon articles so

---

[124] See 'Gilfillan's Literary Portraits: Keats' (1846), *DQW* xv. 305 n.; 'Pope', ibid. xiii. 269 n.; and 'Some Thoughts on Biography', ibid. xxi. 33.

[125] Ibid. xxi. 33.

[126] Ibid. 34.

[127] Ibid. 32–3.

humble as silver spoons; and it was the daily care of a pious daughter, watching over the good name of her father, to have his pockets searched by a confidential valet, and the claimants of the purloined articles traced out.[128]

Coleridge, the plagiarist, is like a man who, by stealing silver spoons, destroys domestic trust, and De Quincey, the discrete discoverer of Coleridge's thefts, projects himself as the 'pious daughter' who mothers her father by searching his pockets. This figures the biographer's discovery of the Coleridgean thefts as a feminine restoration of domestic order, disrupted by a childlike male. It is both sustaining (the daughter searches discreetly and does not attempt to stop her father from stealing) and implicitly critical (she takes the spoons back and replaces them). It is a scenario that De Quincey recurs to in another extended simile for Coleridge's plagiarisms. Did the reader, he asks,

ever amuse himself by searching the pockets of a child—three years old, suppose, when buried in slumber after a long summer's day of out-a-door's intense activity? I have done this; and, for the amusement of the child's mother, have analyzed the contents, and drawn up a formal register of the whole. Philosophy is puzzled, conjecture and hypothesis are confounded, in the attempt to explain the law of selection which *can* have presided in the child's labours: stones remarkable only for weight, old rusty hinges, nails, crooked skewers, stolen when the cook had turned her back, rags, broken glass, tea-cups having the bottom knocked out, and loads of similar jewels, were the prevailing articles in this *procés verbal.*[129]

In this second pocket-searching scenario, Coleridge's thefts are revealed as practically and aesthetically worthless, appearing as jewels only to the deluded poet. As in the Duke of Anc— anecdote, his thieving has been from the domestic realm—garden and kitchen—and again Coleridge's quest for self-substantiation is both discreetly sustained by the feminine picking of his pockets (De Quincey in alliance with the mother), and exposed to view as childlike self-absorption—the boy's deep slumber recalls Coleridge's opium habit, his most notorious dependency.

As the essay on Coleridge proceeds, anecdotes accumulate which replay the scene, in various forms, and at various removes, of Coleridge's quest for autonomy unmasked by the biographer as a violation of the domestic sphere. An unnamed female (perhaps Dorothy Wordsworth) comes in wet after a walk in the rain and laughingly helps herself to Mrs Coleridge's wardrobe. Although this is done in all innocence, Mrs Coleridge is mortified: 'she felt herself no longer the entire mistress of her own house; she held a divided empire'. De Quincey gives more sympathy here to Dorothy than to Mrs Coleridge, but is critical of Coleridge for failing to support his wife in the incident:

it barbed the arrow to her womanly feelings, that Coleridge treated any sallies of resentment which might sometimes escape her, as narrow-mindedness; whilst, on the

---

[128] *DQW* x. 292.
[129] Ibid. 293.

other hand, her own female servant, and others in the same rank of life, began to drop expressions, which alternately implied pity for her as an injured woman, or sneered at her as a very tame one.[130]

Coleridge gives tacit approval to another (this time a female) act of appropriation and thus stands by yet again whilst a household becomes divided against itself. The anecdote is adumbrated by an incident involving his father. The Revd Coleridge, a naïve 'Parson Adams', is characterized as a solipsistic scholar, blind to the effect of his intellectual enthusiasms on others—he peppers his sermons with Hebrew quotations and, in his Latin Grammar, proposes to rename the accusative case the '"*quale-quare-quidditive*"' by way of simplifying it for students. This blindness to his audience (inherited by his son, in his tendency to monologue and his disastrous lecturing technique) is enhanced by literal shortsightedness which leads him to an embarrassing encounter at dinner. He notices that his shirt has become untucked:

The stray portion of his supposed tunic was admonished of its errors by a forcible thrust back into its proper home; but still another *limbus* persisted to emerge, or seemed to persist, and still another, until the learned gentleman absolutely perspired with the labour of re-establishing order. And, after all, he saw with anguish, that some arrears of the snowy indecorum still remained to reduce into obedience. To this remnant of rebellion he was proceeding to apply himself—strangely confounded, however, at the obstinacy of the insurrection—when the mistress of the house, rising to lead away the ladies from the table, and all parties naturally rising with her, it became suddenly apparent to every eye, that the worthy Orientalist had been most laboriously stowing away, into the capacious receptacles of his own habiliments, the snowy folds of a lady's gown, belonging to his next neighbour . . . the lady appeared almost inextricably yoked to the learned theologian.[131]

Coleridge's thefts are again displaced in a clothes-stealing episode which explicates more fully the previous one. Like Dorothy, who took Mrs Coleridge's clothes as if they were her own, Coleridge's father believes he is simply repossessing himself, by tucking his shirt in. The tone is of high comedy, but the figurative language is of violent sexual and social suppression—the 'forcible thrust', the effort 'to reduce into obedience'. Later in the essay the figure of sexual violation is literalized in the story of 'Augustus Hope', a man who lives by constructing a series of false identities by which he is able serially to seduce and abandon young women, including the 'Beauty of Buttermere'.[132] The revelation that his identity is false brings about his downfall (he is tried for forgery). Coleridge is outraged by the man's conduct, but the foregoing chain of anecdotes, allying the poet's own search for self with an intrusion into feminine

[130] *DQW* x. 302–3.
[131] Ibid. 305–6.
[132] Ibid. 312–17.

domestic space, links him to the Lake District impostor, as it does to the impostor Savage.[133]

The first of the essays on Coleridge was published in *Tait's* side by side with 'What shall we do with our Young Fellows?', Johnstone's feminist response to the question, 'What shall we do with our spinsters?'[134] The *Tait's* readership may have found a feminist inflection in De Quincey's account of Coleridge's monstrous, masculine ego. Yet, if De Quincey defends a feminine principle of domestic community in these essays, he is not always a defender of its female representatives. Mrs Coleridge, in particular, is not kindly drawn. They first meet when she enters the drawing room where De Quincey is closeted with her husband. Coleridge receives her coldly and she silently retires:

From this short, but ungenial scene, I gathered, what I afterward learned redundantly, that Coleridge's marriage had not been a very happy one. But let not the reader misunderstand me. Never was there a baser insinuation, viler in the motive, or more ignoble in the manner, than that passage in some lampoon of Lord Byron's, where, by way of vengeance on Mr. Southey, (who was the sole delinquent,) he described both him and Coleridge as having married 'two milliners from Bath.' Everybody knows what is *meant* to be conveyed by that expression . . . However, in this case, the whole sting of the libel was a pure falsehood of Lord Byron's. Bath was not the native city, nor at any time the residence of the ladies in question, but Bristol.[135]

Despite the implied parallels between the situations of Mrs Coleridge and De Quincey—both would-be interlocutors of the great poet, who find themselves silenced by his monologues—the biographer's gossiping anecdote mischievously perpetuates Byron's aristocratic contempt for her mundane origins, and his slur on her sexual reputation.[136] It is another example of the clash between genius and domestic life, but this time, De Quincey suggests that the nature of domestic life may be partly to blame. His biographical essays are marked by such ambivalences. 'Samuel Taylor Coleridge' exposes the self-creating, masculine genius as a myth, yet inevitably it resurfaces in the essay as an object of veneration. This is the case, for instance in the essay's ending, where he has promised an assessment of Coleridge's genius which he signally fails to deliver, citing, as usual, exigencies of the press by way of excuse. This ironic absence might be read as another way of undermining the biographical subject—a refusal to construct biography as monument, and a decision to trail off in anecdote, in keeping with the model of biography as gossip.

---

[133] De Quincey also tells an anecdote relating to Coleridge and theft in 'Coleridge and Opium-Eating', *DQW* xv. 108, where, as a child, he pretends to swim the Hellespont in the street and is falsely accused of pickpocketing. When his accuser learns his mistake he gives Coleridge a free subscription to a circulating library. It is yet another instance of the dependency of genius on the sustaining kindness of others.

[134] Christian Johnstone, 'What shall we do with our Young Fellows?', *Tait's*, 1/8 (Sept. 1834), 527–30.

[135] *DQW* x. 300.

[136] He does go on to defend the sisters' reputation, but the damage has been done.

However, it is also open to being read as a reverential gesture of deference to the power of the poet in conformity with Wordsworth's ideal epitaph—the biographer bows to the mystery of genius in silence. The essays on Wordsworth are no less ambivalent—at once a gossiping critique of the poet who masks his dependencies on female domestic communities, and an act of profound reverence. Here, however, the poet's capacity to disregard his readers becomes a more insistent theme.

5.6 WORDSWORTH

De Quincey's writings on Coleridge frame him as a threatening doppelgänger—a more respected opium-eater, a more acclaimed Germanist and philosopher. But, if Coleridge was always too close to De Quincey for comfort, Wordsworth was too distant. In his first letters to the younger man Wordsworth was friendly and generous, to the extent of confiding his plans for the poems later to become *The Prelude*, *The Recluse*, and *The Excursion* but, following De Quincey's move to the Lakes, tensions began to emerge between De Quincey and the Wordsworth family over matters such as his marriage to Margaret Simspon, a farmer's daughter, and his opium habit.[137] The 'Lake Reminiscences' and the closely related 'Sketches' which follow, tell the story of De Quincey's desire for companionship with the poet as it met Wordsworth's determination gradually to exclude his acolyte from the charmed circle of family and friends. They contain passages, later suppressed, which candidly describe the souring of his early hero worship:

sometimes even I feel a rising emotion of hostility—nay, something, I fear, too nearly akin to vindictive hatred. Strange revolution of the human heart! . . . *now*, I find myself standing aloof, gloomily granting (because I cannot refuse) my intellectual homage, but no longer rendering my tribute as a willing service of the heart, or rejoicing in the prosperity of my idol![138]

Here he warns Wordsworth directly against hubris and, in one of the 'Sketches' which followed the 'Reminiscences', he portrays him as the model for Satan in his 'inhuman arrogance':

insomuch that I used to say, Never describe Wordsworth as equal in pride to Lucifer; no, but if you have occasion to write a life of Lucifer, set down that, by possibility, in respect to pride, he might be some type of Wordsworth . . .[139]

---

[137] See letters from Wordsworth to De Quincey, 29 July 1803; 6 Mar. [1804]; and 19 Mar. [1804], in Wordsworth, *Letters*, i. 399–401, 452–5, 457–8. See 454 for Wordsworth on his poetic projects. For Margaret and opium as sources of tension, see Jordan, *De Quincey to Wordsworth*, 217 ff. and 285 ff.

[138] *DQW* xi. 62–3. De Quincey censored this passage along with much else expressing direct bitterness towards Wordsworth when he revised the essays for his collective edition in the 1850s, see ibid. 40–1.

[139] Ibid. 253, 256.

When De Quincey looked back on his relationship with Wordsworth from the vantage point of 1840, he reflected that 'never after the first year or so from my first introduction, had I felt much possibility of drawing the bonds of friendship tight with a man of Wordsworth's nature'.[140]

De Quincey's own first (and last) relationship with Wordsworth, as described in the 'Lake Reminiscences', is as his reader, but framed in terms that also suggest an intense sexual devotion.[141] In the first of the 'Reminiscences' he looks back to 1803 and his youthful reverence for Wordsworth, as yet only known through his poetry, as a '"nympholepsy"', figuring the poet as the feminine and unattainable object of the reader's desire.[142] At their first meeting in Westmoreland De Quincey compares himself to Semele, incinerated by Zeus' lightning.[143] It is an ominous opening to the reader/writer relationship and one that prefigures De Quincey's claim in the 'Reminiscences' that both he and Professor Wilson— Wordsworth's earliest and for many years, as De Quincey tells it, his only readers—were ultimately treated with indifference.[144] He had hoped, at first, to talk with Wordsworth 'on something like equal terms, as respected the laws and principles of poetry', but Wordsworth eventually failed to make 'those returns of friendship and kindness' he believed he, and Wilson, deserved.[145] The relationship is represented, from the vantage point of 1839, as irretrievably damaged:

by error, more or less, on one side or the other, either on Wordsworth's in doing too little, or on mine in expecting too much . . .[146]

This is a comment on a personal rift between the two men, but the withdrawal of De Quincey's heartfelt tribute cannot be dissociated from his description of Wordsworth's relationship with his other readers too.

---

[140] Ibid. 255.
[141] He collaborated, uneasily, with Wordsworth in editing his pamphlet on the Convention of Cintra and some subsequent essays. For details of this aspect of the writers' relationship see Robert Morrison, Review of Margaret Russet, *De Quincey's Romanticism: Canonical Minority and the Forms of Transmission*, *Romanticism On the Net* 10 (May 1998) at <http://www.erudit.org/revue/ron/1998/v/n10/005803ar.html>.
[142] *DQW* xi. 43.
[143] Ibid. 49.
[144] Wordsworth was, in fact, welcoming and considerate in responding to De Quincey's first fan letters. See Jordan, *De Quincey to Wordsworth* and Lindop, *The Opium-Eater*, 118. De Quincey's later resentments did not prevent him from acknowledging his own responsibility for delaying their first meeting and for burdening their relationship with excessive emotional demands—see *DQW* xi. 43-7. He also acknowledged the kindness and hospitality with which Wordsworth treated him on that first visit—see ibid. 50.
[145] Ibid. 46, 62.
[146] Ibid. 62-3.

Whilst De Quincey, writing in the late 1830s, works from the premiss of Wordsworth's fame, one of his favourite themes is the poet's early failure to attract an audience.[147] With wry humour, De Quincey narrates Wordsworth's life as a fairy tale of liberation from the constraints of the marketplace. Supported by a series of providential windfalls, he inhabits a fantasy world of pre-industrial patronage.[148] That it is an illusion is clear, for his early problems with publishing have never entirely disappeared. De Quincey is careful to inform his readers on several occasions that Wordsworth's great philosophical poem (*The Prelude*) is, for reasons never stated, still in manuscript.[149] In paraphrasing and quoting from this poem, as the basis for a substantial portion of his biographical narrative, he implies Wordsworth's dependency on his ability to publicize his work in the periodical press. It is significant, in this light, that De Quincey reminds his *Tait's* readers that it is not Southey's poetry which '"*made the pot boil*"', but his prose in the *Quarterly Review*, and states that 'with all his immeasurable genius, Wordsworth has not, even yet, and from long experience, acquired any popular talent of writing for the current press'.[150] He clearly believed that Wordsworth needed some help with his marketing decisions. In an unpublished 'Letter to Mr Tait Concerning the Poetry of Wordsworth', written for *Tait's* in May 1838, De Quincey proposed that he should edit a cheap, popular edition of Wordsworth's poetry. A 'literary man', known to him, he writes, had had the original idea

that an edition of Mr. Wordsworth's poems upon coarse paper, and in every other way adapted to purchasers of the lowest rank, would form a most acceptable present to the great number (now annually growing rapidly) of grave meditative men in the class of mechanics and artizans both here and in the . . . American United States, and throughout our vast colonial empire.[151]

Unlike Wordsworth, De Quincey would anticipate the tastes of readers, excluding 'poems not adapted to the . . . taste which is likely to grow up in such classes of society', an editorial decision which will have 'corresponding advantages to the purse of the buyers'. He would also add notes for the benefit of readers 'not classically educated' or 'not familiar by long habit with his style of thinking', for there is 'a Delphic obscurity' in Wordsworth poems, and not just for these classes of readers.[152] 'Delphic obscurity' is a phrase he had used in 1823 to describe Coleridge's explanations of Kant—himself, an 'oracle' of obscurity.[153] In applying the

---

[147] See *DQW* x. 145–6, 239–40, 287 and xi. 83–4.
[148] See *DQW* xi. 96–102. De Quincey alludes here, ironically, to Wordsworth's anxieties of authorship, inspired by Chatterton and Burns, as expressed in 'Resolution and Independence'.
[149] See e.g. *DQW* xi. 80.
[150] Ibid. 122, 98.
[151] Ibid. 586–7.
[152] Ibid. 588.
[153] Ibid. iii. 95.

phrase to Wordsworth, De Quincey impugns the poet's ability to communicate in a particularly pointed manner. He excuses the obscurity as a sublime effect, but also asserts his own critical power to meet the need of all readers, and especially the less well-educated and the newcomer, for clarification of the sublime.[154] In 1838, in the 'Reminiscences' and in the 'Letter to Mr Tait', De Quincey imagined the readership of the future expanding outwards into the British colonies, sustained by the great voices of English literature in popular editions. In the 'Reminiscences' he envisaged these readers as young women, seduced by Shakespeare:

even in the farthest depths of Canada, many a young innocent girl, perhaps, at this very moment—looking now with fear to the dark recesses of the infinite forest, and now with love to the pages of the infinite poet, until the fear is absorbed and forgotten in the love . . .[155]

He predicted here, in his 'Letter' to Tait, and in the concluding sentence of 'On Wordsworth's Poetry', that the poet would find a place beside Shakespeare in the hearts of readers. In 1838 he spoke of this audience as one of self-educating colonialists, for whom Wordsworth's work would become a secular

bead-roll of sentiments . . . teaching him benignity towards man and resignation towards heaven; instructing him finally (in the very words of the Poet) 'To prize the breath we share with human kind.
   And look upon the dust of man with awe.'[156]

This unpublished proposal, from the 'Letter' to Tait, together with the recurring theme of Wordsworth's difficulties with gaining readers, in the published *Tait's* essays, may be read in several ways. They can be seen, in the context of Wordsworth's 'Essay Supplementary to the Preface', as a defence of Wordsworth's own position, that an initial failure in popularity is, itself, a sign of the original genius of a literary work. Yet, in conjunction with the representation of the poet's relationship with De Quincey and other readers, they raise the question of Wordsworth's degree of adaptability to the contemporary readership and his responsibility to his audience, and suggest, by contrast, De Quincey's own critical acuity and market savvy. The people's *Wordsworth*, edited by De Quincey, did not materialize, but it was a project encapsulating his desire to create a role for himself mediating the sublime to a popular audience on the largest possible scale and attracting that readership on behalf of a poet who was, as he saw it, ill-fitted to do so for himself. In his biographical portrait of Wordsworth, De Quincey represents a divergence between his own and the poet's practice of relating to the readership, and does so by suggesting the congruence

---

[154] As part of this De Quincey proposed to restore Wordsworth's poems to their original versions in his edition—see ibid. xi. 588.
[155] Ibid. 61.
[156] Ibid. 594–5.

of a writer's relationship with his public and his private relationships, especially with women.

De Quincey suggests that Wordsworth, like Coleridge, is unable to behave properly to his female relatives and friends. Having presented himself as Wordsworth's spurned lover, he makes the poet's lack of chivalry a keynote of his character and, by implication, of his relationship with his readers more generally. In the 'Lake Reminiscences' Wordsworth's masculinity is presented as unyielding—his 'character, in all its features, wore a masculine and Roman harshness'.[157] De Quincey recalls his own and Professor Wilson's astonishment that he could ever have submitted himself to the 'self-surrender' of courtship:

> That self-surrender—that prostration of mind, by which a man is too happy and proud to express the profundity of his service to the woman of his heart—it seemed a mere impossibility that ever Wordsworth should be brought to feel for a single instant. . . . There never lived the woman whom he would not have lectured and admonished under circumstances that should have seemed to require it; nor would he have conversed with her in any mood whatever without wearing an air of mild condescension to her understanding.[158]

Unlike De Quincey, who rhapsodizes on his own awakening love for Margaret, his future wife, Wordsworth 'had not the feelings within him which make this total devotion to a woman possible'.[159] He could never forget himself sufficiently to indulge in this worship of the opposite sex, 'to burthen himself with a lady's reticule, parasol, shawl, "or anything that was hers"'. He needed '[f]reedom—unlimited, careless, insolent freedom—unoccupied possession of his own arms—absolute control over his own legs and motions'.[160] It is an image of the sublime self-containment of masculine, poetic genius. In a passage directly following this, but cut before publication, he juxtaposed an anecdote illustrating Wordsworth's early lack of success with his public and one revealing his lack of chivalry.[161] At a dinner party in 1810, a stuttering lawyer says Wordsworth has made 'a d-d-damnation fool of himself' in his poems. This is followed by an account of a quarrel between William and Dorothy. De Quincey, walking in the darkness along a Lakeland road, unwillingly overhears an irritable exchange between the poet and his sister. The only phrase he relays to us is from Dorothy: ' "O <brother> William, I will walk by myself" '.[162] In embarrassment, De Quincey avoids

---

[157] *DQW* xi. 197.

[158] Ibid. 93.

[159] Ibid. Part of De Quincey's motivation for these comments derived from his resentment of the coldness of Wordsworth and his circle towards Margaret—see ibid. 64 n. 53 and Lindop, *The Opium-Eater*, 220. Wordsworth's letters to Mary Wordsworth show that, in his private correspondence, at least, he did submit to the self-abnegating role of the courtly lover—see e.g. *The Love Letters of William and Mary Wordsworth*, ed. Beth Darlington (London: Chatto and Windus, 1982), 39.

[160] *DQW* xi. 73.

[161] '[Cancelled Passage from "William Wordsworth"]', ibid. 578–81.

[162] Ibid. 579–81.

joining them. It is, of course, an ironic commentary on the sibling relationship as represented by Wordsworth in 'Tintern Abbey', from which De Quincey quotes earlier in the passage.[163] The excised anecdotes together portray Wordsworth as a man with the capacity to alienate not only the general public but his second self and most loyal, private audience.

A running theme in the later 'Sketches' is the failure of either Coleridge or Wordsworth to impress their female neighbours with their writing. De Quincey's own, amicable relations with the female social networks in the Lakes give him an insight into how unpopular the work of both Coleridge and Wordsworth is with this potential audience of women. Although fully aware of the existence of their work, they refuse to read it. The refusal is politically motivated—the Misses Cullen and Mrs Millar, Scottish sisters, influenced by the *Edinburgh Review*, will not mention either author or have anything to do with them.[164] We might expect some censure of this devotion to the *Edinburgh Review*, which is, earlier in the series, taken to task for its vindictive sabotage of Wordsworth's early career and which was one of *Tait's* main rivals. But De Quincey comments that the prejudices of the Misses Cullen and Mrs Millar would only have been confirmed if they had read Coleridge's *The Friend*, nominated the Delphic Oracle, on account of its obscurity, by the daughter of the Bishop of Llandaff, a judgement De Quincey thinks justified on the grounds of Coleridge's 'shocking want of adaptation to his audience'.[165]

Wordsworth's lack of feeling for his public is most overtly criticized by De Quincey in terms of the poet's deficiencies as a reader and, more specifically, as a reader of contemporary fiction by women. His contempt for books generally is a theme of the essays and clearly one of the means by which De Quincey competitively ingratiates himself with his audience.[166] The 'extreme limitation of his literary sensibilities', helped on by his natural '*one-sidedness, (einseitigkeit)*' means that

Thousands of books, that have given the most genuine and even rapturous delight to millions of ingenuous minds, for Wordsworth were absolutely a dead letter—closed and sealed up from his sensibilities and his powers of appreciation, not less than colours from a blind man's eye...[167]

He is especially dismissive of female novelists. De Quincey, who believes that two of Harriet Lee's *Canterbury Tales* are 'absolutely unrivalled as specimens of fine narration', lends 'The German's Tale' to Wordsworth, who 'for once, having, I suppose, nothing else to read... condescended to run through it'. The poet's verdict is merely that it leaves 'an uncomfortable impression of a woman as being

---

[163] Ibid. 579.
[164] Ibid. 184–5. See also the reaction of Miss Wilkes, future wife of Francis Jeffrey, ibid. 188–9.
[165] Ibid. 186.
[166] See ibid. 117–18 and 132.
[167] Ibid. 96–7.

too clever'. Wordsworth reads Ann Radcliffe's *The Italian*, 'by some strange accident . . . only to laugh at it'. De Quincey's outrage at these reactions chimes with the championship of women's writing encouraged by Johnstone in *Tait's*. The poet's lack of appreciation for women's fiction, combined with his unaccountable preference for the morally 'disgusting' novels of Smollett, Fielding, and Le Sage, convince De Quincey of his 'defective sympathy . . . with the universal feelings of his age'.[168] The passage shows how De Quincey expresses an enthusiasm for contemporary popular fiction by women that is, precisely, directed *against* the Wordsworthian aristocracy of 'Power', and towards engaging the sympathies of a broadly based readership.[169]

By contrast to his portrait of Wordsworth and as a mark of his solicitude towards the readers of *Tait's*, De Quincey sets out to demonstrate throughout the 'Reminiscences', his own chivalrous devotion to women and especially his affinities with Wordsworth's female associates. He arrives in Westmoreland, as the travelling companion of Mrs Coleridge, in the role of protector of women. Temporarily diverted by his first sight of Wordsworth, he confesses that he forgot to hand her down from the carriage, but, having passed into Wordsworth's cottage, his sympathies with the feminine perspective re-establish themselves:

A little semi-vestibule between two doors prefaced the entrance into what might be considered the principal room of the cottage. It was an oblong square, not above eight and a half feet high, sixteen feet long, and twelve broad; very prettily wainscotted from the floor to the ceiling with dark polished oak, slightly embellished with carving.[170]

The 'stunned' poet-worshipper descends to a prosy catalogue of interior decor. De Quincey here, as everywhere in his *Tait's* essays, intercuts the sublime and the prosaic—the mathematical mode (a parody of the famously tedious narrator of 'The Thorn') continues at intervals during these essays—he even counts the stairs ('fourteen in all') as he is led up to the dining room ('It was not fully seven feet six inches high').[171] Such passages make a specific appeal to the female reader. Johnstone included lengthy descriptions of interiors, fabrics, and female fashions in her reviews and valued literature which opened up a feminine, domestic perspective. In her review of *Scenes and Characteristics of Hindoustan*, by Emma

---

[168] *DQW* xi. 257–8. The records we have of Wordsworth's reading from 1770 to 1815 confirm De Quincey's claims. While Wordsworth was an appreciative reader of women's poetry, he seems to have read very little women's fiction. See Duncan Wu (ed.), *Wordsworth's Reading 1770–1799* (Cambridge: Cambridge University Press, 1993) and Wu (ed.), *Wordsworth's Reading 1800–1815* (Cambridge: Cambridge University Press, 1995).

[169] 'Novels' (1830), a piece written for a young lady's album, *DQW* vii. 289–90, is De Quincey's most substantial defence of the novel as a form supplying the desire of readers—and particularly young female readers—for an ideal of sexual love. It also shows him adapting his views carefully to his audience. De Quincey's 'Diary', *DQW* i. 12–69, shows that he was an enthusiastic reader of women's fiction, memoirs, and poetry. In 1803 he read work by Clara Reeves, Mary Robinson, Mary Hopkins Pilkington, Charlotte Smith, and Sophia Lee, amongst others.

[170] *DQW* xi. 50.

[171] Ibid. 54.

Roberts, for instance, she dwelt on the details given of Anglo-Indian domestic life and pointed out that,

From the writings of Forbes, Tod, Malcolm, Monro, Heber, and others, we had obtained very considerable information regarding India; but the lively and minute pen of a woman was still required to give us those in-door details which none save a woman could note, and none describe so well.[172]

De Quincey's own attention to 'in-door details' throughout his *Tait's* essays, challenges this last assumption, but shows a similar, canny eye to the readership.

Having described Wordsworth's home, De Quincey turns his attention to its female inmates, Mary and Dorothy Wordsworth, whose appearance and characters are given, again in some detail, as a preface to Wordsworth's. The order of precedence is significant, for it establishes De Quincey's affiliations with the feminine domestic world by which Wordsworth is sustained but from which he stands apart. In his description of Mary, he draws on Wordsworth's lyric, 'She was a Phantom of Delight', in which the poet describes his future wife as a harmony of angelic femininity and real woman, in such a way as to return her real presence almost completely to a sublimated ideal. De Quincey defers to Wordsworth's description and even imitates his strategy, but also points out that Mary's passive intellect was what made her the perfect wife for Wordsworth. 'She was a Phantom of Delight' is quoted as an illustration of 'how much better this [intellect] was adapted to her husband's taste, how much more adapted to uphold the comfort of his daily life, than a blue-stocking loquacity, or even a legitimate talent for discussion'.[173] This reinstates Mary as a socially situated subject, stresses Wordsworth's dependency on her and suggests an identification between her present situation and De Quincey's own, as it will unfold, since neither is granted an equality of intellectual relationship. His description of Dorothy develops these critical hints much more fully.

He introduces Dorothy with another quotation from one of Wordsworth's lyrics—'The Beggars'.[174] The poem describes a wild but beautiful female beggar, whom the poet encounters whilst walking. The poet judges both her and her sons to be liars, but allows them their difference, admiring them for their beauty and joy. He chooses not to enter sympathetically into the situation of the beggar woman, who is voiceless in the poem. He is content to acknowledge her strangeness as an object of aesthetic contemplation and move on. As in the description of Mary, De Quincey develops and problematizes the Wordsworth lyric, implying here only a limited satisfaction with his sublimated visions of the feminine. He emphasizes Dorothy's uncomfortable Otherness—her foreign appearance, her wild eyes, indicative of future mental instability, her lack of

---

[172] Christian Johnstone, 'Anglo-Indian Society', *Tait's*, 2/22 (Oct. 1835), 684.
[173] *DQW* xi. 51.
[174] 'Her face was of Egyptian brown', ibid. 52.

conventional femininity. The keynote to her character is 'self-conflict'. She is the opposite of Mary's contented femininity: 'some subtle fire of impassioned intellect apparently burned within her', sometimes visible, but at other times 'checked, in obedience to the decorum of her sex and age, and her maidenly condition, (for she had rejected all offers of marriage, out of pure sisterly regard to her brother and his children)'.[175] De Quincey is full of admiration for her self-sacrifice, but he recognizes it as such. Here, as elsewhere in these essays, we find what Angela Leighton has described as his 'quiet undercurrent of criticism of the social and sexual structures, whether "conjugal" or "parental", in which most women are caught'.[176] It was an undercurrent that the *Tait's* context encouraged in his writing. Later, discussing the predicament of Dorothy as an unmarried woman and citing Mrs Trollope in support of his argument, he mounts a passionate defence of the right of women to choose to remain single and not be mocked for it:

> how important it is that the dignity of noble-minded (and, in the lowest case, of firm-minded) women, should be upheld by society in the honourable election they make of a self-dependent state of virgin seclusion, by preference to a heartless marriage![177]

He still, traditionally enough, sees the life of the single woman primarily in terms of service to others, but there are doubts here too.

De Quincey dwells at length on Dorothy's role as her brother's sympathetic nurturer. Her name, 'gift of God', perfectly described

> the mission with which she was charged—to wait upon him as the tenderest and most faithful of domestics; to love him as a sister; to sympathize with him as a confidante; to counsel him as one gifted with a power of judging that stretched as far as his own for producing; to cheer him and sustain him . . .[178]

The catalogue, as always, suggesting De Quincey's identification with Dorothy, slips in her equal 'power' as a critic, in the midst of the more conventionally feminine attributes of loving solicitude. He names her greatest 'service' to her brother as her ability to listen sympathetically. She is the ideal, indulgent reader:

> The pulses of light are not more quick or more inevitable in their flow and undulation, than were the answering and echoing movements of her sympathizing attention. Her knowledge of literature was irregular, and not systematically built up. She was content to be ignorant of many things; but what she knew and had really mastered, lay where it could not be disturbed—in the temple of her own most fervid heart.[179]

---

[175] *DQW* xi. 52.
[176] Angela Leighton, 'De Quincey and Women', in Stephen Copley and John Whale (eds.), *Beyond Romanticism: New Approaches to Texts and Contexts 1780–1832* (London: Routledge, 1992), 167–8.
[177] *DQW* xi. 102.
[178] Ibid. 104.
[179] Ibid. 53.

Despite her irregular knowledge, De Quincey suggests his identification with Dorothy, for both are represented as Wordsworth's best audience. But, again, he does not accept Dorothy's role as passive nurturer unquestioningly. He stresses the active contribution of her sympathizing attention to her brother's poetry. Readers will owe her a debt in futurity, he says, for having

first *couched* his eye to the sense of beauty—humanized him by the gentler charities, and engrafted, with her delicate female touch, those graces upon the ruder growths of his nature, which have since clothed the forest of his genius with a foliage corresponding in loveliness and beauty to the strength of its boughs and the massiness of its trunks.[180]

Where Dorothy has 'engrafted' her sense of beauty onto the masculine austerity of her brother's work, De Quincey has, in his *Tait's* articles, revealed the poet as a man. Both have 'humanized him' for the benefit of the reader.[181] He writes that Wordsworth has acknowledged his debts to his sister for this, but he also casts doubt on the reciprocity of the relationship. He compares the happiness of Dorothy's early life to that promised to Ruth in Wordsworth's poem of the same title. This is a troubling allusion, since Ruth is, of course, a jilted bride. De Quincey's modified quotation reminds the reader of this at the same time as it alludes to Dorothy's single status:

she, like Ruth, was for years allowed

'To run, though *not* a bride,
A sylvan huntress, by the side'

of him to whom, like Ruth, she had dedicated her days; and to whose children, afterwards, she dedicated a love like that of mothers.[182]

Wordsworth appears here in the position of the feckless husband, a man who, in the poem, is devoted to nature and his own will. As a result of her desertion, Ruth falls victim to melancholy, is put in an asylum, and then becomes a vagrant. The link to the earlier allusion to 'The Beggars' is clear, as is the parallel with Dorothy's own life, which, as De Quincey tells us, has been marked by mental illness.[183] The allusions to 'Ruth' question the idyll of Dorothy's self-sacrificing devotion to her brother. Beneath the surface there is inequality and even a betrayal of trust. As always, De Quincey's representation of Dorothy's relationship with her brother suggests his own relationship with the poet, but also that between the poet and his reading public.

Wooing the readership nurtured by Johnstone, De Quincey identifies himself with Dorothy not only as a member of Wordsworth's early, coterie audience, but

---

[180] Ibid.
[181] Ibid.
[182] Ibid. 103.
[183] Ibid. 107–8. De Quincey concluded the third instalment of the 'Reminiscences' with a valediction to Dorothy ('Farewell, Miss Wordsworth! farewell, impassioned Dorothy!...'), that echoed the final stanza of 'Ruth'—see ibid. 108.

also as a fellow author. In keeping with the *Tait's* identity, he gives high praise for Dorothy's prose, comparing it favourably with that of male writers. Her 'Journal of a Tour in Scotland, 1802' is 'a monument to her power of catching and expressing all the hidden beauties of natural scenery with a felicity of diction, a truth, and strength, that far transcend Gilpin, or professional writers on those subjects'.[184] He also acknowledges his own debts to her 'simple but fervid memoir' of the tragedy of George and Sarah Green in his later narrative of these events in the 'Sketches' series.[185] He feels less convinced by her performance as a poet. Her verse is at best 'wild and pretty', at worst, 'feeble and trivial'.[186] The adjectives betray an assumption of the incompatibility of poetic greatness and female genius, but this is accompanied by a conviction of the value of the alternative path chosen by women who have sought a career as professional prose journalists. Alluding to Dorothy's later mental illness, he suggests that she might have been happier if she had been 'in good earnest, a writer for the press'.[187] This career would have produced an emotional and financial stability in her life and at no sacrifice to her femininity—Joanna Baillie, Mary Mitford, and Christian Johnstone are all cited here as examples of women who have followed this path. Johnstone, particularly, is held up as the model of the writer who

has pursued the profession of literature—the noblest of professions, and the only one open to both sexes alike . . . as a *daily* occupation; and, I have every reason to believe, with as much benefit to her own happiness, as to the instruction and amusement of her readers: for the petty cares of authorship are agreeable, and its serious cares are ennobling. More especially is such an occupation useful to a woman without children . . .[188]

In imagining this career for Dorothy, De Quincey suggests an alternative vision of authorship and the author/reader relationship to those represented by Coleridge or Wordsworth. Prose journalism is characterized not only as a profession within which a woman can flourish, but also as a kind of writing attentive to the needs of the readers, imagined here as a surrogate family.

As is already clear from the examples cited, De Quincey's defence of women writers was hampered by his contempt for the 'bluestocking' who claims intellectual equality with men. To some extent, his chivalrous stance also replicated a characteristic manoeuvre of reviewers at the period, who allowed female genius, but at an implicitly lowered estimate.[189] Similarly, it would be wrong to ignore the fact that De Quincey's debts to Wordsworth were clearly profound, and his questioning of the Wordsworthian sublime in his writing for the *Tait's* audience, of course, entailed a homage to the poet. Whilst recognizing these tensions in his

---

184 *DQW* xi. 106.
185 Ibid. 144.
186 Ibid. 106.
187 Ibid. 107.
188 Ibid. 107–8.
189 See Newlyn, *Reading, Writing, and Romanticism*, 38–9.

writing, we need also to acknowledge the extent to which he cultivated a popular, and particularly a female, readership in his biographical articles for *Tait's* in a sharply critical response to the self-containment of masculine Romantic genius.

De Quincey's *Lives* of Coleridge and Wordsworth domesticated their subjects in a number of ways. They opened up their private lives to public scrutiny and in so doing exposed personal failings which De Quincey connected to their heroic flaws as writers. As De Quincey represented them, both were dependent on domestic communities without adequately acknowledging or connecting sympathetically with them. In both cases private shortcomings are presented as indexes of the failure of the masculine genius, who insists on his capacity for self-making, to operate effectively in the contemporary marketplace. Magazine biography was practised by De Quincey as a means to expose and supply this deficiency, so that, within the interdependent relationship between the autobiographical and the biographical in the *Tait's* essays, it was the ideological basis of autobiography which came under scrutiny. His characteristic biographical mode was gossip, a language which displayed his transgression of the boundary between private and public and his democratizing ambitions. I have read De Quincey's *Lives* of the poets as determined in part by his personal and literary relationships with his subjects, but we have also seen how they were products of his position as urban career journalist, in London and Edinburgh in the 1820s and 1830s, experiencing at first hand the diverse models of authorship and the rapidly changing literary marketplace in Britain at the time. His work was permeated with the debates of the day on the nature of authorship in an age when communication with the new readerships became paramount. The portraits of Coleridge and Wordsworth were part of the wave of memorializations of recently deceased or older, established poets in this decade, which at once celebrated the poet's heroism and linked his private, domestic failings, to the lack of a sympathetic relationship with the contemporary audience. De Quincey was also like other literary biographers of the time in constructing himself as mediator of the poet to the modern age, implying that the poet does not own or create himself but is both owned and created by his biographer and the readers his biographer will attract.

De Quincey's alliance with Christian Johnstone and his interest in female authorship suggest affinities with female biographers, although his gossiping style, which embraced low defamation as well as high reverence, sharply distinguishes him from Mary Shelley, and brings him closer to Lady Blessington. For him the domestic space is the site of irony rather than what Anne Mellor describes as a feminine Romantic ideology of 'rational love, an ethic of care, and gender equality' and 'the communal exercise of reason, moderation, tolerance and the domestic affections that can embrace even the alien Other'.[190] Yet, if, as Marlon Ross argues, the male Romantic poets defined their self-possession

---

[190] Anne K. Mellor, *Romanticism and Gender* (New York: Routledge, 1993), 84, 210.

in part as a defensive reaction to the progressive feminization of the literary marketplace, then De Quincey's literary *Lives*, like Mary Shelley's, raised the repressed fears of male Romantic poets. Like her and like Lady Blessington, he championed female genius in the same arena as male and questioned the ideological investment in creative autonomy that he found in male poets. In this he looked to the future. The final chapter, on memorializations of Felicia Hemans in the 1830s, considers biography's construction of the model poet for the modern age: domesticated, popular, and female.

6

The Female Poet: The After*Lives* of Felicia Hemans and Letitia Landon

From the early 1800s there was an increasing awareness amongst women poets and publishers of the selling power of the female author's private life. Dedications to patrons and subscribers in slim volumes of women's verse had long contained biographical hints, but brief prefatory notices of a more directly auto/biographical nature, sometimes accompanied by frontispiece portraits, were becoming the pattern. Such prefaces nearly always underlined the feminine modesty of the poet and her desire, despite publishing, to avoid publicity. They might also establish her social class, stress her Christian virtue and the moral efficacy of her work, and sometimes they revealed, again by hints, the pathos of a life of straitened circumstances or personal tragedy.[1] Some female poets were commemorated posthumously in more substantial biographical essays. Anna Seward's *Poetical Works* (1810) included such a preface, by Sir Walter Scott, and Anna Barbauld's *Works* (1825) were introduced by Lucy Aikin's 'Memoir', advertised in the title.[2] As we have seen, 'Lives' of female poets were also commonly included in collective biographical histories of eminent women, from the later eighteenth century onwards. Two collections devoted exclusively to female literary lives, by Anne Katherine Elwood and Frederick Rowton, appeared in the 1840s.[3] Rowton's *The Female Poets of Great Britain* (1848) was a landmark in the history of women's poetry, with its substantial preface defining and defending the field, followed by selections from poets, from the

[1] See e.g. Charlotte Smith's autobiographical prefaces to several editions of her poems, repr. in *Elegiac Sonnets, and Other Poems* (London: Jones and Company, 1827). See also prefaces to Elizabeth Scot, *Alonzo and Cora, with Other Original Poems, Principally Elegiac* (London: Bunny and Gold, 1801); Emma Lyon, *Miscellaneous Poems* (Oxford: J. Bartlett, 1812); Isabella Lickbarrow, *Poetical Effusions* (Kendal: Branthwaite & Co., 1814); Ellen Robinson, *Poem Written on the Death of The Rev. Thomas Spencer, in Four Parts*, 2 edn. (Liverpool, W. Bethell, 1812).

[2] *The Poetical Works of Anna Seward; with Extracts from her Literary Correspondence, edited by Walter Scott, Esq.*, 3 vols. (Edinburgh: James Ballantyne & Co.; London: Longman, Hurst, Rees and Orme, 1810); *The Works of Anna Laetitia Barbauld, with a Memoir by Lucy Aikin*, 2 vols. (London: Longman, Hurst, Rees, Orme, Brown and Green, 1825).

[3] Mrs [Anne Katharine] Elwood, *Memoirs of the Literary Ladies of England, from the Commencement of the Last Century*, 2 vols. (London: Henry Colburn, 1843), included essays on Anna Laetitia Barbauld, Anna Seward, Hannah More, Charlotte Smith, and Felicia Hemans. Frederic Rowton (ed.), *The Female Poets of Great Britain, Chronologically Arranged: with Copious Selections and Critical Remarks* (London: Longman, Brown, Green, and Longmans, 1848).

fifteenth century to the present day, including Ann Yearsley, Charlotte Smith, Anna Seward, Mary Tighe, Hannah More, Anna Laetitia Barbauld, Felicia Hemans, Letitia Landon, and Elizabeth Barrett Browning. Each selection was accompanied by a brief biographical and critical introduction.[4]

The first two female poets to receive the same degree of sustained biographical attention as their male counterparts were Felicia Hemans (1793–1835) and Letitia Landon (1802–38), also known by her pen name L. E. L. Hemans and Landon were the most celebrated women poets of their day and the most popular and successful of living British poets of either sex from the mid-1820s, when their verse filled the literary annuals. Hemans published prolifically from an early age, gaining high sales by bringing out her poems first in periodicals, magazines and annuals, and then collecting them in volume form.[5] She gathered a large following not only in Britain but also in the United States. Landon's career started with the weekly publication of her 'Poetical Sketches' in The *Literary Gazette* in the early 1820s. Her first volume, *The Improvisatrice and Other Poems* (1824) went into six editions that year, and her second, *The Troubadour, Catalogue of Pictures and Historical Sketches* (1825), into four. She contributed to numerous gift books and annuals throughout the 1820s and 1830s.[6] Readers speculated on the women behind the poems, especially in the case of Landon, whose first editor, William Jerdan, encouraged rumours of the youth and beauty of the enigmatic 'L. E. L.'. Bulwer Lytton recalled the curiosity of Cambridge students reading her early work in the *Literary Gazette*—'We soon learned it was a female, and our admiration was doubled, and our conjectures tripled. Was she young? Was she pretty?'[7] Landon's later career was also marked by gossip—this time about her supposed liaisons with a series of men.[8] Her death, at the age of 36, in exotic and mysterious circumstances, was the final and most lasting cause of biographical curiosity. She sailed to Africa with her new husband in July 1838 and on 15 October her body was discovered, a bottle of prussic acid in her hand. Three years earlier Felicia Hemans had died an

---

[4] Rowton's collection was partly modelled on Alexander Dyce's, *Specimens of British Poetesses; Selected and Chronologically Arranged* (1825; London: T. Rodd, 1827).

[5] For Hemans's fame and considerable earning power, see Susan J. Wolfson (ed.), *Felicia Hemans: Selected Poems, Letters, Reception Materials* (Princeton: Princeton University Press, 2000), p. xiii and pp. xxxvii–xxxix. Her first volume, *Poems* (1808), was published when she was Felicia Browne, aged 14. Others included *The Domestic Affections* (1812), *Tales and Historic Scenes in Verse* (1819), *Welsh Melodies* (1822), *The Siege of Valencia and Other Poems* (1823), *The Forest Sanctuary* (1825), *Records of Woman* (1828), and *Songs of the Affections* (1830).

[6] See *Letitia Elizabeth Landon: Selected Writings*, ed. Jerome McGann and Daniel Riess (Ontario: Broadview Press, 1997), 12.

[7] *NMM*, 32 (1813), quoted in Angela Leighton, *Victorian Women Poets: Writing Against the Heart* (Hemel Hempstead: Harvester/Wheatsheaf, 1992), 47. Jerdan the editor of the *Literary Gazette*, informed readers (inaccurately) that L. E. L. was 'yet in her teens!'—see *Letitia Elizabeth Landon*, ed. McGann and Riess, 12.

[8] For the rumours about Landon's involvement with Jerdan, William Maginn, Daniel Maclise, and Bulwer Lytton, see Glennis Stephenson, *Letitia Landon: The Woman behind L. E. L.* (Manchester: Manchester University Press, 1995), 35–48.

altogether quieter death in Dublin, but equally pathos-laden in its own way, since she was only 41 and the mother of five boys, whose father had left for Italy and never returned.[9] Unsurprisingly publishers saw an opportunity, in both cases, for literary *Lives.*

Posthumous biographies of Hemans rolled quickly from the presses. *A Short Sketch of the Life of Mrs Hemans* appeared in the year of her death, followed in 1836 by two selected editions of her poetry, each with a biographical preface.[10] The first major, full-length *Life,* by the journalist Henry Fothergill Chorley, *Memorials of Mrs Hemans,* was published in the same year.[11] In response to Chorley, Hemans's sister Harriett Hughes brought out another full-length *Memoir* which prefaced the seven-volume collected *Works* in 1839.[12] A further prefatory biography appeared in *Early Blossoms* (1840).[13] In Landon's case, obituary notices in British and American journals were augmented by debates on the possible causes of her death.[14] As part of this controversy, her friend, Emma Roberts, published a 'Memoir' prefacing *The Zenana and Minor Poems of L. E. L.* ([1839]) and this was followed by a two-volume biography by another friend, Laman Blanchard, the *Life and Literary Remains of L. E. L.* (1841).[15] Blanchard's entertaining book was not only the most important of the Landon biographies, but an interesting example of the opportunistic marketing of literary biography, discussed in Chapter 2. From the stables of Henry Colburn, it was

[9] She met Captain Alfred Hemans when she was 15. They married in 1812 and stayed together, unhappily, until 1818 when he left for Rome.

[10] *A Short Sketch of the Life of Mrs. Hemans: With Remarks on her Poetry; and Extracts* (London: James Paul, 1835); W.A.B., 'Introductory Notice of the Life and Writings of Mrs. Hemans', in *National Lyrics and Songs for Music by Felicia Hemans* (1834; 2nd rev. edn., Dublin: William Curry; London: Simpkin, Marshall & Co.; Edinburgh: Fraser & Co., 1836), pp. xi–xlii; [David Macbeth Moir], 'Biographical Memoir of the Late Mrs Hemans', in *Poetical Remains of the Late Mrs Hemans* (Edinburgh: William Blackwood & Sons; London: T. Cadell, 1836), pp. ix–xxxii.

[11] Henry F. Chorley, *Memorials of Mrs. Hemans with Illustrations of her Literary Character from her Private Correspondence,* 2 vols. (London: Saunders and Otley, 1836) [based on Chorley's 'Sketches and Remembrances' of Hemans published in the *Athenaeum* (1835)]. Henry Fothergill Chorley (1808–72), reviewer and author of music journalism for the *Athenaeum,* was a friend of Hemans.

[12] [Harriett Hughes], 'Memoir of Mrs Hemans', *The Works of Mrs Hemans; with a Memoir of her Life, by her Sister,* 7 vols. (Edinburgh: William Blackwood & Sons; London: Thomas Cadell, 1839), i. 1–315. Hemans's sister, Harriett Mary Browne (1798–1858) married the Revd T. Hughes and then the Revd W. Hicks Owen. She has been referred to variously by modern critics as Harriett Browne Owen and Harriett Hughes.

[13] 'Life of Mrs. Hemans', in *Early Blossoms, a Collection of Poems written between eight and fifteen years of Age. By Felicia Dorothea Browne: afterwards Mrs. Hemans. With a Life of the Authoress* (London: T. Allman, 1840), pp. v–lx.

[14] See Glen T. Hines, 'Bibliography of Works about L. E. L.', *Corvey Women Writers 1796–1834 on the Web,* <http://www2.shu.ac.uk/corvey/cw3/ContribPage.cfm?Contrib=22>. For an account of the posthumous debate on the causes of her death see Stephenson, *Letitia Landon,* 175–95.

[15] Emma Roberts (ed.), *The Zenana and Minor Poems of L. E. L. With a Memoir by Emma Roberts* (London: Fisher and Sons; Paris: Quai D'École [1839]); Laman Blanchard, *Life and Literary Remains of L. E. L.,* 2 vols. (London: Henry Colburn, 1841). See also [Sarah Sheppard], *Characteristics of the Genius and Writings of L. E. L. with Illustrations from her Works and from Personal Recollection.* (London: Longman, Brown, Green, and Longman, 1841).

a much expanded version of a brief 'Memoir' that Blanchard had already published in 1837 in Colburn's *New Monthly Magazine*, while Landon was still living. Colburn had lost little time in exploiting the potential of this posthumous life.[16]

This corpus of texts has been of some importance in rescuing Hemans and Landon from the relative obscurity into which they fell in the first half of the twentieth century, and to their reincarnation, from the late 1980s, as the subjects of academic study.[17] The feminist resurrection of Romantic and Victorian women poets, more generally, has often drawn on the early biographical records, and the memoirs by Chorley, Hughes and Blanchard, in particular, were central to the groundbreaking work on Hemans, and Landon, by Marlon Ross, Angela Leighton, Glennis Stephenson, and others, who used these biographies both as historical sources and as bases for their interpretations of the poetry.[18] It is just one instance of the way in which biography has been of particular significance in the survival of women writers. As Angela Leighton comments, it has been a fundamental resource of feminist criticism, which 'by its very nature, needs to ask "Who is this author?" who, far from having to die, has not yet been brought to life in the reader's consciousness'.[19] Nineteenth-century female essayists and novelists, as well as poets, have needed life-writing to keep them alive. As we have seen, the reputation of Mary Wollstonecraft was seriously damaged by Godwin's *Memoirs*, yet Joanne Shattock notes that the fifty-year period subsequent to this publication, during which her name virtually disappeared, was broken by the narrative of her life rather than by reappraisal of her works: 'It was by means of biography, not a discussion of *A Vindication of the Rights of Woman*, or her fiction, that her rehabilitation as a writer and thinker was negotiated and secured'.[20] The first major biography of Jane Austen, published in 1870, was also the turning point in popularizing her work.[21] We only have to think of the succession of *Lives* of Austen that followed, in the twentieth and

---

[16] *NMM* 50 (May 1837), 78–82.

[17] For discussion of their critical neglect and rescue, see e.g. Harriet Kramer Linkin and Stephen C. Behrendt (eds.), *Romanticism and Women Poets: Opening the Doors of Reception* (Lexington, Ky.: University Press of Kentucky, 1999), 1–4; Susan J. Wolfson, 'Felicia Hemans and the Revolving Doors of Reception', ibid. 214–15; Wolfson (ed.), *Felicia Hemans*, pp. xiii–xvi; and Virginia Blain, 'Letitia Elizabeth Landon, Eliza Mary Hamilton, and the Genealogy of the Victorian Poetess', *Victorian Poetry*, 33/1 (Spring 1995), 34–5.

[18] See Marlon B. Ross, *The Contours of Masculine Desire: Romanticism and the Rise of Women's Poetry* (New York: Oxford University Press, 1989); Leighton, *Victorian Women Poets*; and Stephenson, *Letitia Landon*. See also reference to *CM* in Anne K. Mellor, *Romanticism and Gender* (New York: Routledge, 1993), 124–35; and Susan J. Wolfson, '"Domestic Affections" and "The Spear of Minerva": Felicia Hemans and the Dilemma of Gender', in Carol Shiner and Joel Haefner (eds.), *Re-Visioning Romanticism: British Women Writers, 1776–1837* (Philadelphia: University of Pennsylvania Press, 1994), 128–66.

[19] Leighton, *Victorian Women Poets*, 4.

[20] Joanne Shattock, 'The Construction of the Woman Writer', in Joanne Shattock (ed.), *Women and Literature in Britain 1800–1900* (Cambridge: Cambridge University Press, 2001), 15, and see 13–18. She refers to the essay on Wollstonecraft in Elwood, *Memoirs* (1843).

[21] See Shattock, 'The Construction of the Woman Writer', 22. The biography was by James Austen-Leigh.

twenty-first centuries, or the numerous biographies of Virginia Woolf or Sylvia Plath, to see the continuing importance of the biographical afterlife to the woman writer.

Biography has played an important part in forming, reviving, and preserving the reputations of women writers partly because the additional transgression involved in opening a female subject's personal life to public scrutiny has meant that female *Lives* have always held the potential to generate a disproportionate publicity. But it has also attached itself to women's writing, from the early nineteenth century, as part of the construction of female genius as a natural confluence of life and works—as Poe put it in 1845, 'a woman and her book are identical'.[22] We have seen how *Lives* of the male poets depended upon, but also disrupted, a myth of masculine authorial autonomy that constructed the works as a sign of the poet's self-possession—the conception of 'the man of genius . . . [as] wholly his own product'.[23] Sometimes female genius was represented as similar to male in this respect. Sarah Sheppard wrote in 1841, for instance, that '[t]hat most essential and remarkable characteristic of genius, the powerful life-giving imagination by which, at will, the poet identifies himself with his creations, no writer, perhaps, has more displayed than L. E. L.'.[24] More usually the connotations of self-determination and ownership implicit in the conception of masculine authorial autonomy were absent from representations of female authorship. The figure of the 'poetess', as delineated from the 1820s, particularly in the poetry and reception of Hemans and Landon, embodied a gender-specific understanding of the relationship between the life and works of the female poet. She also embodied a conflict between genius and domestic life that was inflected in particular ways. As a prelude to looking at biographies of Hemans and Landon, therefore, I want to consider discussions of the 'poetess', by contemporary reviewers, the poets themselves, and recent feminist critics. My purpose here is to provide a context for the ways in which Hemans and Landon were represented in the early biographies and to suggest how feminist critical resistance to aspects of the poetess tradition has led to a critical devaluation of these literary *Lives*.

6.1 HEMANS, LANDON, AND THE POETESS TRADITION

In 1816 Wordsworth figured the relationship between Burns's character and his art as a deliberate process of construction: 'On the basis of his human character

---

[22] Edgar Allan Poe, Review of Elizabeth Barrett Browning, *Drama of Exile and other Poems* (1845), in *The Works of Edgar Allan Poe*, 4 vols., ed. John H. Ingram (London: A. and C. Black, 1899), iv. 63.

[23] Mary Jean Corbett, *Representing Femininity: Middle-Class Subjectivity in Victorian and Edwardian Women's Autobiographies* (New York: Oxford University Press, 1992), 18.

[24] Sheppard, *Characteristics of the Genius and Writings of L. E. L.*, 35.

he has reared a poetic one'.[25] In 1831 Maria Jewsbury wrote of Hemans that she 'throws herself into her poetry' and added that 'the said self is an English gentlewoman'.[26] Her words suggest that the relationship between self and works is a less conscious, more physical affair for the female poet than for the male and that, in Hemans's case at least, this self fits with a culturally sanctioned model of femininity. For Jewsbury, Hemans's intellectual qualities were beautified by her 'matronly delicacy of thought, her chastened style of expression, her hallowed ideas of happiness as connected with home, and home-enjoyments;— to condense all in one emphatic word, her *womanliness*'. All imaginative readers will agree that 'a poetess ought to be feminine', for

If, after sighing away your soul over some poetic effusion of female genius, a personal introduction took place, and you found the fair author a dashing dragoon-kind of woman—one who could with ease rid her house of a couple of robbers—would you not be startled?[27]

Jewsbury, who spoke from personal knowledge of Hemans, adopted a tongue-in-cheek tone here, but her vision fitted with the more earnest desire of other commentators to counter the monstrous paradox of a female poet by reading Hemans's work as the unmediated expression of her own, domesticated femininity. The supposed congruity of Hemans's personal character and her poetry, and the femininity of both, were reiterated themes in the reviews, from the early 1820s onwards.[28] George Gilfillan, looking back at her from the vantage point of 1847, wrote of this natural interchange of self and works, that 'her life was a poem. Poetry coloured all her existence with a golden light—poetry presided at her needlework—poetry mingled with her domestic and maternal duties'.[29] Landon, too, was identified with her poetry in this way, although her public presence as a professional woman writer on the London literary scene, with attendant scandals, produced a less comfortable vision of the poetess than Hemans's domestic retirement in Wales, Liverpool, and Ireland. The image of Landon inferred from the poetry was nevertheless, like Hemans's, one of artlessly embodied, feminine sensibility. Landon was a melancholy vessel of feelings, the living image of her own representations of the tragic poetess (especially of Sappho, as depicted in *The Improvisatrice*), a fount of spontaneous utterance. A reviewer of *The Vow of the Peacock* in 1835 wrote: 'it is obvious that her personal feeling gives its colour to the whole . . . [it is] too truly expressed not to

---

[25] Wordsworth, 'Letter to a Friend of Robert Burns', *PWW* iii. 123.

[26] 'Literary Sketches No. 1: Felicia Hemans', *Athenaeum*, 172 (12 Feb. 1831), in Wolfson (ed.), *Felicia Hemans*, 565. Jewsbury's essay presents conflicting models of creativity. It also discusses Hemans's early classicism and describes her creative process as one of fashioning or building.

[27] Ibid. 565.

[28] See Wolfson, 'Felicia Hemans and the Revolving Doors of Reception', 216–21.

[29] 'Female Authors. No. 1—Mrs. Hemans', *Tait's*, NS 14 (June, 1847), in Wolfson (ed.), *Felicia Hemans*, 596.

have been keenly felt' and Frederic Rowton in 1848 doubted that Landon's friends could have been speaking the truth when they denied she was, herself, melancholy: 'How otherwise are we to understand her poetry?' 'We must suppose that she *felt* what she wrote'.[30]

Late twentieth-century feminist critics have found the nineteenth-century myth of the poetess problematic. They have acknowledged Hemans's and Landon's own part in creating it, and have conceded that it could be interpreted as, in various ways, empowering to them, but only if conceived as a performance over which they were in control. Angela Leighton, for example, has argued that the nineteenth-century ideal of improvisation 'asserts an easy equivalence of body and text' and that, in adopting the ideal, both Hemans and Landon themselves, like Hélène Cixous, sought 'to reclaim woman's poetic selfhood as a physical identity translated as a kind of writing'.[31] But she and others have struggled with the unselfconscious female creativity and the ideologically conservative model of femininity that the poetess tradition enshrined. They have argued that to a large extent these were ideas imposed upon female poets by male reviewers, such as Francis Jeffrey and George Gilfillan, who were disconcerted by the apparent takeover of the poetry market by women and the spectre of a future feminization of literature, and used the term 'poetess' to rank female genius as inherently lesser than male.[32] Gilfillan, for example, wrote of Hemans that '[s]he is less a maker than a *musician*, and her works appear rather to rise to the airs of the piano than

[30] *New Monthly Review*, quoted in Stephenson, *Letitia Landon*, 6. See ibid. for the 'many examples' of Landon's works being judged, quite literally, 'on the merits of her person rather than on their own intrinsic qualities'. Rowton, *The Female Poets of Great Britain*, 429–30. This is in the context of Rowton's discussion of the artlessness of her genius. Hemans and Landon were sometimes coupled as improvisatrices, see e.g. George W. Bethune in 1848: 'As the line came first to the brain, so it was written; as it was written, so it was printed. Mrs Hemans's melody was as much improvisation as Miss Landon's,' quoted in Glennis Stephenson, 'Poet Construction: Mrs Hemans, L. E. L., and the Image of the Nineteenth-Century Woman Poet', in Shirley Neuman and Glennis Stephenson (eds.), *ReImagining Women. Representations of Women in Culture* (Toronto: University of Toronto Press, 1993), 65.

[31] Leighton, *Victorian Women Poets*, 58. She admits to exasperation at the way that Landon's bodily stream of language dissolves, at its core, into vacuity. See also Blain, 'Letitia Elizabeth Landon', for Hemans's own 'positive' use of the term 'poetess' and on 'L. E. L.' as a 'masquerade' by which Landon could deal with the difficulties of being a public woman; and Stephenson, *Letitia Landon*, 15, arguing that Landon 'deliberately and carefully ... constructed the conventionally female poetic self of L. E. L.'.

[32] See Stephenson, 'Poet Construction', 62: male critics were 'always able to ... reinscribe L. E. L. within conventional gender ideology'; and Stephenson, *Letitia Landon*, 2: Landon's 'persona is to a great extent imposed upon her and therefore has a potentially limiting rather than liberating effect'. The seminal work on the defensive demotion of female poetry is Ross, *The Contours of Masculine Desire*. A clear example of this defensiveness is Francis Jeffrey's Burkean consignment of female poetry to a lesser rank of 'feminine' beauty in the *Edinburgh Review*, 50 (Oct. 1829), in Wolfson (ed.), *Felicia Hemans*, 549–54. For a discussion of Jeffrey's essay and of reviews by H. T. Tuckerman and William Gifford in a similar vein, see Ross, *The Contours of Masculine Desire*, 236–43. See also Wolfson, 'Felicia Hemans and the Revolving Doors of Reception', 216–18; and Stephenson, 'Poet Construction', 65: female poets 'were often seen to exemplify a debased Romanticism'.

that still sad music of humanity'.[33] His metaphors suggested that female poetry, with its lack of original agency, could not go beyond the confines of the bourgeois drawing room to reach the universal truths of the Wordsworthian sublime.

Whilst the poetry of Hemans and Landon suggested a continuity between the poetess's life and her works, it was, in fact, far from representing the relationship as a simple confluence. Following in the tradition of de Staël's *Corinne*, Hemans and Landon explored the ways in which the female poet was a woman divided against herself—torn between fame and love, caught between her public persona and her private attachments. This was the tragic destiny of the poetess, who in so far as she had a choice in the matter, typically ended up putting genius second to love. 'Thou hast a charmed cup, O Fame! | A draught that mantles high', Hemans writes in 'Woman and Fame' (1829), but characteristically refuses to drink: 'Away! To me—a woman—bring | Sweet waters from affection's spring!' In the final stanza she firmly identifies her poetry of the affections as both feminine and domestic: 'let mine—a woman's breast, | By words of home-born love be blessed'. This domestic trajectory in Hemans's verse was not popular with late twentieth-century feminist critics, who preferred to read her poetry as a critique of the domestic sphere, and to celebrate her descriptions of the rift between private and public life, as the only possible way to politicize, and therefore to value, her work. This was the tenor of Ann Mellor's argument when she stated that

Hemans' poetry locates ultimate human value within the domestic sphere. At the same time it emphasizes just how precarious, how threatened, is that sphere—by the passage of time, by the betrayals of family members, by its opposition to the dominant ideology of the masculine public sphere, the domain of ambition, military glory and financial power.[34]

Similarly Susan Wolfson admired the heroines in Hemans's verse who 'rupture the domestic sphere . . . defy male authority and avenge its treachery with violence, and whose protests may even take their children's lives with their own'. She found it 'a sign of Felicia Browne's precocious genius that, in attempting to celebrate the domestic affections [in the volume of that title] as a universal foundation of bliss, she winds up exposing a socially specific scheme so inwrought with suppression and denial for women as to evoke a longing for death as their only release'.[35] Leighton acknowledged that sensibility could operate in the public as well as private realms, in poems such as 'Corinne at the Capitol', but her preferences were clear when she praised this piece for helping 'to shift the tradition of sensibility away from its private domestic context

---

[33] Wolfson (ed.), *Felicia Hemans*, 593.
[34] Mellor, *Romanticism and Gender*, 124.
[35] Wolfson, '"Domestic Affections" and "The Spear of Minerva"', 140–1, 143.

of tearful but tidy femininity towards a public, socially purposeful platform of female inspiration and creative power'. She regretted that Hemans's ultimate legacy was a conservative femininity which set up 'a prison of theme and feeling' from which subsequent women poets struggled to escape.[36]

These comments should prepare us for an ambivalent response to biography from these critics. Indeed, the biographical basis of the poetess tradition seemed, to them, to betray the female poet—to take agency from her, not just by insisting on the identity of the woman and her works and the unreflective nature of her creativity, but by confining her within a feminine, domestic, and depoliticized sphere of influence. Leighton's *Victorian Women Poets* (1992) included biographical sections, often drawing on nineteenth-century sources, in each of her chapters, on the poetry of Hemans, Landon, Elizabeth Barrett Browning, and Christina Rossetti amongst others, but did so nervously. She noted the 'problems of biography' and reassured readers that she would keep these sections separate from her interpretations of the poetry, thereby avoiding Wimsatt's 'intentional fallacy', for '[t]he self who lives is not the same as the self who writes'.[37] She and others plundered the biographies by Chorley, Hughes, and Blanchard as 'factual' sources, but they were also suspected of inaccuracy, manipulation, and bad faith, and lumped together with the reviews as imposing on these poets a simplistic and repressive identification of female poetry with a particular model of feminine virtue.[38] Tellingly, Leighton sympathized with Elizabeth Barrett Browning's view of Landon's biographer, Blanchard, as interposing his voice unnecessarily where all she wanted to hear was the poet herself: 'Barrett Browning was rightly offended by the way "Mr. Blanchard presses his words where we want hers [Landon's], & his commentaries & explanations where we want none at all"'.[39] It is a nice example of the mistrust of the biographer, as third party intervening in the reader/author relationship, ventriloquizing for the creative artist, but with the added dimension of gender, a masculine appropriation of the female voice.

Biography was thus an acknowledged instrument of the feminist critical resurrection of Hemans and Landon, but it also represented everything from

---

[36] Leighton, *Victorian Women Poets*, 40–1. For a different approach to the issue of the relationship between domesticity and public life in women's poetry, see e.g. Emma Francis, 'Letitia Landon: Public Fantasy and the Private Sphere', in Anne Janowitz (ed.), *Romanticism and Gender* (The English Association, 51; Cambridge: D. S. Brewer, 1998), 93–115. Francis argues that Landon conceived of the poetess as exemplifying 'woman's mission'—that is, through her offices, the domestic sphere could extend its benefits to the public world.

[37] Leighton, *Victorian Women Poets*, 4.

[38] See e.g. Stephenson, *Letitia Landon*, 21, complaining that Blanchard's *Life* of L. E. L. is an inadequate factual source, confusing and evasive; or Leighton, *Victorian Women Poets*, 56 on the 'coy mysteriousness' of Blanchard's language, and a story he 'concocts'; and Wolfson, '"Domestic Affections" and "The Spear of Minerva"', 131, on Chorley's counter-feminist insistence on Hemans's domestic femininity.

[39] Leighton, *Victorian Women Poets*, 56. Leighton is also sympathetic with Barrett Browning's disappointment with the myth of the poetess as represented by Chorley and Hughes (41).

which the female poet had to be rescued. The following discussion of the first *Lives* of Hemans and Landon takes account of these dissatisfactions, but also sets out to defend these texts from their hitherto summary and dismissive treatment. It is important to recognize the generic characteristics and affiliations of these biographies. They have been read in ways that fail to differentiate them from the review literature, but they were not reviews and their differences, as biographical narratives, produced some significant divergences from the tradition of the poetess I have been outlining above. In the following discussion I read these texts as they have not been read, perhaps, since the time of their publication, in the context of other *Lives* of the poets, appearing at the period, with attention to the lines of connection, the congruities, as well as the incongruities, that emerge between the biographical representation of male and female poets. Intervening in the wider biographical debate on the nature of genius and its relationship to domestic life, the biographies of Hemans and Landon questioned what it meant to be a female poet and in the process urged the need for a shift away from masculine, Romantic genius towards a model of authorship more adapted to the modern age.

6.2 THE 'CREATURE OF HEARTH AND HOME': FELICIA HEMANS[40]

One way in which the biographical literature on female poets was distinct from the reviews, was in its generic focus on domestic life. As we have seen, there was an existing tradition of female *Lives*, from the later eighteenth century, that drew on and contributed to an ideological understanding of domestic woman. Hemans's own importance as a popularizer of this ideology through her poetry of 'hearth and home' in the 1820s and 1830s made her one of the major contributors to a culture in which biography took root and flourished. It also, in some ways, made her the perfectly adapted biographical subject. The image of the poetess that she projected (and had projected upon her) in her lifetime, might lead us to expect an all too easy opportunity for hagiography. Here was the ideal domestic woman ready-made, even her potentially troubling status as a successful female poet, sanctioned by repeated assurances of the '*womanliness*' of her verse. This certainly had its effect on the biographical literature. The first *Lives* of Hemans underwrote the myth of the poetess, enacting, making explicit, and capitalizing on the conjunction of the self that lives and the self that writes—as Henry Chorley, put it: 'Her works were a part of herself, herself of them'.[41] Several biographers began by depicting her as a child whose super-sensitivity and personal beauty marked her out as a natural poet.[42] Chorley represented the

[40] Felicia Hemans, quoted in *CM* i. 212.
[41] Ibid. 217.
[42] See e.g. W. A. B., *National Lyrics*, pp. xiii–xiv; *CM* i. 12; *HM*, 4; *Early Blossoms*, pp. viii–ix.

Records of Woman as her all but unmediated expression of self: 'In this, to use her own words, "there is more of herself to be found" than in any preceding composition'. It was 'like every line that she wrote, as far as possible from being a studied exercise'.[43] Similarly, biographers insistently underlined the 'femininity' of her genius, but they also showed awareness of an ironic disjuncture between the writer and her works. The first biographies of Hemans capitalized on her status as the embodied ideal of the poetess, but they did so in the context of a narrative of the poet's life and her personal and creative development that challenged the myth in distinctive ways.

One challenge to the myth was found in the simple fact that biography reinscribed the material conditions of authorship that the myth of the poetess effectively effaced. One of these was education. Like female biography more generally from the later eighteenth century, *Lives* of women poets were interested in the formative education of the subject. Scott's 'Life' of Anna Seward began with an account of her education, at the hands of her father, its subsequent withdrawal amidst fears that she would become a bluestocking, and its eventual replacement by her own literary studies and exchanges with male and female literary circles, represented as the vital influences in awakening her poetic powers.[44] Anna Barbauld's education, first at home and then at the Dissenting Academy at Warrington, and her own role as an educator, were the central themes of the 'Memoir' by Lucy Aikin. Biographers of Hemans also gave details of her reading—in Milton, Shakespeare, and the Germans—and her learning in languages, but, more significantly, Chorley and Hughes printed her correspondence with networks of male and female writers, including Wordsworth, Joanna Baillie, Mary Mitford, Mary Howitt, and Maria Jewsbury—letters that were full of references to her literary projects and her reading. Through this correspondence, readers could gain insight into how important Hemans's various intellectual communities were to her formation as a poet. Her biographers also charted her publishing career, her ups and downs, hopes and fears as a writer—the success of *The Sceptic*, the failure of *The Vespers of Palermo*, for instance—together with extracts from reviews.[45] Chorley started his book by stating that he would 'trace out the career of a poetess' at a time when '[w]ith the increase of female authorship, a change has taken place in the position of the authors. Our gifted women must feel themselves less alone in the world than was formerly their case'.[46] The conception of female poetry as a spontaneous expression of self was countered by this alternative, biographical narrative of the female poet as both a product and a producer of contemporary literary culture, one of a growing body of professional women writers.

---

[43] *CM* i. 127–8.
[44] Seward, *The Poetical Works*, pp. iv–xi.
[45] e.g. *HM*, 33, 70.
[46] *CM* i. 8.

Hemans's biographers further challenged the idea that women wrote poetry as unreflective self-expression by telling her story as a narrative of development. Chorley introduced his biography by stating that he would trace in it 'the entire progress of her mind through its several stages'.[47] In this biography she had not simply been born a poet, she had had to learn to become one, and had done so, significantly, by moving away from the dangerous excesses of poetic imagination and sensibility in her earlier years, towards a mature, reflective genius. She had not merely poured herself onto the page, she had had to exercise self-censorship and reflection and gradually discover her better self. It was a version of the maturation narrative that ran through *Lives* of male poets too and Hemans's biographers were conscious of the points of connection as well as contrast between her journey and those of Byron, Shelley, and Wordsworth. They also wrote with a powerful example of the progress of the female author in mind. This was Hannah More, who had died at the age of 88 in 1833, two years before Hemans, and had been memorialized in a best-selling Evangelical biography by William Roberts in 1834.[48] Roberts presented More's life as a moral and spiritual journey away from the vanity fair of the London literary scene towards domestic seclusion but, by that token, social influence. He adulated her in terms that positioned her as antithetical to masculine, Romantic genius—unnamed, male contemporaries who were clearly Byron and Shelley— whose impiety, immorality and revolutionary politics were represented by him as corrupting to society.[49] Unlike them, More was Christian, didactic, audience-orientated and counter-revolutionary. 'She knew it was the first business of an author to get readers' and, unlike '[g]enius in general, [which] requires to be placed at a certain distance', '[h]er genius invited a near approach'.[50] She exemplified the political power of woman's mission: from her retirement at Cowslip Green, her writings had issued forth targeting the sections of society most liable to revolution with home-born truths. Writing in the post-1832 moment, Roberts praised her as an example for his own times, of the power of literature to stabilize a volatile society, through a Christian, counter-revolutionary influence, and described what he hoped would be the 'moral influence' of his own biography on 'the great corporation of the reading public', in an age when we see 'power . . . gradually passing from the few to the many' in a 'great levelling march'.[51]

---

[47] *CM*, p. vi.

[48] William Roberts, *Memoirs of the Life and Correspondence of Mrs Hannah More*, 4 vols. (2nd edn., London: R. B. Seeley and W. Burnside, 1834). See ibid., vol. i, p. ix, where Roberts states that the first edition of 2,000 sold out within three weeks of publication.

[49] See ibid. 6 where he implies that his book is a diversion from recent biographies of Byron and Shelley. See also ibid. 18, on poets who 'spread a moral night around them'.

[50] Ibid. iv. 357, 361.

[51] Ibid., vol. i, p. xiv. For More's counter-revolutionary influence, see ibid. ii. 346–7 and iv. 119.

Hemans's own, popular success and her domestic retirement, meant there were obvious parallels between the two writers' lives, despite the generation gap. However, Hemans did not project herself as the conscience of culture in the way of More, and was much more dangerously close to Shelley and Byron in her self-projections as the passionate and melancholy poetess. Where More opposed the cult of sensibility, Hemans embraced it.[52] Hemans's relative reserve in terms of the social mission of her verse was not itself a problem for her biographers, but they worried that her surrender to the seductions of imagination had affected her own, personal development adversely and detracted from her poetry's moral influence. We saw in the first chapter how female 'Lives' positioned domestic woman, in various ways, in a relationship to public life. One way was inherent in the act of publication itself, another in the framing of the private female subject as a potentially life-changing role model for the female readers, and a third through the thematic representation of the translation of female, domestic virtue into public influence. We also saw how the publication of private life became a particular problem for the female subject, who more fitted than the male to become a domestic exemplum, was, by that very token, less fitted for public exposure. All these factors affected the biographical literature on Hemans. Biographers framed her as a role model for female readers, but were concerned that she might not, necessarily, set a good example. Their narratives variously exposed and compensated for these difficulties.

The literature produced in the first two years after Hemans's death was the most critical. In 'W. A. B.''s biographical introduction to *National Lyrics* (1836), a warning was issued against the dangers of the poetic calling for the young 'female mind': '[g]enius is a fearful dower for a woman; she whose whole early life is so unceasingly invested with illusive colouring, ill requires the additional veil of poetical imagination, to deepen or beautify the illusion'.[53] The first posthumous biography, *A Short Sketch* (1835), was even more disapproving of Hemans's early surrender to sensibility and imagination. It showed an Evangelical sternness in reprimanding her for 'levity' and 'frivolity' and applauded what she described as her transition from 'the feverish and somewhat *visionary* state of mind' often associated with youth 'to higher and holier tasks'.[54] As examples of her deplorable 'weaknesses', letters were quoted in which Hemans archly described a walk with Sir Walter Scott and ridiculed Wordsworth's earnest wedding present of a pair of scales to the daughter of a poet.[55] The biographer feared

---

[52] See More's *Strictures on the Modern System of Female Education. With a View of the Principles and Conduct Prevalent Among Women of Rank and Fortune*, 2 vols. (London: T. Cadell Jun. and W. Davies, 1799). Ross, *The Contours of Masculine Desire*, 207, comments that '[w]e could say that More's project is the converse of the romantic poet's'.

[53] W.A.B., *National Lyrics*, p. xx. The author is less inclined to blame Hemans for her marriage breakdown, but still suggests that her keen imaginative sensibilities didn't help.

[54] *A Short Sketch* (1835), 22, 25, 4. *A Short Sketch* was dedicated to the Revd Thomas Bowdler.

[55] Ibid. 19–25.

that her over-developed imagination had caused the breakdown of her marriage—she might have flourished wedded to an indulgent poet, but not to the
'prosaic and commonplace understanding' of Captain Hemans, 'a strict utilitarian' who 'ill able to bear with the wanderings and fancies of imagination . . . was
once heard to declare, that "it was the curse of having a literary wife that he could
never get a pair of stockings mended"'.[56] The anecdote was not told here in order
to garner sympathy for Felicia Hemans. Like Byron, she had undergone a
separation, and, like him, she posed biographers with the problem of the
apparent incompatibility of poetry and a virtuous married life. Unlike Byron,
she was rarely excused on these grounds.[57] The onus on the female biographical
subject was to be a good role model and make sure that domestic virtue and
poetry *were* compatible.

   The model of the woman writer who, like Hannah More, had managed to
harmonize these areas of her life, was also very much present in the major
biographies of Hemans, by Henry Chorley and Harriett Hughes. Both were
lengthy and sympathetic memoirs in the *Lives and Letters* format. In different
ways, both told the story of a woman who proved that poetic genius and
domestic virtue could be mutually supportive and that poetry's moral influence
could grow eventually from its origins in a life of domestic responsibility and
affection. In Chorley's account, this was not a given, but a long struggle—
indeed, the defining struggle of Hemans's career. In his introduction he wrote
that he wanted to allay current fears that the rise of female genius was interfering
'"with our implanted and imbibed ideas of domestic life and womanly duty"'.[58]
In fact his book did not offer easy reassurances. He traced Hemans's personal
journey from youthful imaginative enthusiasm, to mature, reflective genius, as a
salutary but difficult transition effected by circumstances that forced her to take
on domestic responsibilities. Her childhood environment was described as
nurturing her poetic temperament in a way that wholly indulged her Romantic
sensibility. Her first home, in Wales, was a fantasy landscape, a place of unfettered imagination.[59] Chorley warned that such complete seclusion from the
world was dangerous for Hemans, as a woman poet, and the reason that 'she
did only a partial justice to her powers'. Her poetry as she grew older

breathed more reality and less of romance; the too exclusive and feverish reverence for
high intellectual or imaginative endowment, yielded to a calmness, and a cheerfulness,
and a willingness more and more, not merely to speculate upon, but to partake of 'the
beauty in our daily paths'.[60]

---

[56] *A Short Sketch* (1835), 29, 32.
[57] The author of the 'Life' in *Early Blossoms* (1840) comes the closest to explaining the
breakdown of her marriage in the same terms as Moore had done for Byron.
[58] *CM* i. 8. He was quoting Maria Jewsbury.
[59] Ibid. 16–20.
[60] Ibid. 24–5.

It was the same transition from 'romance' to 'reality' that Mary Shelley wished for her husband in 1839 and that Milnes later made the defining journey of Keats's life. Like theirs, Hemans's poetry had suffered from the author's other-worldliness, but in her case this was framed much more explicitly as a flight from the practicalities of domestic life. She was impeded, Chorley argued, by the 'peculiar' circumstances in which she lived as a young adult. He passed discreetly over the details of the separation from her husband—although her status as a single mother of five boys was clear enough from his book—but focused instead on the fact that it resulted in Hemans's mother becoming the head of the household. This devolved domestic responsibility from Felicia, even as an adult, until her mother's death, and allowed her unusual freedom to concentrate on her poetry. It was not, in Chorley's view, a helpful situation either for her or for her muse. He represented it as a state of affairs that encouraged a regressive, because unreflective, imaginative life. Hemans was, even as an adult, childlike, impulsive, and slightly unstable. She showed a 'personal self-neglect, childish to wilfulness'.[61] She once set a Welsh hillside covered in furze on fire in a 'freak' of humour.[62] Domestic responsibilities might have eroded her genius, Chorley admits, but they also 'might have imparted to her poetry more of masculine health and stamen, at the expense of some of its romance and music'.[63] He held up Maria Jewsbury as a counter-example to Hemans in this respect, as a female poet whose reasoning had been strengthened by the 'responsibilities and diffi-culties of her youth'.[64]

Chorley's narrative thus showed Hemans growing towards an invigorating harmony of imagination and domestic life, but one that did not come naturally to her. He gave full recognition to the hardships she suffered when, after the death of her mother, she had to lead a 'more interrupted and responsible life' and 'make acquaintance with an "eating, drinking, buying, bargaining" world, with which, from her disposition and habits, she was ill-fitted to cope'.[65] At Wavertree she learnt for the first time about 'the cares and vexations of domestic life' which had always previously 'increased her eagerness to escape to those extreme regions of fancy and speculation which nothing earthly or practical was permitted to enter'.[66] He printed letters from her in which she presented herself as entirely fulfilled by domestic life: 'I have been all my life a creature of hearth and home', 'there is *no* enjoyment to compare with the happiness of gladdening hearth and home for others—it is woman's own true sphere', but also letters expressing her difficulties in balancing such responsibilities with her literary career and

---

[61] Ibid. 128.
[62] Ibid. 48.
[63] Ibid. 43.
[64] Ibid. 172.
[65] Ibid. 131.
[66] Ibid. ii 2.

exasperation at household management.[67] Thus, she writes to Jewsbury on reading Wordsworth's *Miscellaneous Poems*:

I had many more things to say respecting all that I have thought and felt during the perusal of these works, but my interruptions, consisting of morning visits from the Bishop down to the tailor of the diocese (which latter guest, to the mother of five boys, is no means an unimportant one), have been incessant, to say nothing of the boys themselves. My mother being unwell, and my sister engaged, all the duties of politeness have devolved upon me for the day.[68]

Chorley also included a letter to Mary Mitford, in which Hemans complained about having to take on her mother's role: 'I am now for the first time in my life holding the *reins of government*, independent, managing a household myself; and I never liked any thing less than "*ce triste empire de soi-même*".[69]

There is, of course, a distinction to be made between domestic affections, which Hemans is shown as always having had in abundance, and household management, a skill which she unwillingly acquired. But, in Chorley's account, as in contemporary conduct literature, for example, by Sarah Stickney Ellis, the second was the necessary expression of the first. As these passages show, for the woman writer the 'domestic' not only bore particular ideological significances but was also literalized in a way that it was not for the male poet. It did not occur to most biographers of Byron, Shelley, Wordsworth, or Coleridge to mention their competence or otherwise at household management (Mary Shelley and Hogg came the nearest). Nevertheless, we can also see how Hemans's struggles between private and public, domestic and literary, might be compared with those of the male poets as represented in biography of the period. Chorley clearly wanted his readers to make such comparisons, and particularly pointed to the ways in which she might be seen in relation to Byron and Wordsworth in this respect. He mistrusted Byron, as he did Shelley, on religious, political, and sexual grounds, and because in all three areas they seemed to embody imaginative self-indulgence. As he represented it, one of the most important stages in Hemans's progress towards poetic maturity was when she decided to drop her early passion for Byron in favour of Wordsworth. The change in allegiances was centred on these poets' different views of the relationship between genius and domestic life. Hemans and her family stayed with the Wordsworths at Rydal Mount in 1830, and Chorley included generous extracts from letters written during the visit. Here she discussed the contrast between her host and Byron, as represented in Moore's *Letters and Journals of Lord Byron*. She observed that Wordsworth's

---

[67] *CM* i. 212, 224.
[68] Ibid. 176.
[69] Ibid. 233.

gentle and affectionate playfulness in the intercourse with all the members of his family, would of itself sufficiently refute Moore's theory in the Life of Byron, with regard to the unfitness of genius for domestic happiness.[70]

In another letter, also quoted, she elaborated on this thought:

It is delightful to see a life in such perfect harmony with all that his writings express, 'true to the kindred points of heaven and home!' You may remember how much I disliked, and I think you agreed with me in reprobating that shallow theory of Mr. Moore's with regard to the unfitness of genius for domestic happiness.

She went on to report, approvingly, Wordsworth's response to her opinion of this theory:

'It is not because they *possess* genius that they make unhappy homes, but because they do not possess genius *enough*; a higher order of mind would enable them to see and feel all the beauty of domestic ties.'[71]

The references to Moore's *Letters and Journals* are interesting because they show, explicitly, the intertextuality that is everywhere implied, in Chorley's *Memorials,* between the life of Hemans and those of her male contemporaries.[72] The particular passage from Moore was important for Chorley because it provided shared ground upon which Hemans and Wordsworth could agree in rejecting Byron and affirming a commitment to a harmony of genius and the domestic which was also the ideological basis of his own biography. In describing her responses to Wordsworth and Byron, Chorley still allowed his readers to see her relationship to domestic life as conflicted. Like the author of *A Short Sketch*, he printed the letter in which Hemans mocked Wordsworth's bridal gift of scales to the daughter of a poet:

You will be thinking of a broach in the form of a lyre, or a butterfly-shaped aigrette, or a Forget-me-not ring, or some 'such small gear.' Nothing of the sort—but a good, handsome, substantial, useful-looking, pair of scales, to hang up in her store-room! 'For you must be aware, my dear Mrs. Hemans,' added he gravely, 'how necessary it is for every lady to see things weighed herself.' *Poveretta me!*—I looked as *good as I could*, and, happily for me, the poetic eyes are not very clear-sighted, so that I believe no suspicion, derogatory to my notability of character, has yet flashed upon the master's mind; indeed, I told him that I looked upon scales as particularly graceful things, and had great thoughts of having my picture taken with a pair in my hand.[73]

---

[70] Ibid. ii. 115.

[71] Ibid. 119.

[72] See also ibid 194, where Hemans comments on reading *PPS* and enjoying 'the earnest eloquence of Mrs. Shelley's preface'.

[73] To Harriett Hughes, July 1830, *CM* ii. 141–2. Leighton, *Victorian Women Poets* and Wolfson, '"Domestic Affections" and "The Spear of Minerva"', both read this letter as a riposte to the male poet.

Unlike the earlier biographer, Chorley did not condemn this as 'levity'. Hemans's self-characterization as a naughty schoolgirl, pretending to be good,
whilst having a lecture on housewifery forced upon her, perfectly accords with
his running theme of her childish resistance to domestic responsibility. Chorley
lets the subversive humour stand. In another letter she praises Wordsworth for
having harmonized domestic happiness and poetic genius:

'There is a daily beauty in his life,' which is in such lovely harmony with his poetry, that
I am thankful to have witnessed and *felt* it. . . . I was much interested by his showing me,
carved deep into a rock, as we passed, the initials of his wife's name, inscribed there many
years ago by himself, and the dear old man, like 'Old Mortality,' renews them from time
to time. I could scarcely help exclaiming '*Esto perpetua!*'.[74]

This letter, like the earlier one, mingles respect with irony and shows her
pitting herself, as lively young woman and rival poet, against the 'old man' and
his conventionally hierarchical model of domestic life. The implicit contrast
between his time-honoured uxoriousness and her brief and disastrous experience
of marriage is an unspoken presence. Chorley allows these disturbing cross-
currents to remain, but what is important for him, as the true index of Hemans's
own progress as a poet, is her ultimate recognition of Wordsworth's value as, in
her words, 'the true *Poet of Home*, and of all the lofty feelings which have their
root in the soil of home affections'.[75] He discusses, at some length, Hemans's
disgust, by contrast, at Byron's sexual incontinence.[76] As he notes, the effect of
the *Life* of Byron was such that, after reading it, she left off wearing a brooch
containing a lock of his hair.[77] Throughout, Chorley represents Wordsworth's
influence on Hemans as a steadying one. Towards the end of his biography, he
writes with satisfaction that '[i]n defining the distinction between the genius of
Wordsworth and that of Byron, I remember her saying, that it required a higher
power to still a tempest than to raise one, and that she considered it the part of
the former to calm, and of the latter to disturb the mind'.[78] Her knowledge of
Wordsworth's poetry and life, and the fact that the two are harmonized, helps
ground her tendency to over-sensitive unworldliness. Wordsworth, in other
words, is part of the domesticating influence which prevents her from becoming
that most horrifying of spectres—a female Shelley or Byron.[79]

   Such passages established a dialogue between Hemans's life, as woman and
poet, and Byron's and Wordsworth's as male poets. This interchange created

---

[74] *CM* ii. 26–7.
[75] Ibid. i. 174.
[76] See ibid. ii. 21–3, 83, 177.
[77] Ibid. 21–3.
[78] Ibid. 263.
[79] Compare Rowton, *The Female Poets of Great Britain*, 410, for a reassuring contrast between
Hemans and Byron: 'Love is with him a selfish and unrestrainable idolatry. . . . Far different is Mrs.
Hemans. Affection is with her a serene, radiating principle, mild and ethereal in its nature, gentle in
its attributes.'

parallels between the situations of male and female genius, but did it do so merely to re-establish conventional hierarchies of gender and poetic genius? To some extent Chorley's account, like Hughes's after him, positioned Wordsworth as a fathering influence for Hemans's poetry.[80] But her relationship with him was shown as compounded of respect for this elder statesman of the literary world and competitiveness with the 'old man' of British poetry. Chorley's biography portrays her as the new blood and future of British poetry in declaring his purpose to be that of catching 'the spirit of the age' in dealing with 'the popularity and prevalence of female authorship'.[81] Wordsworth is introduced as a venerable male poet who will lend gravitas to Hemans's public image, but rather than being in his shade, she emerges from Chorley's narrative, as from subsequent biographies, as Byron's better and Wordsworth's equal.

Three years after Chorley's biography, Hemans's collected works appeared, prefaced by her sister Harriett Hughes's memoir. This was a much more defensive piece of work than Chorley's. It was produced in response to his biography, which seemed to Hughes to have, albeit unintentionally, damaged Hemans's reputation.[82] She began by stressing Hemans's fear of publicity: 'Perhaps there never was an individual who would have shrunk more sensitively from the idea of being made the subject of a biographical memoir'. Her life was uneventful and '[i]n every thing approaching to intrusion on the privacies of domestic life, her favourite motto was *"Implora pace"'*. In a pattern we have observed before, Hughes's response simply took her further into the realms of biographical revelation:

The spell having thus been broken, and the veil of the sanctuary lifted, it seems now to have become the duty of those with whose feelings the strict fulfilment of her own wishes would have been so far more accordant, to raise that veil a little further, though with a reluctant and trembling hand.[83]

As she presented it, Hughes's action in further lifting the veil on her sister's privacy was forced upon her by the particular situation of the famous female subject—once anything at all is known of the private life of a woman a risky addition of potentially redemptive information seems the only feasible defence.

---

[80] *HM* reprints all the letters on Wordsworth and Byron mentioned above in relation to Chorley, except the one on Wordsworth and the scales, perhaps because it is more markedly in contrast to Hughes's portrait of Hemans as feminine devotee of the hearth and home, than any other. Elwood, *Memoirs of the Literary Ladies of England*, ii. 248, also reproduces the exchange of Wordsworth and Hemans on Moore's Byron.

[81] *CM* i. 6.

[82] *HM*, 2. Hughes drew support from a review of Chorley's book in which he was criticized, along with other contemporary biographers, for trying 'to draw an angel *down*', rather than aiming to ' "lift a mortal to the skies" ': see 'The Poetesses of our Day.—No.1. Felicia Hemans', *Dublin University Magazine*, 10/56 (Aug. 1837), 138.

[83] *HM*, 1–2. Other biographers also included less extended prefatory excuses for breaching Hemans's privacy. See e.g. *A Short Sketch* and *CM*.

But Hughes's hesitancies over making personal revelations were titillating as well as conventionally self-protective. The memoir was advertised as a family portrait, entitled 'by her sister' and dedicated to Hemans's brother, Colonel Sir Henry Browne, under whose roof it had been written. It offered the prospect of a combination of sympathy and an unprecedentedly intimate perspective, including the first inside account of the marriage and the reasons for the separation.[84] This was its selling point, and the reason for its place in volume i of Hemans's collected works.

Hughes represents her sister, throughout her memoir, as the embodied ideal of domesticated femininity (Fig. 6.1). The frontispiece portrait shows Hemans in a domestic setting, seated on a chaise longue, her veil suggestive of an Italianate Madonna (the significance of the ring, prominently displayed, remains uncertain). There is still something of the narrative of progression that is so strong a presence in Chorley's book—Hughes, too, emphasizes Hemans's rejection of Byron and friendship with Wordsworth and comments, for instance, that, as she grew to maturity her earlier, classical tastes as a poet 'by degrees gave way to one which suggested a choice of subjects more nearly allied to the thoughts and feelings of daily life'.[85] She also prints some of the letters in which Hemans reveals her dissatisfactions with her domestic world.[86] But, as Marlon Ross has argued, she attempts to minimize this aspect of her sister's character.[87] In Hughes's version of Hemans, a harmony of poetry with family life was naturally and always present, and it was achieved by dint of putting her family first. Hemans was, for Hughes, first of all a loving daughter and mother and only then a poet. She comments that, in her sister, the 'endearing predominance of the mother over the author' was 'one of the loveliest features of her character', 'the tumultuous exultation of her boys, was a far dearer tribute than the praise of the mightiest critic'.[88] Anecdotes are brought forward to illustrate the wisdom of Hemans's priorities. She suspends poetry for Christmas: 'The fate of poetic heroes and heroines would remain in abeyance, whilst juvenile mimes and mysteries were going on at the fireside; and for the moment nothing seemed so important as the invention of different devices for the painted bags of *bonbons* designed to adorn the boughs of the "Christmas Tree"'.[89] It is an image that celebrates the humbler rituals of bourgeois, family life over the grandeur of poetic themes. Seeing the portrait of his mother by West and the bust by Fletcher, one

---

[84] See *HM*, 29–30. Hughes is discreet, but gives more detail than Chorley, telling her readers that no separation was envisaged and that correspondence was kept up but that 'years rolled on—seventeen years of absence, and consequently alienation—and from this time to the hour of her death, Mrs Hemans and her husband never met again'.

[85] See ibid. 28.

[86] See e.g. ibid. 52, 59, 156.

[87] Ross, *The Contours of Masculine Desire*, 251.

[88] *HM*, 76–7, 49–50.

[89] Ibid. 79.

Fig. 6.1. Engraved frontispiece portrait of Mrs Hemans, from a painting by William E. West, in *The Works of Mrs Hemans; with a Memoir of her Life, by her Sister*, [ed. Harriett Hughes], 7 vols. (Edinburgh: William Blackwood and Sons; London: Thomas Cadell, 1839).

of Hemans's sons cries out: '"The bust is the poetess, but the picture is *all mother*"'.[90]

It is easy to mock such sentimental vignettes—and modern critics have not refrained from doing so. Hughes seems to be telling aspiring female poets to do as Hemans did and, as Ella Wheeler Wilcox wrote: 'Make thy life better than thy work'.[91] This is a message that historically has particularly dogged women writers. We have not found male poets being celebrated by their biographers for putting their families before their poetry. Yet, the fact that, in Hughes's memoir, Hemans puts her family first does not imply that her success as a poet is belittled. On the contrary, Hughes presents the family as Hemans's natural element, not only for personal happiness but also for her poetry. Her mother, who had, in Chorley's narrative, been an unwitting impediment to Hemans's creativity, was, in Hughes's, its ultimate and most important source. The young Felicia was educated by their mother whose character

was an exemplification of St. Paul's description of that charity which 'suffereth long and is kind,' 'seeketh not her own,' 'thinketh no evil.' Her piety was sober, steadfast, and cheerful; never displaying itself in high-wrought excitements or ostentatious professions, but silently influencing every action of her life, and shedding a perpetual sunshine over all which came within its sphere.[92]

It is a conventional portrait of the good, Christian woman, but the pious, affective influence, without ostentatious, Evangelical enthusiasm, also evokes a role model for the female poet who wishes to shed light on the world without the self-display of 'high-wrought excitements'. From the seclusion of the family home, Hemans's poetry projects her affections outwards to her audience, and this is the heart of its popular appeal. Like Hannah More before her, she is shown to be an approachable author, without that splendid obliviousness to audience that all the male poets are accused of by their biographers.[93] Hughes suggests her ability to extend her family affections into her local community. Her 'warm attachment for "the green land of Wales"' was also for 'its affectionate, true-hearted people'.[94] When her play *The Vespers of Palermo* failed, not only her family but the whole local community were disappointed.[95] Hughes comments that 'the extending influence of her talents, the growing popularity of her writings, and the warm interest and attachment of many private friends' compensated for the loss of her husband, suggesting Hemans's capacity to create an

[90] *HM*, 130.

[91] Leighton, *Victorian Women Poets*, 41 quotes this phrase as encapsulating Hemans's legacy for Victorian women poets.

[92] *HM*, 5.

[93] Although Hemans's letters show a mixture of excitement and irritation when she speaks of the readers who pursue her in the Lakes—see e.g. *HM*, 219.

[94] Ibid. 5.

[95] Ibid. 70.

alternative family of readers and friends, embraced together so that popularity amongst the one will be mirrored in the other.[96] That her sons' praise is more valued by her than critical adulation is only in keeping with a poet who thinks of her wider audience as her family—sometimes pursuing and plaguing her, like her boys, but ultimately a group whose interests she has at heart and who, in return, sustain her by their affection. Hughes describes how the poem she regards as Hemans's most important work, *The Forest Sanctuary*, was composed not merely within a domestic context, but as, in some senses, a family effort:

The progress of this work was watched with great interest in her domestic circle, and its touching descriptions would often extract a tribute of tears from the fireside auditors. When completed, a family consultation was held as to its name.[97]

It is another sentimental vignette, but with a pragmatic heart. The poem which springs from domestic affections, raising tears by the hearth, will also go out into the world to be read by Hemans's *other* family, her audience, who, as Hughes tells us on the next page, are widening daily and clamouring for more.[98]

Hughes thus develops the aspect of the poetess tradition that sanctions the woman writer's public influence as 'woman's mission'. It is a gentler, less overtly politicized model of influence than that exemplified by Hannah More, but it is quietly empowering. In representing Hemans's ability to translate her private life into public poetry, neither Hughes nor Chorley wrote in the spirit of reviewers such as Jeffrey or Gilfillan who subtly demoted the poetess, in relation to the poet, by demarcating her influence as operating within a 'feminine' sphere. Hemans emerged in the biographies of the 1830s as a signal instance of a poet who, by grounding her work in the domestic affections, had achieved a poetry of genuine popularity in a way that her male contemporaries had not. Indeed, it is the figure of the successful female writer who haunts male literary *Lives* in this decade. Moore's defence of Byron's masculinity may be read in part, as it has been by Marlon Ross, as a response to the rise of the literary woman and the spectre of a future feminization of literature. Mary Shelley's essays on Shelley in many respects produced a portrait of the tragic poet which was the converse of Hemans—her fabulous success rooted in a happy home, Shelley's struggle for recognition mirrored in his peripatetic lifestyle, his withdrawal from the social going hand in hand with the retreat of his poetry from the real concerns of a potential readership. De Quincey stressed the success of contemporary female novelists and journalists and the self-confidence of the mutually supportive, female literary communities of the Lakes, by contrast with the failures of Coleridge and Wordsworth to communicate with their readers—failures which he read as symptomatic of Coleridge's blindness to his dependency on the

---

[96] Ibid. 30.
[97] Ibid. 80.
[98] Ibid. 82 and see 93–4 on her 'widely extending fame' in the mid-1820s, esp. in America.

domestic affections and Wordsworth's inability to extend his love for his family and closest friends to the wider circle of friends and neighbours. Within this context it seems that Hemans, as portrayed by Chorley and Hughes, became the model of the poet as she, *or he*, should be.

Chorley clearly had in mind the contrast between Shelley and Byron, on the one hand, and Wordsworth and Hemans, on the other, when he wrote that

> There is no subject of contemplation more interesting or more impressive than the last years of the lives of poets. It is saddening, indeed, to consider how many gifted ones have been summoned from earth before their mission was accomplished; some, as it were, snatched away in the midst of a whirlwind, leaving nothing behind them save wild and forlorn fragments of song.... But, in proportion as these examples of noble spirits quenched—wasted—shattered—humble our pride in human genius and human intellect, it is gladdening to regard the progress of those, too sensitive or scornful by nature, who were permitted to live till calmness, and thought, and humility, had taken the places of passion, and waywardness, and self-approval;—who became not only willing to wait their appointed time, but earnest to do their part in serving their fellow-men, by opening the innermost treasure-chambers of truth and poetry, to the few who have eyes to see and hearts to conceive; or by singing simple and fanciful songs in the ear of the plainer day-labourer, winning him by gentle influences from the too exclusive and narrowing cares of his mechanical calling.[99]

It is interesting that, amongst the younger generation of poets, it is Hemans who is considered most nearly to achieve this redemptive narrative of the poet who makes the transition from youthful sensibility to mature reflection, from wasted effort to 'serving' her 'fellow-men', her mission to extend her 'gentle influences' to the hearts of readers—both the few and the many. She is, for Chorley, a poet against whom all but Wordsworth, amongst the contemporary male poets, are measured and found wanting. Both Chorley and Hughes end with the death scene, but neither make it, as Mary Shelley and Milnes did, a presiding theme. The premature deaths of Shelley and Keats, proleptically figured throughout the narratives of their lives, were made to signify their perpetual immaturity, their fated, or, in Shelley's case, partly willed, failure to leave 'romance' behind and arrive at a poetry of 'real' life. Hemans's death, although similarly premature, was not represented as such by Chorley or Hughes, nor was it obsessively prefigured. It came at the end of a life fulfilled and was described in the tradition of so many pious female *Lives*, before and after, as the result of illness, borne with Christian fortitude and womanly patience. Hughes also used the death scene to reaffirm her belief that there were higher things than poetry in her sister's life:

> The dark and silent chamber seemed illumined by light from above, and cheered with songs of angels; and she would say, that, in her intervals from pain, 'no poetry could

---

[99] *CM* ii. 255.

express, nor imagination conceive, the visions of blessedness that flitted across her fancy'[100]

Instead of verse, she tells us, Hemans read pious biography to comfort her, taking particular pleasure in *Lives of Sacred Poets* by R. A. Willmott and the death of Madame de Mornay from *Lives of Eminent Christians*.[101] By including this detail, Hughes promoted her own art and its capacity to touch the reader's heart through the life and death of an exemplary woman. Her prolonged and sentimental narrative of her sister's suffering particularly recalled the extended account of Hannah More's saintly death, at an advanced age, which ended the Roberts biography. Indeed, both Chorley and Hughes presented Hemans's death as if she, like More, had lived to a ripe old age. Unlike the deaths of Shelley or Keats, Hemans's was not framed as the tragic expression of an inchoate genius. She died young, but after the crucial moment of mature realization.

6.3 DEATH OF THE POETESS: LETITIA LANDON

Letitia Landon's death, unlike Hemans's, dominated the narratives of her life and her posthumous reputation as a poet. Her most influential biographer, Laman Blanchard, told her story, in part, as a whodunnit. Was it suicide or an accident? Was it death by natural causes, or murder? Blanchard's quest for the culprit turned up a range of possible explanations, all of which had significance for Landon's reputation but also for the image of the poetess that she embodied. Angela Leighton reads the death of Landon, as mythologized by her biographers, as depressingly destructive in both respects:

her life, whatever the true facts, disturbingly and quite shockingly reinforced the conclusions of the Sappho-Corinne myth: 'the fruits of a successful literary career for a woman' are, ultimately, death. Whether or not Letitia killed herself, the shady and much publicised nature of her end only intensified the punishing moral which lies at the core of the myth. Woman's creative success leads to moral and domestic disaster.

Leighton sees this 'punishing moral' as directed at Landon, rather than at Hemans, because she ventured more in living her life as a professional woman poet:

Hemans, as a woman, though not always as a poet, played safe and stayed at home; L. E. L. as both woman and poet, openly embraced the public stage of her professional success, and died. The comparison would not have been missed by their successors.[102]

---

[100] *HM*, 299.
[101] Ibid. 309–10.
[102] Leighton, *Victorian Women Poets*, 57.

This does not do justice to the first biographies of Landon, which were both more ambivalent and more enlightened than it suggests. The vigorous and enduring tradition of the depiction of suffering and death in biography, from medieval saints' lives onwards, particularly exploits the erotic potential of female suffering. But it would be wrong to assume that the death and suffering of the female literary subject always or simply signifies punishment for her creative ambition. Neither Emma Roberts, Landon's first memoirist, nor Blanchard expressed or suggested hostility to Landon's achievement as a poet, and neither invited readers to infer from her death that '[w]omen's creative success leads to moral and domestic disaster'. Rather, the circumstances of her death led both to question the simplistic equation of the life and work that was integral to the myth of the poetess, and in the process to explore the nature of creative ambition and its different models—from Byronic hubris on the one hand, to the more pragmatic ambitions of the professional writer on the other.

Roberts and Blanchard, both friends of Landon, wrote their posthumous memoirs in order to defend her against the rumours that, having made an unhappy marriage, and pent up in an African castle, far away from her friends, she had taken her own life. The religious and social stigma of suicide, as well as the potential for pathos and eroticism, was enhanced when the perpetrator was a woman. Mary Wollstonecraft's suicide attempt, after her abandonment by Gilbert Imlay, had been vividly and sympathetically described by Mary Hays in her brief 'Memoirs' of the author in 1800, but this was a mark of Hays's unusual daring in confronting social taboos.[103] Her account was partly based on Godwin's in chapter 8 of his *Memoirs* of Mary Wollstonecraft, but Godwin had included a disquisition on the irrationality of suicide and, in the second edition of the *Memoirs*, he had added a paragraph pointing to the failure of Wollstonecraft's 'moral judgement' in seeking to end her life as a result of a doomed relationship.[104] Landon, as a new bride, was particularly vulnerable to the imputation that she had committed suicide as a way of escaping an unhappy marriage. But, as a female poet, had the verdict of suicide been accepted it would also have placed her awkwardly in the company of her male literary forebears. By the 1830s a death wish was enshrined as part of the mythology of male Romantic genius, as exemplified by the suicide of Chatterton (also by prussic acid in some accounts) or the willed self-destruction of Burns, Shelley, and Byron. In poems such as Shelley's 'Alastor' or Byron's *Manfred*, suicide was represented as the ultimate act of solipsistic despair, but also the final declaration of the godlike self-determination of masculine genius. For a recently married, female poet to have taken her own life in 1838 would have signified not merely the usual social,

[103] Hays, 'Memoirs of Mary Wollstonecraft', *The Annual Necrology for 1797–8* (London: R. Phillips, 1800), 448–9.
[104] See *Collected Novels and Memoirs of William Godwin*, gen. ed. Mark Philp, 8 vols. (London: Pickering and Chatto, 1992), i. 154.

religious, and gender transgressions, but also a regressive imitation of a model of the life and death of the male poet, by then outmoded.

In order to keep the rumours of suicide at bay, both Roberts and Blanchard had to persuade their readers that Landon was not predisposed to such a desperate act. Their difficulty here was that her poetry suggested otherwise. Her melancholy heroines, some of them poetesses, and her reiterated themes of lost love, death, and despair, led readers who assumed an identification between the woman and her works, to see a death by suicide, with the Gothic trappings of a lonely, exotic castle, and a cruel husband, as her natural end. The temptation was to read this death, as so many had read Shelley's or Byron's, as prescribed by the poetry. To deny that this was the case—as Roberts and Blanchard were determined to do—thus had the effect of forcing them to deny the equation between life and works that was so fundamental to the mythology of the poetess. They did not do so consistently. Their biographical narratives veered between opposing models of female poetry as naïve self-expression and as self-conscious performance.

In her 'Memoir', prefacing her edition of *The Zenana* (1839), Roberts wrote as one of Landon's intimate circle of female friends. From this perspective she valued the poetry as the resurrection of a loved one now lost. In editing Landon's poems from the *Drawing Room Scrap Book*, she found that '[s]he seems indeed to live again in the glowing pages of her song'.[105] This subscribed to the view that the poetess was embodied in her poetry, as did Roberts's identification of Landon with her own improvisatrice. Her verse, in the early days, was the unpremeditated outpouring of a poetess oblivious to the harsh realities of the literary world:

Living completely in a world of her own, constructed from materials found in those agreeable fictions which had been her study and her solace, she rushed fearlessly into print, not dreaming for a moment, that verses which were poured forth like the waters from a fountain, gushing, as she has beautifully expressed it, of their own sweet will, could ever provoke stern or harsh criticism.

Yet, Roberts argues, even at this stage, Landon was unprepared for her work to be read as autobiographical expression. Her poetry was about thwarted love, but this was something Landon, herself, had never experienced:

While dwelling with apparently earnest tenderness upon the sorrows of love, its disappointments and treacheries, L. E. L. identified herself with the beings of her fancy, lamenting frequently in the first person, over miseries which she had never felt, and to which she was by no means likely to be subjected....While generally supposed to be the pining victim of unrequited love, her heart remained untouched, its overflowing tenderness being lavished upon the faithless heroes of her own creation.[106]

[105] Roberts, *The Zenana*, 27.
[106] Ibid. 9–11.

Coming back to England after some years abroad, and reading the poetry Landon had published in the interim, Roberts was pleased to be able 'to trace the maturer views of a mind always progressing'. As a child, the 'infant genius' had lived so much in a world of imagination that it seemed she was 'domesticated in Fairy-land'.[107] But the 'maturer' Landon 'appealed less to the imagination, she spoke more strongly to the heart'. She still belied her own 'gaiety' in the despondency of her poetry, but even this was ameliorating in her very last works which would have 'exhibited far less gloomy pictures of human life'.[108] Roberts projected a cheerful Landon—the frontispiece engraved portrait was of a smiling, even coquettish young woman (Fig. 6.2)—and she was careful to paint the marriage, to George Maclean in 1838, as a happy one. Landon admired Maclean's heroic qualities, 'the chivalric energy with which he strove to put an end to the slave-trade', and 'she quitted England a gay and happy bride'. 'At our last interview, a very short time before her departure, she assured me of her perfect happiness with a sincerity of look and manner which could not be doubted'.[109] Roberts's eagerness to assert an incongruity between Landon's subject matter and her life, and to place her poetry within a narrative that moved gradually away from gloom as it progressed from imagination to the 'heart', was clearly motivated by her wish to deny the possibility that her melancholy nature had led inevitably to suicide (her death was, on the contrary, 'wholly accidental').[110] Yet it also had the effect of disrupting the easy equation of the woman with the work. Landon, in this brief 'Life', was a woman who composed poetry as an escape from self, her improvisation a performance, and one that was ever changing and developing in the course of her career. The personal insight of the biographer thus allowed her both to read her friend into her work, and to read the work as antithetical to her friend. To Landon's 'small circle of female friends', who knew Landon as 'a bright, blithe being, affectionate and glad', the assumption of the critics that Landon was, herself, a love-lorn heroine, was a source of amusement or annoyance. Ironically, her only genuine experience of melancholy as a poet was due to the hardships of the literary marketplace:

the trials, great as they are, which every author, however distinguished and successful, must encounter. The necessity of fulfilling engagements to the day—of writing against time, often under the infliction of indisposition or mental anxiety, form some of the numerous drawbacks which those who cannot command literary leisure experience; with which she was frequently compelled to combat, though borne with cheerfulness, could not fail to produce occasional depression of spirits, and to give to her first views of the realities of life, somewhat of a melancholy character.[111]

[107] Roberts, *The Zenana*, 27, 8.
[108] Ibid. 27–8.
[109] Ibid. 29, 32–3.
[110] Ibid. 31.
[111] Ibid. 11–13.

Fig. 6.2. Engraved frontispiece portrait of Letitia Landon, from a drawing by Daniel Maclise, in *The Zenana and Minor Poems of L. E. L. With a Memoir by Emma Roberts* (London: Fisher and Sons [1839]).

As in the *Lives* of Hemans, the myth of the poetess was countered here by insight into the female poet as a professional writer.

Blanchard's was a much fuller biography than Roberts's, anecdotal and lively, based partly on the childhood reminiscences of Landon's brother, and including extracts from Landon's own correspondence. Yet he took his cue from Roberts in suggesting, on the one hand, that she was a natural genius and, on the other, that her poetry was a performance.[112] The latter argument was now more developed and insistent. Blanchard denied the autobiographical basis of Landon's early sketch 'The History of a Child', which would lead readers to believe that she was 'a shy, melancholy, lonely, unloved child. . . . Now the real L. E. L. was anything on earth but this'.[113] He supplied anecdotes illustrating her close relationship with her brother and their high-spirited and tomboyish games—they attacked a gardener with 'Spartan' arrows and he threw them into a hedge.[114] She was, says her brother, '"a strong healthy child, a joyous and high-spirited romp"'. In later life this was not lost but mutated into '"the milder and less childish form of playful wit and social cheerfulness"'.[115] Grappling, as Roberts had done, with the problem of the melancholy nature of her poetry, he was adamant:

there was not the remotest connection or affinity, not indeed a colour of resemblance, between her every-day life or habitual feelings, and the shapes they were made to assume in her poetry. No two persons could be less like each other in all that related to the contemplation of the actual world, than 'L. E. L.' and Letitia Elizabeth Landon.[116]

After composing a melancholy piece '[t]he spectres she had conjured up vanished as the wand dropped from her hand', 'Sorrow and suspicion, pining regrets for the past, anguish for the present, and morbid predictions for the future, were, in L. E. L., not moral characteristics, but merely literary resources'.[117] As with Roberts, Blanchard was preparing his case against suicide here, and in doing so he, like Roberts before him, began to develop an insight into the nature of Landon's public persona as 'L. E. L.' that has also informed contemporary feminist approaches to her work. Stephenson, for example, takes essentially the same line as these biographers when she argues that Landon adopted a 'public image' as 'the melancholy romantic poetess', an image that was at odds with the realities of her life as a professional writer.[118]

The generic tendency of biography to reveal the life/works relationship as one compounded of congruity and incongruity, was potentially liberating for the

[112] For Landon the natural genius see Blanchard, *Life*, i. 17: 'Her genius seems to have sprung up "Just as the grass grows that sows itself"'.
[113] Ibid. 22–3.
[114] Ibid. 15–16.
[115] Ibid. 24.
[116] Ibid. 34.
[117] Ibid. 35, 38.
[118] Stephenson, *Letitia Landon*, 28. See also Emma Francis and Virginia Blain on Landon's performance as 'poetess'.

female literary subject. It posited but also questioned the model of feminine creativity as unreflective self-expression and implied the possibility of a more knowing negotiation of her public persona. It also recognized the material contexts within which her poetry was composed. Yet, in Roberts and more so in Blanchard, this went along with some reservations about the kind of poetry that resulted. As we have already seen, Roberts, like Chorley, Hughes, and Mary Shelley, was uncomfortable not just with the concentration on melancholy subject matter but also with the conception of poetry as an imaginative flight from the real. For Blanchard, too, Landon's tendency to romance—her escapist aesthetic—was problematic. His conflicted response to her poetry, on these grounds, is present throughout the biography. It comes into play, for instance, in a passage reporting an eyewitness account of Landon's bedroom, given to him by one of her female friends. It is another in the long line of biographical closet scenes, here with the added titillation of granting an intimate view of the most private space of the female writer:

the description is 'graphic.' 'Genius,' says our accomplished informant, 'hallows every place where it pours forth its inspirations. Yet how strongly contrasted, sometimes, is the outward reality around the poet, with the visions of his inward being. Is it not D'Israeli, in his "Curiosities of Literature," referring to this frequent incongruity, who mentions, among other facts, that Moore composed his "Lalla Rookh" in a large barn? L. E. L. remarks on this subject, "A history of the *how* and *where* works of imagination have been produced, would often be more extraordinary than the works themselves." Her own case is, in some degree, an illustration of perfect independence of mind over all external circumstances. Perhaps, to the L. E. L. of whom so many nonsensical things have been said—as "that she should write with a crystal pen dipped in dew upon silver paper, and use for pounce the dust of a butterfly's wing," a *dilettante* of literature would assign, for the scene of her authorship, a fairy-like boudoir, with rose-coloured and silver hangings, fitted with all the luxuries of a fastidious taste. How did the reality agree with this fancy sketch? Miss Landon's drawing-room, indeed, was prettily furnished, but it was her invariable habit to write in her bed-room. I see it now, that homely-looking, almost uncomfortable room, fronting the street, and barely furnished—with a simple white bed, at the foot of which was a small, old, oblong-shaped sort of dressing-table, quite covered with a common worn writing-desk heaped with papers, while some strewed the ground, the table being too small for aught besides the desk; a little high-backed cane-chair which gave you any idea rather than that of comfort—a few books scattered about completed the author's paraphernalia.'[119]

The passage positions the reader as a voyeuristic literary tourist (the 'graphic' account even includes a description of her bed), but also as one whose visit to the inner sanctum, guided by one close friend of L. E. L., quoting the account of another, even closer, will reveal the real woman behind her public persona. The popular conception of a poet will always be out of keeping with the truth and the

---

[119] Blanchard, *Life*, i. 78–9.

case of L. E. L. is no exception. The reader who imagines her bedroom to be an extension of her poetry will be disappointed. It is no gaudy, fairy grotto (or kept woman's 'boudoir'), but an ordinary, modest space, in which her desk, her chair, and her papers—the traces of a hard-working professional writer—are an unpretentious part of her mundane, domestic environment.[120] The point of the passage is the incongruity of poets' 'external circumstances' with their internal imaginative life. The exoticism of *Lalla Rookh* issued from a barn and from L. E. L.'s unremarkable, cell-like bedroom came poetry which was other-worldly, luxurious, even, perhaps, sexually suspect. Here the biographer asserts his power to go behind the scenes and mediate the reality of the poet to the reader, but the slippage between the life and the works has troubling implications for the poetry. By contrast to the moving simplicity of her life, her poetry looks gaudy and superfluous. Would it have been better, both for her and for her work, if she had grounded her imagination in reality rather than romance? This is a question that hovers throughout the biography, but which is focused most clearly in Blanchard's central theme: the causes of Landon's death.

His biography is, as I have said, a whodunnit, but one that offers conflicting solutions to the murder mystery. One story he tells is of a happily married bride, who is just beginning to progress away from her earlier Romantic excesses to a mature poetic vision when she is cut off in her prime. By the end of her life,

High and solemn thought had found the place where wild fancy or extravagant sentiment alone had revelled before; knowledge had succeeded to mere impulse or reckless speculation; the feelings had become more deeply seated, as the heart beat less feverishly; the sportive child had sprung into the woman. . . . The ideal became purer as her knowledge of the actual advanced; and her dreams deepened in loveliness from her intercourse with the world.[121]

Her progress is marked for him by the fact that she had started to lean away from poetry completely and towards prose. In response to criticism of her earlier poetry 'Reality, in short, grew as familiar to her as Romance. She led Prose captive, as she had led Poetry'.[122] At the time of her death she was engaged on a cheerful work in prose—essays on the female characters from Scott.[123] Her death, in this version of events, could therefore have had nothing to do with her husband, her alleged melancholy disposition, or her career as a poet. It was simply an unfortunate stroke of fate. He proves this in a lengthy, forensic investigation of the evidence, as revealed in Landon's letters, at the inquest

---

[120] Compare Mary Robinson's account of her writing room: 'In a small basket near my chair slept my little Maria; my table was spread with papers; and every thing around me presented the mixed confusion of a study and a nursery', *Memoirs of the Late Mrs Robinson, written by Herself. A New Edition, with an Introduction* (1801; London: Cobden-Sanderson, 1930), 87.

[121] Blanchard, *Life*, i. 275.

[122] Ibid. 277. He alludes here to Landon's novel, *Romance and Reality* (1831).

[123] Blanchard, *Life*, i. 299–300.

and, more importantly, in Blanchard's view, by witnesses whose testimony was not taken into account. Having weighed this evidence up, his explanation is that her death was by natural causes—an abscess in the ear led to a 'suffusion on the brain' and caused the fit from which she died.[124]

This is one conclusion to the murder mystery, but by no means the only one his biography offers. There is an alternative narrative, lurking behind the forensic explanation, in which Landon's death has nothing to do with an abscess. In this version of events her end is much more like Shelley's as represented in the 1839 *Poetical Works*. It is a death foretold, foreshadowed early in the story of her life and linked to her tendency for escapist imaginative fantasy. Her father made a voyage to Africa as a young man and conferred on her a lifelong fascination with exotic travel. Her childhood reading fed this imaginative yearning.[125] Her father gave her *Silvester Tramper*, a novel about travels in Africa, as well as *The Arabian Nights*.[126] She also loved *Robinson Crusoe* and made her brother play games of imaginary travel to her own Robinson Crusoe island.[127] These details prepare us for her actual voyage to Africa, as a fatal fulfilment of childhood fantasy. A letter, written to Blanchard from the Cape, refers to her surroundings in terms of this childhood reading: 'It is like living in the "Arabian Nights," looking out upon the palm and cocoa-nut trees'.[128] In another she writes, '[t]he solitude here is very Robinson Crusoe-ish' and her very last letter, written on the day of her death, describes 'how I enact the part of a feminine Robinson Crusoe'.[129] As a child she had built 'wonderful castles . . . in her imagination'.[130] As an adult the imaginary castle materializes, with catastrophic effects.

In this narrative, Landon's mistake is to journey backwards into her childhood fantasy towards a country which can only be a land of imagination to her English friends. Her journey to Africa is, in fact, represented as a regression into pure fantasy—significantly Blanchard quotes Landon's sea journal in which she compared herself to the Ancient Mariner. Africa, as the imaginary continent, is not only linked with the visionary, Romantic quest, but with darkness, anarchy and seduction. The 'dark outline of the wild and far-off coast' is a presage of violence. Maclean, Blanchard informs us, had an African mistress who, according to one rumour, had killed Landon in a jealous rage. He discounts this rumour, but still uses it as an excuse for commenting on 'the hot blood and the fierce habits of the natives of Western Africa'.[131] Although Blanchard, like Roberts

---

[124] Ibid. 232.
[125] Ibid. 3.
[126] Ibid. 20–1.
[127] Ibid. 18.
[128] Ibid. 197.
[129] Ibid. 199, 213.
[130] Ibid. 9.
[131] Ibid., 171–2, 217. See also ibid. 189 for the confusion of their arrival on the coast in the darkness, leading to the death of one of their fellow travellers.

before him, defends the reputation of Maclean and argues that Landon was a willing and happy bride, his revelations suggest otherwise. He mentions no names, but alludes much more fully than Roberts to Landon's previously unhappy experiences with men, suggesting that she was to some extent driven to accept Maclean. He quotes from letters in which she showed ambivalent feelings towards her husband, even if jokily expressed: 'it would be a very fine thing to be married if it were not for the husband!'[132] Blanchard's revelation that Maclean had kept an African mistress inevitably raises questions about his intentions towards his bride, as does the comparison of the couple to Desdemona and Othello.[133] Ominously their major shared interest is Africa: 'African habits, African horrors, and African wonders—the sea, the coast, the desert, the climate and the people'.[134] The marriage, in this light, appears as a death-wish. She is a female victim, an innocent betrayed, first by her father, then by her husband, in alliance with Africa itself, the country of unfettered imaginative desire.

Both Roberts and Blanchard quote Landon's last, poignant letter home, in which she mixes cheerful chattiness with self-dramatizing melancholy:

The castle is a fine building—the rooms excellent. I do not suffer from heat; insects there are few, or none; and I am in excellent health. The solitude, except an occasional dinner, is absolute.... On three sides we are surrounded by the sea. I like the perpetual dash on the rocks—one wave comes up after another, and is for ever dashed in pieces, like human hopes that only swell to be disappointed. We advance—up springs the shining froth of love or hope, 'a moment white, and gone for ever.'[135]

The letter starts in the manner of a Jane Austen heroine and ends in the style of Radcliffe. It recalls both Mary Shelley's description of the Casa Magni, and the uncanny beach house where Ellena di Rosalba awaits her murder in *The Italian*. Blanchard is unsure how to deal with it. It does not fit with his argument that Landon was not really a depressive, despite the evidence of her poetry, so he dismisses it as in 'the vein poetical'.[136] But it fits with his other narrative of her death, as an awkward contradiction to the story of her progress towards enlightenment. In the first story, Landon is the maturing, Victorian poetess. In the second, she has made, for her, a fatal return to the Romantic imagination. Blanchard notes that Landon was not alone amongst young women writers in meeting her death in exotic lands—Jewsbury and then Emma Roberts, Landon's own biographer, died in India.[137] In this company, Landon appears, as presented by Blanchard, as one of a band of women poets who have gone astray, but her story is not therefore a warning to women against literary ambition. The poetess

---

[132] Blanchard, *Life*, i. 168.
[133] Ibid. 137.
[134] Ibid. 136.
[135] Ibid. 213–14, and see Roberts, *The Zenana*, 34–5.
[136] Blanchard, *Life*, i, 199.
[137] Ibid. 261, 264.

who dies in this biography is very specifically the Romantic author—the female Byron. Death, in this narrative, is not a punishment for Landon's career, but for her turning away from it, her move from the domestic to the exotic, from London and the life of the professional woman writer to a remote and solitary castle of the imagination.

Bibliography

MANUSCRIPTS

Letter from De Quincey to John Johnstone, 22 September 1827 (Pierpont Morgan, MS MA3007).

Letter from William Tait to Christian Johnstone, 22 August 1840 (National Library of Scotland MS 1670, fos. 74/5 and 73).

Letter from Christian Johnstone to William Tait, 22 August 1840 (National Library of Scotland MS 1670, fos. 71/72).

PRIMARY

[Allsop, T. (ed.)], *Letters, Conversations and Recollections of Coleridge*, 2 vols. (London: Edward Moxon, 1836).

Anderson, Robert, *The Works of the British Poets, with Prefaces Biographical and Critical*, 13 vols. (Edinburgh 1793–1807).

Arnold, Matthew, *The Complete Prose Works of Matthew Arnold*, ed. R. H. Super, 11 vols. (Ann Arbor: University of Michigan Press, 1960–77).

B., W. A. (ed.), *National Lyrics and Songs for Music by Felicia Hemans*, [2nd edn., *With an Introductory Notice of her Life and Writings*] (Dublin: William Curry; London: Simpkin, Marshall & Co.; Edinburgh: Fraser & Co., 1836).

Barbauld, Anna Laetitia, *The Works of Anna Laetitia Barbauld, with a Memoir by Lucy Aikin*, 2 vols. (London: Longman, Hurst, Rees, Orme, Brown and Green, 1825).

Benson, Joseph, *A Short Account of the Death of Mrs Mary Hutton, of Sunderland, who Died February 24, 1777* ([Newcastle upon Tyne?], 1777).

Bertram, J. G., *Some Memories of Books, Authors and Events* (Westminster: A. Constable, 1893).

Betham, Mathilda, *Biographical Dictionary of the Celebrated Women of Every Age and Country* (London: B. Crosby, 1804).

Biographium Faemineum. The Female Worthies: or, Memoirs of the Most Illustrious Ladies, of all Ages and Nations, who have been Eminently distinguished for their Magnanimity, Learning, Genius, Virtue, Piety, and other Excellent Endowments, conspicuous in all the various Stations and Relations of Life, public and private, 2 vols. (London: S. Crowder and J. Payne, J. Wilkie and W. Nicoll, J. Wren, 1766).

Blanchard, Laman, *Life and Literary Remains of L. E. L.*, 2 vols. (London: Henry Colburn, 1841).

Blessington, Lady. *See* Gardiner, Marguerite.

Boswell, James, *The Life of Samuel Johnson, LL.D. Including a Journal of a Tour to the Hebrides, A New Edition. With Numerous Additions and Notes, by John Wilson Croker, LL.D. F.R.S.*, 5 vols. (London: John Murray, 1831).

—— *Boswell's Life of Samuel Johnson, Together with Boswell's Journal of a Tour to the Hebrides*, ed. George Birkbeck Hill and L. F. Powell, 6 vols. (Oxford: Oxford University Press, 1934–50).

'Bull, John'. *See* Lockhart.

Byron, A. I. Noel, *Remarks Occasioned by Mr. Moore's Notices of Lord Byron's Life* (London: Richard Taylor, [1830]).

Byron, Gordon George Lord, 'Lord Byron's Poems on His Own Domestic Circumstances', *The Champion* (14 Apr. 1816).

—— *Poems on his Domestic Circumstances. By Lord Byron. I. Fare Thee Well! II. A Sketch from Private Life. With the Star of the Legion of Honour, and Other Poems. To Which is Prefixed, The Life of the Noble Author*, 11th edn. (London: R. Edwards, 1816).

—— *The Works of Lord Byron: With his Letters and Journals, and his Life, by Thomas Moore, Esq.*, 17 vols. [advertised in vol. i as 14 vols.] (London: John Murray, 1832–3).

—— *Works* [in 1 volume with biographical notes] (London: John Murray, 1837) accompanied by a 1-volume reprint of Moore's *Journals and Letters*.

—— *Byron's Letters and Journals*, ed. Leslie A. Marchand, 12 vols. (London: John Murray, 1973–82).

Carlyle, Thomas, *The Works of Thomas Carlyle*, Centenary Edition, ed. H. D. Traill, 30 vols. (1st edn., London: Chapman and Hall, 1896–9; repr. New York: Charles Scribner's Sons, n.d.).

—— *The Collected Letters of Thomas and Jane Welsh Carlyle*, Duke-Edinburgh Edition, gen. ed. Charles Richard Sanders (Durham, NC: Duke University Press, 1970–).

Chorley, Henry F., *Memorials of Mrs. Hemans with Illustrations of her Literary Character from her Private Correspondence*, 2 vols. (London: Saunders and Otley, 1836).

—— *The Authors of England: A Series of Medallion Portraits* (London: C. Tilt, 1838).

[Coleridge, Derwent, and Coleridge, Sara (eds.)], *The Poetical and Dramatic Works of S. T. Coleridge. With a Memoir* (Boston: Little, Brown, 1854).

Coleridge, H. N., *Specimens of the Table Talk of the Late Samuel Taylor Coleridge*, 2 vols. (London: John Murray, 1835).

[—— and Coleridge, Sara (eds.)], *Biographia Literaria*, 2 vols. (London: William Pickering, 1847).

Coleridge, Samuel Taylor, 'A Prefatory Observation on Modern Biography' [Prefacing his 'Sketches and Fragments of the Life and Character of The Late Admiral Sir Alexander Ball'], *The Friend*, 21 (Thursday, 25 Jan. 1810).

—— *The Poetical and Dramatic Works of Samuel Taylor Coleridge, with a Life of the Author* (London: John Thomas Cox, 1836).

—— *The Friend*, ed. Barbara E. Rooke, 2 vols. [no. 4 in *The Collected Works of Samuel Taylor Coleridge*, Bollingen Series LXXV, gen. ed. Kathleen Coburn] (London and Princeton: Routledge and Kegan Paul and Princeton University Press, 1969).

Corry, John, *The Life of William Cowper* (London: B. Crosby and Co., 1803).

Cottle, Joseph, *Early Recollections, Chiefly Relating to the Late Samuel Taylor Coleridge, During his Long Residence in Bristol*, 2 vols. (London: Longman, Rees & Co. and Hamilton, Adams & Co., 1837).

Croker, John Wilson. *See* Boswell.

Currie, James (ed.), *The Works of Robert Burns: With an Account of his Life, and a Criticism on his Writings*, 4 vols. (Liverpool and Edinburgh: J. McCreery and W. Creech, 1800).

Dallas, R. C., *Recollections of the Life of Lord Byron, from the year 1808 to the End of 1814; Exhibiting his Early Character and Opinions, Detailing the Progress of his Literary Career, and Including Various Unpublished Passages of his Works, taken from Authentic Documents in the Possession of the Author* (London: Charles Knight, 1824).

De Quincey, Thomas, 'Samuel Taylor Coleridge. By the English Opium-Eater', *Tait's Edinburgh Magazine*, 1/8 (Sept. 1834), 509–20; 1/9 (Oct. 1834), 588–96; 1/10 (Nov. 1834), 685–90; 2/13 (Jan. 1835), 3–10.

——'Lake Reminiscences, from 1807 to 1830, by the English Opium-Eater. No. I.— William Wordsworth', *Tait's Edinburgh Magazine*, 6/61 (Jan. 1839), 1–12; '[No. II.] William Wordsworth', 6/62 (Feb. 1839), 90–103; 'No. III.—William Wordsworth', 6/64 (Apr. 1839), 246–54; 'No. IV.—William Wordsworth and Robert Southey', 6/67 (July 1839), 453–64; 'No. V—Southey, Wordsworth, and Coleridge', 6/68 (Aug. 1839), 513–17.

—— *The Posthumous Works of Thomas De Quincey*, ed. A. H. Japp, 2 vols. (London: Heinemann, 1891).

—— *The Works of Thomas De Quincey*, gen. ed. Grevel Lindop, 21 vols. (London: Pickering and Chatto, 2000–3).

Dixon, Thomas, *A Brief Account of the Life and Death of Barbara Walker* ([London?]: 1777).

Dowden, Edward, *The Life of Percy Shelley*, 2 vols. (London: Kegan Paul, Trench & Co., 1886).

Dyce, Alexander, *Specimens of British Poetesses; Selected and Chronologically Arranged* (1825; London: T. Rodd, 1827).

Early Recollections, Chiefly Relating to the Late Samuel Taylor Coleridge, During his Long Residence in Bristol, 2 vols. (London: Longman, Rees & Co. and Hamilton, Adams & Co., 1837).

Eccentric Biography; or the Memoirs of Remarkable Female Characters, Ancient and Modern. Including Actresses, Adventurers, Authoresses, Fortune-Tellers, Gipsies, Dwarfs, Swindlers, Vagrants, and Others who have Distinguished themselves by their Chastity, Dissipation, Intrepidity, Learning, Abstinence, Credulity, &c. &c. Alphabetically Arranged. Forming a Pleasing Mirror of Reflection to the Female Mind, 2nd edn. (London: T. Hurst, 1803).

Ellis, Sarah Stickney, *The Women of England, Their Social Duties and Domestic Habits. By Mrs. Ellis* (London: Fisher, Son & Co. [1839]).

Elwood, Mrs [Anne Katharine], *Memoirs of the Literary Ladies of England, from the Commencement of the Last Century*, 2 vols. (London: Henry Colburn, 1843).

Engels, Friedrich, *The Condition of the Working-Class in England in 1844*, trans. Florence Kelley Wischnewetzky (1st English edn. 1892; London: George Allen & Unwin Ltd., 1936).

—— *The Condition of the Working Class in England*, ed. and trans. W. O. Henderson and W. H. Chaloner (Oxford: Basil Blackwell, 1971).

Froude, James Anthony (ed.), *Reminiscences by Thomas Carlyle*, 2 vols. (London: Longmans, Green and Co., 1881).

Galt, John, *The Life of Lord Byron* (London: Henry Colburn and Richard Bentley; Edinburgh: Bell and Bradfute; Dublin: Cumming, 1830).

——'Pot versus Kettle. Remarks on Mr. Hobhouse and Mr. Galt's Correspondence respecting Atrocities in the Life of Lord Byron', *Fraser's Magazine*, 2/2 (Dec. 1830), 533–42.

'Galt's *Life of Byron*', *Fraser's Magazine*, 2/19 (Oct. 1830), 347–70.

[Gardiner, Marguerite, Lady Blessington], 'Journal of Conversations with Lord Byron, by the Countess of Blessington', *New Monthly Magazine and Literary Journal*, 35–9 (July 1832–Dec. 1833).

—— *Conversations of Lord Byron* (London: Henry Colburn, 1834).

—— *Lady Blessington's Conversations of Lord Byron*, ed. Ernest J. Lovell (Princeton: Princeton University Press, 1969).

[Gilfillan, George], 'Miscellaneous', *The Critic*, 2 (1854), 157.

Gilman, James, *The Life of Samuel Taylor Coleridge*, 2 vols. [only 1 pub.] (London: William Pickering, 1838).

Godwin, William, *Memoirs of the Author of A Vindication of the Rights of Woman* (London: J. Johnson, 1798).

—— *Life of Geoffrey Chaucer, The Early English Poet: Including Memoirs of his near Friend and Kinsman, John of Gaunt, Duke of Lancaster: With Sketches of the Manners, Opinions, Arts and Literature of England in the Fourteenth Century* (1st edn. [2 vols.], London: Richard Phillips,1803; 2nd edn. [4 vols.], London: Richard Phillips, 1804).

—— *Collected Novels and Memoirs of William Godwin*, gen. ed. Mark Philp, 8 vols. (London: Pickering and Chatto, 1992).

Gordon, Cosmo, *Life and Genius of Lord Byron* (London: Knight and Lacey, 1824).

Grimshawe, T. S. (ed.), *The Life and Works of William Cowper. His Life and Letters by William Hayley Esq. Now First Completed with an Introduction of Cowper's Private Correspondence*, 8 vols. (London: Saunders and Otley, 1835).

[Grimstone, Mary Leman], 'Men and Women', *Tait's Edinburgh Magazine*, 1/2 (Mar. 1834), 101–3.

Guiccioli, Theresa Countess, *My Recollections of Lord Byron and those of Eye-Witnesses of his Life*, new edn., trans. [from the French by] Hubert E. H. Jerningham (London: Richard Bentley, 1869).

[Hare, Julius], 'Samuel Taylor Coleridge and the English Opium-Eater', *The British Magazine*, 7 (1835), 15–27.

Hayley, William, *The Life and Posthumous Writings of William Cowper*, 3 vols. (London: J. Johnson, 1803–4).

[Hays, Mary], 'Memoirs of Mary Wollstonecraft', *The Annual Necrology for 1797–1798* (London: R. Phillips, 1800), 411–60.

—— *Female Biography; or, Memoirs of Illustrious and Celebrated Women, of all Ages and Countries. Alphabetically Arranged*, 6 vols. (London: Richard Phillips,1803).

—— *Memoirs of Queens* (1821).

Hazlitt, William, *The Complete Works of William Hazlitt*, ed. P. P. Howe, 21 vols. (London: Dent, 1930–4).

Hemans, Felicia, *Memorials of Mrs. Hemans* [see Chorley, Henry Fothergill].

—— *National Lyrics and Songs for Music by Felicia Hemans*, 2nd edn., *With an Introductory Notice of her Life and Writings* [see B., W. A.].

—— *Poetical Remains of the Late Mrs. Hemans* [see Moir, Daivd Macbeth].

—— *The Works of Mrs. Hemans; with a Memoir of her Life by her Sister*. See Hughes, Harriett.

—— *Early Blossoms, a Collection of Poems Written between eight and fifteen years of Age. By Felicia Dorothea Browne: afterwards Mrs. Hemans, With a Life of the Authoress* (London: T. Allman, 1840).

—— *Felicia Hemans. Selected Poems, Letters* [see Wolfson, Susan J.].

[Hobhouse, John Cam], 'Dallas's "Recollections" and Medwin's "Conversations"', *Westminster Review*, 3/5 (Jan. 1825), 1–35.

Hogg, James, *The Domestic Manners and Private Life of Sir Walter Scott, with a Memoir of the Author* (New York: Harper and Brothers, 1834; repr. Glasgow: John Reid & Co., 1834).

[Hogg, Thomas Jefferson], 'Percy Bysshe Shelley at Oxford', *New Monthly Magazine and Literary Journal*, 34–5 (Jan.–Dec. 1832).

—— 'The History of Percy Bysshe Shelley's Expulsion from Oxford', *New Monthly Magazine and Literary Journal*, 38 (May 1833).

—— *The Life of Percy Bysshe Shelley*, 4 vols. [only 2 pub.] (London: Edward Moxon, 1858).

—— *The Life of Percy Bysshe Shelley, by Thomas Jefferson Hogg, with an Introduction by Professor Edward Dowden* (London: George Routledge and Sons; New York: Edward Dutton, 1906).

Holmes, Richard, *Shelley: The Pursuit* (London: Weidenfeld and Nicolson, 1974; Penguin Books, 1987).

[Hook, Theodore], 'My Wedding Night; the Obnoxious Chapter in Lord Byron's Memoirs', *John Bull Magazine and Literary Recorder*, 1/1 (July 1824), 19–21.

[Hughes, Harriett], 'Memoir of Mrs Hemans', *The Works of Mrs Hemans; with a Memoir of her Life, by her Sister*, 7 vols. (Edinburgh: William Blackwood and Sons; London: Thomas Cadell, 1839), i. 1–315.

Hunt, James Henry Leigh, *Lord Byron and Some of his Contemporaries; with Recollections of the Author's Life, and of his Visit to Italy* (London: Henry Colburn, 1828).

—— 'Mr. Shelley. With a Criticism on his Genius, and Mr. Trelawny's Narrative of his Loss at Sea', in *Lord Byron and Some of his Contemporaries; with Recollections of the Author's Life, and of his Visit to Italy* (London: Henry Colburn, 1828), 174–229.

[Jeffrey, Francis], Review of *The Excursion*, *Edinburgh Review*, 24 (Nov. 1814), 1–30.

—— Review of *Memoirs of the Life of the Right Honourable Sir James Mackintosh*, *Edinburgh Review*, 62 (Oct. 1835), 205–55.

Johnson, John (ed.), *The Works of the Late William Cowper*, 10 vols. (London: Baldwin, Cradock and Joy, 1817) [vol. iii contained 'A Sketch of his Life by his Kinsman' by Johnson].

Johnson, Samuel, *The Yale Edition of the Works of Samuel Johnson*, gen. ed. J. H. Middendorf, ii. *The Idler* and *The Adventurer*, ed. W. J. Bate, J. Bullitt, and L. F. Powell (New Haven: Yale University Press, 1963); iii–v. *The Rambler*, ed. W. J. Bate and A. B. Strauss (New Haven: Yale University Press, 1969).

—— *Life of Savage*, ed. Clarence Tracy (Oxford: Clarendon Press, 1971).

—— *The Lives of the Most Eminent English Poets; With Critical Observations on their Works*, ed. Roger Lonsdale, 4 vols. (Oxford: Clarendon Press, 2006).

Johnstone, Christian, Review of Catherine Gore, *The Hamiltons, or the New Era*, 'Literary Register', *Tait's Edinburgh Magazine*, 1/3 (Apr. 1834), 208.

—— 'The Duchess D'Abrantès and the Countess of Blessington', *Tait's Edinburgh Magazine*, 1/3 (Apr. 1834), 204–6.

—— 'Life of Mrs. Siddons. By Thomas Campbell Esq.', *Tait's Edinburgh Magazine*, 1/7 (Aug. 1834), 467–9.

—— 'What shall we do with our Young Fellows?', *Tait's Edinburgh Magazine*, 1/8 (September 1834), 527–30.

Johnstone, Christian, 'Anglo-Indian Society' [Review of *Scenes and Characteristics of Hindoustan*, by Emma Roberts], *Tait's Edinburgh Magazine*, 2/22 (Oct. 1835), 683–93.

——'Mr De Quincey, and the Literary Society of Liverpool in 1801', *Tait's Edinburgh Magazine*, 4/41 (May 1837), 337–40.

——'Mrs Postans' Cutch; or, Random Sketches of Western India', *Tait's Edinburgh Magazine*, 6/61 (Jan. 1839), 28–35.

——'Mrs Jameson's Winter Studies and Summer Rambles in Canada', *Tait's Edinburgh Magazine*, 6/62 (Feb. 1839), 69–81.

——'Mrs Broughton's Six Years' Residence in Algiers', *Tait's Edinburgh Magazine*, 6/66 (June 1839), 399–406.

——'Lady Morgan's "Woman and her Master"', *Tait's Edinburgh Magazine*, 7/78 (June 1840), 390–7.

Johnstone, J., *Specimens of the Lyrical, Descriptive . . . Poets . . . With Biographical and Critical Notices* (Edinburgh, 1828).

K.[elty], M.[ary] A.[nn], *Biography for Young Ladies* (London: John Kendrick, 1839).

[Kilgour, Alexander], *Anecdotes of Lord Byron from Authentic Sources; with Remarks Illustrative of his Connection with the Principal Literary Characters of the Present Day* (London: Knight and Lacey; Aberdeen: W. Gordon, A. Stevenson, D. Wylie and L. Smith, 1825).

Knight, William, *The Life of William Wordsworth*, 3 vols. (Edinburgh: William Paterson, 1889).

Landon, Letitia [L. E. L.], *The Zenana and Minor Poems of L. E. L.* [see Roberts, Emma].

——*Letitia Elizabeth Landon: Selected Writings*, ed. Jerome McGann and Daniel Riess (Ontario: Broadview Press, 1997).

Lawrence, D. H., *The Letters of D. H. Lawrence*, gen. ed. James T. Boulton, 8 vols. (Cambridge: Cambridge University Press, 2002).

Lickbarrow, Isabella, *Poetical Effusions* (Kendal: Branthwaite & Co., 1814).

The Life and Memoirs of the Late Miss Ann Catley, The Celebrated Actress: with Biographical Sketches of Sir Frances Blake Delaval, and the Hon. Isabella Pawlet, Daughter to the Earl of Thanet, by Miss Ambross (London: J. Bird, n.d.).

[Lockhart, John Gibson], 'John Bull', *Letter to the Right Hon. Lord Byron* (London: William Wright, 1821).

——*Life of Robert Burns*, vol. xxiii of Constable's Miscellany (Edinburgh: Constable, 1828).

——Review of *The Life of Samuel Johnson. . . . By John Wilson Croker*, *Quarterly Review*, 46 (Nov. 1831 and Jan. 1832), 1–46.

——*Memoirs of the Life of Sir Walter Scott*, 7 vols. (Edinburgh: Cadell, 1837–8).

'Lord Byron's Letters', *John Bull Magazine and Literary Recorder*, 1/2 (Aug. 1824), 41–2; 'Lord Byron's Memoirs', ibid. 1/5 (Nov. 1824), 165; 'His Marriage', ibid. 165–6; 'His Departure', ibid. 166–7.

Lyon, Emma, *Miscellaneous Poems* (Oxford: J. Bartlett, 1812).

[Macaulay, Thomas Babbington], Review of *The Life of Samuel Johnson . . . by John Wilson Croker*, *Edinburgh Review*, 107 (Sept. 1831), 1–38.

Mahony, Joseph Francis ['Father Prout'], 'Gallery of Literary Characters', no. 41, 'Miss Landon', *Fraser's Magazine*, 8 (Oct. 1833), 433.

Martineau, Harriet, *Biographical Sketches. 1852–1875*, new edn. (London: Macmillan, 1893).

Medwin, Thomas, *Journal of the Conversations of Lord Byron. Noted During a Residence with his Lordship at Pisa, in the Years 1821 and 1822* (London: Henry Colburn, 1824).

—— *The Shelley Papers. Memoir of Percy Bysshe Shelley and Original Poems and Papers by Percy Bysshe Shelley. Now First Collected* (London: Whittaker, Treacher and Co., 1833).

Memes, John S. (ed.), *The Miscellaneous Works of William Cowper*, 3 vols. (Edinburgh: Fraser and Co; London: Smith, Elder and Co.; Dublin: W. Curry, Jun. and Co., 1834).

Memoirs of Mrs. Billington, from her Birth: Containing a Variety of Matter, Ludicrous, Theatrical, Musical, and —— (London: James Ridgway, 1792).

Milnes, Richard Monckton (ed.), *Life, Letters, and Literary Remains, of John Keats*, 2 vols. (London: Edward Moxon, 1848).

Mitford, J.[ohn], *The Private Life of Lord Byron; Comprising his Voluptuous Amours, Secret Intrigues, and Close Connection with Various Ladies of Rank and Fame in Scotland and London, at Eton, Harrow, Cambridge, Paris, Rome, Venice, &c., &c., With a Particular account of the Countess Guiaccoli* [sic.]*, and, never before Published, Details of the Murder at Ravenna, which caused his Lordship to leave Italy; Various Singular Anecdotes of Persons and Families of the Highest Circles of Haut Ton; compiled from Authentic Sources. With Extracts from Unburnt Documents! And Familiar Letters; from his Lordship to his Friends; being an Amusing and Interesting Expose of Fashionable Frailties, Follies, and Debaucheries. With Numerous Engravings* (London: H. Smith, n.d. [1836?]).

[Moir, David Macbeth], pseud. 'Delta', Obituary essay on Felicia Hemans, *Blackwood's*, 38 (July 1835), 96–7.

——'Biographical Memoir of the Late Mrs Hemans' in *Poetical Remains of the Late Mrs Hemans* (Edinburgh: William Blackwood & Sons; London: T. Cadell, 1836), pp. ix–xxxiii.

Moore, Thomas, *Letters and Journals of Lord Byron: with Notices of his Life*, 2 vols. (London: John Murray, 1830).

More, Hannah, *Strictures on the Modern System of Female Education. With a View of the Principles and Conduct Prevalent Among Women of Rank and Fortune*, 2 vols. (London: T. Cadell Jun. and W. Davies, 1799).

A Narrative of the Circumstances which attended the Separation of Lord and Lady Byron; Remarks on his Domestic Conduct, and a complete refutation of the calumnies circulated by Public Writers (London: R. Edwards, 1816).

Onwhyn, Thomas, ['Peter Paul Palette'], 'The Green Lane—No. 1', *Tait's Edinburgh Magazine*, 7/78 (June 1840), 341–6.

Peacock, Thomas Love, 'Memoirs of Percy Bysshe Shelley', 1st pub. in *Fraser's Magazine* (1858–60), in H. F. B. Brett-Smith and C. E. Jones (eds.), *the Works of Thomas Love Peacock*, Halliford Edition, viii. *Essays Memoirs, Letters and Unfinished Novels* (London: Constable and Co. Ltd.; New York: Gabriel Wells, 1934), 39–131.

'Personal Character of Lord Byron', *The London Magazine* (Oct. 1824), 337–47.

Pilkington, Mrs. [Mary], *Biography for Boys; or, Characteristic Histories, Calculated to Impress the Youthful Mind with an Admiration of Virtuous Principles and Detestation of Vicious Ones* (1st edn., London: Vernor & Hood, 1799; 3rd edn., London: J. Harris, 1808).

Pilkington, Mrs. [Mary], *Biography for Girls; or, Moral and Instructive Examples for the Female Sex* (1st edn., London: Vernor & Hood, 1799; 3rd edn., London: Vernor and Hood, Poultrey, 1800).

Poe, Edgar Allan, *The Works of Edgar Allan Poe*, ed. John H. Ingram, 4 vols. (London: A. and C. Black, 1899).

'The Poetesses of our Day.—No.1. Felicia Hemans', *Dublin University Magazine*, 10/56 (Aug. 1837), 123–41.

Redding, Cyrus, 'Memoir of Percy Bysshe Shelley', in *Poetical Works of Coleridge, Shelley, and Keats* (Paris: Galignani, 1829).

Roberts, Emma (ed.), *The Zenana and Minor Poems of L. E. L. With a Memoir by Emma Roberts* (London: Fisher and Sons; Paris: Quai D'École [1839]).

Roberts, William, *Memoirs of the Life and Correspondence of Mrs Hannah More*, 4 vols. (2nd edn, London: R. B. Seeley and W. Burnside, 1834).

Robinson, Ellen, *Poem Written on the Death of The Rev. Thomas Spencer, in Four Parts*, 2nd edn. (Liverpool: W. Bethell, 1812).

Robinson, Mary, *Memoirs of the Late Mrs Robinson, written by Herself. A New Edition, with an Introduction* (1801; London: Cobden-Sanderson, 1930).

Rowton, Frederic, *The Female Poets of Great Britain, Chronologically Arranged: with Copious Selections and Critical Remarks* (London: Longman, Brown, Green, and Longmans, 1848).

Scot, Elizabeth, *Alonzo and Cora, with Other Original Poems, Principally Elegiac* (London: Bunny and Gold, 1801).

Seward, Anna, *The Poetical Works of Anna Seward; with Extracts from her Literary Correspondence, edited by Walter Scott, Esq.*, 3 vols. (Edinburgh: James Ballantyne & Co.; London: Longman, Hurst, Rees and Orme, 1810).

Shelley, Lady [Jane] (ed.), *Shelley Memorials: From Authentic Sources. To Which is Added An Essay on Christianity, by Percy Bysshe Shelley; now First Printed* (London: Smith, Elder & Co., 1859).

Shelley, Mary Wollstonecraft, 'Life of Shelley' (*c.*1823) in *A Facsimile and Full Transcript of Bodleian MS. Shelley adds.c.5*, ed. Alan M. Weinberg, vol. 22, pt. 2 of *The Bodleian Shelley Manuscripts. A Facsimile Edition, with Full Transcripts and Scholarly Apparatus*, gen. ed. Donald H. Reiman (New York: Garland Publishing Inc., 1997), 267–87.

[—— (ed.)], *Posthumous Poems of Percy Bysshe Shelley* (London: John and Henry L. Hunt, 1824).

—— 'Memoirs of William Godwin', in William Godwin, *Caleb Williams*, Standard Novels, no. 2 (London: Henry Colburn and Richard Bentley; Edinburgh: Bell and Bradfute; Dublin: Cuming, 1831), pp. iii–xiii.

—— (ed.), *The Poetical Works of Percy Bysshe Shelley*, 4 vols. (London: Edward Moxon, 1839).

—— (ed.), *Essays, Letters from Abroad, Translations and Fragments, by Percy Bysshe Shelley*, 2 vols. (London: Edward Moxon, 1840 [1839]).

—— *The Letters of Mary Wollstonecraft Shelley*, ed. Betty T. Bennett, 3 vols. (Baltimore: Johns Hopkins University Press, 1980–8).

—— *The Journals of Mary Shelley, 1814–1844*, ed. Paula R. Feldman and Diana Scott-Kilvert (Oxford University Press, 1987; Baltimore: Johns Hopkins University Press, 1995).

—— *The Novels and Selected Works of Mary Shelley*, gen. ed. Nora Crook, with Pamela Clemit, introd. Betty T. Bennett, 8 vols. (London: William Pickering, 1996).

—— *Mary Shelley's 'Literary Lives' and Other Writings*, gen. ed. Nora Crook, 4 vols. (London: Pickering and Chatto, 2002).

—— *The Mary Shelley Reader*, ed. Betty T. Bennett and Charles E. Robinson (New York: Oxford University Press, 1990).

[Sheppard, Sarah], *Characteristics of the Genius and Writings of L. E. L. with Illustrations from her Works and from Personal Recollection* (London: Longman, Brown, Green, and Longman, 1841).

A Short Sketch of the Life of Mrs. Hemans: With Remarks on her Poetry; and Extracts (London: James Paul, 1835).

Simmons, J. W., *An Inquiry into the Moral Character of Lord Byron* (London: John Cochran, 1826).

Smith, Charlotte, *Elegiac Sonnets, and Other Poems* (London: Jones and Company, 1827).

Southey, Robert (ed.), *The Remains of Henry Kirke White: With an Account of his Life*, 2 vols. (London: Vernor, Hood & Sharpe, 1807).

—— *The Life of Nelson*, 2 vols. (London: John Murray, 1813).

——(ed.), *Attempts in Verse, by John Jones, an Old Servant: with some Account of the Writer, written by Himself; and an Introductory Essay on the Lives and Works of our Uneducated Poets* (London: John Murray, 1831).

——(ed.), *Select Works of the British Poets, from Chaucer to Jonson, with Biographical Sketches* (London: Longman, Rees, Orme, Brown and Green, 1831).

——(ed.), *Horae Lyricae. Poems... by Isaac Watts. With a Memoir of the Author* (Sacred Classics, ix, London: 1834).

——(ed.), *The Life and Works of William Cowper*, 15 vols. (London: Baldwin and Cradock, 1835–7).

Stanfield, James Field, *An Essay on the Study and Composition of Biography* (Sunderland: printed by George Garbutt; London: sold by Gale, Curtis, Fenner, Cradock and Joy; Edinburgh: sold by Constable and Co., and John and James Robertson, 1813).

[Stewarton, G. L.], *The Female Revolutionary Plutarch, containing Biographical, Historical, and Revolutionary Sketches, Characters, and Anecdotes. By the Author of the Revolutionary Plutarch and Memoirs of Talleyrand*, 3 vols. (London: John Murray, 1806).

Stowe, Harriet Beecher, 'The True Story of Lady Byron's Life', *Macmillan Magazine*, 20 (Sept. 1869), 377–96.

—— *Lady Byron Vindicated: a History of the Byron Controversy from its beginning in 1816 to the Present Time* (London: Sampson, Low, Son, and Marston, 1870).

Strachey, Lytton, *Eminent Victorians. Cardinal Manning, Florence Nightingale, Dr. Arnold, General Gordon* (London: Chatto and Windus, 1918).

Styles, Revd John D. D., *Lord Byron's Works Viewed in Connexion with Christianity, and the Obligations of Social Life: A Sermon, Delivered at Holland Chapel, Kennington, July 4th, 1824* (London: Knight and Lacey, 1824).

Symons, A. J. A., *The Quest for Corvo* (London: Cassell, 1934).

Taylor, Thomas, *The Life of William Cowper Esq.* (London: Smith, Elder and Co., 1833).

'Thomas De Quincey and his Works', *Westminster Review*, 5 NS (Apr. 1854), 519–37.

Thompson, Henry, *The Life of Hannah More: With Notices of Her Sisters* (London: T. Cadell; Edinburgh: Blackwood, 1838).

Trelawny, Edward John, *Recollections of the Last Days of Shelley and Byron* (London: Edward Moxon, 1858).

——*Records of Shelley, Byron and the Author* (London: Basil Montagu Pickering, 1878).

——*Records of Shelley, Byron, and the Author*, ed. David Wright (1973; 2nd edn., Harmondsworth: Penguin, 1982).

'Tyro', *A Sketch from Public Life, and A Farewell: A Poem* (London: J. Hatchard, 1816).

[Watkins, John], *Memoirs of the Life and Writings of the Right Honourable Lord Byron, with Anecdotes of some of his Contemporaries* (London: Henry Colburn, 1822).

[Wilson, John], 'Observations on Mr Wordsworth's Letter Relative to a New Edition of Burns' Works; By a Friend of Robert Burns', *Blackwood's Magazine*, 1/3 (June 1817), 261–6.

——'Vindication of Mr Wordsworth's Letter to Mr Gray, on a New Edition of Burns', *Blackwood's Magazine*, 2 (Oct. 1817), 65–73.

——'Letter Occasioned by N's Vindication of Mr Wordsworth in Last Number', *Blackwood's Magazine*, 2 (Oct. 1817), 201–4.

Woolf, Virginia, *The Common Reader*, 2nd ser. (London: The Hogarth Press, 1932).

——*Collected Essays by Virginia Woolf*, 4 vols. (London: Hogarth Press, 1966–7).

——*The Essays of Virginia Woolf*, ed. Andrew McNeillie, 4 vols. (London: The Hogarth Press, 1986–94).

Wordsworth, Christopher, *Memoirs of William Wordsworth, Poet-Laureate, D. C. L.*, 2 vols. (London: Edward Moxon, 1851).

Wordsworth, William, *A Letter to a Friend of Robert Burns: Occasioned by an Intended Republication of the Account of the Life of Burns, by Dr. Currie; and of the Selection Made by him from his Letters* (London: Longman, Hurst, Rees, Orme and Brown, 1816).

——*The Prose Works of William Wordsworth*, ed. Alexander B. Grossart, 3 vols. (London: Edward Moxon, 1876).

——*The Letters of William and Dorothy Wordsworth*, ed. E. de Selincourt, 8 vols. (Oxford: Clarendon Press, 1967–93).

——*The Prose Works of William Wordsworth*, ed. W. J. B. Owen and Jane Worthington Smyser, 3 vols. (Oxford: Clarendon Press, 1974).

——*The Love Letters of William and Mary Wordsworth*, ed. Beth Darlington (London: Chatto and Windus, 1982).

SECONDARY

Alec-Smith, Alex, 'Appendix: Byron in Fiction. A List of Books', in Wilson (ed.), *Byromania*, 221–6.

Altick, Richard D., *Lives and Letters: A History of Literary Biography in England and America* (New York: Knopf, 1965; repr. Westport, Conn.: Greenwood Press, 1979).

Armstrong, Nancy, *Desire and Domestic Fiction: A Political History of the Novel* (New York: Oxford University Press, 1987).

Barcus, James E. (ed.), *Shelley: The Critical Heritage* (London: Routledge and Kegan Paul, 1975).

Barrell, John, *The Infection of Thomas De Quincey: A Psychopathology of Imperialism* (New Haven: Yale University Press, 1991).

Battersby, James L., 'Life, Art, and the *Lives of the Poets*', in David Wheeler (ed.), *Domestick Privacies: Samuel Johnson and the Art of Biography* (Lexington, Ky.: University Press of Kentucky, 1987), 26–56.

Bennett, Betty T., 'Machiavelli and Mary Shelley's Castruccio: Biography as Metaphor', *Romanticism*, 3/2 (1997), 139–51.

Bertram, J. G., *Some Memories of Books, Authors and Events* (London: A. Constable and Co., 1893).

Blain, Virginia, 'Letitia Elizabeth Landon, Eliza Mary Hamilton, and the Genealogy of the Victorian Poetess', *Victorian Poetry*, 33/1 (Spring 1995), 31–51.

Booth, Alison, *How to Make It as a Woman: Collective Biographical History from Victoria to the Present* (Chicago: University of Chicago Press, 2004).

Bostridge, Mark (ed.), *Lives for Sale: Biographers' Tales* (London: Continuum, 2004).

Boulton, James T. (ed.), *Samuel Johnson: The Critical Heritage* (London: Routledge, 1995).

Bowlby, Rachel, 'Domestication', in Diane Elam and Robyn Wiegman (eds.), *Feminism Beside Itself* (New York: Routledge, 1995), 71–91.

Bradley, Arthur, and Rawes, Alan (eds.), *Romantic Biography* (Aldershot: Ashgate, 2003).

Bruss, Elizabeth, *Autobiographical Acts: The Changing Situation of a Literary Genre* (Baltimore: Johns Hopkins University Press, 1976).

Butler, Marilyn, 'Satire and the Images of Self in the Romantic Period: The Long Tradition of Hazlitt's *Liber Amoris*', *Yearbook of English Studies*, 14 (1984), 209–25.

Cafarelli, Annette Wheeler, *Prose in the Age of Poets: Romanticism and Biographical Narrative from Johnson to De Quincey* (Philadelphia: University of Pennsylvania Press, 1990).

Chew, Samuel C., *Byron in England: His Fame and After-Fame* (1924; New York: Russell and Russell, 1965).

Churchwell, Sarah, 'Secrets and Lies: Plath, Privacy, Publication and Ted Hughes's *Birthday Letters*', *Contemporary Review*, 42/1 (2001), 102–48.

Clarke, Norma, *Dr Johnson's Women* (London: Hambledon and London, 2000).

Clifford, James L., 'How Much Should a Biographer Tell? Some Eighteenth-Century Views', in Philip B. Daghlian (ed.), *Essays in Eighteenth-Century Biography* (Bloomington, Ind.: Indiana University Press, 1968), 67–126.

Clingham, Greg (ed.), *New Light on Boswell: Critical and Historical Essays on the Occasion of the Bicentenary of the 'Life of Johnson'* (Cambridge: Cambridge University Press, 1991).

——*James Boswell: The Life of Johnson* (Cambridge: Cambridge University Press, 1992).

——'Life and Literature in Johnson's *Lives of the Poets*', in Greg Clingham (ed.), *The Cambridge Companion to Samuel Johnson* (Cambridge: Cambridge University Press, 1997), 161–91.

Clubbe, John, 'George Gordon, Lord Byron', in Frank Jordan (ed.), *The English Romantic Poets*, 4th edn., 465–592.

Conger, Syndy MacMillen, 'Multivocality in Mary Shelley's Unfinished Memoirs of her Father', *European Romantic Review*, 9/3 (1998), 303–22.

Corbett, Mary Jean, *Representing Femininity: Middle-Class Subjectivity in Victorian and Edwardian Women's Autobiographies* (New York: Oxford University Press, 1992).

Cronin, Richard, *Romantic Victorians: English Literature, 1824–1840* (Basingstoke: Palgrave, 2002).

Curran, Stuart, 'Percy Bysshe Shelley', in Frank Jordan (ed.), *The English Romantic Poets*, 593–663.

Davidoff, Leonore, and Hall, Catherine, *Family Fortunes: Men and Women of the English Middle Class 1780–1850.* (Hutchinson Education, 1987; rev. repr., London: Routledge, 2002).

De Man, Paul, 'Autobiography as De-Facement', in *The Rhetoric of Romanticism* (1979; New York: Columbia University Press, 1984), 67–81.

Devlin, D. D., *De Quincey, Wordsworth and the Art of Prose* (London: Macmillan, 1983).

Duffy, Cian, '"His *Canaille* of an Audience": Thomas De Quincey and the Revolution in Reading', *Studies in Romanticism*, 44/1 (2005), 7–22.

Easley, Alexis, *First-Person Anonymous: Women Writers and Victorian Print Media, 1830–1870* (Aldershot: Ashgate, 2004).

Elfenbein, Andrew, *Byron and the Victorians* (Cambridge: Cambridge University Press, 1995).

Eliot, T. S., 'Shelley and Keats', in *The Use of Poetry and The Use of Criticism: Studies in the Relation of Criticism to Poetry in England* (1933; London: Faber and Faber, 2nd edn., 1964), 87–102.

Ellis, Kate Ferguson, *The Contested Castle: Gothic Novels and the Subversion of Domestic Ideology* (Urbana and Chicago: University of Illinois Press, 1989).

—— 'Subversive Surfaces: The Limits of Domestic Affection in Mary Shelley's Later Fiction', in Fisch, Mellor, and Schor (eds.), *The Other Mary Shelley Beyond Frankenstein*, 220–34.

Elwin, Malcolm, *Lord Byron's Wife* (London: Macdonald, 1962).

Engelberg, Karsten Klejs, *The Making of the Shelley Myth: An Annotated Bibliography of Criticism of Percy Bysshe Shelley 1822–1860* (London: Mansell; Westport, Conn.: Meckler, 1988).

Epstein, William H. (ed.), *Contesting the Subject: Essays in the Postmodern Theory and Practice of Biography and Biographical Criticism* (West Lafayette, Ind.: Purdue University Press, 1991).

Erickson, Lee, *The Economy of Literary Form: English Literature and the Industrialization of Publishing, 1800–1850* (Baltimore: Johns Hopkins University Press, 1996).

Favret, Mary, 'Mary Shelley's Sympathy and Irony: The Editor and her Corpus', in Fisch, Mellor, and Schor (eds.), *The Other Mary Shelley: Beyond Frankenstein*, 17–38.

Feldman, Paula R., 'Mary Shelley and the Genesis of Moore's *Life* of Byron', *Studies in English Literature, 1500–1900*, 20/4 (1980), 611–20.

Fisch, Audrey A., Mellor, Anne K., and Schor, Esther H. (eds.), *The Other Mary Shelley Beyond Frankenstein* (New York: Oxford University Press, 1993).

Folkenflik, Robert, *Samuel Johnson, Biographer* (Ithaca, NY: Cornell University Press, 1978).

Fraistat, Neil, 'Illegitimate Shelley: Radical Piracy and the Textual Edition as Cultural Performance', *PMLA* 109/3 (May, 1994), 409–23.

Francis, Emma, 'Letitia Landon: Public Fantasy and the Private Sphere', in Anne Janowitz (ed.), *Romanticism and Gender* (The English Association, 51; Cambridge: D. S. Brewer, 1998), 93–115.

Garraty, John A., *The Nature of Biography* (1957; 2nd edn., London: Jonathan Cape, 1958).

Gill, Stephen, *Wordsworth and the Victorians* (Oxford: Clarendon Press, 1998).

Gleadle, Kathryn, and Richardson, Sarah (eds.), *Women in British Politics, 1760–1860: The Power of the Petticoat* (Basingstoke: Macmillan; New York: St Martin's Press, 2000).

Gordon, Eleanor, and Nair, Gwyneth, *Public Lives: Women, Family and Society in Victorian Britain* (New Haven: Yale University Press, 2003).

Graham, Peter W., 'His Grand Show: Byron and the Myth of Mythmaking', in Wilson (ed.), *Byromania*, 24–42.

Guerra, Lia, 'Mary Shelley's Contributions to Lardner's *Cabinet Cyclopaedia: Lives of the Most Eminent Literary and Scientific Men of Italy*', in Laura Bandiera and Diego Saglia (eds.), *British Romanticism and Italian Literature: Translating, Reviewing, Rewriting* (Amsterdam: Rodopi, 2005), 221–35.

Hamilton, Ian, *Keepers of the Flame: Literary Estates and the Rise of Biography* (London: Pimlico/Random House, 1992).

Harding, Anthony John, ' "Domestick Privacies": Biography and the Sanctifying of Privacy, from Johnson to Martineau', *Dalhousie Review*, 85/3 (Fall 2005), 371–89.

Hart, Francis R., *Lockhart as Romantic Biographer* (Edinburgh: Edinburgh University Press, 1971).

Heiland, Donna, 'Remembering the Hero in Boswell's *Life of Johnson*', in Clingham (ed.), *New Light on Boswell*, 194–206.

Higgins, David, *Romantic Genius and the Literary Magazine: Biography, Celebrity and Politics* (Abingdon: Routledge, 2005).

Hogle, Jerrold E., 'Percy Bysshe Shelley', in O'Neill (ed.), *Literature of the Romantic Period*, 118–42.

Holmes, Richard, 'Death and Destiny', *Guardian*, Review section (24 Jan. 2004).

Houghton, W. E., Houghton, E. R., and Singerland, J. H. (eds.), *The Wellesley Index to Victorian Periodicals 1824–1900*, 5 vols. (Toronto: University of Toronto Press, 1987).

Hunt, Margaret R., *The Middling Sort: Commerce, Gender, and the Family in England, 1680–1780* (Berkeley and Los Angeles: University of California Press, 1996).

Hyde, Michael, 'The Role of "Our Scottish Readers" in the History of *Tait's Edinburgh Magazine*', *Victorian Periodicals Review*, 14/4 (Winter, 1981), 135–40.

Jackson, J. R. De J. (ed.), *Coleridge: The Critical Heritage*, 2 vols. (London: Routledge, 1970–91).

Jones, Christine Kenyon (ed.), *Byron: The Image of the Poet* (Newark, Del.: University of Delaware Press/Rosemont Publishing and Printing Corp./Associated University Presses, 2008).

Jones, Deborah, 'Gossip: Notes on Women's Oral Culture', in Deborah Cameron (ed.), *The Feminist Critique of Language: A Reader* (London: Routledge, 1990), 243–50.

Jordan, Frank (ed.), *The English Romantic Poets: A Review of Research and Criticism*, 4th edn. (New York: Modern Language Association of America, 1985).

Jordan, John E., *De Quincey to Wordsworth: A Biography of a Relationship, with the Letters of Thomas De Quincey to the Wordsworth Family* (Berkeley and Los Angeles: University of California Press, 1962).

Kelly, Gary, *Revolutionary Feminism: The Mind and Career of Mary Wollstonecraft* (Basingstoke: Macmillan; New York: St Martin's Press, 1992).

Kipperman, Mark, 'Absorbing a Revolution: Shelley becomes a Romantic, 1889–1903', *Nineteenth-Century Literature*, 47/2 (Sept. 1992), 187–211.

Kremmerer, Kathleen Nulton, 'Domestic Relations in Samuel Johnson's *Life of Milton*', *The Age of Johnson: A Scholarly Annual*, 15 (2004), 57–82.

Kucich, Greg, 'Mary Shelley's *Lives* and the Reengendering of History', in Betty T. Bennett and Stuart Curran (eds.), *Mary Shelley in Her Times* (Baltimore: Johns Hopkins University Press, 2000), 198–213.

Langland, Elizabeth, *Nobody's Angels: Middle-Class Women and Domestic Ideology in Victorian Culture* (Ithaca, NY: Cornell University Press, 1995).

—— 'Women's Writing and the Domestic Sphere', in Joanne Shattock (ed.), *Women and Literature in Britain, 1800–1900* (Cambridge: Cambridge University Press, 2001), 119–41.

Leavis, F. R., 'Shelley', in *Revaluation: Tradition and Development in English Poetry* (1936; London: Chatto and Windus, 1962), 203–40.

Leighton, Angela, 'De Quincey and Women', in Stephen Copley and John Whale (eds.), *Beyond Romanticism: New Approaches to Texts and Contexts 1780–1832* (London: Routledge, 1992), 160–77.

—— *Victorian Women Poets: Writing Against the Heart* (Hemel Hempstead: Harvester/Wheatsheaf, 1992).

Lindop, Grevel, *The Opium-Eater: A Life of Thomas De Quincey* (London: J. M Dent and Sons, 1981).

Linkin, Harriet Kramer, and Behrendt, Stephen C. (eds.), *Romanticism and Women Poets: Opening the Doors of Reception* (Lexington, Ky.: University Press of Kentucky, 1999).

Little, Geoffrey (ed.), *Barron Field's Memoirs of Wordsworth* (Australian Academy of the Humanities, Monograph, 3; Sydney: Sydney University Press, 1975).

Lustig, Irma S., and Pottle, Frederick A. (eds.), *Boswell: The Applause of the Jury 1782–1785* London: Heinemann, 1982 edn.).

MacCarthy, Fiona, *Byron: Life and Legend* (London: John Murray, 2002).

McDayter, Ghislaine, 'Conjuring Byron: Byromania, Literary Commodification and the Birth of Celebrity', in Wilson (ed.), *Byromania*, 43–62.

McElderry, B. R., Jr., 'Boswell in 1790–91: Two Unpublished Comments', *Notes and Queries* (July 1962), 266–8.

Martin, Philip W., *Byron: A Poet Before His Public* (Cambridge: Cambridge University Press, 1982).

Marcus, Laura, *Auto/biographical Discourses: Theory, Criticism, Practice* (Manchester: Manchester University Press, 1994).

Matthews, Samantha, *Poetical Remains: Poets' Graves, Bodies, and Books in the Nineteenth Century* (Oxford: Oxford University Press, 2004).

Mellor, Anne K., *Romanticism and Gender* (New York: Routledge, 1993).

—— *Mary Shelley: Her Life, her Fiction, her Monsters* (London: Methuen, 1988).

Melnyk, Veronica, '"Half Fashion and Half Passion": The Life of Publisher Henry Colburn', unpub. PhD thesis, University of Birmingham, 2002.

Millgate, Michael, *Testamentary Acts: Browning, Tennyson, James, Hardy* (Oxford: Clarendon Press, 1992).

Miller, J. Hillis, *The Disappearance of God: Five Nineteenth-Century Writers* (1963; Cambridge, Mass.: Belknap Press of Harvard University Press, 1979).

Moore, Doris Langley, *The Late Lord Byron: Posthumous Dramas* (1961; 2nd rev. edn., London: John Murray, 1976).

Mole, Tom, *Byron's Romantic Celebrity: Industrial Culture and the Hermeneutic of Intimacy* (Basingstoke: Palgrave Macmillan, 2007).

Morrison, Lucy, 'Writing the Self in Others' Lives: Mary Shelley's Biographies of Madame Roland and Madame de Staël', *Keats-Shelley Journal*, 53 (2004), 127–51.

Morrison, Robert, 'Red De Quincey', *Wordsworth Circle*, 29/2 (1998), 131–6.

——Review of Margaret Russet, *De Quincey's Romanticism: Canonical Minority and the Forms of Transmission, Romanticism On the Net*, 10 (May 1998) at <http://www.erudit.org/revue/ron/1998/v/n10/005803ar.html>

Motion, Andrew, *Keats* (London: Faber and Faber, 1997).

Newey, Vincent, and Shaw, Philip (eds.), *Mortal Pages, Literary Lives: Studies in Nineteenth-Century Autobiography* (Aldershot: Scolar Press, 1996).

Newlyn, Lucy, *Reading, Writing, and Romanticism: The Anxiety of Reception* (Oxford: Oxford University Press, 2000).

Nitchie, Elizabeth, 'Shelley at Eton: Mary Shelley vs. Jefferson Hogg', *Keats-Shelley Memorial Bulletin*, 11 (1960), 48–54.

North, Julian, 'Leeches and Opium: De Quincey replies to "Resolution and Independence" in *Confessions of an English Opium-Eater*', *Modern Language Review*, 89/3 (July 1994), 572–80.

——'Autobiography as Self-Indulgence: De Quincey and his Reviewers', in Newey and Shaw (eds.), *Mortal Pages, Literary Lives*, 61–70.

——*De Quincey Reviewed: Thomas De Quincey's Critical Reception, 1821–1994* (Columbia, S.C.: Camden House, 1997).

——'Self-Possession and Gender in Romantic Literary Biography', in Bradley and Rawes (eds.), *Romantic Biography*, 109–38.

——'"I change but I cannot die": The Metamorphoses of P. B. Shelley', in Carla Dente et al. (eds.), *Proteus: The Language of Metamorphosis*, Studies in European Cultural Transition, 26, gen. eds. Martin Stannard and Greg Walker (Aldershot: Ashgate, 2005), 165–71.

——'Wooing the Reader: De Quincey, Wordsworth and Women in *Tait's Edinburgh Magazine*', in Robert Morrison and Daniel Sanjiv Roberts (eds.), *Thomas De Quincey: New Theoretical and Critical Directions* (New York: Routledge, 2008), 99–121.

O'Neill, Michael (ed.), *Literature of the Romantic Period: A Bibliographical Guide* (Oxford: Clarendon Press, 1998).

——'"Trying to make it as good as I can": Mary Shelley's Editing of Shelley's Poetry and Prose', *Romanticism*, 3/2 (1997), 185–97.

O'Rourke, James, '"Nothing more unnatural": Mary Shelley's Revision of Rousseau', *English Literary History*, 56/3 (Fall 1989), 543–69.

Parker, Fred, 'Johnson and the "Lives of the Poets"', *Cambridge Quarterly*, 29/4 (2000), 323–37.

Peterson, Linda H., *Traditions of Victorian Women's Autobiography: The Poetics and Politics of Life Writing* (Charlottesville, Va.: University Press of Virginia, 1999).

Pollitt, Charles, *De Quincey's Editorship of the Westmoreland Gazette* (Kendal: Atkinson and Pollitt, 1890).

Poovey, Mary, *The Proper Lady and the Woman Writer: Ideology as Style in the Works of Mary Wollstonecraft, Mary Shelley, and Jane Austen* (Chicago: University of Chicago Press, 1984).

Raven, James, *Judging New Wealth: Popular Publishing and Responses to Commerce in England, 1750–1800* (Oxford: Clarendon Press, 1992).

Ready, Robert, 'Flat Realities: Hazlitt on Biography', *Prose Studies*, 5/3 (Dec. 1982), 309–17.

Reed, Joseph W., *English Biography in the Early Nineteenth Century: 1801–1838* (1965; New Haven: Yale University Press, 1966).

Reiman, Donald H., *Romantic Texts and Contexts* (Columbia: University of Missouri Press, 1987).

Ross, Marlon B., *The Contours of Masculine Desire: Romanticism and the Rise of Women's Poetry* (New York: Oxford University Press, 1989).

Russell, Norma, *A Bibliography of William Cowper to 1837* (Oxford: Clarendon Press, 1963).

Rutherford, Andrew (ed.), *Byron: The Critical Heritage* (London: Routledge and Kegan Paul; New York: Barnes and Noble, 1970).

Sanders, Valerie, *The Private Lives of Victorian Women: Autobiography in Nineteenth-Century England* (New York: Harvester/Wheatsheaf, 1989).

Schor, Esther (ed.), *The Cambridge Companion to Mary Shelley* (Cambridge: Cambridge University Press, 2003).

Seymour, Miranda, *Mary Shelley* (London: John Murray, 2000).

Shattock, Joanne, 'The Construction of the Woman Writer', in Joanne Shattock (ed.), *Women and Literature in Britain 1800–1900* (Cambridge: Cambridge University Press, 2001), 8–34.

Smith, Johanna M., *Mary Shelley* (Twayne's English Authors Series, 526; New York: Twayne Publishers; London: Prentice Hall International, 1996).

Soderholm, James, *Fantasy, Forgery, and the Byron Legend* (Lexington, Ky.: University Press of Kentucky, 1996).

Spacks, Patricia Meyer, *Gossip* (1985; Chicago: University of Chicago Press, 1986).

Stauffer, Donald A., *The Art of Biography in Eighteenth-Century England, Bibliographical Supplement* (Princeton: Princeton University Press, 1941).

Stephenson, Glennis, 'Poet Construction: Mrs Hemans, L. E. L., and the Image of the Nineteenth-Century Woman Poet', in Shirley Neuman and Glennis Stephenson (eds.), *ReImagining Women: Representations of Women in Culture* (Toronto: University of Toronto Press, 1993), 61–73.

——*Letitia Landon. The Woman behind L.E.L.* (Manchester: Manchester University Press, 1995).

St Clair, William, *The Reading Nation in the Romantic Period* (Cambridge: Cambridge University Press, 2004).

Stillinger, Jack, *Multiple Authorship and the Myth of Solitary Genius* (New York: Oxford University Press, 1991).

Stott, Ann, 'Women and Religion', in Hannah Barker and Elaine Chalus (eds.), *Women's History, Britain, 1700–1850: An Introduction* (London: Routledge, 2005), 100–23.

Strickland, Margot, *The Byron Women* (London: Peter Owen, 1974).

Sutherland, John, 'Henry Colburn, Publisher', *Publishing History*, 19 (1986), 59–84.

Taylor, Charles H., *The Early Collected Editions of Shelley's Poems: A Study in the History and Transmission of the Printed Text* (New Haven: Yale University Press, 1958).

Tosh, John, *A Man's Place: Masculinity and the Middle-Class Home in Victorian England* (New Haven: Yale University Press, 1999).

Treadwell, James, *Autobiographical Writing and British Literature, 1783–1834* (Oxford: Oxford University Press, 2005).

Tucker, Herbert F., 'House Arrest: The Domestication of English Poetry in the 1820s', *New Literary History*, 25/3 (Summer, 1994), 521–48.

Tuite, Clara, 'Domesticity', *An Oxford Companion to The Romantic Age: British Culture 1776–1832*, gen. ed. Iain McCalman (Oxford: Oxford University Press, 1999), 125–33.

Webb, Timothy, *Shelley: A Voice not Understood* (Manchester: Manchester University Press, 1977).

Whale, John C., '"In a Stranger's Ear": De Quincey's Polite Magazine Context', in Robert Lance Snyder (ed.), *Thomas De Quincey: Bicentenary Studies* (Norman, Okla.: University of Oklahoma Press, 1985), 35–53.

White, Newman I., (ed.), *The Unextinguished Hearth: Shelley and His Contemporary Critics* (1938; New York: Octagon Books, 1966).

——'The Beautiful Angel and his Biographers', in Frank Jordan (ed.), *The English Romantic Poets*, 73–85.

Williams, John, *Mary Shelley: A Literary Life* (Basingstoke: Macmillan, 2000).

Wilson, Frances (ed.), *Byromania: Portraits of the Artist in Nineteenth- and Twentieth-Century Culture* (Basingstoke: Macmillan; New York; St Martin's Press, 1999).

Wolfson, Susan J., 'Editorial Privilege: Mary Shelley and Percy Shelley's Audiences', in Fisch, Mellor, and Schor (eds.), *The Other Mary Shelley: Beyond Frankenstein*, 39–72.

——'"Domestic Affections" and "The Spear of Minerva": Felicia Hemans and the Dilemma of Gender', in Carol Shiner and Joel Haefner (eds.), *Re-Visioning Romanticism: British Women Writers, 1776–1837* (Philadelphia: University of Pennsylvania Press, 1994), 128–66.

——'Felicia Hemans and the Revolving Doors of Reception', in Linkin and Behrendt (eds.), *Romanticism and Women Poets*, 214–41.

——(ed.), *Felicia Hemans: Selected Poems, Letters, Reception Materials* (Princeton: Princeton University Press, 2000).

Wolstenholme, Susan, 'Voice of the Voiceless: Harriet Beecher Stowe and the Byron Controversy', *American Literary Realism*, 19/2 (Winter 1987), 48–65.

Wu, Duncan (ed.), *Wordsworth's Reading 1770–1799* (Cambridge: Cambridge University Press, 1993).

——(ed.), *Wordsworth's Reading 1800–1815* (Cambridge: Cambridge University Press, 1995).

Yolton, John W., Porter, Roy, et al. (eds.), *The Blackwell Companion to the Enlightenment* (1991; Oxford: Blackwell, 1995).

Index

828.8809

NOR

#534666